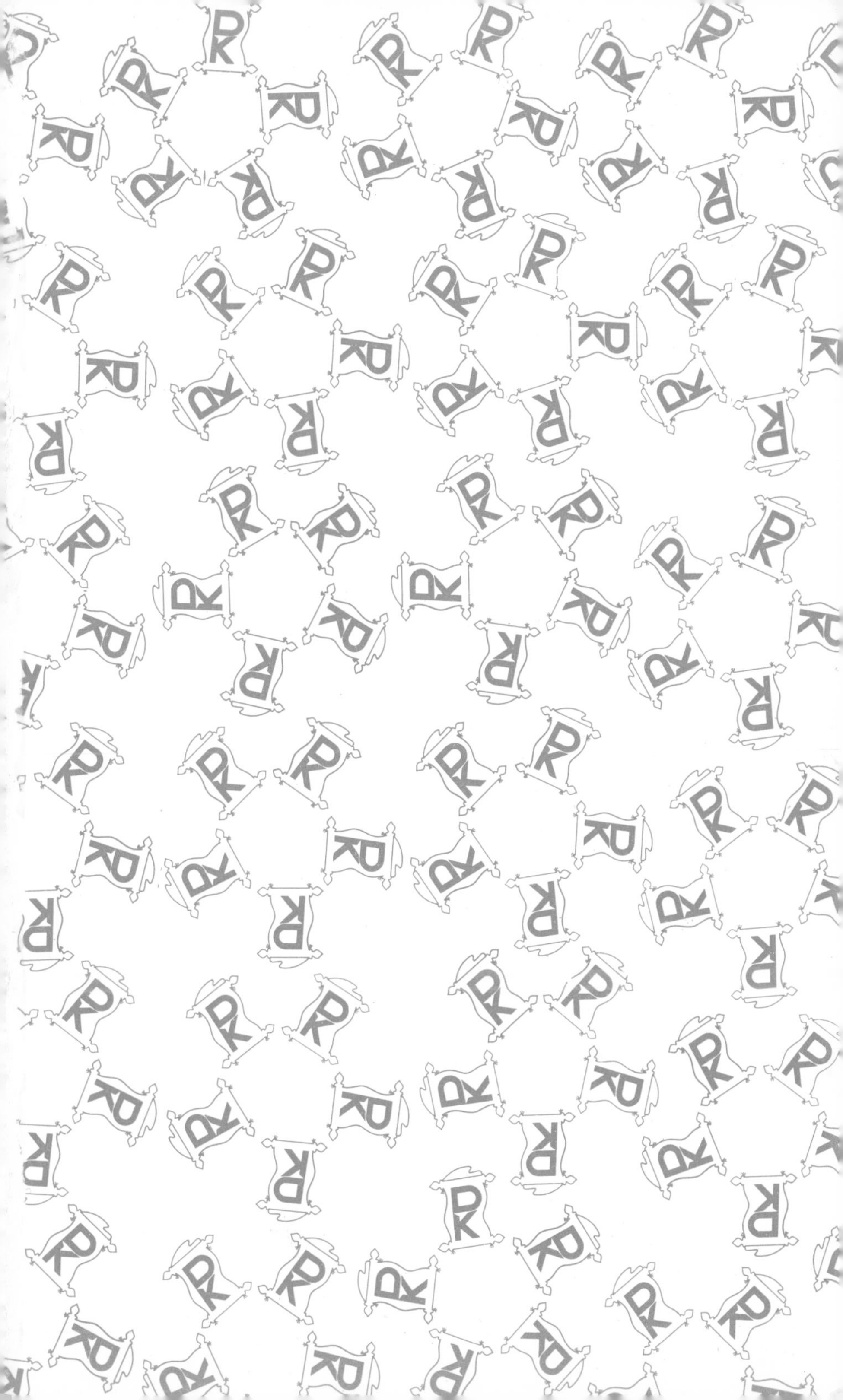

# Dictionary
# of
# Hindu Gods and Goddesses

# Dictionary
# of
# Hindu Gods and Goddesses

*by*

**T.R.R. Iyengar**

D.K. Printworld (P) Ltd.
New Delhi

**Cataloging in Publication Data — DK**

Iyengar, T.R.R. (T.Renga Rajan), 1962 –
Dictionary of Hindu gods and goddesses.
Includes index.

1. Gods, Hindu — Dictionaries. 2. Goddesses, Hindu — Dictionaries. 3. Mythology, Hindu — Dictionaries. I. Title.

**ISBN 81-246-0232-8 (HB)**
**ISBN 81-246-0233-6 (PB)**

*First Published in India in 2003*


*Published and printed by*:
**D.K. Printworld (P) Ltd.**
*Regd. office* : *'Sri Kunj'*, F-52, Bali Nagar
New Delhi - 110 015
*Phones* : (011) 2545-3975; 2546-6019
*Fax* : (011) 2546-5926
*E-mail*: dkprintworld@vsnl.net
*Web*: www.dkprint.com

# Introduction

The Hindu pantheon is unique among those of ancient religions and mythologies; there are diverse gods and goddesses, each with his or her own attributes and functions. The world of Hindu gods and goddesses is, as noted by scholars, very similar to the ancient Greek pantheon of deities, both personifying the basic elements of nature and what ancient man saw as unexplainable natural phenomena — that he feared and was in awe of — as deities. He evolved interesting stories concerning them where they appear, feel, interact with each other and behave in general very much like ordinary human beings. But the Indian tradition is believed to be far more ancient; rather its antiquity which can be traced to the *Ṛgveda* cannot be dated just as the text itself. The gods and goddesses of the Indian pantheon, moreover, are still a living tradition they are believed in, worshipped and appeared like they were eons ago and they are part and parcel of the daily social and cultural life of the Hindus.

The early Āryans were pastoral and agricultural people who lived close to nature, experiencing its benign and destructive influences everyday of the their lives and trying to question and understand the powers of nature and their effect upon themselves. In the process, they invested them — the rain, fire, clouds, storms as well as the beauties of nature that thrilled their hearts — with a distinct personality and invoked them in hymns. Without holding anyone god as superior to the others, they exalted some more than others depending on whose bounties they desired the most at a particular time. Later, however, the triad of Agni, Sūrya and Vāyu or Indra came to be acknowledged as the most supreme.

In the Hindu conception of gods, the idea of one Supreme Being was of a later evolution: it is only in some late hymns of the *Ṛgveda Saṁhitā* that we find traces of this thought. Between the time of the *Saṁhitā* and the *Brāhmaṇa* portion of the Veda — emphasising the ritual and liturgy which obscured the simplicity of the Vedic myths — this idea gained prominence, now one Great Being was seen as the soul of the Universe — the quiescent universal soul, *Brahman* who also look as a creative form as Brahmā, the Prajāpati.

In the epic poems *Rāmāyaṇa* and *Māhābhārata* we find a marked change though they deal more with mortal men than the strength and majesty of the gods. Here, clearly, the triad, Brahmā, Viṣṇu and Śiva are the major gods, with the old Vedic deites disappearing or being relegated to the background. Viṣṇu, friend and companion of Indra in the Vedas, is the foremost deity, the god of preservation, and Śiva is now the terrible deity Rudra of the Vedas. These two gods contend with each other, each in turn receiving homage and honoured as the greatest of gods. It was only in the Purāṇas that the complex and diverse pattern of deities, as we know it today, came into existence. The Vedic deities then received no importance and the *trimūrti* of Brahmā.

Viṣṇu and Śiva was prominent with soon the former falling into obscurity. Fantastic legends were woven around Viṣṇu and Śiva and a plethora of other deities; each had myriad epithets which, in terms, had distinctive fetures in terms of appearance, qualities and actions. Devī, Śiva's female consort for instance was devoutly worshipped (laying the foundation for the bloody rites that later developed in the Tantras) in many forms as Durgā, Kālī, Mahiṣāsuramardinī and so on, each form placed in a definite setting with specific myths, stories and meanings. The Purāṇas and other later writings are the authorities of modern Hinduism; their mythology and gods and goddesses form the care of contemporary Hindu pantheon. The fact that Hindu religious literature especially the Purāṇas are many and extensive and elaborately deal with the stories, the mode of worship and belief in deities means that a study of gods and goddesses in Hinduism is well reveal interesting yet complex pattern of diverse proportions and myriad meanings along with a certain amount of contradictions.

The making of this dictionary of Hindu gods and goddesses has been a stupendous affair. It has involved references to diverse ancient sources to accurately and systematically trace the evolutionary and physical aspects of each deity and its actions, its metaphysical significance, nature of its worship and so on. Such a study is rendered complicated and, at the same time, it intrigues the mind of the readers as it involves citing of different works referring to the same deity or one of its forms, the account in one work at times varying from the details in another. Such instances need to be further researched in a broader discussion — something that cannot be undertaken in a dictionary. Another matter that is of great interest in compiling such a dictionary is the nature of the entries included. In Hinduism, gods and goddesses need not be only personified beings with great physical and spiritual powers that make them superhuman. They may be represented as different creatures and inanimate objects as well relating to the form of a god/goddess or closely associated with a particular deity. So these become sacred and are worshipped with reverence accorded to gods and goddesses. That is why the essence of Hinduism is said to lie in its ability to absorb and would different thought streams and ideas and as a result, its broad and all-encompassing framework. So we have animals, plants, trees, stones considered sacred and worshipped: the elephant, the snake and the cow are particularly important; the *tulasī* plant is worshipped and stories relate why *tulasī* is revered; trees like the banyan and the *pīpal* are worshipped as a daily basis; stones like the *śāligrāma*s and *bāṇaliṅga*s are esteemed by the Vaiṣṇvaites and Śaivites respectively.

Our ancient religious works and mythology relate stories describing the characteristics and actions of gods and goddesses that involve interplay of various characters and events — concerning *apsarās*es, sages and men and women associated in kinship with the heroes of these stories and their antogonists and others. A dictionary such as this cannot afford not mentioning same of these 'sacred' characters who if not actually worshipped like gods and goddesses are nevertheless considered 'holy' and venerated. Thus, this dictionary describes, apart from the gods and goddesses themselves, the ancient seers of great knowledge and mystical powers, and the kin of mythological gods like Rāma and Kṛṣṇa.

The Hindu tradition of belief in gods and goddesses is not only a thing of the past; it forms the modern Indian's religious link to the other and superior world of deities and his spiritual link with the universe and the beyond. It is not only a matter of study for scholars but a constant source of inspiration for the men and women in their daily life. So a dictionary compiling information on Hindu gods and goddesses has a persevering importance. The scope of study being vast, it can only sincerely attempt to capture and highlight the entire canvas of deities with their myriad representations, cannotations and associations.

# Contents

# A

**Abhasvaras**: A class of deities, sixty-four in number, of whose nature little is known.

**Abhimānī**: An Agni. The eldest son of Brahmā. By his wife Svāhā he had three sons, Pāvaka, Pavamāna and Sucī. They had forty-five sons who, along with the original son of Brahmā and his three descendants, constitute the forty-nine fires.

**Acyuta**: [Unfallen] A name of Viṣṇu. It has been variously interpreted as signifying 'he who does not perish with created things'; in the *Mahābhārata* as 'he who is not distinct from final emancipation'; and in the *Skanda Purāṇa* as 'he who never declines from his proper nature'.

**Aditi**: [Free, unbounded, infinite] The boundless heaven as compared with the finite earth; or, according to Muller, 'the visible infinite, visible by the naked eye; the endless expanse beyond the earth, beyond the clouds, beyond the sky'. In the *R̥gveda* she is frequently implored 'for blessings on children and cattle, for protection and for forgiveness'. Aditi is called Devamātr̥, 'mother of the gods' and is represented as being the mother of Dakṣa and the daughter of Dakṣa. On this statement Yāska remarks in the *Nirukta*: 'How can this be possible? They may have had the same originator, according to the nature of the gods, they may have been born from each other, have derived their substance from one another.' 'Eight sons were born from the body of Aditi; she approached the gods with seven but cast away the eighth, Mārttaṇḍa.' These seven were the Ādityas.

In the *Yajurveda* Aditi is addressed as 'supporter of the sky, sustainer of the earth, sovereign of this world, wife of Viṣṇu'; but in the *Mahābhārata* and *Rāmāyaṇa*, as well as in the Purāṇas, Viṣṇu is called the son of Aditi. In the *Viṣṇu Purāṇa* she is said to be the daughter of Dakṣa and wife of Kāśyapa, by whom she was mother of Viṣṇu in his dwarf incarnation and also of Indra, and she is called 'mother of the gods' and 'the mother of the world'. Indra acknowledged her as mother and Viṣṇu, after receiving the adoration of Aditi, addressed her in these words 'Mother, goddess, do thou show favour unto me and grant me thy blessing.' According to the *Matsya Purāṇa,* a pair of ear-rings was produced at the churning of the ocean, which Indra gave to Aditi, and several of the Purāṇas tell a story of these ear-rings being stolen and carried off to the city of Prāgjyotiṣa by the *asura* king named Naraka, from whence they were brought back and restored to her by Kṛṣṇa. Devakī, the mother of Kṛṣṇa, is represented as being a new birth or manifestation of Aditi. [*Hindu Mythology*, T.R.R. Iyengar; *A Classical Dictionary of Hindu Mythology and Religion*, J. Dowson]

**Ādityas**: The group of gods called Ādityas, i.e., sons of Aditi or Infinity, is celebrated in six whole hymns and in parts of two others in the *Ṛgveda*. In the early Vedic times the Ādityas were six or more frequently seven celestial deities, of whom Varuṇa was chief; consequently, he was 'the Āditya'. They were the eight sons of Aditi who approached the gods with seven, having cast away the eighth, Mārttaṇḍa. Later the number was increased to twelve, as representing the sun in the twelve months of the year. Āditya is one of the names of the sun. Dr. Muir quotes the following from Professor Roth:

> There dwell and reign those gods who bear in common the name of Adityas. We must, however, if we would discover their earliest character, abandon the conceptions which in a later age, and even in that of the heroic poems, were entertained regarding these deities. According to this conception they were twelve sun gods, bearing evident reference to the twelve months. But for the most ancient period we must hold fast the primary signification of their name.

As for their number the *Ṛgveda* says that Aditi at first presented only seven sons to the gods, but afterwards brought the eighth Mārttaṇḍa, i.e., the Sun. The *Atharvaveda* states that Aditi had eight sons. The *Ṛgveda*, at one place only, enumerates all the

Ādityas except Sūrya. They are Mitra, Aryaman, Bhaga, Tuvijata, Varuṇa, Dakṣa and Aṁśa. That the third of these, Bhaga was only an epithet of Savitṛ is proved not only by a passage which enumerates four of the Ādityas as Savitṛ, the Bhaga, Varuṇa, Mitra, and Aryaman, but also by numerous other passages. As for the fourth Amity, Tuvijata, he is clearly none other than Indra. This identification is proved by the fact that Indra has been called Tuvijata elsewhere in the *Ṛgveda*, and also that a verse of a Vālakhilya hymn, basing its statement on this hymn of the *Ṛgveda*, invokes Indra as the fourth Āditya. That the eighth Āditya, Mārttaṇḍa is none other than Sūrya is proved by the fact that Sūrya is called Āditya in several hymns of the *Ṛgveda*. The *Taittirīya Brāhmaṇa* also regards the Ādityas as eight, but in enumerating them it seems to have called Dakṣa by the name Dhātṛ, and to have substituted Vivasvat for Sūrya. In the *Śatapatha Brāhmaṇa* and in post-Vedic literature, the number of Ādityas swelled to twelve, the four that were added being Viṣṇu, Pūṣan, Vivasvat and Tvaṣṭṛ, with Viṣṇu being regarded as the greatest of them. The Ādityas have some common characteristics. They are the inviolable, imperishable, eternal beings. Aditi, eternity or the eternal, is the element which sustains or is sustained by them. The eternal and inviolable element in which the Ādityas dwell, and which forms their essence, is the celestial light. The Ādityas, the gods of this light, do not therefore by any means coincide with any of the forms in which light is manifested in the universe. They are neither sun, nor moon, nor stars, nor dawn, but the eternal sustainers of this luminous life, which exists, as it were, behind all these phenomena. It is difficult to say what the Ādityas originally denoted but since most, if not all, of the gods coming in this category are clearly connected with the sun, they must have been conceived as gods of light. Later, of course, they were regarded as solar gods. Dakṣa is frequently excluded and Indra, Savitṛ and Dhātṛ are added. The names of the twelve Ādityas are variously given, but many of them are names of the sun. [*Hindu Mythology*, T.R.R. Iyengar; *India in the Vedic Age*, P.L. Bhargava]

**Agni**: Agni is the chief terrestrial god and second in importance God, and he is celebrated in at least 200 hymns in the *R̥gveda*. The physical phenomenon of fire being always present before the poets, anthropomorphism in the case of Agni is not much developed and his bodily parts are seen as various aspects of the sacrificial fire itself. Thus, he is called butter-faced, butter-backed and beautiful-tongued. He is likened to a bull, a horse, bird, an eagle or a ham. His food is said to be ghee and he eats thrice a day. He also eats and chews the forests with sharp teeth or eats and blackens them with his tongues. He is sometimes spoken of as the mouth by which the gods eat the sacrifice. He is also invited to drink the *soma* juice and in one hymn he is called *Somagopa*, 'guardian of *soma*'.

Agni is represented as having seven tongues, each of which has a distinct name for licking up the butter used in sacrifice. He is described in the *Harivaṁśa* as clothed in black, having smoke for his standard and head-piece, and carrying a flaming javelin. He has four hands, and is borne in a chariot drawn by red horses, and the seven winds are the wheels of his car. A ram accompanies him, and sometimes he is represented riding on that animal. He is the guardian of the south-east quarter, being one of the eight *lokapāla*s, and his region is called Puraj-jyotiṣ. In a celebrated hymn of the *R̥gveda* attributed to Vasiṣṭha, Indra and other gods are called upon to destroy the *kravyād*s, 'the flesh-eaters' of the gods. Agni himself is also a *kravyād*, and as such he takes an entirely different character. He is represented in a form as hideous as the beings he is invoked to devour. He sharpens his two iron tusks, puts his enemies into his mouth and swallows them. He heats the edges of his shafts and sends them into the hearts of the *r̥ṣi*s. Agni's brightness is often described. He is of brilliant colour, bright-flamed and bright-coloured. But when he rushes through the forest, shaving the earth like a barber does the beard, his path is black. His flames roar terribly and shoot into the sky, while his smoke rises above them, owing to which he is called smoke-bantered. He is borne on a luminous car, drawn by two or more horses, in which he brings the gods to receive the offerings of men.

Agni is often called the son of Dyaus and Pr̥thivī. Indra is also said to have generated Agni between two stones. Elsewhere he is said to be born from two fire-sticks regarded as his parents. With reference to his production by friction he is said to be produced by the ten maidens. As force is need for his production he is called the son of Sūrya. He has also been brought into existence by the Dawn; because he is kindled at dawn he is called Usuarbudha, 'walking at dawn'. Being kindled everyday, he is ever young, though ancient form of Agni. Agni is said to have been brought down from the heaven by Mātarisvan and established on the earth in the form of the sacrifice by the Bhr̥gus, who were therefore called Atharvans, fire-priests. Being thus connected with both heaven and earth in his birth he is often called Dvijanman. Sometimes, however, Agni is given a triple birth: in the heaven, on earth and in waters. The triple nature of Agni probably explains the practice of worshipping Agni on three altars in rituals.

Agni is often connected with other gods. Varuṇa is spoken of as his brother. Indra is said to be his twin-brother, and in the Puruṣa-Sūkta both are said to have sprung from the mouth of Puruṣa. It is because of this association that Agni is described as vanquishing the Paṇis and is called breaker of forts and the slayer of Vr̥tra. In one hymn Agni is also coupled with Soma. Agni is occasionally identified with Varuṇa and Mitra. He is also successively identified with about a dozen gods in one of the hymn. Agni is more intimately connected with human life than any other god is. He dwells in every abode and is frequently called lord of the house. Besides he is regarded as a guest in every house, for he is an immortal who has taken his abode among mortals. As leader of the people he is also called Viṣpati. He is often described as the father and sometimes as the brother of his worshipper. He takes the offerings of men to gods and brings the gods to the sacrifice. He is thus characteristically a messenger appointed by gods, and by men, to be an oblation-bearer. Being common to all men he is called Vaiśvānara. As a protector of his worshippers he consumes with iron teeth the sorcerers as well as goblins; and so he is referred to by the epithet *rakṣo'ham*. Dr. Muir in the following verse explains the nature and function of the deity:

Great Agni, though thine essence be but one,
Thy forms are three; as fire thou blazest here,
As lightning flashest in the atmosphere.
In heaven thou flames as the golden sun.

It was in heaven thou had'st thy primal birth;
By art of sages skilled in sacred lore.
Thou wast drawn down to human hearths of yore,
And thou abid'st a denizen of earth.

Sprung from the mystic pair, by priestly hands,
In wedlock joined, forth flashes Agni bright;
But, oh! ye heavens and earth, I tell you right,
The unnatural child devours the parent brands.

But Agni is a god; we must not deem
That he can err or dare to comprehend,
His acts, which far our reason's grasp transcend;
He best can judge what deeds a god beseem.

And yet this orphaned god himself survives:
Although his hapless mother soon expires,
And cannot nurse the babe as babe requires;
Great Agni wondrous infant, grows and thrives.

Smoke-bantered Agni, god with crackling voice,
And flaming hair, when thou dost pierce the gloom
At early dawn, and all the world illume
Both heaven and earth and gods and men rejoice.

In every home thou art a welcome guest,
The household tutelary lord, a son;
A father, mother, brother, all in one,
A friend by whom thy faithful friends are blest.

A swift-winged messenger, thou callest down
From heaven to crowd our hearths the race divine,

To taste our food, our hymns to hear, begin,
And all our fondest aspirations crown.

Thou, Agni art our priest: divinely wise,
In holy science versed, thy skill detects
The faults that mar our rites, mistakes corrects,
And all our acts completes and sanctifies.

Thou art the cord that stretches to the skies,
The bridge that scans the chasm, profound and vast,
Dividing earth from heaven, o'er which at last,
The good shall safely pass to Paradise.

Thou levellest all thou touchest; forests vast
Thou shear'st like beards which barber's razor shaves.
Thy wind-driven flames roar loud as ocean's waves,
And all thy track is black when thou hast past.

But thou great Agni, dost not always wear
That direful form; thou rather love'st to shine
Upon our hearths, with milder flame benign,
And cheer the homes where thou art nursed with care.

'Yes! thou delightest all those men to bless
Who toil unwearied to supply the food
Which thou so lovest — logs of well-dried wood,
And heaps of butter bring, thy favourite men.

Though I no cow possess and have no store
Of butter, nor an axe fresh wood to cleave,
Thou, gracious god, wilt my poor gift receive:
These few dry sticks I bring — I have no more.

Preserve us, lord; thy faithful servants save
From all the ills by which our bliss is marred;
Tower like an iron wall our homes to guard,
And all the boons bestow our hearts can crave.

And when away our brief existence wanes,
When we at length our earthly homes must quit,
And our freed souls to worlds unknown shall flit,
Do thou deal gently with our cold remains.

And then, thy gracious form assuming, guide
Our unborn part across the dark abyss
Aloft to realms serene of light and bliss,
Where righteous men among the gods abide.

The reason why Agni consumes everything yet remains pure as specified in the *Mahābhārata*.

The sage Bhṛgu, it is said once, carried away a woman betrothed to an *asura*, and this person in his search for his beloved went to Agni and asked him where she was, as Agni, in his nature of fire, had access to all places. Agni with his characteristic truthfulness told him where she was and the *asura* brought back his beloved. Bhṛgu came to know of Agni's part in the affair and cursed him to eat everything pure and impure. Agni remonstrated with him and said that in speaking the truth he only did what was becoming of a god and that the whole attitude of Bhṛgu in the affair was anything but proper. Bhṛgu was appeased and he added a blessing to the curse; accordingly, though Agni was to eat everything, he could still remain pure. Hence even impure things when consumed by fire become pure. Agni is a divine monarch and is sometimes praised for his mighty deeds but his priesthood is the most salient feature of his character. He is often called the domestic priest, ministrant, invoker, officiating priest and praying priest. He is in fact the great priest, as Indra is the great warrior. The name Agni is Indo-European and is cognate with Latin 'igneous' and Slavonic 'omni'. The sacrificial fire is an Indo-European institution since the Greeks and Italians as well as the Indians and Iranians had the custom of offering fidgets to gods in the fire.

The names and epithets of Agni are as follows: Vahni; Anala; Pāvaka; Vaiśvānara, 'son of Viśvanara, the sun'; Abja-hasta, 'lotus in hand'; Dhūmaketu, 'whose sign is smoke'; Hutasa, 'devourer of offerings'; Sūci, 'the bright'; Rohitāśva, 'having red horses'; Chāgaratha, 'Ram-rider'; Jātavedas; Saptajihvā,'seven-tongued'; Tomaradhara, 'javelin-bearer'; Huta-bhuj, 'devourer of offerings'; and Śukra, 'the bright'.

[*Hindu Mythology*, T.R.R. Iyengar; *Epics, Myths and Legends of India*, P. Thomas; *A Classical Dictionary of Hindu Mythology and Religion*, J. Dowson; *Glossary of Hinduism*, T. Rengarajan]

**Āgneya**: Son of Agni, a name of Kārttikeya or Mārs; also an appellation.

**Agni-dagdhas**: Pitṛs or Manes, who when alive kept up the household flame and presented oblation with fire.

**Agniṣvāttas**: Pitṛs or Manes of the gods, who when living upon earth did not maintain their domestic fire or offer burnt sacrifices. According to some authorities they are descendants of Marīci. They are also identified with the seasons.

**Ahi**: A serpent. A name of Vṛtra, the Vedic demon of drought; but Ahi and Vṛtra are sometimes 'distinct, and mean most probably, differently formed clouds'.

**Aindrī**: [Son of Indra] An appellation of Arjuna.

**Airāvata**: [A fine elephant] An elephant which is produced at the churning of the ocean, and appropriated by the god Indra. The derivation of this name is referred to the word 'Iravat' signifying 'produced from water'. He is the guardian of one of the points of the compass.

**Aja**: [Unborn] An epithet applied to many of the gods. A prince of the solar race, sometimes said to be the son of Raghu, and at other times the son of Dilīpa, the son of Raghu. He was the husband chosen by Indumatī, daughter of the Rājā of Vidarbha, at her *svayaṁvara* and he was the father of Daśaratha and grandfather of Rāma. The Raghuvaṁśa relates how on his way to the *svayaṁvara* he was annoyed by a wild elephant and ordered it to be shot. When the elephant was mortally wounded a beautiful figure issued from it, which declared itself a *gandharva* who had been transformed into a mad elephant for deriding a holy man. The *gandharva* was delivered, as Aja had foretold it to him, and he gave the prince some arrows, which enabled him to excel in the contest at the *svayaṁvara*. When Daśaratha grew up, Aja ascended to Indra's heaven. (See, Candra, for genealogy). [*A*

*Classical Dictionary of Hindu Mythology and Religion*, J. Dowson]

**Ajagava**: The primitive bow of Śiva, which fell from heaven at the birth of Pṛthu.

**Akita**: [Unconquered] Name of Viṣṇu, Śiva and many others. There were classes of gods bearing this name in several *manvantaras*.

**Akṣa**: Name of Garuḍa.

**Akṣamālā**: Name of Arundhati.

**Akūti**: A daughter of Manu Svayambhuva and Śatarūpā whom he gave to the patriarch Rūci. She bore twins, Yajña and Dakṣiṇā, who became husband and wife and had twelve sons, the deities called Yamas.

**Amareśvara**: [Lord of the immortals] A title of Viṣṇu, Śiva and Indra. Name of one of the twelve great *liṅgas*.

**Ambā**: [Mother] Name of Durgā.

**Ambarīṣa**: An appellation of Śiva.

**Ambikā**: A sister of Rudra, but in later times identified with Umā. Savanna explains Ambikā as one with Pārvatī. In the earlier literature, she is the sister and subsequently the wife of Rudra. In the *Taittirīya Brāhmaṇa* it is said: 'This is thy portion, Rudra, with thy sister Ambikā'. According to the commentator, Ambikā represents autumn which kills by producing disease.

**Āmbikeya**: A metronymic applicable to Gaṇeśa, Skanda and Dhṛtarāṣṭra.

**Amṛta** [Immortal] A god. The water of life.

**Anakadundubhi Drums**: Anakadundubhi is a name of Vāsudeva who was so-called because the drums of heaven resounded at his birth.

**Ānanda**: [Joy, happiness] An appellation of Śiva; also of Balarāma.

**Anaṅgaṇu**: [The bodiless] A name of Kāma, god of love.

**Ananta**: [The infinite] A name of the serpent Śeṣa. The term is also applied to Viṣṇu and other deities.

**Aṅgiras**: A *ṛṣi* to whom many hymns of the *Ṛgveda* are attributed. He was one of the seven *maharṣi* and also one of the ten Prajāpatis. In later times Aṅgiras was one of the inspired lawgivers and also a writer on astronomy. As an astronomical personification he is Bṛhaspati, the regent of the planet Jupiter, or the planet itself. He is also called 'the priest of the gods' and 'the lord of sacrifice'. There is much ambiguity about the name. It comes from the same root as Agni, 'fire' and resembles that word in sound. This may be the reason why the name Aṅgiras is used as an epithet of Agni. The name is also employed as an epithet for the father of Agni and it is found especially connected with the hymns addressed to Agni, Indra and the luminous deities.

According to one statement, Aṅgiras is the son of Uru by Āgneyī, the daughter of Agni, although, as above-stated, the name is sometimes given to the father of Agni. Another account states that he was born from the mouth of Brahmā. His wives are Smṛti, 'memory', daughter of Dakṣa; Śraddhā, 'faith', daughter of Kardama; and Svadhā, 'oblation', and Satī, 'truth', two other daughters of Dakṣa. His daughters are the Ṛcās and his sons are the Manes called Haviṣmats. But he had other children as well; among them are sons Utathya, Bṛhaspati and Mārkaṇḍeya. According to the *Bhāgavata Purāṇa*, 'he begot sons possessing Brāhmaṇical glory on the wife of Rathitara, a kṣatriya who was childless, and these persons were afterwards called descendants of Aṅgiras'. [*Hindu Mythology*, T.R.R. Iyengar]

**Aṅgirasas, Aṅgirases**: Descendants of Aṅgiras. They share in the nature of the legends attributed to Aṅgiras. Aṅgiras being the father of Agni, they are considered as descendants of Agni himself, who is also called the first of the Aṅgirasas. Like Aṅgiras they occur in hymns addressed to the luminous deities, and, at a later period, they become for the most part personifications of light, of luminous bodies, of division of time, of celestial phenomena, and fires adapted to peculiar occasions, as the full moon and change of the moon or to particular rites, such as the *aśvamedha* and *rājasūya*. In the *Śatapatha Brāhmaṇa* they and the Ādityas are said to have descended from Prajāpati and 'they strove together for the priority in ascending to heaven'. Some descendants of Aṅgiras by the kṣatriya wife of a childless king are mentioned in the Purāṇas as two tribes of Aṅgiras who were brāhmaṇas as well as kṣatriyas. The hymns of the *Atharvaveda* are called Aṅgirasas, and the descendants of Aṅgiras were specially charged with the protection of sacrifices performed in accordance with the *Atharvaveda*. From this cause, or from their being associated with the descendants of Atharvans, they are called distinctively Atharvāṅgirasas. [*Hindu Mythology*, T.R.R. Iyengar]

**Āṅgirasas**: A class of *pitṛ*s.

**Anila**: Name of wind god.

**Anilas**: A *gaṇa* or class of deities, forty-nine in number, connected with Anila, the wind.

**Animiṣa**: A general epithet of all gods.

**Aniruddha**: [Uncontrolled] Son of Pradyumna and grandson of Kṛṣṇa.

**Añjana**: The elephant of the west or south-west quarter.

**Añjanā**: Mother of Hanumān by Vāyu, god of wind.

**Annapūrṇā**: Annapūrṇā is one of the popular forms of Pārvatī when she distributed food to Śiva and other gods. She is represented as a standing image with two hands, holding a pot full of food in the left hand and a spoon in the right one with which to serve the food. This is a widely worshipped manifestation of Pārvatī. It was occasioned by a domestic quarrel between Śiva and Pārvatī. Śiva, as a mendicant, supported the family by begging; but due to excessive smoking he could not go on his daily rounds. The hungry children, the rat of Gaṇeśa and the peacock of Kārttikeya consumed the previous day's provision. But the elder member of the family had to starve. While Śiva was wondering why he was fated to starve like this when all other gods lived in opulence, Nārada appeared before him. On enquiring of the sage if he knew the cause of his misery, Nārada told Śiva that it was all on account of Pārvatī. An auspicious wife, said the learned sage, brings good fortune to her husband and an inauspicious one misfortunes. He pointed out Viṣṇu who, he said, had married Śrī and had ever since lived in plenty. After imparting this information to Śiva the sage repaired to the kitchen where he saw the starving Pārvatī sitting in a melancholy mood. She asked the sage if he knew why she was condemned to such penury, and Nārada told her that it was all on account of her husband. He said,

> A capable husband supports his family and keeps them in opulence. Look at Sarasvatī, she married the creator and lives in a heaven the likes of which does not exist in the three worlds. It pains me to say so, noble lady, but there is no getting away from the fact that the tendencies of your husband are essentially destructive, and he cares not for his wife and children.

Pārvatī brooded over the words of Nārada and decided to desert her husband. Next day, while Śiva was out begging, she called her children and proceeded towards her father's house. Nārada, however, did not want things to go that far and so he appeared before her. He told her that though Śiva had many faults he had some redeeming features as well which the other gods envied. He advised her to go to the house where Śiva went for begging, in advance of her husband, and collect all the food from them. She did so with the result that her husband returned home hungry with his begging bowl empty. Pārvatī now fed him with the food she collected, and Mahādeva was so pleased with her that he embraced her violently and became one with her. The form of Pārvatī feeding her husband is known as Annapūrṇā Devī while the combined form — in which Śiva became one with his wife — is called Ardhanārī. [*Epics, Myths and Legends of India*, P. Thomas]

**Antaka**: [The ender] A name of Yama, judge of the dead.

**Āpaḥ**: Āpaḥ or the water are lauded in four hymns of the *Ṛgveda* as well as in a few scattered verses. Their personification is only incipient, hardly extending beyond the notion of their being mothers and goddesses who confer boons and come to the sacrifice. Indra, armed with the bolt, dug out a channel for them, and they never infringe his ordinances. They are celestial as well as terrestrial and the sea is their goal. King Varuṇa moves in the midst, looking down on the truth and falsehood of men. Agni is also described as dwelling in them. They drip honey, and are bright and purifying. They bestow health, wealth, strength, long life and immortality. [*India in the Vedic Age*, P.L. Bhargava, *Hindu Mythology*, T.R.R. Iyengar]

**Apām-Napāt**: The deity Apām-Napāt is lauded in one entire hymn besides being invoked in two verses of a hymn to the waters and is mentioned by name nearly thirty times in the *Ṛgveda*. Apām-Napāt is described as brilliant and youthful and is said to shine without fuel in the waters, which surround and nourish him. He is golden in form, appearance and colour. Steeds swift as thought carry this son of the waters. He is, in a few passages, identified with Agni, but elsewhere he is distinguished from him. The name of Apām-Napāt occurs in the *Avesta* also where he is a spirit of the waters who lives in their depths, is surrounded by females and drives with swift steeds, and is said to have seized the brightness in the depth of the ocean. [*Hindu Mythology*, T.R.R. Iyengar; *India in the Vedic Age*, P.L. Bhargava]

**Aparṇā**: According to the *Harivaṁśa*, the eldest daughter of Himavatī and Menā. She and her two sisters, Ekaparṇā and Ekapāṭalā, gave themselves up to austerity and practised extraordinary abstinence; but while her sisters lived, as their names denote, upon one leaf or on one *paṭala* respectively, Aparṇā managed to subsist upon nothing. This so distressed her mother that she cried out, 'Umā', i.e., 'Oh, don't'. Aparṇā thus became the beautiful Umā, the wife of Śiva.

**Āpava**: [Who sports in the waters] A name of the same import as Nārāyaṇa, and having a similar though not an identical application. According to the *Brahma Purāṇa* and the *Harivaṁśa*, Āpava performed the office of the creator Brahmā, and divided himself into two parts, male and female, the former begetting offspring upon the latter. The result was the production of Viṣṇu, who created Virāj, who brought the first man into the world. According to the *Mahābhārata*, Āpava is a name of the Prajāpati Vasiṣṭha. The name of Āpava is of late introduction and has been vaguely used. Wilson says: 'According to the commentator, the first stage was the creation of Āpava or Vasiṣṭha or Virāj by Viṣṇu, through the agency of Brahmā and the next was that of the creation of Manu by Virāj.' [*A Classical Dictionary of Hindu Mythology and Religion*, J. Dowson]

**Apsaras**: The *apsaras*es are the celebrated nymphs of Indra's heaven. The name signifies 'moving in the water'.

**Araṇyāni**: In the *Ṛgveda*, the goddess of woods and forests.

**Ardhanārī**: [Half-woman] A form of Śiva in which he is represented as half-male and half-female, typifying the male and female energies.

**Argon**: Son of Kṛtavīrya, king of the Haihayas. He is better known by his patronymic, Kārttavīrya.

**Aruṇa**: [Red, rosy] The dawn personified as the charioteer of the sun. This is of later origin than the Vedic Uṣas. He is said to be the son of Kaśyapa and Kadru. He is also called *rumra,* 'tawny' and by two other epithets of which the meaning is not obvious — *an-uru*, 'thighless' and *asmana*, 'stony'.

**Arundhatī**: The morning star, personified as the wife of the *ṛṣi* Vasiṣṭha and a model of conjugal excellence.

**Aruṣa**: [*aruṣī* meaning 'red'] A red horse. In the *Ṛgveda* the red horses or mares of the sun or of fire. The rising sun.

**Arvan**: [A horse] One of the horses of the moon.

**Aryaman**: (1) Chief of the *pitṛ*s. (2) One of the Ādityas. (3) One of the Viśvadevas.

**Aśvamukha**: Horse-faced.

**Aśvapati**: Lord of horses.

**Aśvins**: [Horsemen] Two Vedic deities, twin sons of the sun or the sky. They are ever young and handsome, bright and of golden brilliance, agile, swift as falcons, possessing many forms, and they ride in a golden car drawn by horses or birds, as harbingers of Uṣas, the dawn. 'They are the earliest bringers of light in the morning sky, who in their chariot hasten onwards before the dawn and prepare the way for her.' As personification of the morning twilight, they are said to be children of the sun by a nymph who concealed herself in the form of a mare; hence she was called Aśvan, and her sons Aśvins. But inasmuch as they precede the rise of the sun, they are called his parents in his form Pūṣan. The twin deities called Aśvins are next to Indra, Agni and Soma, the most prominent. In the *Ṛgveda* they claim more than fifty hymns and are mentioned over 400 times. The name Aśvan, which is the common title of these twin gods, means 'horse-rider' and in most of the hymns addressed to them they are shown as riding on chariots. A few verses show that they were originally conceived as ever on the backs of horses ready to venture forth to rescue their devotees. The two most distinctive epithets of the Aśvins are Nāsatyas and Dasras; even in the period of the *Ṛgveda*, the two words were sometimes regarded as separate proper names of the Aśvins. The word *dasra* means wondrous, while the word *nāsatya* is generally explained to mean 'not untrue'. The physical basis of the Aśvins has been a puzzle from the time of the earliest interpreters.

One probable theory accepted by Oldenberg and some other scholars is that they represent the morning and evening stars. A most probable explanation suggested by Hopkins and others and supported by their description in the *Ṛgveda* is that the Aśvins represent the morning twilight as half-night and half-dark. This is confirmed by a verse quoted by Yāska in which one of the Aśvins is called the son of night, the other the son of dawn. The Aśvin twins known in these latter-day texts as Aśvinikumāras are similar to the twin gods Castor and Pollux of Grecian mythology. Many hymns have been addressed to them. The *sūkta* I.3.1 speaks of them as having large arms. They are also called Dasras and Nāsatyas in *ṛk* 3. The Aśvins ride on chariot with three wheels. Again this chariot is a triangular one. The Aśvins blow conch at the time of battles. The Aśvins do not age. The donkeys carry the chariot of the Aśvins. The Aśvins were mechanics: they prepared substitute metalloid leg for Vispalā, the wife of Khela. They restored the eyesight of Ṛjrasva and they are called medical men. In *Ṛgveda* 69.4 the poet says that at night, Joṣitā, daughter of Sun covers the chariot of the Aśvins. Again *ṛk* 8 says that they are always young. As regards the physical description of the Aśvins, the *Ṛgveda* is silent about it. Mythologically they are the parents of the Pāṇḍava princes, Nakula and Sahadeva. Their attributes are numerous, but relate mostly to youth and beauty, light and speed, duality, the curative power, and active benevolence. The number of hymns addressed to them testifies to the enthusiastic worship they received. They were the physicians and in this character are called Dasras and Nāsatyas, Gadagadau and Svarvaidyau. Other appellations are 'Abdhijau', 'ocean born': 'Puṣkara-srajau', 'wreathed with lotuses'; 'Baḍaveyau', 'sons of the submarine fire', Baḍava. Many instances are recorded of their benevolence and their power of healing. They restored the sage Cyavana to youth, and prolonged his life when he had become old and enfeebled, and through his instrumentality they were admitted to partake of the libations of Soma, like the other gods, although Indra strongly opposed them. 'The Aśvins', says Muir, 'have been a puzzle to the oldest commentators', who have differed widely in their explanations. According to different interpretations quoted in the *Nirukta*, they are 'heaven and earth', 'day and night', 'two kings' and 'performers of holy acts'. [*India in the Vedic Age*, P.L. Bhargava; *Hindu Mythology*, T.R.R. Iyengar]

**Atharvan**: Name of a priest mentioned in the *Ṛgveda* where he is represented as having 'drawn to fire' and to have 'offered sacrifice in early times'. He is mythologically represented as the eldest son of Brahmā, to whom that god revealed the *brahma-vidyā*, as a Prajāpati and as the inspired author of the fourth Veda. At a later period he is identified with Aṅgiras. His descendants are called Atharvanas, and they are often associated with the Aṅgirasas.

**Avatāra**: [A descent] The incarnation of a deity, especially of Viṣṇu. The first indication, not of an *avatāra*, but of what subsequently developed into an *avatāra*, is found in the *Ṛgveda*, in the 'three steps' of 'Viṣṇu, the unconquerable preserver', who strode over this (universe) and in three places planted his step. The early commentators understood the 'three places' to be the earth, the atmosphere, and the sky; that on the earth Viṣṇu was fire, in the air lightning and in the sky the solar light. One commentator, Aurṇavābha, whose name deserves mention, took a more philosophical view of the matter, and interpreted 'the three steps' as being the different positions of the sun at his rising, culmination, and setting. Sāyaṇa, the great commentator, who lived at a time when god Viṣṇu had obtained pre-eminence, understood 'the three steps' to be the three steps taken by that god in his incarnation of Vāmana, the dwarf. Another reference to 'three strides' and to a sort of *avatāra* is made in the *Taittirīya Saṁhitā*, where it is said 'Indra, assuming the form of a she-jackal, stepped all round the earth in three (strides). Thus the gods obtained it.' The *avatāra*s of Viṣṇu are numerous, but ten are considered to be the most prominent. They are 1. Matsya, 2. Kūrma, 3. Varāha, 4. Narasiṁha, 5. Vāmana, 6. Paraśurāma, 7. Rāma, 8. Kṛṣṇa, 9. Buddha and 10. Kalki. But the number is extended in the *Bhāgavata Purāṇa* to include twelve more incarnations: 11. Puruṣa, 12. Nārada, 13. Nara-Nārāyaṇa, 14. Pṛthu, 15. Kapila, 16. Vyāsa, 17. Ṛṣabha, 18. Yajña, sacrifice, 19. & 20. Dhanvantari, 21. Balarāma, and 22. Dattātreya. A detailed account of these *avatāra*s are as follows:

1. ***Matsya***: The fish. This is an appropriation to Viṣṇu of the ancient legend of the fish and the deluge, as related in the *Śatapatha Brāhmaṇa*, and quoted above. The details of this *avatāra* vary slightly in different Purāṇas.

The object of the incarnation was to save Vaisvasvata, the seventh Manu, and progenitor of the human race, from destruction by a deluge. A small fish came into the hands of Manu and besought his protection. He carefully guarded it, and it grew rapidly until nothing but the ocean could contain it. Manu then recognised its divinity, and worshipped the deity Viṣṇu thus incarnate. The god apprised Manu of the approaching cataclysm, and bade him prepare for it. When it came, Manu embarked in a ship with the *ṛṣi*, and with a most stupendous horn. The ship was bound to this horn with a great serpent, as with a rope, and was secured in safety until the waters had subsided. The *Bhāgavata Purāṇa* introduces a new feature. In one of the nights of Brahmā, and during his repose, the earth and the other worlds were submerged in the ocean. Then the demon Hayagrīva drew, near and carried off the Veda which had issued from Brahmā's mouth. To recover the Veda thus lost Viṣṇu assumed the form of a fish, and saved Manu as above related. But this Purāṇa adds that the fish instructed Manu and the *ṛṣi*s in the true doctrine of the soul of the eternal Brahmā and, when Brahmā awoke at the end of this dissolution of the universe, Viṣṇu slew Hayagrīva and restored the Veda and Brahmā. In the *Mahābhārata*, Brahmā is said to have appeared before Manu in the form of a fish. The Purāṇas assert that it was Viṣṇu who did so and predicted the deluge and saved Manu from the universal cataclysm. The fish that propelled Manu's ship across the waters to the Himālayas is said to have been of golden colour, having a horn, and a body extending over ten million *yojana*s (one *yojana* is equivalent to four miles). In this *avatāra*, Viṣṇu is represented as half-fish and half-man, the human form having the usual attributes of Viṣṇu — four hands, the back ones carrying *śaṅkha* and *cakra*, and the front ones depicted in *abhaya* and *varada* poses, while the lower half of the body has the shape of a fish. There are no main temples dedicated to this *avatāra* except that images of this form are usually seen in the *gopurams* and pillars of temples.

2. ***Kūrma***: The tortoise. The germ of this *avatāra* is found in the *Śatapatha Brāhmaṇa*, as above noticed. In the *Śatapatha Brāhmaṇa* it is said, 'Prajāpati, having assumed the form of a tortoise, created offspring. That which he created, he made', hence the word *kūrma*. In its later and developed form, Viṣṇu appeared in the form of a tortoise in the *satya-yuga* to recover some things of value, which had been lost in the deluge. In the form of a tortoise he placed himself at the bottom of the sea of milk, and made his back the base or pivot of the mountain Mandāra. The gods and demons twisted the great serpent Vāsuki round the mountain, and dividing into two parties, each took an end of the snake as a rope, and thus churned the sea until they recovered the desired objects. These were *amṛta*, the water of life; Dhanvantari, the physician of gods and bearer of the cup of *amṛta*; Lakṣmī, goddess of fortune and beauty, and consort of Viṣṇu; Surā, the goddess of wine, Candra, the moon, Rambhā, a nymph and the epitome of a lovely and amiable woman; Ucchaiḥsravas, a wonderful and model horse; *kaustubha*, a celebrated jewel; *pārijāta*, a celestial tree; Surabhi, the cow of plenty; Airāvata, a wonderful model elephant; *śaṅkha*, a shell, the conch of victory; *dhanuṣ*, a famous bow; and *viṣa*, poison. As soon as Dhanvantari appeared with the bowl of ambrosia, the gods and the *asuras* left the churning rope and madly rushed towards the physician. In the scuffle, the *asuras* succeeded in seizing the bowl, and they made away with it. But a quarrel broke out among the *asuras* themselves on the question as to who should be served first. Then appeared in their midst a damsel of celestial beauty, with her face like a lotus in efflorescence, waist like an island, and her person, adorned with necklaces, bangles and anklets. She stepped merrily into the midst of the *asuras*, her anklets jingling,

and smiled sweetly on them. The *asura*s now forgot all about ambrosia and stood wondering at the beauty of Mohinī. Mohinī threw her glances at the bowl of ambrosia and a gallant *asura* suggested that she should decide how they share the ambrosia, and all the *asura*s cheered him. Mohinī smiled and asked them whether it would be prudent to leave such a momentous decision to a woman. Mohinī with a mischievous smile stated that wise men have said women are unreliable. All the *asura*s laughed heartily and were now convinced without any doubt that she could be trusted, and swore that they would abide by her decision unconditionally. Mohinī remarked that the gods and *asura*s had toiled equally hard in raising the ambrosia and should get an equal share, and made them sit in two rows. She took the bowl and served the row of gods first. After the last god had been served Mohinī disappeared with the bowl. A terrible uproar ensued on her departure and the gods and the *asura*s fought a fierce battle. But the gods who were strengthened by the draughts of ambrosia they had drunk easily defeated the *asura*s and put them to flight. One of the *asura*s had disguised himself as a god and sat in the row of the gods. He had just quaffed a mouthful of ambrosia when Sūrya and Candra who were sitting on either side of him detected the fraud and pointed him out to Viṣṇu. This deity immediately cut him into two with his weapon, but by virtue of the nectar he had drunk, both the portions of the demon remained animate and Brahmā translated them into the heavens as planets. The upper portion is called Rāhu and the other Ketu. It is said that Rāhu is even now the mortal enemy of the sun and the moon and that eclipses are caused by his trying to devour them. It may be added that Śiva became enamoured of the Mohinī form of Viṣṇu and hence he went to Vaikuṇṭha and requested his crony to assume that shape again. Viṣṇu obliged him but Śiva chased Mohinī with the intention of doing violence on her. On this, Viṣṇu assumed his male form but the infatuated Śiva caught him, embraced him and became one with him.

3. ***Varāha***: Varāha is fabled to have once raised the earth from primal waters under which it lay submerged. For accomplishing this feat he had to take the form of a boar. In the *Taittirīya Saṁhitā* and *Taittirīya Brāhmaṇa* and also in the *Śatapatha Brāhmaṇa*, the creator of Prajāpati, afterwards known as Brahmā, took the form of a boar for the purpose of raising the earth out of the boundless waters. The *Taittirīya Saṁhitā* says this universe was formerly water, fluid. On it, Prajāpati becoming wind, moved. He saw this earth. Becoming a boar, he took her up. Becoming Viśvakraman, he wiped the moisture from her. She extended. She became the extended one. From this, the earth derives her designation as the extended one. The *Taittirīya Brāhmaṇa* is in accord as to the illimitable waters, and adds, Prajāpati practised arduous devotion as to how shall this universe be (developed)? He beheld a lotus leaf standing. He thought, there is somewhat on which this rests. He, as a boar, having assumed that form, plunged beneath towards it. He found the earth down below. Breaking off (a portion of) her, he rose to the earth. He then extended it on the lotus leaf. Inasmuch as he extended it, that is the extension of the extended one. From this the earth derives its name 'Bhūmi'. Further, in the *Taittirīya Āraṇyaka* it is said that the earth was raised by a black boar with a hundred arms. The *Śatapatha Brāhmaṇa* states that formerly the earth was only the size of a span. A boar called Emuṣa raised her up. In the *Rāmāyaṇa* also it is stated that Brahmā 'became a boar and raised up the earth'. In the beginning all was water through which the earth was formed. Thence arose Brahmā, the self-existent, the imperishable Viṣṇu. He then becoming a boar, raised up this earth and created the whole world. The *Viṣṇu*

*Purāṇa* gives the following exposition: 'At the close of the last age, the divine Brahmā endowed with the quality of goodness awoke from his night of sleep and beheld the universal void. He, the supreme Nārāyaṇa, invested with the form of a Brahmā concluding that within the water lay the earth and being desirous to raise it up, created another form for the purpose. And as in the preceding ages he had assumed the shape of a fish or a tortoise, so in this he took the form of a boar. Having adopted a form universal soul plunged into the ocean. According to *Vāyu Purāṇa*, the form of a boar was chosen, because it is an animal delighting in water. Another version of this myth is that a demon named Hiraṇyākṣa propitiated Brahmā by penance and received a boon that exempted him from harm by god, man or beast. But while enumerating all possible forms of beings from whom he claimed exemption, he omitted, through an oversight, to include the boar. While Brahmā was asleep he stole the Vedas and dragged the earth into his abode in the nether region under the waters; and Viṣṇu assuming the form of a boar, killed him with his tusks, regained the Vedas and caused the earth to float once again. The boar is described in the *Vāyu Purāṇa* as ten *yojana*s in breadth and a thousand *yojana*s in height; his colour dark and his roar like thunder. His bulk was vast as a mountain; his tusks were white, sharp and fearful; fire flashed from his eyes like lightning; and he was as radiant as the sun. His shoulders were round, fat and large, he strode along like a powerful lion, and his haunches were fat, his loins slender, and his body was smooth and beautiful. The *avatāra* is represented as a human being except for the face, which is that of a boar, having four arms and bearing the usual *āyudha*s. The image of *varāha* is almost invariably associated with Bhūdevī, the earth goddess. In addition to iconographical details of Varāha, *Padma Purāṇa* gives an esoteric meaning to this form, indicating that the form and various limbs of Varāha represent the components of a sacrifice giving significance to each and every part of the body of this deity. Varāha is represented in various forms, the more important being the following:

*Bhū Varāha*: *Vaikhānasāgama* indicates that this form has the face of a boar with the body of a man, the right leg being bent, resting on the hoods of Ādiśeṣa on which is seated Bhūmadevī, whom the deity would be embracing with his lower right hand with the other left hand holding her legs.

*Lakṣmī Varāha*: Here the main image is seated on a pedestal, having the right leg hanging down and the left bent to seat Lakṣmī on his thigh, embracing her with his left hand while the right is in *abhaya* pose.

*Yajña Varāha*: Seated image on a *siṁhāsana* just as Lakṣmī Varāha, but instead of Lakṣmī, Bhūdevī is shown as seated on his left thigh.

*Kevala Varāha*: Standing image of Varāha alone, having the two lower arms bent at the elbow so that they would be shown as resting on the hips.

4. ***Narasiṁha***: Viṣṇu assumed the form of a man-lion to kill Hiraṇyakaśipu, the brother of Hiraṇyākṣa who had been slain by Varāha. Hiraṇyakaśipu too, like his brother, propitiated Brahmā and obtained a boon, which gave him immunity from all conceivable forms of danger. He could not be killed by god, man or beast. He could die neither by day nor by night; neither inside nor outside his home. Thus protected, he proceeded to claim divine honours for himself and prohibited all forms of worship in his kingdom. But his own son Prahlāda was an ardent a devotee of Viṣṇu, and the lad was caught red-handed in the act of worshipping that deity. Hiraṇyakaśipu advised his son to give up his devotional exercises, but Prahlāda refused. He was flogged and sent to a preceptor notorious for his atheistic doctrines. On his return from his

teacher, Prahlāda was however found to be as ardent devotee of Viṣṇu as ever. This enraged Hiraṇyakaśipu beyond all measure and, highly exasperated, he commanded serpents to fall upon his disobedient and insane son and bite him to death. The serpents did their worst, but Prahlāda felt them not. The snakes cried out to the king, 'Our fangs are broken, our jewelled crests are burst; there is fever in our hoods, and fear in our hearts; but the skin of the youth is still unscathed. Have recourse, O King of the *daityas*, to some other expedient.' Other forms of torture followed. One day, while Hiraṇyakaśipu was sitting in his palace and speaking to his son on the fallacy of Viṣṇu worship, the latter began to chant the praises of Viṣṇu. 'Where is your Viṣṇu?' asked Hiraṇyakaśipu in a rage. 'Everywhere', replied Prahlāda. 'Is he in this pillar?' 'Yes', replied Prahlāda. 'Then I kill him', said the demon-king and getting up kicked the pillar. Out of the pillar sprang forth Narasiṁha, and he tore Hiraṇyakaśipu to pieces. It is said the incident took place by evening and since man-lion is neither god, beast nor man, the provisions of Brahmā's boon were respected to the letter. The Narasiṁha *avatāra* is represented with the body of a man having the face of a lion. There are many forms of Narasiṁha.

*Girijā Narasiṁha*: Girijā Narasiṁha is represented as in the form of *sthaṅka* and *āsana*. In standing form, he is represented with four hands, having the *cakra* and the *śaṅkha* in the upper ones while the lower are in *abhaya* and *varada* poses, and he has a ferocious lion's face.

*Yoga Narasiṁha*: He is also represented as a seated *mūrti* in *sukhāsana* when he is named Yoga Narasiṁha.

*Lakṣmī Narasiṁha*. Here Narasiṁha is represented with Devī seated on his left thigh.

*Ugra Narasiṁha*: It is more ferocious with Narasiṁha represented as tearing the demon, having him on his thigh. The *Pañcarātrāgama* describes this Ugra Narasiṁha form as terrible: like flaming fire, he has a lion face, with a human body, furious fangs, a protruding tongue, an open mouth, a thick mane and muscular chest. He stands in the *ālīḍha* posture in an angry mood and splits the breast of the giant, thrown flat upon his thigh, with the sharp nails of his hands. Sometimes this variety has more than four hands, up to even sixteen hands.

*Yanaka Narasiṁha*: He is depicted as seated on the shoulder of Garuḍa.

5. ***Vāmana***: Bali, grandson of Prahlāda, ruled his kingdom well and wisely but was ambitious. He decided to enlarge the frontiers of his kingdom and began to perform a great sacrifice. Indra, the king of the gods, was troubled as it was evident that Bali's object was to acquire the celestial kingdom and drive away the gods from their abode. He consulted his preceptor Bṛhaspati who confirmed his fears and added that as Bali's sacrifice had gone too far, nothing could be done to prevent his conquest of Indra just then, and the gods would be well-advised to leave their kingdom. This was done. Afterwards penances and prayers propitiated Viṣṇu and he took birth as the son of Bṛhaspati. The child was a deformed dwarf. When he reached boyhood he went to Bali begging for alms and Bali, famous for his generosity, told the dwarf he could have anything he wanted. The dwarf made Bali promise on oath that he would give him three paces of land. The pigmy then grew to inconceivable proportions and measured the three worlds in two paces. There was no more land for the third pace and Bali was accused of not having kept his promise and sent to the nether region. A legend tells us that Bali was much devoted to his subjects and begged Viṣṇu to permit him to visit his lost

kingdom once a year and that Viṣṇu agreed. Images of Vāmana or dwarf aspect of this *avatāra* in the lower panel are very rare. According to Hemādri, the dwarf is a fat young *brahmacārin* with ill-formed limbs, having two arms holding a staff in one hand and a *kamaṇḍalu* in the other. There are no important shrines dedicated to this aspect. However the form of Trivikrama is more popular and well-represented. There are three forms in this particular aspect according to the level up to which the left leg of the deity is raised up to the right knee, navel or forehead. Trivikrama images have two to eight hands carrying the usual weapons of Viṣṇu. In some sculptural representations Brahmā could be shown with offerings at the uplifted toe of Viṣṇu's leg, with Śiva on the other side in *añjalī* pose. Down below, representation of King Bali, his queen, and Śukrācārya, his preceptor, are also known.

6. ***Paraśurāma***: The story of this *avatāra* indicates a caste-conflict between brāhmaṇas and kṣatriyas in which the former were victorious. Viṣṇu is said to have been born as a militant brāhmaṇa to annihilate the kṣatriyas who had become proud and begun oppressing brāhmaṇas. Jamadagni, a brāhmaṇa hermit, who lived in the woods, had a faithful and virtuous wife who was the mother of five sons. One day she went to the river to bathe and, as ill-luck would have it, saw in the river a handsome man sporting with a damsel. She looked at the amorous pair, took pleasure in voluptuous thoughts and even desired to enjoy the company of the handsome man. On her return to the hermitage her husband 'beholding her failed from her perfection and shorn of the lustre of her sanctity' reproached her. All the sons of the hermit were, at that time, out in the woods gathering berries. They came home one by one and Jamadagni asked each of them to kill his mother. Four sons refused to become matricides. The angry sage cursed his disobedient sons and they

became idiots. Lastly came Paraśurāma, the youngest, to whom Jamadagni said, 'Kill thy mother, who has sinned; and do it without repening'. Rāma promptly took his axe and cut off his mother's head. Jamadagni greatly pleased with his son asked him to demand of him any boons he wished. Rāma begged for these boons. The restoration of his mother to life with forgetfulness of having been slain and purification from all defilement; the return of his brothers to their natural condition; and for himself invincibility in single combat, and length of days. These were granted. He is represented as an elderly person with beard, moustache, *jaṭā-mukuṭa*, having normally two hands carrying an axe and sword. *Agni Purāṇa* states that he has four hands bearing *paraśu*, *khaḍga*, *bāṇa* and *dhanuṣ*. There are no particular temples for this deity.

7. ***Rāmacandra***: The moon like or gentle Rāma, the hero of the *Rāmāyaṇa*. He was son of Daśaratha, king of Ayodhyā, of the solar race, and was born in the *tretā-yuga*, for the purpose of destroying the demon Rāvaṇa. (*See* Rāmacandra).

8. ***Kr̥ṣṇa***: [The black or dark coloured] This is the most popular of all the later deities, and has obtained such pre-eminence, that his votaries look upon him not simply as an incarnation, but as a perfect manifestation of Viṣṇu. When Kr̥ṣṇa is thus exalted to the full godhead, his elder brother Balarāma takes his place as the eighth *avatāra*. (*See* Kr̥ṣṇa).

9. ***Buddha***: The great success of Buddha as a religious teacher seems to have induced the brāhmaṇas to adopt him as their own, rather than to recognise him as an adversary. So Viṣṇu is said to have appeared as Buddha to encourage demons and wicked men to despise the Vedas, reject caste, and deny the existence of the gods, and thus to effect their own destruction. In the *Skanda Purāṇa* the doctrines he taught are thus summarised:

Viṣṇu as the Buddha taught that the universe was without a creator. It is false therefore to assert that there is one universal and supreme spirit, for Brahmā, Viṣṇu and Śiva and the rest are names of mere corporeal beings like ourselves. Death is a peaceful sleep, why fear it? He also taught that pleasure is the only heaven and pain the only hell, and liberation from ignorance the only beatitude. Sacrifices are acts of folly. Lakṣmī is also mentioned as having assumed the form of a woman and taught the female disciples to place all happiness in sensual pleasures.

**10.** ***Kalki***: [The white horse] The incarnation of Viṣṇu is to appear at the end of the *kali* or Iron age seated on a white horse, with a drawn sword blazing like a comet, for the final destruction of the wicked, the renovation of creation and restoration of purity. In the *Viṣṇu Purāṇa* the need for destroying the world and building it anew is thus vividly described:

The kings of the earth will be of churlish spirit, violent in temper, and ever addicted to falsehood and wickedness. They will inflict death on women, children, and cows; they will seize the property of subjects, be of limited power, and will, for the most part, rapidly rise and fall; their lives will be short, their desires insatiable, and they will display but little piety. The people of various countries intermingling with them will follow their example; and the barbarians being powerful under the patronage of princes, whilst purer tribes are neglected, the people will perish. Wealth and piety will decrease day by day until the world shall be wholly depraved. Property alone will confer rank, wealth will be the only source of devotion, passion will be the sole bond of union between the sexes, falsehood will be the only means of success in litigation and women will be objects merely of sensual gratification. Earth will be venerated only for its mineral treasures; the Brāhmaṇical thread will constitute a brāhmaṇa; external types will be the only distinctions of the several orders of life, dishonesty will be the universal means of subsistence, weakness will be the cause of dependence, menace and presumption will be the subterfuge for learning, liberality will be devotion, and simple ablution will be purification. Mutual assent will be marriage, fine clothes will be dignity, and water afar off will be esteemed a holy spring. The people, unable to hear the heavy burdens imposed upon them by their avaricious sovereigns, will take refuge among the valleys and be glad to feed upon wild honey, herbs, roots, fruits, flowers and leaves, their only covering will be the dark of trees, and they will be exposed to cold and wind, and sun and rain. No man's life will exceed three-and-twenty years. Thus in the *kali* age shall decay flourish, until the human race approaches annihilation.

11. ***Puruṣa***: He is shown as a seated image with four hands having Śrīdevī and Medinī Devī on either side.

12. ***Nārada***: The great sage (*see* under 'Nārada').

13. ***Nara-Nārāyaṇa***: See under 'Nara-Nārāyaṇa'.

14. ***Pṛthu***: *See* under 'Pṛthu'.

15. ***Kapila***: Kapila is represented as an old man with beard in *dhyāna* pose, having a *jaṭā-mukuṭa*, carrying *śaṅkha*, and *cakra* and also *sruk*, *ajyabharata*, having goddesses Svāhā and Svadhā at his sides.

16. ***Vyāsa***: [An arranger] This title is common to many old authors and compilers, but it is especially applied to Veda-Vyāsa, the arranger of the Vedas, who, from the imperishable nature of his work, is also called Śāśvatas, the immortal. The name is given also to the compiler of the *Mahābhārata*, the founder of the Vedānta philosophy, and the arranger of the Purāṇas; all these persons being held to be identical with Veda-Vyāsa. But this is impossible, and the attribution of all these works to one

person has arisen either from a desire to heighten their antiquity and authority, or from the assumed identity of several 'arrangers'. Veda-Vyāsa was the illegitimate son of the *ṛṣi*s Parāśara and Satyavatī, and the child, who was of a dark colour, was brought forth on an island in the Yamunā. Being illegitimate he was called Kanina, the 'bastard', from his complexion he received the name Kṛṣṇa, and from his birthplace he was called Dvaipāyana. His mother afterwards married king Śāntanū, by whom she had two sons. The elder was killed in battle, and the younger, named Victiravīrya, died childless. Kṛṣṇa Dvaipāyana preferred a life of religious retirement, but in accordance with law and at his mother's request, he took the two childless widows of her son, Victiravīrya. By them he had two sons, Dhṛtarāṣṭra and Pāṇḍu, between whose descendants the Great War of the *Mahābhārata* was fought. Vyāsa is another form of Viṣṇu depicted as a sage with *jaṭā* having by his side four well-known disciples Sumantu, Jaiminī, Paila and Vaiśampāyana. The periodic incarnation doctrine of Vyāsa according to *Liṅga Purāṇa*. (*See* Table on page 33.)

17. ***Ṛṣabha***: Son of Nābhi and Meru and 'father of a hundred sons, the eldest of whom was Bharata. He gave his kingdom to his son and retired to a hermitage, where he led a life of such severe austerity and abstinence, that he became a mere collection of skin and fibres, and went the way of all flesh. The *Bhāgavata Purāṇa* speaks of his wanderings in the western part of the Peninsula and connects him with the establishment of the Jaina religion in those parts.

18. ***Yajña***: Sacrifice personified in the Purāṇas as son of Rūci and husband of Dakṣiṇā. He had the head of a deer, and was killed by Vīrabhadra at Dakṣa's sacrifice. According to the *Harivaṁśa*, he was raised to the planetary sphere by Brahmā, and made into the constellation Mṛgaśiras.

19-20. ***Dhanvantari***: He is the divine physician having four hands, with *śaṅka*, *cakra* and the *amṛta-kalaśa* in the lower left hand and a *sruva* in the right hand. (*See* 'Dhanvantari'.)

21. ***Balarāma***: *See* 'Balarama'.

22. ***Dattātreya***: He is a combination of the *trimūrti*s, the image having three heads and six hands carrying the representative of *āyudha*s of Brahmā, Viṣṇu and Śiva. He is also known as Hariharapitāmahamūrti, and is in standing posture. Usually the vehicles, Haṁsa, Garuḍa and Ṛṣabha are also represented on the pedestal.

Of the other *avatāra*s, the following are important:

***Dharma***: He is a minor incarnation, supposed to be the son of Brahmā, having four faces, four arms and four legs.

***Ādimūrti***: Viṣṇu is shown as seated on the coils of Ādiśeṣa, the left leg hanging and the right one folded and resting on the serpent seat, with four hands and the company of two Devīs. Sometimes Bhṛgu, Mārkaṇḍeya, Brahmā and Śiva standing by his side in *añjalī* pose are also shown.

***Mohinī***: He is represented as a female *avatāra* that Viṣṇu took once when he distributed the *amṛta* to Devas and secondly at the request of Śiva, when the latter wanted to curb the arrogance of the *ṛṣi*s of Tāraka forest. She is represented as a fine well-built woman, almost nude.

***Hayagrīva***: He is the god of learning, whom *Viṣṇu-dharmottara* describes is white in colour having the face of a horse, sometimes having Lakṣmī on his left lap. He has four hands and carries *śaṅkha*, a *cakra* and a book in his left hand. The lower right hand is in *jñāna-mudrā* with a rosary. He is seated in *padmāsana*.

[*Hindu Mythology*, T.R.R. Iyengar; *Glossary of Hinduism*, T. Rengarajan; *South Indian Image*, T.N. Srinivasan; *Epics, Myths and Legends of India*, P. Thomas; *A Classical Dictionary of Hindu Mythology and Religion*, J. Dowson]

## List of Vyāsa's Incarnation

| *Name of yuga* | *Vyāsa of the yuga* | | *Incarnation* |
|---|---|---|---|
| | *Disciple 1* | *Disciple 2* | *Disciple 3* |
| 1st Cycle — Dvāpara | Lord | Śveta | Śveta |
| | Śvetaśikhā | Śvetasya | |
| 2nd cycle — Kali | Prajāpati | Sutara | |
| | Dundubhi | Śatarūpā | Ṛcikā |
| 3rd cycle — Dvāpara | Bhārgava | Damana | Vikeśa |
| | Vikośa | Vipāśā | |
| 4th cycle — Dvāpara | Aṅgiras | Suhotra | |
| | Sumukha | Durmukha | Dardura |
| 5th cycle — Dvāpara | Savitar | Kaṅka | |
| | Sanaka | Sanandana | Sanātana |
| 6th cycle — | Mṛtyu | Laugākṣī | |
| | Sudhuman | Virājas | Śaṅkhapāda |
| 7th cycle — Dvāpara | Śatakratu | Jaigiśavya | |
| | Sārasvata | Meghā | Meghavāhana |
| 8th cycle — | Vasiṣṭha | Dadhivāhana | Kapila |
| | Āsuri | Pañcaśikhā | |
| 9th cycle | Sārasvata | Ṛṣabha | |
| | Parāśara | Garga | Bhārgava |
| 10th cycle | Tripāda | Brahma sage | |
| | Balabandhu | Niramitra | Ketubhṛṅga |
| 11th cycle — Dvāpara | Trivrata | Ugra | |
| | Lambodara | Lambakṣa | Lambakeśa |
| 12th cycle — Dvāpara | Śatatejas | Atri | |
| | Sarvajña | Samabuddhi | Sandhyā |
| 13th cycle | Nārāyaṇa | Vali | |
| | Sudhaman-2 | Kaśyapa-1 | Vasiṣṭha |
| 14th cycle | Tarakṣu | Gautama | Atri |
| | Devasada | Śravaṇa | |

| | | | |
|---|---|---|---|
| 15th cycle | Trayyāruṇī | Vedaśiras | Kuni |
| | Kunibāhu | Kuśarīra | |
| 16th cycle | Deva | Gokarṇa | |
| | Kaśyapa-2 | Uśanas | Cyavana |
| 17th cycle | Kṛtañjaya | Guhavasa | |
| | Utatya | Vāmadeva | Mahāyoga |
| 18th cycle | Ṛtañjaya | Śikhaṇḍin | |
| | Vācaśravas | Ṛcikā | Syāvāśva |
| 19th cycle | Bharadvāja | Jātamālin | |
| | Hiraṇyanābha | Kauśalyā | Laugākṣī |
| 20th cycle | Gautama | Aṭṭahāsa | |
| | Sumantu | Barbari | Kabandha |
| 21st cycle | Vācaśravas | Dāruka | Plākṣa |
| | Darbhayāṇi | Ketuman-2 | |
| 22nd cycle | Suṣmayāna | Lāṅgalin | |
| | Bhālavin | Madhupiṅgā | Śvetaketu |
| 23rd cycle | Tṛṇabindu | Śveta-2 | Uśika |
| | Bṛhadaśva | Devala | |
| 24th cycle | Ṛkṣa | Sulin | |
| | Śālihotra | Agniveśa | Yuvanaśa |
| 25th cycle | Śakti | Daṇḍin | |
| | Chagala | Kundakaraṇ | Kumbhaṇḍa |
| 26th cycle | Parāśara | Sahiṣṇu | Ulūka |
| | Vidyuta | Śambūka | |
| 27th cycle | Jātukarṇya | Somaśarman | |
| | Akṣapāda | Kumāra | Ulūka |
| 28th cycle | Dvaipāyana | Lakuli | |
| | Kuśika | Garga | Mitra |

# B

**Bādarāyaṇa**: A name of Veda-Vyāsa, especially used for him as the reputed author of the Vedānta philosophy. He was the author of the *Brahma-Sūtras*, published in the *Bibliotheca Indica*.

**Bādari**: A place near the Ganges in the Himālayas sacred to Viṣṇu, particularly in his dual form of Nara-Nārāyaṇa. Thus in the *Mahābhārata*, Śiva addressing Arjuna says, 'Thou wast Nara in a former body, and with Nārāyaṇa for thy companion, didst perform dreadful austerity at Bādari for many myriads of years'. It is now known as Badrīnātha, though this is properly a title of Viṣṇu as lord of Bādari.

**Balabhadra**: *See* Balarāma.

**Bāla-gopāla**: The boy Kṛṣṇa.

**Balarāma**: [Balabhadra and Baladeva are other forms of this name]. The elder brother of Kṛṣṇa. When Kṛṣṇa is regarded as a full manifestation of Viṣṇu, Balarāma is recognised as the seventh *avatāra* of incarnation in his place. According to this view, which is the favourite one of the Vaiṣṇavas, Kṛṣṇa is a full divinity and Balarāma an incarnation, but the story of their birth, as told in the *Mahābhārata*, places them more in equality. It says that Viṣṇu took two hairs, a white and a black one, and that these became Balarāma and Kṛṣṇa, who was very dark. As soon as Balarāma was born he was carried away to Gokula so that his life could be preserved from the tyrant Kaṁsa, and there Nanda nurtured him as a child of Rohiṇī. He and Kṛṣṇa grew up together, and he took part in many of Kṛṣṇa's boyish freaks and adventures. His earliest exploit was the killing of the great *asura* Dhenuka who had the form of an ass. This demon attacked him, but Balarāma seized his assailant, whirled him round by his legs till he was dead, and cast his carcass into a tree. Another *asura* attempted to carry off Balarāma on his shoulders, but the boy beat out the demon's brains with his fists. When Kṛṣṇa went to Mathurā, Balarāma accompanied him, and manfully supported him till Kaṁsa was killed. Once when Balarāma was intoxicated he called upon the Yamunā river to come to him, that he might bathe but his command not being heeded, he plunged his ploughshare into the river, and dragged the waters with severe he went, until they were obliged to assume a human form and beseech his forgiveness. This action gained for him the title 'Yamunā-bhid' and 'Kālindī-karṣaṇa', breaker or dragger of the Yamunā. He killed Rukmiṇī in a gambling brawl. When Duryodhana detained Śāmba, son of Kṛṣṇa, as a prisoner at Hastināpura, Balarāma demanded his release, and being refused, he thrust his ploughshare under the ramparts of the city, and drew them towards him, thus compelling the Kauravas, to give up their prisoner. Lastly, he killed the great ape Dvivida, who had stolen his weapons and derided him. Such are some of the chief incidents of the life of Balarāma, as related in the Purāṇas, and as popular among the votaries of Kṛṣṇa. In the *Mahābhārata* he has more of a human character. He taught both Duryodhana and Bhīma the use of the mace. Though inclining to the side of the Pāṇḍavas, he refused to take an active part either with them or the Kauravas. He witnessed the combat between Duryodhana and Bhīma, and beheld the foul blow struck by the latter, which made him so indignant that he seized his weapons and was with difficulty restrained by Kṛṣṇa from falling upon the Pāṇḍavas. He died before Kṛṣṇa, as he sat under a banyan tree in the outskirts of Dvārakā. The 'wine-loving' Balarāma was as much addicted to wine as his brother Kṛṣṇa was devoted to the fair sex. He was also irascible in temper, and sometimes quarrelled even with Kṛṣṇa. The Purāṇas represent them as having a serious difference about the *syamantaka* jewel. He had but one wife, Revatī, daughter of King Raivata, and was faithful to her. By her he had two sons Niśatha and Ulmuka. He is represented as of fair complexion, and as Nīlavastra, 'clad in the dark-blue vest'. His especial weapons are a club, the ploughshare, and the pestle from which he is called *phāla* and *hala*. He is also called Halayudha, 'plough-armed'; Halabhṛt; 'plough-bearer'; Lāṅgali and Saṅkarṣaṇa, 'ploughman'; and Mūsali, 'pestle-holder'. As he has a palm for a banner, he is called Tāladhvaja. Other appellations are 'Guptacara', 'who goes secretly'; Kāmpāla and

Samvartaka. [*Mahābhārata*; *A Classical Dictionary of Hindu Mythology and Religion*, J. Dowson]

**Bāṇaliṅgas**:Bāṇaliṅgas are important for the Śaivites. They are mostly clear quartz pebbles, which are rounded as a result of erosion and look white spherical or ovoid bodies. These are dedicated to Śiva and are worshipped at home. Bāṇaliṅgas have several varieties like Śāligrāmas, and have various colours, from jet colour to crystal colour. [*South Indian Image*, T.N. Srinivasan.]

**Barhiṣads**: A class of *pitṛs*, who, when alive, kept up the household flame and presented offerings with fire.

**Bhadracāru**: A son of Kṛṣṇa and Rukmiṇī.

**Bhadra-Kālī**: Name of a goddess.

**Bhadraśva**: A celebrated horse, son of Ucchaiḥsravas.

**Bhaga**: A deity mentioned in the Vedas, but of very indistinct personality and powers. He is supposed to bestow wealth and to preside over marriages, and he is classed among the Ādityas and Viśvadevas.

**Bhaganetraghna**: [Destroyer of the eyes of Bhaga] An appellation of Śiva.

**Bhāgīrathī**: Name of river Ganges. The name is derived from Bhagīratha, a descendant of Sagara, whose austerities induced Śiva to allow the sacred river to descend to the earth for the purpose of bathing the ashes of Sagara's sons, who had been consumed by the wrath of the sage Kapila. Bhagīratha named the river Sagara, and after leading it over the earth to the sea, he conducted it to *pātāla*, where the ashes of his ancestors were laved with its waters and purified. [*A Classical Dictionary of Hindu Mythology and Religion*, J. Dowson]

**Bhairava (mas.)**, **Bhairavī (fem.)**: The terrible. Names of Śiva and his wife Devī. The Bhairavas are eight inferior forms or manifestations of Śiva, all of them of a terrible character.

1. Asītāṅga Black-limbed

2. Candracūḍa — Moon-crested
3. Kālā — Black
4. Krodha — Anger
5. Mahā — Great
6. Ruru — Dog
7. Saṁhāra — Destruction
8. Tāmracūḍa — Red-crested

Other names are met with as variant: Kapāla, Rudra, Bhīṣaṇa, Unmatta and Kupati. In these forms Śiva often rides upon a dog, wherefore he is called Svaśva, 'whose horse is a dog'.

The eight gates of Śiva's city are watched by Bhairavas and the following list of this watchman, obtained from a Madrāsī mendicant in Garhwal, may be of interest.

| *Name* | *Colour of the body* | *Vehicle* | *Śakti* |
|---|---|---|---|
| Gaṇanetra | Golden | Swan | Brāhmī |
| Caṇḍa<br>Maheśvarī | The sky at dawn | He-goat | |
| Kapa | Blood | Peacock | Kaumāri |
| Unmatta<br>Vaiṣṇavī | Yellow | Lion | |
| Naya | Blue | Buffalo | Vārāhī |
| Kapāli<br>Mahendri | Ruby | Elephant | |
| Bhīṣaṇa<br>Cāmuṇḍī | Black | Crow | |
| Śaṅkara | Molten gold | Rat | Kālī |

[*Hindu Mythology*, T.R.R. Iyengar; *Glossary of Hinduism*, T. Rengarajan; *Religion in the Himalayas*, E.T. Atkinson]

**Bhairavī**: Goddess. She is represented as riding on a bull, with three eyes and ten arms, and is decorated with a crescent.

**Bhāratī**: A name of Sarasvatī.

**Bhāratī**: Goddess. She is a member of the Vedic triad of goddess. She is also called Mahi. Her individuality is vague in the *R̥gveda*. Sāyaṇa following Yāska interprets the name 'Bhāratī' as meaning the wife of Bharata (i.e.) Āditya. The Āditya *par excellence* in post-Vedic literature is Viṣṇu, and his wife is Lakṣmī.

**Bhūmadevī**: Goddess. Bhūmadevī is not often individually represented except as the other Ubhayanaciar of Viṣṇu, when she stands on his left side. She has a *nīlotpala* flower in her right hand, while the left one hangs loose. Bhūmadevī is also represented as being seated on the lap of Viṣṇu as Varāhāvatāra, when she was brought back from the depths of the ocean after slaying Hiraṇyākṣa, the demon who stole the earth and hid it in the ocean. [*South Indian Image*, T.N. Srinivasan]

**Bhava:** A Vedic deity often mentioned in connection with Sarva, the destroyer. A name of Rudra or Śiva, or of a manifestation of that god.

**Bhavānī**: One of the names of the wife of Śiva.

**Bhīmaśaṅkara**: Name of one of the twelve great *liṅgas*.

**Bhīṣmaka**: An appellation of Śiva.

**Bhr̥gus**: [Roasters, consumers] A class of mythical beings who belonged to the middle or aerial class of gods. They are connected with Agni, and are spoken of as producers and nourishers of fire, and as makers of chariots. They are associated with the Aṅgirasas, the Atharvans, the R̥bhus and others.

**Bhū**: The earth.

**Bhūta**: [A ghost, imp, goblin] Malignant spirits which are found near cemeteries, lurk in trees, animate dead bodies, and delude and devour human beings. According to the *Vāyu Purāṇa* they are 'fierce beings and eaters of flesh' whom the creator created when he was incensed. In the *Vāyu Purāṇa* their mother is said to have been Krodha, 'anger'. The Bhūtas are attendants of Śiva, and he is held to be their king. [*Hindu Mythology*, T.R.R. Iyengar]

**Bhūteśa**: [Lord of beings or of created things] A name applied to Viṣṇu, Brahmā and Kṛṣṇa; as 'lord of the *bhūta*s or goblins' it is applied to Śiva.

**Bībhatsu**: [Loathing] An appellation of Arjuna.

**Brahmā:** In the *Yajurveda*, the Supreme Being is introduced speaking thus: From me Brahmā was born; he is above all; he is Pitāmaha, or the father of all men; he is Aja and Svayambhū or self-existing. He is described as the first of the gods; framer of the universe; guardian of the world. From him all things proceeded and in him pre-existed the universe; comprehending all material forms which he at once called into creation or arranged existence, as they are now seen; although perpetually chaining their appearances by the operation of the reproductive powers the oak exists in the carrion, as the fruit is in the seed, awaiting the development and expansion, so all material forms existed in Brahmā and their germs were at once produced by him. The first member of the Hindu triad; the supreme spirit manifested as the active creator of the universe. He sprang from the mundane egg, deposited by the supreme first cause and is the Prajāpati, or father of all creatures, and in the first place of the *ṛṣi*s. When Brahmā has created the world it remains unaltered for one of his days, a period of 2,16,00,00,000 years. The world and all that is therein is then consumed by fire, but the sages, gods, and elements survive. When he awakes he again restores creation, and this process is repeated until his existence of a hundred years is brought to a close, a period which it requires fifteen figures to express. When this period is ended he himself expires and he and all the gods, and sages, and the whole universe are resolved into their constituent elements. His name is invoked in religious services but Puṣkara, near Ajmer, is the only place where he receives worship though Prof. Williams states that 'he has heard of homage begin paid to him at Idar'.

The name Brahmā is not found in the Vedas and *Brāhmaṇa*s,

in which the active creator is known as Hiraṇyagarbha and Prajāpati, but there is a curious passage in the *Śatapatha Brāhmaṇa* which says, 'He created the gods. Having created the gods, he placed them in these worlds: in this world Agni, Vāyu in the atmosphere, and Sūrya in the sky.' The points connected with Brahmā are remarkable. As the father of men he performs the work of procreation by incestuous intercourse with his own daughter, variously named Vāc or Sarasvatī Sandhyā and Śatarūpā. Secondly, his powers as creator have been arrogated to the other gods, Viṣṇu and Śiva, while Brahmā has been thrown into the shade. In the *Aitareya Brāhmaṇa* it is said that Prajāpati was in the form of a buck and his daughter was Rohit, a deer. According to the *Śatapatha Brāhmaṇa* and Manu, the supreme soul, the self-existent lord created the waters and deposited in them a seed, which seed became a golden egg, in which he himself was born as Brahmā, the progenitor of all the worlds. As the waters were 'the place of his movement, he (Brahmā) was called Nārāyaṇa'. Here the name Nārāyaṇa is referred distinctly to Brahmā, but it afterwards became the name of Viṣṇu. The account of the *Rāmāyaṇa* is that

> All was water only, in which the earth was formed. Thence arose Brahmā, the self-existent, with the deities. He then, becoming a boar, raised up the earth and created the whole world with the saints, his sons. Brahmā, eternal and perpetually undecaying, sprang from the ether, from him was descended Marīcī; the son of Marīcī was Kāśyapa. From Kāśyapa sprang Vivasvat, and Manu is declared to have been Vivasvat's son.

A later recension of this poem alters this passage so as to make Brahmā a mere manifestation of Viṣṇu. Instead of 'Brahmā, the self-existent, with the deities', it substitutes for the last three words, 'the imperishable Viṣṇu'. The *Viṣṇu Purāṇa* says that the 'divine Brahmā called Nārāyaṇa created all beings' that Prajāpati 'had formerly, at the commencement of the *kalpa*s, taken the shape of a fish, a tortoise, &c., (so now), entering the body of a boar, the lord of creatures entered the water'. But this 'lord of creatures' is clearly shown to be Viṣṇu, and these three forms, the fish, the tortoise, and the boar, are now counted among the *avatāras* of Viṣṇu. This attribution of the form of a boar to Brahmā had been made before by the *Śatapatha Brāhmaṇa*, which also says, 'Having assumed the from of a tortoise, Prajāpati created offspring'. The *Linga Purāṇa* is quite exceptional among the later works in ascribing the boar form to Brahmā. The *Mahābhārata* represents Brahmā as spraining from the navel of Viṣṇu or from a lotus which grew thereout, hence he is called Nābhija, 'navel-born'; Kañja, 'the lotus'; Sarojin, 'having a lotus'; Abjaja, Abjayoni, and Kañjaja, 'lotus-born'. This is, of course, the view taken by the Vaiṣṇavas. The same statement appears in the *Rāmāyaṇa* although this poem gives Brahmā a more prominent place than usual. It represents Brahmā as informing Rāma of his divinity, and of his calling him to heaven in 'the glory of Viṣṇu'. He bestowed boons on Rāma while that hero was on earth, and he extended his favours also to Rāvaṇa and other *rākṣasas* who were descendants of his son Pulastya. In the Purāṇas also he appears as a patron of the enemies of the gods, and it was by his favour that the *daitya* king Bali obtained that almost universal dominion which required the incarnation of Viṣṇu as the dwarf to repress. He is further represented in the *Rāmāyaṇa* as the creator of the beautiful Ahalyā, whom he gave as wife to the sage Gautama. Brahmā, being thus inferior to Viṣṇu, is represented as giving homage and praise to Viṣṇu himself and to his form Kr̥ṣṇa, but the Vaiṣṇava authorities make him superior to Rudra, who, they say, sprang from his forehead. The Śaiva authorities make Mahādeva to be the creator of Brahmā, and represent Brahmā as worshipping the *liṅga* and as the charioteer of Rudra.

Brahmā was the father of Dakṣa, who is said to have sprung from his thumb, and he was present at the sacrifice of that patriarch, which was rudely disturbed by Rudra. Then he had to humbly submit and appease the offended god. The four Kumāras, the chief of whom was called Sanatkumāra or by the patronymic Vaidhatra, were later creations or sons of Brahmā.

Brahmā is also called Vidhi, Vedhas, Druhina and Sraṣṭṛ, 'creator'; Dhātṛ and Vidhātṛ, 'sustainer'; Pitāmaha, 'the great father'; Lokeśa, 'lord of the world'; Parameśa, 'supreme in heaven'; Sanat, 'the ancient'; Ādi-kavi, 'the first poet'; and Drughana, 'the axe'. According to Rūpamanyana, Brahmā is depicted as standing or sitting in *padmāsana* with four heads — symbolic of the four Vedas, facing the four quarters. It appears Brahmā at one time had five heads but Śiva removed the top one in anger. Brahmā has four hands. He is called Caturānana, 'four-faced' and Aṣṭakarṇa, 'eight-eared'. The *āyudha*s that Brahmā often carries are *kamaṇḍalu*, *akṣamālā*, *sruva* (spoon), *sṛka*, *ajuasthan* (ghee pot), *pustaka*, and *kuśa* grass in his two upper hands. The lower right and left hands are often held in *abhaya* and *varada* poses. While *Viṣṇu Purāṇa* and *Suprabhedāgama* state that Brahmā is red in colour, he is described as white in *Śilparatna*. He is often given a beard and moustache and his hair is matted in a *jaṭā-mukuṭa*. As one of the principal deities, he is adorned with jewels. Sometimes he is represented as riding in a chariot drawn by seven swans with the goddess Sarasvatī by his side and also at times with Sāvitrī on the other side. His residence is called Brahmā-vṛnda. [*Hindu Mythology*, T.R.R. Iyengar; *The World Mythology*, T.R.R. Iyengar; *Glossary of Hinduism*, T. Rengarajan; *Epics, Myths and Legends of India*, P. Thomas; *A Classical Dictionary of Hindu Mythology and Religion*, J. Dowson]

**Brahmādikas**: The Prajāpatis.

**Brahmaṇaspati**: A Vedic equivalent of the name Bṛhaspati.

**Brāhmaṇī**: The female form or the daughter of Brahmā, also called Śatarūpā. The goddess has four faces, six arms and the swan as vehicle.

**Bṛhaspati**: In the *Ṛgveda*, the names Bṛhaspati and Brahmaṇaspati alternate, and are equivalent to each other. They are names 'of a deity in whom the action of the worshipper upon the gods is personified'. He is the suppliant, the sacrificer, and the priest, who intercedes with gods on behalf of men and protects mankind against the wicked. Hence he appears as the prototype of the priests, and priestly order and is also designated as the *purohita* of the divine community. He is called in one place 'the father of the gods', and a widely extended creative power is ascribed to him. He is as designated as 'the shining' and 'the gold-coloured', and as 'having the thunder for his voice'. This god is addressed in eleven entire hymns and in two others conjointly with Indra. He is also but less frequently called Brahmaṇaspati, the two forms of the name alternating in the different verses of the same hymn. Though Bṛhaspati is enumerated among aerial gods in the *Naighaṇṭuka* it would be better to refer to him as a terrestrial god as done by Macdonell. The physical features of Bṛhaspati are few. He is golden coloured and ruddy, bright, pure and charming-tongued. He is armed with bow and arrows and wields a golden hatchet. He has a car drawn by ruddy steeds, which slays the goblins and bursts open the cow stall. He is often invoked with Indra, some of whose epithets such as Maghnavana, 'bountiful' and Vājin, 'wielder of the bolt' he shares. Bṛhaspati like Agni is called a brāhmaṇa and a *purohita* as well as Aṅgiras. In some passages he appears to be identified with Agni. But he is much more commonly distinguished from him. Bṛhaspati is the lord of prayers, as his epithet Brahmaṇaspati clearly shows. He is also called as Pūrvabhaj and without him sacrifice does not succeed. He is described as the supreme king of prayers. Bṛhaspati is sometimes directly invoked with the Maruts, but at other times he is said to be accompanied by a singing host, by whom undoubtedly the Maruts are meant — who are well-known as singers. This is doubtless the reason why he is called Gaṇapati, lord of a host. Bṛhaspati was probably originally an aspect of Agni as a divine priest presiding over devotion of god Gaṇapati. This is clear from many things. In the first place Gaṇapati, the name of the later Hindu god, is already an epithet of Bṛhaspati. Secondly the later Gaṇapati like Bṛhaspati is the leader of prayers and just as sacrifice does not succeed without Bṛhaspati so also sacrifice and other undertakings are believed not to succeed without prayers to Gaṇapati. Thirdly the later Gaṇapati is a god of wisdom and Bṛhaspati is also called the wisest of the wise and one whom the wise persons placed at their head. Fourthly the later Gaṇapati carries an axe in his hand like Bṛhaspati. Since Bṛhaspati was regarded as the leader of the host of Maruts, the sons of Rudra, it is easy to understand why Gaṇapati came to be regarded as a son of Rudra. But the physical appearance of the later Gaṇapati is totally un-Vedic and was the result of identifying this Vedic god with non-Āryan elements and the elephant head.

In later times, he is a *ṛṣi*. He is also regent of the planet Jupiter, and the name is commonly used for the planet itself. In this character his car is called Nītighoṣa and is drawn by eight pale horses. He was son of the *ṛṣi* Aṅgiras, and he bears the patronymic Aṅgirasa. As preceptor of the gods he is called Animiṣācārya, Cakṣus, Ijyā and Indrejyā. His wife Tārā was carried off by Soma, the moon, and this gave rise to a war called the Tārakamaya. Soma was aided by Uśanas, Rudra and all the *daitya*s and *dānava*s, while Indra and the gods took the part of Bṛhaspati. 'Earth, shaken to her centre' appealed to Brahmā who interposed and restored Tārā to her husband. She was delivered of a son which Bṛhaspati and Soma both claimed, but Tārā, at the command of Brahmā to tell the truth, declared Soma to be the father, and the child was named Budha. There is an extraordinary story in the Purāṇas off the *ṛṣi*s having milked the earth through Bṛhaspati. Bṛhaspati was the father of Bharadvāja by Mamatā, wife of Utathya. An ancient code of law bears the name of Bṛhaspati, and he is represented as being the Vyāsa of the fourth, *dvāpara* age. There was a *ṛṣi* of the name in the second *manvantara*, and one who was the founder of a heretical sect. Other epithets of Bṛhaspati are Jīva, 'the living'; Didivis, 'the bright', Dhīṣaṇa, 'the intelligent'; and for his eloquence, Giṣpati, 'lord of speech'. [*A Classical Dictionary of Hindu Mythology and Religion*, J. Dowson; *Vedic Index Macdonell and Keith*; *Glossary of Hinduism*, T. Rengarajan]

**Budha**: [Wise, intelligent.] The planet Mercury, son of Soma, the moon, by Rohiṇī or by Tārā, wife of Bṛhaspati. He married Ilā, daughter of the Manu Vaivasvata and by her had a son Pururavas. Budha was author of a hymn in the *Ṛgveda*. From his parents he is called Saumya and Rauhineya. He is also called Praharṣaṇa, Rodhana, Tuṅga, and Śyāmāṅga, 'black-bodied'. The intrigue of Soma with Tārā was the cause of a great quarrel, in which the gods and the *asuras* fought against each other. Brahmā compelled Soma to give up Tārā, and when she returned to her husband she was pregnant. A son was born, who was so beautiful that Bṛhaspati and Soma both claimed him. Tārā for a long time refused to tell his paternity, and so excited the wrath and nearly incurred the curse of her son. At length, upon the command of Brahmā, she declared Soma to be the father, and he gave the boy the name Budha. [*A Classical Dictionary of Hindu Mythology and Religion*, J. Dowson]

# C

**Cakra**: *Cakra* is also known as Sudarśana in Sanskrit and Cakaratha Alwar in Tamil. It is the discus or the fast revolving wheel that Viṣṇu always carries and with which he destroys his enemies. In iconography, it is represented as a human being with several hands standing inside a circular hollow ring, carrying several weapons.

**Cakravartī**: A universal emperor described by the *Viṣṇu Purāṇa* as one who is born with the mark of Viṣṇu's discus visible in his hand.

**Cakṣuṣa**: The sixth Manu.

**Cāmuṇḍā**: An emanation of the goddess Durgā, sent forth from her forehead to encounter the demons Caṇḍa and Muṇḍa. She is thus described in the *Mārkaṇḍeya Purāṇa*:

> From the forehead of Ambikā, contracted with wrathful frowns, sprang swiftly forth a goddess of black and formidable aspect, armed with a scimitar and noose, bearing a ponderous mace, decorated with a garland of dead corpses, robed in the hide of an elephant, dry and withered and hideous, with yawning mouth, and lolling tongue, and bloodshot eyes, and filling the regions with her shouts.

When she had killed the two demons, she bore their heads to Durgā, who told her that she should henceforth be known, by a contraction of their names, as Cāmuṇḍā. [*Hindu Mythology*, T.R.R. Iyengar]

**Cāmuṇḍī**: Goddess. Cāmuṇḍā and Caṇḍikā represent Kālī in her most terrible forms. She is represented in black and is frightening with protruding teeth, swollen red eyes. She rides on a corpse, wearing a garland of skulls and jewels of serpents. Having slain the demons Caṇḍa and Muṇḍa she brought their heads to Durgā, who told her that having slain them she should henceforth be known on earth as Cāmuṇḍā. She is termed Kālī owing to her black colour and Karāli owing to her hideous face, but the latter name is not used in hymns. In the Mālatī and Mādhava her place of worship is near the public cemetery and she is thus addressed by her priest Aghoraghaṇṭā:

Hail, hail, Chamunda, mighty goddess hail,
I glorify thy sport, when the dance,
That fills the court of Śiva with delight,
Thy foot descending spurns the earthly globe. From the torn orb,

The trickling nectar falls, and every skull
Those germs thy necklace laughs with horrid life
Attendant's spirits tremble and applaud
The mountain falls before the powerful arms

Around whose length the sable serpents twine
They are swelling forms, and knit terrific bands,
While from the hood expanded frequent flash enveloped flames.
As rolls thy awful head,

Thy lowering eye that glows amidst thy brow fiery circle designates, that wraps
The spheres within its terrible circumference;
Whilst by the banner of thy dreadful staff;
High waved, the stars are scattered from their orbits;

The three-eyed god, exults the embrace
Of his fair spouse, as Gauri sinks appalled
By the distracting cries of countless flends
Who shot thy praise? Oh may such dance afford

What'er we need, what'er may yield us happiness.

According to some Cāmuṇḍā sprang from Pārvatī, but others say that the mild portion of Pārvatī issued from her side, leaving the wrathful portion whence arose Kālī, Śyāmā, Durgā and Cāmuṇḍā. [*Epics, Myths and Legends of India*, P. Thomas]

**Caṇḍa, Caṇḍī**: The goddess Durgā, especially in the form she assumed for the destruction of the *asura* called Mahiṣa.

**Candra**: The moon worshipped as a deity. Also, a planet (one of the *navagrahas*).

**Candravaṁśa**: [The Lunar race] The lineage which claims descent from the moon. It is divided into two great branches, the Yādavas and Pauravas, respectively descended from Yadu and Puru. Kṛṣṇa belonged to the line of Yadu. The lineage of Yādavas, according to the *Viṣṇu Purāṇa*, comprised Āyu, Āyus, Nahuṣa, Yayāti, Yadu, Kroṣṭu (and three others), Vṛjinivat, Svāhī, Ruṣadgu, Citraratha, Śaśabindu, Pṛthusravas, Tamas, Uśanas, Sitāyus, Rukmakavaca, Paravṛt, Jyāmagha, Vidarbha, Kratha, Kuntī, Vṛṣṇi, Nirvṛti, Daśārna, Vyoman, Jimūta, Vikṛti, Bhīmaratha, Navaratha, Daśaratha, Śakuni, Karambhi, Devarāṭa, Devakṣattra, Madhu, Anavaratha, Kuruvatsa, Anuratha, Puruhotra, Aṁśu, Satvata, Andhaka, Bhajamāna, Viduratha, Sura, Samin, Pratikṣattra, Svayambhoja, Hṛdika, Devamidhuṣa, Sūra, Vasudeva, Kṛṣṇa and Balarāma.

**Cāraṇas**: [Panegyrists] The panegyrists of the gods.

**Cāru, Cārudeha, Cāru-Deṣṇa, Cāru-Gupta**: Sons of Kṛṣṇa and Rukmiṇī. [*Dictionary of Hinduism*, T.R.R. Iyengar]

**Cāruhāsinī**: [Sweet-smiler] This epithet is used for Rukmiṇī and for Lakṣmaṇa, and perhaps for other wives of Kṛṣṇa.

**Cārumatī**: Daughter of Kṛṣṇa and Rukmiṇī.

**Chāyā**: [Shade] A handmaid of the sun. Saṁjñā, wife of the sun, being unable to bear the fervour of her lord, put her handmaid Chāyā in her place. The sun, believing Chāyā to be his wife, had three children by her: Śani, the planet Saturn; the Manu Sāvarṇi; and a daughter, the Tāpti river. As mother of Saturn, Chāyā is known as Śanipraśu. The partiality that she showed for these children provoked Yama, the son of Saṁjñā, and he lifted his foot to kick her. She cursed him to have his leg affected with sores and worms. This made it clear that she was not Saṁjñā and the mother of Yama, so the son went in search of Saṁjñā and brought her back. According to a Purāṇa, Chāyā was a daughter of Viśvakarmā, and sister of Saṁjñā, the wife of the sun. [*Dictionary of Hinduism*, T.R.R. Iyengar]

**Ciranjīvin**: [Long lived] Gods or deified mortals, who live for long periods.

**Cow**: The cow does not appear to have been particularly sacred in the Vedic times. References in the Vedas and even in the epics indicate that ancient Hindus considered beef a desirable item of food. There are passages in the epics that describe how even holy sages entertained their guests with beef and venison. The slaughter of cows was probably prohibited for the advancement of agriculture at a time when there was a difficult situation and men were compelled to leave off their ancient habit of killing cattle and feeding on their meat. Whatever the origin of the worship, the cow is at present held to be a sacred animal by the Hindus. She is not only venerated but also actually worshipped as a goddess. According to current belief *go-hatyā* is as great a sin as *brahma-hatyā*. The dung and urine of the cow are also held sacred and are supposed to possess cleansing and magical properties. The ashes of cow-dung are often used to put sectarian marks. Brahmā created the cow together with the brāhmaṇa on the first day of Vaiśākha and hence this day is sacred to her. One of the heavens is named after the cow. The boon-granting cow Surabhi, as already related, rose from the Milk Ocean. There is some confusion as to her nature and identity. Kāmadhenu, Nandinī and Śabalā are said to be her different names in some accounts while others maintain that they are her daughters. The milch-cow calf is a favourite subject with Hindu artists and she is symbolic of felicity and plenty. Nandī, Śiva's bull, is an object of worship among the Śaivas. [*Hindu Mythology*, T.R.R. Iyengar; *Epics, Myths and Legends of India*, P. Thomas]

# D

**Dakṣa**: The name generally carries with it the idea of a creative power. Dakṣa is a son of Brahmā; he is one of the Prajāpatis and is sometimes regarded as their chief. There is a great deal of doubt and confusion about him, which of old the sage Parāśara could only account for by saying that in every age Dakṣa and the rest are born and are again destroyed. In the *Ṛgveda* it is said, 'Dakṣa sprang from Aditi and Aditi from Dakṣa.' Upon this marvellous mutual generation Yāska in the *Nirukta* remarks,

> How can this be possible? They may have had the same origin; or, according to the nature of the gods, they may have born from each other, and have derived their substance from each other.

Roth's view is that Aditi is eternity, and that Dakṣa is the male energy which generates the gods in eternity. In the *Śatapatha Brāhmaṇa*, Dakṣa is identified with Prajāpati, the creator. As son of Aditi, he is one of the Ādityas, and he is also reckoned among the Viśvadevas.

According to the *Mahābhārata*, Dakṣa sprang from the right thumb of Brahmā, and his wife from that deity's left thumb. The Purāṇas adopt this view of his origin, but state that he married Prasūti, daughter of Priyavrat and granddaughter of Manu. By her he had, according to various statements, twenty-four, fifty or sixty daughters. The *Rāmāyaṇa* and the *Mahābhārata* agree in the large number, and according to Manu and the *Mahābhārata* he gave ten of his daughters to Dharma and thirteen to Kaśyapa, who became the mothers of gods and demons, men, birds, serpents and all living things. Twenty-seven were given in marriage to Soma, the moon, and these became the twenty-seven Nakṣatras or lunar mansions. One of the daughters, named Satī, married Śiva and killed herself in consequence of a quarrel between her husband and father. The Kāśī Khaṇḍa represents that she became a *satī* and burnt herself.

Another legend of the *Mahābhārata* and Purāṇas represents

Dakṣa as begin born a second time, in another *manvantara*, as son of the Pracetasas and Mariṣa, and that he had seven sons, the allegorical persons Krodha, Tamas, Dama, Vikr̥ta, Aṅgiras, Kardama and Aśva. This second birth is said to have happened through his having been cursed to it by his son-in-law Śiva. Dakṣa was in a certain way, by his mother Mariṣa, an emanation of Soma, the moon; and as twenty-seven of his daughters were married to that luminary, Dakṣa is sometimes referred to as being both the father and the offspring of the moon, thus reiterating the duality of his nature. According to the *Harivaṁśa*, Viṣṇu himself became Dakṣa, and formed numerous creatures, or, in other words, he became the creator. Dakṣa, the first of male, by virtue of *yoga*, himself took the form of a beautiful woman, by whom he had many fair daughters, whom he disposed of in marriage in the manner related by Manu and above-stated. An important event in the life of Dakṣa, and very frequently referred to, is Dakṣa's sacrifice, which was violently interrupted and broken up by Śiva. The germ of this story is found in the *Taittirīya Saṁhitā*, where it is related that the gods having excluded Rudra from a sacrifice, he pierced the sacrifice with an arrow, and that Pūṣaṇ, attempting to eat a portion of the oblation, broke his teeth. The story is found both in the *Rāmāyaṇa* and *Mahābhārata*. According to the latter, Dakṣa was engaged in sacrifice, when Śiva in a rage, and shouting loudly, pierced the offering with an arrow. The gods and *asura*s were alarmed and the whole universe quaked. The *r̥ṣi*s endeavoured to appease the angry god, but in vain. 'He ran up to the gods, and in his rage knocked out the eyes of Bhaga with a blow, and, incensed, assaulted Pūṣaṇ with his foot and knocked out his teeth as he was eating the offering.' The gods and *r̥ṣi*s humbly propitiated him, and when he was appeased 'they apportioned to him a distinguished share in the sacrifice, and through fear resorted to him as their refuge. In another part of the same work the story is again told with considerable variation. Dakṣa instituted a sacrifice and apportioned no share to Rudra. Instigated by the sage Dadhici, the god hurled his blazing trident, which destroyed the sacrifice of Dakṣa and fell with great violence on the breast of Nārāyaṇa. It was hurled back with violence to its owner, and a furious battle ensued between the two gods, which was not intermitted till Brahmā prevailed upon Rudra to propitiate Nārāyaṇa. The god was gratified, and said to Rudra, 'He who knows thee knows me; he who loves thee loves me.' The story is reproduced in the Purāṇas with many embellishments. Dakṣa instituted a sacrifice to Viṣṇu, and many of the gods repaired to it but Śiva was not invited, because the gods had conspired to deprive him of the sacrificial offerings. The wife of Śiva, the mountain goddess Umā, perceived what was going on. Umā was a second birth of Satī, daughter of Dakṣa who had deprived herself of life in consequence of her father's quarrel with herself and her husband, Śiva. Umā urged her husband to display his power and assert his rights. So he created Vīrabhadra, 'a being like the fire of fate', and of most terrific appearance and powers. He also sent with him thousands of powerful demi-gods, whom he called into existence. A terrible catastrophe followed: 'the mountains tottered, the earth shook, the winds roared, and the depths of the sea were disturbed.' The sacrifice was broken up and, in the words of Wilson,

> Indra is knocked down and trampled on, Yama has his staff broken, Saraswati and the Matris have their nose cut off, Mitra has his eyes pulled out, Pushan has his teeth knocked down his throat, Chandra is pummelled, Vahini's hands are cut off, Bhr̥gu loses his beard, the Brāhmaṇs are pelted with stones, the Prajāpatis are beaten, and the gods and demigods are run through with swords. . . .

Dakṣa then, in great terror, propitiated the wrathful deity and acknowledged his supremacy.

According to some versions, Dakṣa himself was decapitated and his head thrown into the fire. Śiva subsequently restored him and the other dead to life, and as Dakṣa's head could not be found, it was replaced by that of a goat. The *Harivaṁśa*, in its glorification of Viṣṇu, gives a different finish to the story. The sacrifice was destroyed and the gods fled in dismay, till Viṣṇu intervened, and seizing Śiva by the throat, compelled him to desist, and acknowledge his master. 'This,' says Wilson 'is a legend of some interest, as it is obviously intended to intimate a struggle between the worshippers of Śiva and Viṣṇu, in which at first the latter, but finally the former, acquired the ascendancy.' [*A Classical Dictionary of Hindu Mythology and Religion*, J. Dowson; *Dictionary of Hinduism*, T.R.R. Iyengar]

**Dakṣa-sāvarṇa**: The ninth Manu.

**Dākṣāyaṇī**: A name of Aditi as daughter of Dakṣa.

**Dāmodara**: A name given to Kṛṣṇa because his foster mother tried to tie him up with a rope round his belly.

**Daṇḍadhara**: [The rod-bearer] A title of Yama, the god of death.

**Daśaratha**: A prince of the solar race, son of Aja, a descendant of Ikṣavāku, and king of Ayodhyā. He had three wives but being childless, he performed the sacrifice of a horse and, according to the *Rāmāyaṇa*, the chief queen, Kauśalyā, remained in close contact with the slaughtered horse for a night, and the other two queens beside her. Four sons were then born to him from his three wives. Kauśalyā bore Rāma, who was an *avatāra* of Viṣṇu. [*The World Mythology*, T.R.R. Iyengar]

**Daśārha**: A title of Kṛṣṇa.

**Dasras**: [Beautiful] The elder of the two Aśvins, or in the dual, the two Aśvins.

**Dattātreya**: Son of Atri and Anasūyā. A brāhmaṇa saint in whom a portion of Brahmā, Viṣṇu and Śiva, or more particularly Viṣṇu, was incarnate. He had three sons, Soma, Datta and Durvāsas, to whom also a portion of the divine essence was transmitted. He was the patron of Kārttavīrya, and gave him a thousand arms.

**Deva**: [God, a deity] The gods are spoken of as thirty-three in number, eleven for each of the three worlds.

**Devaka**: The father of Devakī and brother of Ugrasena.

**Devakī**: Wife of Vasudeva, mother of Kṛṣṇa and cousin of Kaṁsa. She is sometimes called an incarnation of Aditi, and is said to have been born again as Pṛṣnī, the wife of King Sutapas.

**Devaloka**: The world of the gods.

**Devamātṛ**: [Mother of the gods.] An appellation of Aditi.

**Devaratha**: A royal *ṛṣi* of the solar race, who dwelt among the Videhas and had charge of Śiva's bow, which descended to Janaka and was broken by Rāma.

**Devarṣis**: *Ṛṣi*s or saints of the celestial class, who dwell in the regions of the gods, such as Nārada. Sages who have attained perfection upon earth and have been exalted as demi-gods to heaven.

**Devatā**: [A divine being or god] The name *devatā*s includes the gods in general, or, as most frequently used, the whole body of inferior gods.

**Devayoni**: [Of divine birth] A general name for the inferior gods, the Ādityas, Vasus, Viśvadevas and others.

**Devī**: 'The goddess' or Mahādevī, 'the great goddess' wife of god Śiva, and daughter of Himavat, i.e., the Himālaya mountains. She is mentioned in the *Mahābhārata* under a variety of names and with several of her peculiar characteristics, but she owes her great distinction to the Purāṇas and later works. As the Śakti or female energy of Śiva she has two characters, one mild and the other fierce; and it is under the latter that she is especially worshipped. She has a great variety of names referable to her various forms, attributes, and actions, but these names are not always used accurately and distinctively. There include

***Name of the Goddess Attributes***: Umā, Light; a type of beauty; Gaurī, the yellow or brilliant; Pārvatī, the mountaineer; Haimavatī, Himālayā; Jaganmātā, the mother of the world; Bhavānī; the Mother of the World; Durgā, the inaccessible; Kālī, the black; Śyāmā, the black; Caṇḍī, the fierce; Caṇḍikā, the fierce; Bhairavī, the terrible; Adrijā, the mountain-born; Girijā, the mountain-born; Kujā, the earth-born; Dakṣajā, sprung from Dakṣa; Kanyā, the virgin; Kanyākumārī; the youthful virgin; Ambikā, the mother; Avarā, the youngest; Anantā, the everlasting; Nityā, the everlasting; Āryā, the revered; Vijayā, victorious; Ṛddhi, the rich, Satī, virtuous; Dakṣiṇā, right-handed; Piṅgalā, tawny, dark; Karburi, spotted; Bhrāmarī, the bee, Koṭarī, the naked; Karṇamotī, the pearl-eared; Padma-Lāñchanā, distinguished by a lotus; Sarvamaṅgalā, always auspicious; Śākambharī, nourisher of herbs; Śivadūti, Śiva's messenger; Siṁharathī, riding on a lion; Gaṇanāyakī, the leader of the *gaṇa*s; Kāmākṣī, wanton-eyed; Kāmākhyā, called by the name of Kāma (desire).

Other names applicable to her terrible forms are Bhadrakālī; Bhīmādevī; Cāmuṇḍā; Mahākālī; Mahāmārī; Mahāsurī; Mātaṅgī; Rājasī; 'the fierce' and Raktadantī, 'red or bloody toothed'.

The names of Devī obtained from her husband are Bhagavatī, Īśānī, Īśvarī, Kālañjarī, Kapālinī, Kauśikī, Kirātī, Māheśvarī, Mṛḍā, Mṛḍānī, Rudrāṇī, Sarvāṇī, Śivadūtī and Tryambakī.

The names of Durgā are Daśabhujā, ten-armed — destroyed the *asura*s; Siṁhavāhinī, riding on a lion — destroyed the *asura*s; Mahiṣamardinī, destroyer of Mahiṣa *asura*; Jagadhātrī, fosterer of the World; Kālī, destroyed Raktabīja; Muktakeśī, dishevelled hair — destroyed the *asura*s; Tārā, star — destroyer of *asura* Śumbha; Chinnamastakā, decapitated — destroyed *asura* Niśumbha; Jagadgaurī, the world's fair one.

[*A Classical Dictionary of Hindu Mythology and Religion*, J. Dowson; *Glossary of Hinduism*, T. Rengarajan]

**Devī-māhātmya**: The greatness of Devī.

**Dhanadā**: [Giver of wealth] Kubera, the god of riches.

**Dhanañjaya**: [Conqueror of riches] A title of Arjuna.

**Dhanapati**: [Lord of wealth] Kubera.

**Dhaneśvara**: [Lord of wealth] Kubera.

**Dhanvantari**: (1) Name of a Vedic deity to whom offerings at twilight were made in the north-east quarter. (2) The physician of the gods, who was produced at the churning of the ocean. He was a teacher of medical science, and the *Āyurveda* is attributed to him. In another birth he was son of Dīrghatamas, and his 'nature was exempt from human infirmities, and in every existence he had been master of universal knowledge'. He is called also Sudhāpāṇi, 'carrying nectar in his hands' and Amṛta, 'the immortal'. Other physicians seem to have had the name applied to them, as Bhela, Divodāsa, and Palakapya. [*India in the Vedic Age*, P.L. Bhargava]

**Dharaṇī**: [The earth] The wife of Paraśurāma.

**Dharma**: [Justice] A name of Yama, the judge of the dead.

**Dharma**: An ancient sage sometimes classed among the Prajāpatis. He married thirteen of the daughters of Dakṣa, and had a numerous progeny; but all his children 'are manifestly allegorical, being personification of intelligences and virtues and religious rites, and being therefore appropriately wedded to the probable authors of the Hindu code of religion and morals, or the equally allegorical representation of that code *dharma*, 'moral and religious duty.'

**Dharmaputra**: Son of Dharma.

**Dharmarāja**: Yama, the god of dead.

**Dharmasāvarṇi**: The eleventh Manu.

**Dhātrī**: [Maker, creator] In the later hymns of the *Ṛgveda*, Dhātrī is a deity of no very defined powers and functions, but he is described as operating in the production of life and the preservation of health. He promotes generation, brings about matrimony, presides over domestic life, cures diseases, and heals broken bones. He is said to 'have formed the sun, moon, sky, earth, air and heaven as before'. He appears also as one of the Ādityas, and this character he still retains. In the later mythology he is identified with Prajāpati or Brahmā, the creator; and in this sense of 'maker' the term is used as an epithet of Viṣṇu and Kṛṣṇa. Sometimes he is a son of Brahmā. [Macdonnell and Keith,

*Vedic Index*]

**Dhruva**: [The pole star]. According to the *Viṣṇu Purāṇa*, the sons of Manu Svayambhuva were Priyavrata and Uttānapāda. The latter had two wives; the favourite Suruci, was proud and haughty and the second, Sunīti was humble and gentle. Suruci had a son named Uttama, and Sunīti gave birth to Dhruva. While quite a child Dhruva was contemptuously treated by Suruci, and she told him that her own son Uttama alone would succeed to the throne. Dhruva and his mother submitted, and he declared that he wished for no other honours than such as his own actions should acquire. He was a kṣatriya, but he joined a society of *ṛṣi*s, and becoming a *ṛṣi* himself, he went through a rigid course of austerities, notwithstanding the efforts of Indra, to distract him. At the end he obtained the favour of Viṣṇu, who raised him to the skies as the pole star. He has the patronymic Auttānapadī, and he is called Grahadrara, 'the stay or pivot of the planets'.

**Dhurjaṭī**: [Having heavy matted locks.] A name of Rudra.

**Digambara**: [Clothed with space] A naked mendicant. A title of Śiva.

**Diggajas**: The elephants who protect the eight points of the compass. 1. Airāvata, 2. Puṇḍarīka, 3. Vāmana, 4. Kumuda, 5. Añjana, 6. Puṣpadanta. 7. Sārvabhauma, 8. Supratīka.

**Dikpālas**: *See* under 'Lokapālas'.

**Dilīpa**: Son of Aṁśumat and father of Bhagīratha. He was of the solar race and ancestor of Rāma.

**Dīrghasravas**: Son of Dīrghatamas, and therefore a *ṛṣi*, but as in a time of famine he took to trade for a livelihood, the *Ṛgveda* calls him 'the merchant'.

**Dīrghatamas**: [Long darkness.] A son of Kāśīrāja, according to the *Mahābhārata*; of Ucathya, according to the *Ṛgveda*; and of Utathya and Mamatā in the Purāṇas. His appellation of Aucathya and Māmateya favour the latter parentage. He was born blind but is said to have obtained sight by worshipping Agni.

**Diti**: A goddess or personification in the Vedas, who is associated with Aditi and seems to be intended as an antithesis or as a complement to her. In the *Rāmāyaṇa* and in the Purāṇas she is daughter of Dakṣa, wife of Kāśyapa and mother of the *daityas*. The *Viṣṇu Purāṇa* relates that having lost her children, she begged of Kāśyapa a son of irresistible prowess, who should destroy Indra. The boon was granted, but with this condition: 'If, with thoughts wholly pious and person entirely pure, you carefully carry the babe in your womb for a hundred years.' She assiduously observed the condition; but Indra knew what was preparing for him. So he went to Diti and attended upon her with the utmost humility, watching his opportunity. In the last year of the century, Diti retired one night to rest without washing her feet. Indra then with his thunderbolt divided the embryo in her womb into seven portions. Thus mutilated, the child cried bitterly, and Indra being unable to pacify it, became angry and divided each of the seven portions into seven, thus forming the swift-moving deities called Maruts, from the words *mā-rodiḥ*, 'weep not' which Indra used to quieten them. [Macdonell and Keith,*Vedic Index; Glossary of Hinduism*, T. Rengarajan]

**Durgā**: [Inaccessible] The wife of Śiva. According to the *Bhāgavata Purāṇa*, she was born of Yaśodā, the wife of Nanda in order to save the life of Kṛṣṇa, her brother. She was taken by Vasudeva, exchanging her place with Kṛṣṇa's and when Kaṁsa attempted to dash the female child, she flew up in the air announcing her identity. A story is told of how she killed Śumbha and Niśumbha, two *asura* brothers. These demons performed austerities for 11,000 years and received a boon from Śiva by the power of which they could be slain by no god. After receiving the boon, they declared war on the gods, who in their distress, went to Brahmā, Viṣṇu and Mahādeva for protection. Mahādeva advised them to address their complaint to his consort as no god could kill the demons but a goddess could. So Durgā was propitiated by a religious ceremony and she agreed to destroy the demons. Durgā then assumed the shape of a woman of celestial beauty and proceeded to the Himālayas where Caṇḍa and Muṇḍa, two spies of Śumbha and Niśumbha, saw her. They sent word to their masters of the presence of the lovely lady in the forest, and added that she would be a desirable addition to their women's apartments. On hearing this Śumbha sent a messenger to Durgā with a polite invitation to her to visit him and be his wife. Durgā told the envoy that she had taken a vow to marry only the person who could defeat her in a single combat and added that Śumbha might try his luck. The messengers returned to Śumbha but he paid no heed to the message of Durgā and sent his general Dhūmralocana to seize Durgā and bring her to him. Dhūmralocana set out with a huge army but Durgā set-up a dreadful roar, which destroyed practically the whole army and the general. This news reaching Śumbha and Niśumbha, they sent Caṇḍa and Muṇḍa to capture the goddess. Durgā first devoured the armies of these in easy mouthfuls of thirty to hundred demons, and, after thus destroying the whole army, she caught Caṇḍa by the hair and cut off his head. Seeing this Muṇḍa advanced and was also slain in a similar manner. Now Śumbha and Niśumbha themselves proceeded to the Himālayas with an army consisting of legions of demons. Durgā produced several goddesses from her locks and a terrible combat between the demons and the goddess took place. The goddess destroyed the armies of the demons when Śumbha engaged Durgā in single combat. Śumbha was slain after a fierce fight; then Niśumbha engaged her but he too was killed. After this, the goddess celebrated the victory by feasting on the carnage. It is said that she received her name Durgā on account of her having killed an *asura* named Durga. This demon conquered the three worlds and dethroned Indra, Vāyu, Candra, Yama, Varuṇa, Agni, Kubera, Īśāna, Rudra and Sūrya. The wives of the *ṛṣis* were compelled to celebrate his praises. He sent all the gods from their heavens to live in forests, and at his nod they came and worshipped him. He abolished all religious ceremonies. The brāhmaṇas through fear of him gave up the reading of the Veda, all changes took place during his period of regime. The gods in their distress approached Śiva who conducted them to his wife. Pārvatī undertook to destroy the demon and created Kālarātrī whom she sent to flight. Then Pārvatī herself came out of Mount Kailāsa, and a celebrated contest took place. Durga's army consisted of 1000000 chariots, 12000000000 elephants, 1000000 swift-footed horses and innumerable soldiers. As soon as the giant drew near, Pārvatī assumed one thousand arms, and called to her assistant different kinds of beings. The troops of the giant poured their arrows on Pārvatī, thick as the drops of rain in a storm; they tore up the trees, the mountains and hurled them at the goddess; she, however, threw a weapon which carried away many of the arms of the giant. Then he, in return, hurled a flaming dart on the goddess; she turned it aside. He discharged another; but this also she resisted by a hundred arrows. He next let fly an arrow at Pārvatī's breast; but this too she repelled as well as two other instruments, a club and a spike. At last Pārvatī seized Durga and caused a dreadful shower of hail to descend, the effect of which Pārvatī counteracted by an instrument called Śoṣṇu. He next broke off a piece of a mountain and threw it at Pārvatī who cut it into seven pieces by her arrows. The giant now assumed the shape of an elephant as large as a mountain and approached the goddess but she tied his legs and, with her nails, which were like scimiters, tore him into pieces. He then arose in the form of a buffalo, and with his horns cast stones, trees and mountains at the goddess, tearing up the trees by the breath of his nostrils. The goddess next pierced him with her trident when he reeled to and fro and renouncing the form of a buffalo assumed his original body as a giant with a thousand arms and weapons in each. The goddess seized him by his thousand arms and carried him into the air, whence she threw him down with dreadful force. Perceiving, however, that this had no effect she pierced him in the breast with an arrow, when the blood issued in streams from his mouth and he expired. Durgā is represented in art as a woman of gentle countenance with ten arms in each of which she holds a weapon. With one foot she presses on the body of Mahiṣa and the other rests on her *vāhana,* the lion, that is depicted as lacerating the body of Mahiṣa. She wears a crown on her head and her clothes are magnificently jewelled. So in many types of Durgā though she is represented with Śaivite symbols she has the *cakra* and *śaṅkha*, characteristics of Viṣṇu. The older types of Durgā are more or less calm-featured images having *cakra* and *śaṅkha* in the upper arms, and *pāśa*, *aṅkuśa* and *śūla*. [*Hindu Mythology*, T.R.R. Iyengar; *A Classical Dictionary of Hindu Mythology and Religion*, J. Dowson; *Bhāgavata Purāṇa*]

**Dyaus**: [The sky, heaven] In the Vedas he is a masculine deity and is called occasionally Dyauspitṛ, 'heavenly father', the earth being regarded as the mother. He is father of Uṣas, the dawn. Dyaus-Pṛthivī, 'heaven and earth' are represented as the universal parents, not only of men but also of gods, but in other places they are spoken of as having been themselves created; and then, again, there are speculations as to their origin and priority. In one hymn it is asked, 'Which of these two was the first and which the last? How have they been produced? Who knows?' The *Śatapatha Brāhmaṇa* declares in favour of the earth, saying, 'This earth is the first of created beings.' [*India in the Vedic Age*, P.L. Bhargava]

# E

**Earth**: In the Vedas and the Purāṇas the earth is often referred to as the goddess Pṛthivī. In the *Ṛgveda* Dyaus is said to be her husband and in the Purāṇas, Pṛthu. Pṛthu was an *avatāra* of Viṣṇu, born of the arm of the dead body of Vena and the sages found that a wicked king was better than none. So they opened the thigh of Vena and from there sprang forth a black demon. The wickedness of Vena thus leaving him his arm was opened and Pṛthu came out of the gaping arm. He married Pṛthivī but she refused to yield her treasures. When there was a famine in the land Pṛthu decided to kill Pṛthivī and chased her. She took the form of a cow and fled to Brahmā for protection. The creator refused her asylum but asked her to return to her husband and give him what he wanted. She returned and Pṛthu beat and wounded her in memory of which all the races of men have ever since been wounding her with ploughs, spades and other implements of agriculture. In course of time Pṛthivī came to be considered a symbol of patience, bearing all the misdeeds of men without complaint. She is said to be the example of correct behaviour, as she returns good for evil and gives those who tear her bowels the desirable treasures of the earth. [*Epics, Myths and Legends of India*, P. Thomas]

**Ekaparṇā, Ekapāṭalā**: These, with their sister Aparṇā, were, according to the *Harivaṁśa*, daughters of Himavat and Menā. They performed austerities surpassing the powers of gods and *dānava*s, and alarmed both worlds. Ekaparṇā took only one leaf for food, and Ekapāṭalā only one *paṭala*. Aparṇā took no sustenance at all and lived *a-parṇa*, 'without a leaf'. Her mother being distressed at her abstinence, exclaimed in her anxiety, 'U-mā' — 'O don't'. Through this she became manifest as the lovely goddess Umā, the wife of Śiva. [*Dictionary of Hinduism*, T.R.R. Iyengar]

**Ekāṣṭakā**: A deity mentioned in the *Atharvaveda* as having practised austere devotion, and being the daughter of Prajāpati and mother of Indra and Soma.

**Ekadaṁṣṭra**: [Having one tusk] A name of Gaṇeśa. The *Liṅga Purāṇa* relates the origin of this deity. It is mentioned that as a result of austerities, the *asura*s became very powerful and they began to fight with the *deva*s and defeat them. When the gods appealed to Śiva, he created an *asura* out of himself and named him Vigheśvara, who became the chieftain of the *bhūta-gaṇa*s of Śiva. Thirty-two forms of Gaṇapati are mentioned in the *Mudgala Purāṇa*. The *Śilpasāra* refers to some of these types. Ordinarily Gaṇapati is represented as a sitting or standing image in *avibhaṅga* pose, having the head of an elephant with the trunk usually turned towards the left. In rare cases it is turned to right and such images are called Valamburi Vināyaka. Though ordinarily he has only two eyes, the Āgamas prescribe three eyes to him in some particular aspects. He has normally four arms, but at times he may have up to sixteen arms, carrying an *āyudha*. The more important characteristics of Gaṇeśa are *pāśa*, *aṅkuśa*, and a ball of special form of food — *modaka* cake. He has an enormously big belly — which gives him the name Lambodara — and it is tied up with a snake. His favourite vehicle is the rat, which is invariably represented in miniature on the pedestal of the deity. A single image of Gaṇapati is either seated or standing and there are some varieties like Bāla-Gaṇapati where he is represented as a child. [*Hindu Mythology*, T.R.R. Iyengar]

# G

**Gadā**: A younger brother of Kṛṣṇa.

**Gādhi, Gāthin**: A king of the Kuśika race, and father of Viśvāmitra. He was son of Kuśāmba, or, according to the *Viṣṇu Purāṇa*, he was Indra, who took upon himself that form.

**Gaja**: Elephant God.

**Gajapati**: A title meaning the protector or Lord of elephants. Another name for Lord Gaṇeśa.

**Gaṇa**: A class of deities often associated with Śiva or his aspects, connoting a group of minor gods or followers. Among the attendant *gaṇa*s of Śiva may be mentioned Caṇḍeśa, Bhṛṅgīśa and Nandīśa. The first is considered the foremost among Śiva's servants and hence is named Ādidāsa Caṇḍeśa; he is called, in the *kṛta-yuga*, Pracaṇḍa, with a fierce countenance and sixteen arms. In the *tretā-yuga* he is named Caṇḍa, depicted as smiling, with eight arms and dishevelled braids of hair. In the *dvāpara-yuga* he has only four hands, rides a lion with a frightful face, has protruding teeth and holds in his hands, the tanks, trident noose and hook. In the *kali-yuga* he is depicted with a peaceful face, has hair made into a *jaṭā-mukuṭa* and stands in the *abhaṅga* pose. His weapon is the axe. The *gaṇa*s sometimes are associated with aspects of Śiva like Vīrabhadra. The *Śilparatna* depicts this deity as having eight hands, riding a demon and surrounded by *gaṇa*s or his followers. These Śaiva *gaṇa*s have certain legends about them. The *Varāha Purāṇa* relates how Nandīśa was once merely an ascetic but, through the performance of severe penances, was blessed by Śiva with a form like that of Śiva himself and made the leader of the *gaṇa*s attending on that god. Bhṛṅgīśa was also such a fervent devotee of Śiva that he ignored the feminine aspect of Śiva, namely, Pārvatī and worshipped Śiva alone. Śiva to test this devotee adopted his Ardhanārī form in which Śiva and Pārvatī are united in one form. Bhṛṅgīśa, not to be outdone, became a bee, and boring a hole into this form went round Śiva alone, ignoring Pārvatī who was so enraged that she cursed him with emaciation, which reduced him to such helplessness that he was unable to either stand or help himself. Śiva discovering this provided Bhṛṅgīśa with a third leg. [*Hindu Mythology*, T.R.R. Iyengar; *Glosssary of Hinduism*, T. Rengarajan; *South Indian Image*, Harish Sastri Kṛṣṇa]

**Gaṇa-devatās**: [Troops of deities] Deities who generally appear, or are spoken of, in classes. Nine such classes are mentioned: Ādityas, Viśvas, Vasus, Tuṣitas, Abhasvaras, Anilas, Majarājikas, Sādhyas and Rudras. These inferior deities are attendant upon Śiva, and under the command of Gaṇeśa. They dwell on Gaṇa-parvata i.e., Kailāsa and under the command of Gaṇeśa attend on Śiva. Their chief, Gaṇeśa was also called Gaṇapati. In sculpture the god Gaṇapati according to the *Śilparatna* is to be surrounded by gods and *gaṇa*s. The *gaṇa-devatā*s sometimes attend the images of Mahālakṣmī carrying weapons, usually a round buckler and a curved sword. [*A Classical Dictionary of Hindu Mythology and Religion*, J. Dowson]

**Gaṇapati**: See 'Gaṇeśa'.

**Gaṇas**: See 'Gaṇa-devatās'.

**Gandharvas**: The heavenly *gandharva* of the Veda was a deity who knew and revealed the secrets of heaven and divine truths in general. He is thought by Goldstücker to have been a personification of the fire of the sun. The *gandharva*s generally had their dwelling in the sky or atmosphere, and one of their offices was to prepare the heavenly *soma* juice for the gods. They had a great partiality for women, and had a mystic power over them. The *Atharvaveda* speaks of 'the 6333 *gandharavas*'. The *gandharva*s of later times are similar in character: they have charge of the *soma*, are skilled in medicine, regulate the asterisms and are fond of women. [*A Classical Dictionary of Hindu Mythology and Religion*, J. Dowson]

**Gaṇeśa**: Lord of the *gaṇa*s or troops of inferior deities, especially those attendant upon Śiva. Son of Śiva and Pārvatī or of Pārvatī only. One legend represents that he sprang from the scurf on Pārvatī's body. He is the god of wisdom and remover of obstalces;

hence he is invariably propitiated at the beginning of any important undertaking. He is said to have written down the *Mahābhārata* from the dictation of Vyāsa. Vyāsa in his turn stipulated that Gaṇapati should never write down anything, which he did not understand. Vyāsa found that he had to pause while he was dictating, but recollecting his counter stipulation, purposely dictated a rather tough verse which while the shrewd god was pondering over, aided the poet to keep ahead of the god's writing down the verses dictated. According to *Matsya Purāṇa*, Pārvatī produced Gaṇeśa to cure her husband of his habit of surprising her while she was in the bathtub. One day, she took the oil and ointment used at the bath, and together with other impurities that came from her body, formed them into the figure of a man to which she gave life by sprinkling it with the water of the Ganges. She then kept him as the door-keeper of her bathing apartments. Presently Śiva came, and seeing Gaṇeśa he was considerably surprised. He, however, tried to force an entry and a quarrel broke out between the two in which Śiva cut off Gaṇeśa's head. When Pārvatī came out and saw that her son was killed, she gave herself up to lamentations, and to conciliate her, Śiva ordered the first head to be found of any living being to be brought to him. This happened to be an elephant's and Śiva clapped it on the trunk of Gaṇeśa and gave him life. The *Brahmavaivartta Purāṇa*, which is devoted to the history of Gaṇeśa, relates how Pārvatī desiring a son was told by her husband to propitiate Viṣṇu, who allowed a portion of himself (Kṛṣṇa) to be born as Gaṇeśa. When the gods came to congratulate Pārvatī, Śani, who had been doomed to destroy everything he looked upon, turned his gaze away, but, on being permitted by Pārvatī, took a peep at Gaṇeśa, on which the child's head was severed from its body and 'flew away to the heaven of Kṛṣṇa where it reunited with the substance of him of whom it was a part'. Pārvatī was inconsolable until Viṣṇu appeared and placed an elephant's head instead of the lost one and hence Gaṇeśa is always represented with an elephant's head. Another version is that his mother formed him so to suit her own fancy, and a further explanation is that Śiva slew Āditya the sun, but restored him to life again. For this violence Kāśyapa doomed Śiva's son to lose his head; and when he did lose it, the head of Indra's elephant was used to replace it. A legend is introduced to account for the loss of one of his tusks. Paraśurāma, who was a favourite disciple of Śiva, came to the Himālayas to see his master, but was denied entrance by Gaṇeśa, on which a quarrel arose. Gaṇeśa had at first the advantage and seizing Paraśurāma by his trunk shook him so that he fell senseless. The hero when he recovered hurled the axe of Śiva at Gaṇeśa, who recognising his father's weapon simply received it on one of his tusks which it immediately severed. Hence Gaṇeśa has but one tusk, and is known by the name of Ekadanta or one-tusked. In the *Varāha Purāṇa* Śiva alone is said to have produced Gaṇeśa. The immortals and holy sages observing that no difficulty occurred in accomplishing good or evil deeds which they and others commenced consulted together respecting the means by which obstacles might be opposed to the commission of bad actions and repaired to Śiva for counsel to whom they said, 'O Mahādeva, god of gods, three-eyed, bearer of the trident, it is thou alone who canst create a being capable of opposing obstacles to the commission of improper act.' Hearing these words Śiva looked at Pārvatī, and whilst thinking how he could effect the wishes of the gods, from the splendour of his countenance there sprang up to existence a youth shedding radiance around, endowed with the qualities of Śiva, and evidently another Rudra, and captivating by his beauty the female inhabitants of heaven. Umā seeing his beauty was excited with jealousy, and in her anger pronounced this curse, 'Thou shall not offend my sight with the form of a beautiful youth; therefore assume an elephant's head and a large belly, and thus shall all thy beauties vanish.' Śiva then addressed his son saying, 'The name shall be Gaṇeśa, and the son of Śiva; thou shall be chief of the Vināyakas and the games; success and disappointment shall spring from thee; and great shall be thine influence amongst the gods, and in sacrifices and all affairs. Therefore shalt thou be worshipped and invoked the first on all occasions; . . .' Śiva also said that one who omits to do shall fail in his object and prayers. In the *Skanda Purāṇa* yet another account of the origin of Gaṇeśa is given. During the twilight that intervened between the *dvāpara* and *kali-yuga*s, women, barbarians and śūdras and other workers of sin obtained entrance to the heaven by visiting the shrine of Somanātha, and heaven became overcrowded and hells were without inhabitants. Seeing this predicament Indra and the other gods appealed to Śiva for help who asked them to address their complaints to Pārvatī. Pārvatī was propitated and she rubbed her body and produced a wondrous being with four arms and an elephant's head who created obstacles for men going to heaven by diverting their longing for pilgrimage to desire for the acquisition of wealth.

Gaṇeśa is represented or described in various ways:

***Bāla-gaṇapati***: Gaṇapati is represented as a child.

***Taura-Gaṇapati***: Gaṇapati is represented in the form of a youth with four hands.

***Mahāgaṇapati***: Gaṇapati is represented as an elderly person seated on the pedestal or on the back of his vehicle, the rat.

***Nṛtya-Gaṇapati***: Here Gaṇapati is in a dance pose, with one leg slightly raised and the other bent inwards to indicate the dancing attitude.

***Śakti-Gaṇeśa***: The general characteristics of Śakti-Gaṇeśa, according to the *Vighneśvara-pratiṣṭhā-vidhi* that he is seated on the *padmāsana* with a green-coloured Śakti by his side, whom he is embracing about her waist, and that there no contact between the hips of the god and the goddess. His colour is the crimson of the setting sun. He is represented as holding the weapons, *pāśa* and *vajra* and is made to look terrific. The *Mantramahārṇava*, on the other hand, has it that *danta*, *aṅkuśa*, *pāśa* and *akṣamālā* should be placed in the hands and the *modaka* in the trunk of this Gaṇapati, and that Śakti, decked with ornaments and clothed in gold-laced cloth, should be seated by his side. There are several types of which the more popular are Lakṣmī, Ucchiṣṭa, Ūrdhava and Piṅgalā Gaṇapati.

***Lakṣmī-Gaṇapati*** shows Gaṇapati having eight hands carrying a parrot, a pomegranate, lotus, *aṅkuśa*, *pāśa*, *kalpakalaśa*, *bāṇa* and a water vessel in them. He embraces Lakṣmī or a Devī image that is shown seated on his left lap. [Also see 'Ucchiṣṭa Gaṇapati']

***Heramba-Gaṇapati***: He is a special type of Vināyaka represented as having five heads — the four facing the four directions and the other one, placed above these heads, looking upwards. He is seated upon a powerful lion and has ten arms — the two lowest being in *abhaya* and *varada* poses while the others carry the *pāśa*, *danta*, *akṣamālā*, *paraśu*, a three-headed *mudgara* and *modaka*. The figure of Heramba is very different from all the other figures of Vighneśvara. The colour of Heramba-Gaṇapati has to be golden yellow.

***Prasanna-Gaṇapati***: This Gaṇapati is described as a standing figure that has either a few bends in the body or is perfectly erect. One authority says that the figure should be *abhaṅga* while another says that it should be *samabhaṅga*. The bends on the body are generally three. The seat or pedestal upon which this figure should stand is the *padmāsana*. The Gaṇeśa has to be scarlet in colour, like the rising sun, and should be draped in red cloth.

***Dhvaja-Gaṇapati***: Dhvaja-Gaṇapati should have four hands carrying a book, an *akṣamālā*, *daṇḍa* and a *kamaṇḍalu* and be of terrific look.

Gaṇeśa is also called by the following names: Gajānana, elephant-faced; Gajavadana, elephant-faced; Karimukha, elephant-faced; Harimukha, boastful; Heramba, boastful; Lambakarṇa, long-eared; Lambodara, pendant-bellied; Dvideha, double-bodied; Vighneśa, remover of obstacles; Vighnahārī, remover of obstacles; Dvaimātura, having two mothers.

The following is the list of Gaṇeśa and Śakti specified in the *Nārada Purāṇa*:

| *Name of Gaṇeśa* | *Śakti (1)* | *Śakti(2)* |
|---|---|---|
| Amoda | Bhūti | |
| Caturmūrti | Kāmadā | |
| Dīrghajihvā | Jaratinī | Kālikā |
| Divadanta | Kāntī | Bhaginī |
| Durmukha | Bhautikī | |
| Dvijihvā | Vikīrṇā | |
| Dvijihvā | Jambhiṇī | |
| Dviranda | Grāmaṇī | |
| Ekadanta | Sumedhā | Bhaga |
| Ekapāda | Mahiṣī | |
| Gajavakra | Kāminī | Bhajinī |
| Gajendra | Umā | |
| Gaṇanātha | Svāhā | Śivā |
| Gaṇanāyaka | Karmarūpiṇī | |
| Kaparddī | Pārvatī | Kālarātrī |
| Lambodara | Vigneivi | |
| Mahāṇanda | Svarūpiṇī | |
| Nirañjara | Naṭī | Subhagā |
| Pramoda | Ramā | |
| Sadāśiva | Madajihvā | |
| Śankukarṇaka | Nandā | |
| Ṣaṇmukha | Dīrghagagohnā | |
| Senānī | Śaśiprabhā | |
| Śivottama | Svasti | Subhagā |
| Sumukha | Sītā | |
| Sura | Bhṛkuṭi | |
| Sūrpakarṇa | Tejarati | |
| Vakratuṇḍa | Rati | |
| Vāmadeveśa | Yāminī | |

| | | |
|---|---|---|
| Varada | Dhanurdhanī | |
| Vighakṛta | Sarasvatī | Durbhajā |
| Vighnarāja | Puṣṭi | Cañcalā |
| Vighneśa | Hrī | Lolanetrā |
| Vināyaka | Śānti | Diptī |
| Vīra | Lajjā | |
| Virocana | Satyā | |
| Vṛṣadhvaja | Sureśī | |

He is represented as a short fat man of a yellow colour, with a protuberant belly, four hands and the head of an elephant, which has only one tusk. In one hand he holds a shell, in another a discus, in the third a club and in the fourth hand, a water lily. Sometimes he is depicted riding upon a rat or attended by one, hence his appellation Akuratha. His temples are very numerous in India. [*Epics, Myths and Legends of India*, P. Thomas; *Hindu Mythology*, T.R.R. Iyengar; *Dictionary of Hinduism*, T.R.R. Iyengar]

**Gaṅgā**: The sacred river Ganges. It is said to be mentioned only twice in the *Ṛgveda.* The Purāṇas represent the heavenly Ganges as flowing from the toe of Viṣṇu and to have been brought down from heaven by the prayers of the saint Bhagīratha to purify the ashes of the sixty thousand sons of king Sagara, who had been burnt by the angry glance of the sage Kapila. From this earthly parent the river is called Bhāgīrathī. Gaṅgā was angry at being brought down from heaven, and Śiva, to save the earth from the shock of her fall, caught the river on his brow, and checked its course with his matted locks. From this action he is called Gaṅgā-dhara, 'upholder of the Ganges'. The river descended from Śiva's brow in several streams, four according to some, and ten according to others, but the number generally accepted is seven, being the *sapta-sindhava*, the seven rivers. The Ganges proper is one of the number. The descent of the Ganges disturbed the sage Jahnu as he was performing a sacrifice, and in his anger he drank up the waters, but them relented and allowed the river to flow from his ear, hence, the Ganges has the name of Jāhnavī. Personified as a goddess, Gaṅgā is the eldest daughter of Himavat and Menā, and her sister was Umā. She became the wife of King Śāntanu and bore a son, Bhīṣma, to whom the metronymic Gāṅgeya applies. Being also, in a peculiar way, the mother of Kārttikeya, she is called Kumārasu. Gold, according to the *Mahābhārata*, was borne by the goddess Gaṅgā to Agni, who had impregnated her.

The names and titles of the Gaṅgā are: Bhadrasoma, produced in heaven; Gāndinī, produced in heaven; Kirātī, produced in heaven; Devabhūti, produced in heaven; Haraśekhara, crest of Śiva; Khapaga; flowing form heaven; Mandākinī, gently-flowing; Tripathagā, triple flowing — running in heaven, earth and hell; Trisrotaḥ, triple flowing — running in heaven, earth and hell. [*Hindu Mythology*, T.R.R. Iyengar; *A Classical Dictionary of Hindu Mythology and Religion*, J. Dowson]

**Gaṅgādhara**: A name of Śiva.

**Gāṅgeya**: Name of Kārttikeya.

**Gardabhila**: This is referred to as an inferior animal in comparison with the horse in the *R̥gveda*. Its capacity to bear heavy burden is not forgotten. It is depicted as a vehicle of the deity of Śītalā, goddess of small pox.

**Garga**: One of the priests of Kr̥ṣṇa.

**Garuḍa**: A mythical bird, or vulture, half-man, half-bird on which Viṣṇu rides. He is the king of birds, and descended from Kāśyapa and Vinatā, one of the daughters of Dakṣa. He is the great enemy of serpents, inheriting the hatred from his mother who had a quarrel with her co-wife and superior, Kadru, the mother of serpents. His lustre was so brilliant that soon after his birth the gods mistook him for Agni and worshipped him. He is represented as having the head, wings, talons, and beak of an eagle, and the body and limbs of a man. His face is white, his wings red, and his body golden. He had a son named Sampāti, and his wife was Unnati. According to the *Mahābhārata*, his parents gave him liberty to devour bad men, but he was not to touch brāhmaṇas. Once, however, he swallowed a brāhmaṇa and his wife but the brāhmaṇa so burnt his throat that he was glad to disgorge them both.

In the *Viṣṇu Purāṇa* he is stated to be the son of Kāśyapa by Vinatā and is king of the feathered tribes and the remorseless enemy of the serpent race. Kāśyapa had by Kadru, another of his wives, one thousand powerful, many-headed serpents, of immeasurable might, subject to Garuḍa. But Kadru and Vinatā quarrelled regarding the colour of the horse that was produced at the churning of the ocean, and they laid a wager by which the loser was to be the other's slave. Garuḍa's mother lost, and the serpents in the nether regions imprisoned her. Garuḍa prayed for her release but the serpents asked him, by way of ransom, to bring the moon to them so that they could feast on the nectar in the moon. Garuḍa started for the regions of the moon but on the way felt hungry. While passing the regions of the Pole Star he met his father Kāśyapa and asked him if anything edible could be obtained there. Kāśyapa directed his son to a lake where Garuḍa saw a tortoise and an elephant fighting. 'The tortoise was eighty miles long and the elephant one hundred and sixty. Garuḍa with one claw seized the elephant, with the other the tortoise and perched with them on a tree eight hundred miles high. But the tree was unable to bear his ponderous weight, and, unhappily, thousands of pigmy brāhmaṇas were then worshipping on one of its branches. Trembling lest he should destroy any of them, he took the bough in his beak, continued to hold the elephant and tortoise in his claws, and flew to a mountain in an uninhabited country where he finished his repast on the tortoise and elephant.' Garuḍa is said to have stolen the *amṛta* from the gods in order to purchase with it the freedom of his mother from Kadru. Indra discovered the theft and fought a fierce battle with Garuḍa. The *amṛta* was recovered, but Indra was worsted in the fight, and his thunderbolt was smashed. After many more adventures of a like nature, Garuḍa reached the regions of the moon, seized him, concealed him under his wings and started on his return flight. The gods determined to regain the moon, attacked Garuḍa and, after an indecisive action, came to terms with him. Viṣṇu made him immortal and promised him a higher seat than his own. Garuḍa, on his part, agreed to become the charger of Viṣṇu. Since then 'Viṣṇu rides upon Garuḍa while the latter in the shape of a flag, sits at the top of Viṣṇu's car'. In the Satvata list of the thirty-nine incarnations of the god he appears as Vihaṅgama and Amṛtaharaṇa, the god's ninth and eighteenth *avatāras*. He was originally the sun conceived as a bird. A Ṛgvedic hymn describes the celestial Garutman as endowed with beautiful wings. Garuḍa's another name is Tārkṣya in the epic and Paurāṇika literature. Garuḍa was of immense help to Rāma in the battle of Laṅkā, when Rāma and Lakṣmaṇa and the monkey heroes were struck down by the Nāgāstra of Indrajit. Garuḍa appeared before Rāma and gave him Garuḍāstra which counteracted the effects produced by Nāgāstra. The approach of Garuḍa and the help rendered by him is thus described in the *Rāmāyaṇa:*

The rushing wind grew loud,
Red lightnings flashed from banks of cloud,
The mountains shook, the wild waves rose,
And, smitten by resistless blows,

Uprooted fell each stately tree
That fringed the margin of the sea
All life within the waters feared:
Then, as the vānaras gazed, appeared

King Garuḍa's self, a wondrous sight,
Disclosed in flames of fiery light.
From his fierce eye in sudden dread
All serpents in a moment fled;

And those transformed to shafts, that bound
The princes, vanished in the ground.

Garuḍa is also referred to as Kāśyapī, Vainateya, Tārkṣya and Vināyaka. His other names are as follows: Amṛtaharaṇa, stealer of the *amṛta*; *cirād*, eating long; Gaganeśvara, lord of the sky;

Garutman, chief of birds; Kāmacārin, who goes where he will; Kāmāyus, who lives at pleasure; Khageśvara, king of birds; Nāgāntaka, destroyer of serpents; Pannaganāśana, destroyer of serpents; Raktapakṣa, red-winged; Rasāyana, who moves like quicksilver; Sarparāti, enemy of serpents; Sītānana, white-faced; Sudhāhara, stealer of *amṛta;* Suparṇa, chief of bird; Surendrajit, vanquisher of Indra; Suvarṇakāvya, golden-bodied; Śvetarohita, white and red; Tarasvin, the swift; Vajrajit, subduer of the thunderbolt; Viṣṇuratha, vehicle of Viṣṇu.

The image of Garuḍa is always placed at the corners of parapet walls in Viṣṇu temples and also placed opposite to the shrine of the main dieites. He is also represented in a seated position as well as the vehicle Garuḍavāhanam. But usually he is represented in images as a standing human figure having a beaked nose with protruding eyes and a pair of outspreading wings from the back. He has two hands having a *krīṭam* and ornaments but the more conspicuous is the serpent ornaments. As *vāhanam*, he is represented as a seated image kneeling on his left knee and having his two hands spread out to hold the feet of Viṣṇu. In some places Garuḍa is represented as a standing figure carrying the *amṛta-kalaśa,* the pot of nectar, in one hand and the other raised near the head, with legs parted in the posture of running. [*The World Mythology*, T.R.R. Iyengar; *Epics, Myths and Legends of India*, P. Thomas; *South Indian Image*, T.N. Srinivasan; *Hindu Mythology*, T.R.R. Iyengar]

**Gaurī**: The 'yellow' or 'brilliant', a name of the consort of Śiva. Varuṇa's wife also is called Gaurī.

**Gautameśa**: [Lord of Gautama] Name of one of the twelve great *liṅgas*.

**Gautamī**: An epithet of Durgā.

**Gāyatrī**: A most sacred verse of the *Ṛgveda*, which it is the duty of every brāhmaṇa to repeat mentally in his morning and evening devotions. It is addressed to the sun as Savitṛ, the generator, and so it is called also Savitṛ. Personified as a goddess, Sāvitrī is the wife of Brahmā, mother of the four Vedas, and also of the twice born. Colebrooke's translation of the Gāyatrī is 'Earth, sky, heaven. Let us meditate on the most excellent light and power of that generous, sportive and resplendent sun, it may guide our intellects.' Wilson's version is, in his translation of the *R̥gveda*, 'We meditate on that desirable light of the divine Sāvitrī who influences our pious rites.' In the *Viṣṇu Purāṇa* he had before given a somewhat different version. 'We meditate on that excellent light of the divine sun; may he illuminate our minds.' A later version by Benfey is 'May we receive the glorious brightness of this, the generator, of the god who shall prosper our works'. Wilson observes of it:

> The commentators admit some variety of interpretation; but it probably meant, in its original use, a simple invocation of the sun to shed a propitious influence upon the customary offices of worship; and it is still employed by the Unphilosophical Hindus with merely that signification. Later notions, and especially those of the Vedanta, have operated to attach to the text an import it did not at first possess, and have converted it into a mystical propitiation of the spiritual origin and essence of existence.

It is considered so holy that copyists often refrain from transcribing it.

It is also the name given to Śatarūpā Brahmā's female half, daughter and consort, as 'the declarer of sacred knowledge'. It is applied to the consort of Śiva in the *Harivaṁśa.* [*Glossary of Hinduism*, T. Rengarajan; Macdonnell and Keith *Vedic Index; R̥gveda*]

**Ghaṭotkaca**: Ghaṭotkaca is worshipped in what is one of the oldest temples at Cakuī in Kālī Kumaon. The *Mahābhārata* relates how the Pāṇḍavas, on escaping from the burning house at Vārṇāvata, wandered through the forest southwards along the western bank of the Ganges. Here they met Hiḍimba, the terrible man-eating *asura*, and his beautiful sister Hiḍimbā. Hiḍimba was slain by Bhīma, and his sister followed the

Pāṇḍavas through the forests. She prayed to Kuntī, the mother of the Pāṇḍavas, to command her son Bhīma to take her as his wife and threatening to kill herself if her request were not complied with. So Kuntī, believing that the strong *asura* woman's experiences in the jungle would greatly help them in their sojourns, desired Bhīma to marry her, and he married her and in due time a son was born who was as robust as his parents and named Ghaṭotkaca. Later on we learn that Karṇa, the Kaurava champion, had received a lance from Indra, which was fated to kill whomsoever it struck, and this he reserved for Arjuna, but at a critical moment of the conflict, when Ghaṭokaca was causing dire destruction among the Kauravas, Karṇa used it to kill Ghaṭotkaca. [*Hindu Mythology*, T.R.R. Iyengar; *Mahābhārata*]

**Ghoṣā**: It is said in the Veda that the Aśvins 'bestowed a husband upon Ghoṣā growing old', and the explanatory legend is that she was a daughter of Kakṣivat, but being a leper, was incapable of marriage. When she was advanced in years the Aśvins gave her health, youth and beauty, so that she obtained a husband. [*Mahābhārata*]

**Ghṛtāci:** An *apsaras* or celestial nymph. She was mother of ten sons by Raudrāśva, a descendant of Puru, and the *Brahmavaivartta Purāṇa* attributes the origin of some of the mixed castes to her issue by the sage Viśvakarman.

**Girijā**: [Mountain born] A name of Pārvatī.

**Gopāla**: A name of the youthful Kṛṣṇa.

**Gopatirṣabha**: A title of Śiva.

**Gopīs** : The cowherd damsels and wives with whom Kṛṣṇa sported in the youth.

**Govardhanadhara**: [Upholder of Govardhana] A name of Kṛṣṇa.

**Govinda**: A name of Kṛṣṇa.

**Guha:** Secret. A name of the god of war.

**Guhyakas**: [Hidden beings] Inferior divinities attendant upon Kubera and guardians of his hidden treasures.

# H

**Halabhṛt**: [Bearing a plough] Name of Balarāma.

**Halāyudha**: [Who has a ploughshare for his weapon] Name of Balarāma.

**Haṁsa**: Name of Kṛṣṇa.

**Hanumān**: [A celebrated monkey chief] He was son of Pavana 'the wind', by Añjanā, wife of a monkey named Keśarī. He was able to fly, and is a conspicuous figure in the *Rāmāyaṇa*. He is represented usually standing with hands in *añjalī* pose and the tail hanging down loose on the back, and with the face of a monkey. He is also represented as Garuḍa, carrying the Mahendra mountain in one hand. He and the other monkeys who assisted Rāma in his war against Rāvaṇa were of divine origin, and their powers were superhuman. Hanumān jumped from India to Ceylon in one bound; he tore up trees, carried away the Himālayas, seized the clouds, and performed many other wonderful exploits. His form is as vast as a mountain and as tall as a gigantic tower. His complexion is yellow and glowing like molten gold. His face is red as the brightest ruby while his enormous tail spreads out to an interminable length. He stands on a lofty rock and roars like thunder. He leaps into the air and flies among the clouds with a rushing noise, while the ocean waves are roaring and splashing below. In one of his fights with Rāvaṇa and the *rākṣasa*s, they greased his tail and set it on fire but to their own great injury, for with it he burnt down their capital city Laṅkā. This exploit obtained for him the name Laṅkādāhī. His services to Rāma were great and many. He acted as his spy and fought most valiantly. He flew to the Himālayas, from whence he brought medicinal herbs with which he restored the wounded, and he killed the monster Kālanemi and thousands of *gandharva*s who assailed him. He accompanied Rāma on his return to Ayodhyā, and there he received from him the reward of perpetual life and youth.

The exploits of Hanumān are favourite topics among Hindus

from childhood to old age and paintings of them are common. In the famous temple at Sholigar, Tamil Nadu, he has four hands having *cakra* and *śaṅkha* in the two upper ones, while the lower ones are in *abhaya* and *varada* poses. He is seated in *yoga* aspect. A rare type of Hanumān known as Pañcamukha Hanumān is also worshipped. In this aspect he is depicted as having five heads each representing Garuḍa, Narasiṁha, Hanumān, Varāha and Hayagrīva, together with ten hands, carrying different *āyudha*s. He is the most powerful of the monkey chiefs. Hanumān's loyalty to Rāma has become proverbial and he is held up as the symbol of faithfulness and self-surrender. He is the ideal of the perfect servant, the servant who finds full realisation of manhood, of faithfulness, he is the subordinate whose glory is in his own inferiority. When Rāma on his return to Ayodhyā asked Hanumān what boon he desired as a reward for his great service, the faithful monkey only asked for permission to live so long as the story of Rāma would be told in this world. The boon was granted and it is believed that Hanumān still lives in some inaccessible mountain. Hanumān was born of an *apsarā* who due to a curse had been transformed into a monkey. In one account of his birth it is said that Hanumān's mother was impregnated by a cake. The story of this cake is that Daśaratha who inadvertently killed a brāhmaṇa performed a sacrifice in expiation and on the advice of the sage Vasiṣṭha made three cakes out of the ghee, sugar and rice used in the sacrifice, and gave a cake to each of his wives so as to beget children, as at that time he had none. Kaikeyī, the favourite wife, was served last as she was the youngest, but this lady took it as a slight and looked at the cake in her hand with disdain. A kite made a sweep and carried off the cake. This kite flew over a mountain where Añjanā, the *apsarā* monkey, was praying to Śiva for progeny and dropped it in her hand. Śiva appeared before Añjanā and asked her to eat the cake. This she did and conceived Hanumān. According to this story the function of Marut, the wind god, was confined to directing the cake in its fall to Añjanā's hand. It may be mentioned here that Kaikeyī repented of her misconduct and the two cakes were shared among the three ladies. Another account of Hanumān's birth is that while Añjanā was wandering in the forest the wind god saw the beautiful damsel and ravished her. After everything was over, Añjanā protested, but Marut pacified her by observing that a son would be born to her and he would be great. Wild tales of Hanumān's physical strength are told. He could course through the sky with the swiftness of the wind, assume any size he pleased, uproot trees and hills and make himself invisible. He himself speaks of his might as follows:

Sprung from that glorious Father, I
In power and speed with him may vie.
A thousand times, with airy leap,
Can circle loftiest Meru's steep.

With my fierce arms can stir the sea
Till from their beds the waters flee,
And rush at my command to drown
This land with grove and tower and town.

I through the fields of air can spring
Far swifter than the feathered king,
And leap before him as he flies
On sounding pinions through the skies.

I can pursue the Lord of Light
Uprising from the eastern height,
And reach him ere his course be sped,
With burning beams engarlanded.

As soon as he was born, Hanumān felt hungry; the mother's breast could not satisfy his fierce hunger, and looking about for something edible the babe saw the rising sun which he mistook for a fruit and leapt into the sky to catch it. The terrified luminary took to flight and Hanumān chased him into Indra's heaven. Indra hurled a thunderbolt on Hanumān that wounded him in the jaw and felled him to the earth. The wind god bent upon avenging his son entered the stomachs of all the gods and they were afflicted with colic. The ailing Indra now apologized to Pavana, and granted Hanumān a boon of immortality. Then Pavana left the gods who were relieved of their pain. When searching for Sītā, Sugrīva, the monkey king, divided his army into four divisions and sent each division to search in one of the four directions. Hanumān was specially selected to take charge of the southern division as, from available evidence, it was surmised that Rāvaṇa had carried off Sītā southwards. He was also given the signet ring of Rāma. The monkeys had but a hazy notion of where Laṅkā was nor could they be sure that Rāvaṇa had carried off Sītā to Laṅkā and nowhere else. So Hanumān and the monkeys made a vigorous search in the sector under their charge till they came to the ocean. Here was an element the simians dreaded. They sat dejected in the woods near the seashore not knowing what to do. Then they saw Sampāti, the vulture, brother of Jaṭāyu and the bird told them of Laṅkā, its fortifications and its distance from the sea. But who would cross the sea? 'One monkey said he could bound over twenty leagues, and another fifty and one eighty and Aṅgada son of Bālī could cross over a hundred but his power would not avail for the return.' Now an old monkey related to Hanumān the feats of his childhood and observed that he could jump over to Laṅkā and back if he would only draw on his strength and divine origin. Hanumān meditated and drew strength from his meditation and felt confident of performing the task. He climbed to the top of the mountain Mahendra, shook his powerful body which began to increase in size and, when he felt he was equal to the task, roared like thunder and hurled through the sky like a mountain — his flashing eyes like forest fires, his lifted tail like Sakara's. While he was coursing through the sky a *rākṣasī* named Surasā opened her mouth to swallow him. The width of her distended mouth was one hundred leagues. Hanumān suddenly contracted himself to the size of a thumb, entered her mouth, assumed his vast form again and came out of her right ear, leaving her a ponderous carcass that crashed into the sea. On reaching Laṅkā, Hanumān reduced his size to that of a cat and wandered over the forts of Laṅkā. He saw the marvellous palace of Rāvaṇa built by Viśvakaramā himself. He even stole into the gaily-decorated bedchamber of Rāvaṇa where he saw the king of Laṅkā sporting with the beautiful Mandodarī and several other ladies.

After many adventures and hairbreadth escapes in the well-guarded palace and pleasure groves of Rāvaṇa, Hanumān at last saw Sītā and delivered his message. He also destroyed the park of Rāvaṇa, set fire to Laṅkā as mentioned elsewhere and returned to Rāma.

In the battle of Laṅkā, Rāma and Lakṣmaṇa were mortally wounded by the *rākṣasa* and nothing but the leaves of a herb that grew in the Himālayas could restore them to health. Hanumān was despatched to bring the herb. But Rāvaṇa had promised half his kingdom to anyone who could kill Hanumān and Kālanemi, an ambitious giant, flew over to the Himālayas in advance of Hanumān and invited this hero, when he reached the mountain, to dinner. An *apsaras*, whom Hanumān had accidentally released from the effect of a curse, told him who his host was and Hanumān caught Kālanemi by the leg and whirled him through the air to Laṅkā where he fell before the throne of Rāvaṇa. After thus disposing of Kālanemi, Hanumān began to look for the herb. But due to a machination of Indra he experienced some difficulty in distinguishing the herb and hence he tore down the whole hill and flew with it towards Laṅkā. While he was passing Ayodhyā the cyclone his course generated was mistaken by Bharata for the work of some evil spirit and this king let fly an arrow which brought Hanumān down. Grieved at his mistake Bharata told Hanumān that he could take him to Laṅkā by means of another arrow, which offer the hero declined. Hanumān flew on his own strength with the hill but on nearing Laṅkā saw from his elevated position that the moon was about to rise. As the herb could have effect only before moonrise he swallowed the moon, reached Laṅkā in time and revived the wounded heroes. Hanumān was famous not only for his physical strength but also for his learning. 'The chief of the monkeys', says the *Rāmāyaṇa*, 'is perfect: no one equals him in the Śāstras, in learning and in ascertaining the sense of scriptures. In all sciences, in the rules of austerity he rivals the preceptor of the gods, Rāma.' When Rāma first met Hanumān in Sugrīva's residence, he was much impressed by the learned discourse of Hanumān. He says:

One whose words so sweetly flow,
The whole *Ṛgveda* needs must know,
And in his well trained memory store
The Yajush and the Saman's lore.

He must have bent his faithful ear
All grammar's varied rules to hear!
For his long speech how well he spoke!
In all its length no rule he broke.

In the *Mahābhārata* is an interesting account of a meeting between Hanumān and his half-brother Bhīma. After Rāma's death, Hanumān was living in a mountain spending his days in contemplation of his great master. Bhīma, in his search for a mythical flower Draupadī wished to possess, happened to pass this forest and saw an old monkey sleeping across his path. He haughtily asked the monkey to get out of his way. The monkey wished to know who he was. Bhīma gave a boastful account of himself and the greatness of the Pāṇḍava heroes; upon this, the monkey asked him how such wonderful people happened to wander in the forests without a kingdom and how the beloved wife of such heroes was suffered to be insulted by Duryodhana. Bhīma disdained to make answer but asked the monkey to clear the road. The monkey said that he was ailing and requested Bhīma to step across him. But Bhīma would not pass by the head-side. After some argument Bhīma agreed to pass by the tail-side, but as he started to pass the tail this appendage of the monkey began to lengthen. After walking along the tail for some time the Pāṇḍava knew he was not dealing with an ordinary ape and so he came back to Hanumān and asked him respectfully who he was. Hanumān smiled and disclosed his identity. He entertained Bhīma with many tales of ancient days, and described to him the feats performed by the monkeys in the *Rāmāyaṇa* battle. Bhīma requested Hanumān to show him the form he had assumed for jumping over to Laṅkā. Hanumān now stood up and began to increase in size; but before he reached his full stature Bhīma got frightened of the enormity of the form, fainted and fell down. Hanumān assumed a smaller size, revived his brother, and gave him directions as to how to get the flower he was seeking and set him on his adventurous task. He is called Marutputra and he has the patronymics Anilī, Māruti and the metronymic Āñjaneya. He is also *yogācāra* from his power in magic or in the healing art, and Rajatadyuti, 'the brilliant'. Among his other accomplishments, Hanumān was a grammarian, and the *Rāmāyaṇa* says, 'The chief of monkeys is perfect; no one equals him in the śāstras, in learning, and in ascertaining the sense of the scriptures. In all sciences, in the rules of austerity, he rivals the preceptor of the gods. . . . It is well known that Hanumān was the ninth author of grammar.' — Muir. [*Rāmāyaṇa*; *South Indian Images*, H.S. Kṛṣṇa; *Hindu Mythology*, T.R.R. Iyengar; *Hindu Dictionary*, T. Rengarajan]

**Hara**: Name of Śiva.

**Hari**: A name which commonly designates Viṣṇu, but it is exceptionally used for other gods.

**Hari-Hara**: A combination of the names, Viṣṇu and Śiva, and representing the union of the two deities in one, a combination which is differently accounted for.

**Hārīta**: A son of Yuvanāsva of the solar race, descended from Ikṣavāku. In the *Liṅga Purāṇa* it is said, 'The son of Yuvanāsva's was Hārīta, of whom the Hārītas were sons. They were on the side of Aṅgiras, twice-born men of kṣatriya lineage.

**Harits**: In the *Ṛgveda* the horses, or rather mares, of the sun, seven or ten in number, and typical of his rays.

**Harṣaṇa**: A deity who presides over the *śrāddha* offerings.

**Havirbhuj**: *Pitṛ*s or Manes of the kṣatriyas, and inhabitants of the solar sphere.

**Hayagrīva**: [Horse-necked] According to one legend a *daitya* who stole the Vedas as it slipped out of the mouth of Brahmā while he was sleeping at the end of a *kalpa*, and was killed by Viṣṇu in the fish *avatāra*. According to another, Viṣṇu himself, who assumed this form to recover the Veda that had been carried off by two *daitya*s.

**Hayaśiras**: [Horse-head] in the *Mahābhārata* it is recorded that the sage Aurva 'cast the fire of his anger into the sea', and that it there 'became the great Hayaśiras, known to those acquainted with the Veda, which vomits forth that fire and drinks up the waters'. A form of Viṣṇu.

In the *Bhāgavata Purāṇa* Brahmā is represented as saying, 'In my sacrifice Bhāgavata himself was Hayaśīrṣa, the male of the sacrifice, whose colour is that of gold, of whom the Vedas and the sacrifices are the substance and the gods the soul'. When he respired charming words came forth from his nostrils.

**Horse:** Although the horse is very often mentioned in the *Ṛgveda*, this animal has never been an object of worship. But *aśvamedha* is the greatest sacrifice a king can perform. Only those monarchs who aspire to universal dominion can perform it. Prior to the performance of the sacrifice a horse, with auspicious marks, is let loose to wander at will for a year. An army follows the horse and anyone who stops the horse is considered an enemy and his act a challenge to the owner of the horse. He has to be conquered. After a year the horse is led back, and a grand sacrifice and feasting take place. Rāma in the *tretā-yuga* and Yudhiṣṭhira in the *dvāpara-yuga* performed this sacrifice and were acclaimed world victors. [*Hindu Mythology*, T.R.R. Iyengar].

**Hṛṣikeśa**: A name of Kṛṣṇa.

# I

**Iḍā**: In the *Ṛgveda* Iḍā is primarily food, refreshment, or a libation of milk; thence a stream of praise personified as the goddess of speech. She is called butter-handed. In one passage she is called the mother of a troop which, according to Sāyaṇa, means the troop of Maruts, the sons of Rudra. She is called the instructress of Manu, and frequent passages ascribe to her the first institution of the rules of performing sacrifices. According to Sāyaṇa, she is the goddess presiding over the earth. A legend in the *Śatapatha Brāhmaṇa* represents her as springing from a sacrifice, which Manu performed for the purpose of obtaining offspring. She was claimed by Mitra-Varuṇa, but remained faithful to him who had produced her. Manu lived with her, and praying and fasting to obtain offspring, he begat upon her the race of Manu. In the Purāṇas, she is daughter of the Manu Vaivasvata, wife of Budha, and mother of Pururavas. The Manu Vaivasvata, before he had sons, instituted a sacrifice to Mitra and Varuṇa for the purpose of obtaining one, but the officiating priest mismanaged the performance, and the result was the birth of a daughter, Iḍā. Through the favour of the two deities her sex was changed, and she became a man, Sudyumna. Under the malediction of Śiva, Sudyumna was again turned into a woman, and, as Ilā, married Budha. After she had given birth to Pururavas, she under the favour of Viṣṇu once more became Sudyumna, and was the father of three sons. According to another version of the legend, the Manu's eldest son was named Ilā. He having trespassed on a grove sacred to Pārvatī was changed into a female, Ilā. Upon the supplications and prayers of Ilā's friends, Śiva and his consort conceded that the offender should be a male one month and a female another. There are other variations in the story that is apparently ancient.

In the later Sanskrit literature Iḍā is one of the well-known names of Durgā who, like her, is a goddess of plenty and is called Annapūrṇā. Durgā is associated with Sarasvatī and Lakṣmī in the same way as Iḍā is associated with Sarasavatī and Bhāratī.

It is therefore not improbable that Durgā was a successor, howsoever removed, of the Vedic Iḍā.

**Idavida**: Daughter of Tṛṇabindu and the *apsaras* Alambuṣā.

**Indra**: The word Indra is derived from Indha, meaning 'kindled', says thet *Śatapatha Brāhmaṇa*. In the *Ṛgveda* he is distinctly mentioned as one born without a fellow. In the *Taittirīya Saṁhitā*, Indra is seen contesting his supremacy with Viṣṇu, the Yajñapuruṣa. The same *Śatapatha Brāhmaṇa* mentions that Indra, Agni, and Sūrya strove hard to secure the supreme positions among the gods and succeeded; this statement gives us an insight into the origin of the Trimūrtis of the later times. In the *Ṛgveda*, Indra is described as the wielder of the Vajra, as encompassing the sky and the waters, and reaching up to heaven and is said to have fixed the earth, the luminaries, propped up the sky and so on, and it is said that these acts were all done under the exhilirating influence of the drink quaffed off from three cups. Though praised as unequalled by together gods and mortals, Indra is not a self-existing being but born of a mother. While he as the chief of the gods churned the ocean of milk in company with the *asuras*, the white elephant named Airāvata came out of it and this was taken for himself by Indra. The name of the wife of Indra is Indrāṇī or Śaci.

In the *Mahābhārata*, Indra is said to be the father of Arjuna and to have a thousand eyes spread all over his body because he seduced Ahalyā, the wife of the *ṛṣi* Gautama. He is also classed as one of the twelve Ādityas. It is thus seen how Indra, one of the supreme gods of the Vedic period, deteriorated into the chief of the minor gods, the leader of the army of the gods, and finally into one of the guardian deities of the eight regions. He was receiving from the human beings some sort of worship on earth, but Kṛṣṇa was the first to put a stop to it. It was on this occasion that Indra caused havoc in Gokula by sending down torrents of rain and it was also then that Kṛṣṇa protected the cowherds and their belongings by lifting up the Govardhana mountain. In spite of Kṛṣṇa's protest against the worship of Indra, it was still existing in the seventh to the tenth centuries of the Christian era.

It is stated in the *Aṁśumadbhedāgama* that the colour of the image of Indra should be dark and that it should have two eyes and two arms; the image should possess very handsome features and be adorned with the *kirīṭa*, *kuṇḍala*s, *hāra*, *keyūra* and other ornaments and be draped in red garments. Indra should carry in his right hand the *śakti* and in the left the *aṅkuśa*. The neck of the figure of Indra should be thick and the belly rather big; the image might be sitting or standing upon a *siṁhāsana* or be seated upon his elephant, the Airāvata. In this figure Indra should be seated with his consort Indrāṇī, decorated with all ornaments and carrying a flower in the hand and with features of a gay and joyful young woman. On either side of this celestial pair should be represented two *gandharva* women waving multi-coloured *cāmara*s. The authorities have practically the same description but differ in that while one states the articles held in the hand by Indra are the Aṅkara or a *nīlotpala* flower, the other states that the colour of Indra should be white and that he should have a third eye lying horizontally in the middle of the forehead and four arms, one of the right hands of which is to carry the *vajra*, the other right hand a *padma*, while one of the left arms should pass round the figure of Indrāṇī in an embrace and the remaining left hand should carry the *aṅkuśa*. Indrāṇī should be of the colour of gold and be clad in blue garments. She should be embracing Indra and, in the other hand, carry a *santānamañjarī*. The *Viṣṇudharmottara* adds that she should be seated upon the left lap of her lord. The elephant Airāvata should have four tusks, two on either side.

Indra is undoubtedly the greatest of the Vedic *deva*s, being invoked in 250 hymns or about one-fourth of *R̥gveda*. As his name does not designate any phenomenon of nature, he has become more anthropomorphic and more invested with mythological imagery than any other member of the pantheon. He is an important deity of the middle region, being the representative of the air in the triad Agni, Indra and Sūrya. The *Naighaṇṭuka* mentions him among the gods of the air alone. He is preeminently a god of power and valour, his most outstanding achievement being the destruction of the demon of drought and the release of waters. He is also the one who grants victory to the believers over their foes. Indra's physical features and gigantic size are much more vividly described than those of any other god. When he grasped the two boundless worlds they were but a handful for him. He surpasses in greatness heaven, earth and air. The two worlds are but equal to half of him. Heaven and earth do not suffice for his girdle and ten earths are not equal to him. His arms are long, far extended, great, strong and well-shaped. In consonance with his size his belly has also unbounded capacity. It is compared when full of *soma* to a lake. Elsewhere Indra is said to have drunk three lakes of *soma* for the slaughter of Vr̥tra but also to have performed great cosmic actions such as supporting earth and sky or spreading out the earth. The epithet Somapa is therefore characteristic of him. Indra's favourite weapon is the thunderbolt. It is generally described as fashioned for him by Tvaṣṭr̥ from the bones of Dadhici. It is made of metal or gold with four or a hundred angles and a thousand points. With the *vajra*, he killed the *asura* Vr̥tra. Only once Rudra and the Maruts also receive such epithets. Sometimes Indra is said to be armed with a bow and arrows. He also carries a hook and the *Atharvaveda* gives him a net wherewith he overwhelms his foes. His chariot is drawn by two tawny steeds. In a few passages his horses are said to be hundred or a thousand or eleven hundred. Indra is associated with various other deities. His chief allies are the Maruts who constantly help him in his war-like exploits. Hence the epithet 'Marutvant' — accompanied by the Maruts — is characteristic of him. Agni is the god most often conjoined with him as a dual divinity. Indra is further often coupled with Varuṇa and Vāyu, and also with Soma, Br̥haspati, Pūṣaṇ and Viṣṇu. The latter is a faithful friend of Indra and helps him in his conflict with Vr̥tra.

Indra's greatness and power is constantly dwelt upon in the hymns addressed to him. Neither gods nor men have attained to the limit of his might. No one like him is known among the gods. No one born, past or present can equal him. Indra alone is king of the whole world. He is the lord of all that moves and breathes. He bears several characteristics attributes expressive of power and greatness such as *śakra*, *saipati*, *śatakratu*, and *puruhuta*. At times he receives the epithet *asura*. He is often compared to the lion in strength. The essential myth, which is the basis of Indra's nature, is described in the hymns with great frequency and much variation. Exhilirated by Soma and generally aided by Maruts, he attacks the demon of drought called Vr̥tra, the obstructer, and conceived as an Ahi or dragon. Heaven and earth tremble with fear when Indra strikes the demon with his bolt. He shatters the demon that encompasses the waters, hence receiving the exclusive epithet 'Apsujit', 'conquering in the waters'. After the combat that is regarded as being constantly renewed, Indra pierces the mountain and sets free the waters like imprisoned cows. It is clear that the mountain, which Indra cleaves to release the waters, is none other than the cloud. The clouds sometimes appear as the fortresses of the aerial demons. Indra shatters them and is thence called the fort-destroyer. But the chief epithet that Indra earns as a result of his conflict with the demon of drought is Vr̥trahan. In this fight the Maruts are his regular allies, but Agni, Soma and Viṣṇu also often assist him. Indra engages in conflict with many minor demons also. One of these, Uraṇa mentioned only once is described as having 99 arms, while another Viśvarūpa is three-headed and six-eyed. Some other demons crushed by Indra are Arbuda, Rauhīna and Vala. Another myth relates the capture by Indra of the cows of the Paṇis, with the help of a bitch called Śaramā. Sometimes Indra is described as destroying demons in general. The release of waters is connected with winning of light, sun and dawn. It is said that when Indra had slain Vr̥tra he placed the sun visible in the heaven. He produces the dawn as well as the sun. The cows mentioned along with the sun and dawn are probably the morning beams that are less where compared with cattle coming out of their dark stalls. Great cosmic actions are often attributed to Indra. He is said to have settled the quaking mountains. In the *Maitrāyaṇī Saṁhitā* Indra is where ever they please. The wings become the clouds. He stretches out two wheels which are kept apart by the axle. He is the generator of heaven and earth. He made the non-existent into the existent in a moment. As the great god of battle Indra is more frequently invoked than any other god as the helper of the Āryas in their conflict with terrestrial enemies. He is said to have rent the citadels of the dark aborigines, subjugated them to the Āryas and given land to the Āryas. He turns away from the Ārya the weapon of the Dasa in the land of the seven rivers. He helped a number of his proteges in overcoming their foes. He vanquished Śambara in the interest of King Divodāsa Atithigva. He conquered Pipru for the sake of R̥ṣisvan. He struck down Namuci for the protection of Namisapya. He crushed Dhūnī and Cumurī in favour of Dadhiti. He safely brought Yadu and Turvasta across the rivers. He helped Sudās in the battle of ten kings. More generally Indra is praised as a protector, helper and friend of his worshippers. He bestows goods and wealth on the pious man. His liberality is so characteristic that the frequent attribute Maghavan, 'bountiful', is almost exclusively his.

Indra's names are many, as Arha, Datteya, Maghavān, Mahendra, R̥bhukṣa, Śakra and Vasava.

His epithets are as follows: Devapati, chief of the gods; Divaspati, ruler of the atmosphere; Jiṣṇu, leader of the celestial host; Marutvan, lord of the winds; Meghavāhana, borne upon the clouds; Pākaśāṣana, the subduer of Pāka; Purandara, destroyer of cities; Śatakratu, of a hundred sacrifices; Suradhipa, chief of the gods; Svargapati, lord of the paradise; Ugradhanvan, of the terrible bow; Ulūka, the owl; Vajrapāṇi of the thunderbolt hand; Vr̥trahan, destroyer of Vr̥ta.

**Indrāṇī**: Wife of Indra, and mother of Jayanta and Jayantī. She is also called Śaci and Aindrī. She is mentioned a few times in the *R̥gveda*, and is said to be the most fortunate of females, 'for her husband shall never die of old age'. The *Taittirīya Brāhmaṇa* states that Indra chose her for his wife from a number of competing goddesses because she surpassed them all in voluptuous attractions. In the *Rāmāyaṇa* and Purāṇas, she appears as the daughter of the *daitya* Puloman from whom she has the patronymic Paulomī. Indra, who killed her father to escape his curse, ravished her. According to the *Mahābhārata*, king Nahuṣa became enamoured of her and she escaped from him with difficulty. Indrāṇī has never been held in very high esteem as a goddess.

**Īśa**: A title of Śiva.

**Īśāna**: A name of Śiva or Rudra, or of one of his manifestations. He is guardian of the north-east quarter.

**Īśvara**: 'Lord'. A title given to Śiva.

# J

**Jagaddhātrī**: [Sustainer of the world]. An epithet given to both Sarasvatī and Durgā.

**Jaganmātṛ**: [Mother of the world] One of the names of Śiva's wife.

**Jalaśāyin**: [Sleeping on the waters]. An appellation of Viṣṇu as he is supposed to sleep upon his serpent couch on the waters during the rainy season, or during the submersion of the world.

**Jaiminī**: Jaiminī is the most prominent disciple of Vyāsa who wrote about 1400 BC a philosophy called Pūrva-Mīmāṁsā in defiance of the Vedic rites. He admits the authority of the Vedas but not their revelation. According to him, an intelligent performance of the Vedic rites leads to salvation. His work has 12 chapters. He admits of Brahmā, but never uses the word Īśvara in his book. Jaiminī asserts that the gods are not separate powers but the *mantras*, i.e., hymns alone are gods. Professor E.B. Cowell here observes:

> In the course of its critical investigations, Purva Mimamsa discusses, however, various philosophical doctrines. It appears to have been originally atheistic, the sacrifices and other ceremonies which it so zealously upholds being said to produce their fruit by an inherent law or fate. One of its most curious speculations is the doctrine of an eternal sound underlying all temporary sounds. This is by some identified with Brahma. The grammarians have naturally adopted this doctrine.

Jaiminī adopts the sound theory of creation as given in the *Ṛgveda* book X. The vast world had its origin in *vāk*, i.e., sound. This sound is Veda; this sound is Vedic hymns. All gods are really sounds. The Vedas have adopted nominalism; all existence are names in sounds. Vākdevī, daughter of seer Abhṛṇa, in her Devī-Sūkta in the *Ṛgveda* says that sound is Brahmā; sound is the origin of all creation.

**Jāmadagnya**: The patronymic of Paraśurāma.

**Jāmbavan**: The King of the bears. The part he played in the battle of Laṅkā was not so noteworthy as that of Hanumān or Sugrīva. After the victory Rāma granted him a boon by which he could be killed only by Viṣṇu. The following is the story of his death. Śatrājit, a Yādava who dwelt in Dvārakā, by a rigorous course of austerities, obtained the solar gem *syamantaka* from Sūrya which yielded him eight stones of gold a day. Kṛṣṇa happened to see the gem and expressed a desire to possess it. Śatrājit, for obvious reasons, did not like to part with it and gave him an evasive reply. Soon after this Prasena, Śatrājit's brother went out on a hunting expedition wearing the gem. Prasena strayed from the main party, and was killed by a lion, which took the gem and went about the forest wearing the brilliant booty. Jāmbavat who was living in a cave in the forest happened to see *syamantaka* and he killed the lion and took possession of the gem. But wild rumours spread in Dvārakā. Śatrājit told people that Kṛṣṇa had once asked him to make a present of the gem to him and circulated rumours by which Kṛṣṇa came to be believed as the murderer of Prasena. Kṛṣṇa decided to find out the real cause of Prasena's death and clear his conduct. With a party of followers he set out on the trial of Prasena and came upon the forest where Prasena had been killed by the lion. There he followed the footprints of the lion and came upon the forest in which that animal had been killed by the bear. He started on the trail of the bear and reached the mouth of the cave where Jāmbavat lived. Kṛṣṇa asked his followers to remain outside and entered the cave. Jāmbavat challenged the intruder and the two fought fiercely in the cave for 21 days at the end of which Jāmbavat was mortally wounded. Realisation now dawned upon the bear and he recognised in Kṛṣṇa his master Rāma. He surrendered the gem, gave his daughter in marriage to Kṛṣṇa and died singing the praises of Viṣṇu. Kṛṣṇa with his party returned to Dvārakā and gave the gem to Śatrājit. This slanderer begged to be pardoned and, by way of atonement, gave his daughter Satyabhāmā in marriage to Kṛṣṇa. [*Hindu Mythology*,

T.R.R. Iyengar; *Epics, Myths and Legends of India*, P. Thomas]

**Jāmbavatī**: Daughter of Jāmbavat, king of the bears, wife of Kr̥ṣṇa and mother of Śāmba.

**Jānakī**: A patronymic of Sītā.

**Janārdana**: [The adored of mankind]. A name of Kr̥ṣṇa, but other derivations are offered as extirpator of the wicked, by Śaṅkarācārya.

**Jātavedas**: [A Vedic epithet for fire] The meaning is explained in five ways:

1. Knowing all created beings.
2. Possessing all creatures or everything existent.
3. Known by created beings.
4. Possessing Vedas, riches.
5. Possessing Vedas, wisdom.

Other derivations and explanations are found in the *Brāhmaṇa*s, but the exact sense of the word seems to have been very early lost, and of the five explanations given, only the first two would seem to be admissible for the Vedic texts.

**Jaṭāyu**: Jaṭāyu, the aged king of the vultures, a descendant of Vinatā, is prompted by his friendship with Daśaratha to offer himself to Rāma as *vāsasahāya* and protector of Jānakī in his and Lakṣmaṇa's absence. He is characterised as a self-sacrificing hero who, out of compassion for Sītā and his friendship with Rāma, fights Rāvaṇa valiantly to the extent of sacrificing his life in order to save Sītā. Aroused from his sleep by the pleading voice of Sītā he first appeals to the moral conscience of Rāvaṇa to release Sītā, exposing his sinfulness of touching another's wife, particularly the wife of a virtuous king like Rāma who was devoted so much to the welfare of others. As he warns Rāvaṇa of the dire consequence which this ignoble act will result in, he also tells him of his intention to prevent him from taking away Sītā even if necessary by giving up his life, for the sake of Rāma and Daśaratha. Jaṭāyu fights valiantly with his beak, claws and wings, notwithstanding the injuries inflicted by Rāvaṇa. The vulture king points out that Rāvaṇa's act will bring about the destruction of the entire *rākṣasa* race and arousing his belligerent ire, he vigorously attacks him, fighting at the risk of his life for Rāma. Rāvaṇa with cruel hands cuts off Jaṭāyu's wings, feet and sides, leaving him near to lifeless on the ground.

**Jayakara**: A Hindu deity who appears in the Buddhist Vajrayāna pantheon as depicted in the *Niṣpannayogāvalī*. This god, in the Hindu pantheon, is along with Balabhadra, Madhukara and Vasanta, a companion of love god, Kāmadeva.

**Jayanta**: Son of Indra, also called Jaya.

**Jayantī**: Daughter of Indra. She is called also Jayanī, Devasenā and Taviṣī.

**Jyeṣṭhādevī**: The worship of this goddess appears to be of ancient origin and the *Bodhāyana Gṛhyasūtras* indicate the nature of worship that must be offered to her. By some, she is considered to be the elder sister of Lakṣmī, as she came out of the ocean of milk, when it was churned and no one wished to marry her on account of her ugliness. But the *ṛṣi* Kapila took her for his wife and so she is also known as Kapilapatnī. She is represented as a grotesque looking female deity with hanging lips, stunted nose, pendant breasts and a huge belly. She revels in blood and has two hands in one of which she holds a lotus. The other hand rests down on the seat. A pair of crows represents her banner. The worship of Jyeṣṭhā is quite common in south India. As she is supposed to be the goddess of misfortune and poverty, her shrines are almost in desolate ruin and neglect.

# K

**Ka**: The interrogative pronoun 'who?' This word has been raised to the position of a deity. In the words of Max Müller,

> The authors of the *Brāhmaṇa*s had so completely broken with the past, that forgetful of the poetical character of the hymns and the yearning of the poets after the unknown god, they exalted the interrogative pronoun itself into a deity and acknowledged a god Ka or who? In the *Taittirīya Brāhmaṇa*, the *Kauṣitakī Brāhmaṇa*, the *Tāṇḍya Brāhmaṇa* and the *Śatapatha Brāhmaṇa*, wherever interrogative verses occur the author states that Ka is Prajāpati or the lord of creatures. Nor did they stop here. Some of the hymns in which the interrogative pronoun occurred were called Kadvat, i.e., having *kad* or *quid*. But soon a new adjective was formed and not only the hymns but also the sacrifice offered to the god were called Kaya or Who-ish. . . . At the time of Pāṇini, this word had acquired such legitimacy as to call for a separate rule explaining its formation. The commentator here explains Ka by *Brahman*. After this we can hardly wonder that in the later Sanskrit literature of the Purāṇas Ka appears as a recognised god, as a supreme god, with a genealogy of his own, perhaps even with a wife; and that in the laws of Manu one of the recognised forms of marriage, generally known by the name of Prajāpati marriage, occurs under the monstrous title of Kaya.

The *Mahābhārata* identifies Ka with Dakṣa and the *Bhāgavata Purāṇa* applies the term to Kāśyapa, no doubt in consequence of their great generative powers and similarity to Prajāpati. [*A Classical Dictionary of Hindu Mythology and Religion*, J. Dowson; *Hindu Mythology*, T.R.R. Iyengar]

**Kadru**: A daughter of Dakṣa and one of the thirteen that were married to Kāśyapa. She was mother of 'a thousand powerful many headed serpents, the chief amongst whom were Śeṣa, Vasukī, and many other fierce and venomous serpents.' The *Viṣṇu Purāṇa* from which this is taken names twelve, the *Vāyu Purāṇa* forty. Her offspring bear the metronymic Kadraveya. [*A Classical Dictionary of Hindu Mythology and Religion*, J. Dowson]

**Kailāsa**: A mountain in the Himālayas, north of the Manasā lake. Śiva's paradise is said to be on Mount Kailāsa, so also is Kubera's abode. It is called also Gaṇaparvata and Rajatādri, 'silver mountain'.

**Kāla**: [Time] A name of Yama, the judge of the dead. In the *Atharvaveda* time is addressed as the source and ruler of all things. 'It is he who drew forth the worlds and encompassed them. Being their father he became their son. There is no other power superior to him.' The *Viṣṇu*, *Bhāgavata* and *Padma Purāṇa*s state that Brahmā existed in the form of Time but the Purāṇas do not generally recognise Time as an element of the first cause.

There is a Purāṇic legend of Kālaharamūrti,the destroyer of the god of death, narrated in connection with the sage Mārkaṇḍeya. Kāla wanted to take away the young Mārkaṇḍeya who was deeply attached to god Śiva and when Kāla arrived the young devotee clung fast to the image of Śiva, out of which Śiva himself issued forth as Kālahara, the conqueror of Death, and piercing Kāla with his trident, hurled him away and then rescued the devout Mārkaṇḍeya. In the Āgamas Śiva is represented as the dancing Naṭarāja treading with his right foot on the *liṅga* while his left one is thrust on the breast of Kāla,who has fallen. In scripture Kāla and Yama are not generally identical. An image of Kāla, as indicated in the Āgamas, can be seen in south Indian temples. Kāla is also shown as an attendant of Yama, standing to his left, with a fierce mien, holding death's noose in his hand, while to Yama's right appears Citragupta. [*South Indian Images*, S.M. Krishna; *Atharvaveda*; *Bhāgavata Purāṇa; Padma Purāṇa*]

**Kālakañjas**: Sons of Kāśyapa by his wife Kālaka. There were many thousands of them, and they were distinguished *dānava*s, who were powerful, ferocious and cruel.

**Kālī**: [The black] In Vedic days this name was associated with Agni, who had seven flickering tongues of flame for devouring oblations of butter. Of these seven Kālī was the black or terrific tongue. This meaning of the word is now lost, but it has developed into the goddess Kālī, the fierce and bloody consort of Śiva. The most formidable aspect of the consort of Śiva is Kālī, who it is said destroyed Kāla, time, itself. Kālī is widely worshipped in India as the goddess of terror and the lower classes are particularly devoted to her. Most of the devil dances, dark rites and obscene ceremonials practised in India by the lower order can be traced to her. She is the goddess of epidemics and cataclysms. She is evidently of non-Āryan origin, a relic of aboriginal savagery which has outlived its time. Kālī is propitiated by sacrifices of animals and birds. The *Kālikā Purāṇa* gives details of sacrifices, including those of humans, to propitiate Kālī. It says,

> By a human sacrifice, Devī is pleased for a thousand years, and by the sacrifice of three men, a hundred thousand years. By human flesh Kāmākhyā, Caṇḍikā, and Bhairava who assume my shape are pleased a thousand years. An oblation of blood, which has been rendered pure by holy texts, is equal to ambrosia; the head and flesh also afford much delight to the goddess Caṇḍikā.

The proper method of sacrifice is thus described. Let the sacrificer repeat the word Kālī twice and say, 'Hail, Devī! goddess of thunder; hail, iron-sceptre goddess!' Let him then take the axe in his hand and again invoke the same by the Kālarātrīya text as follows: 'Let the sacrificer say Hraṅg, Hraṅg! Kālī, Kali! O, horrid-toothed goddess! Eat, cut, destroy all the malignant; cut with this axe; bind, bind; seize, seize; drink blood! Spheng, spheng! secure, Salutation to Kālī.' Thus ends the *kālarātrīya mantra*. Kālī's insatiable thirst for blood was occasioned by the circumstances of her having killed an *asura* named Raktabīja whose blood she drank. This *asura* had received a boon from Brahmā by the power of which every drop of his blood that fell on the ground became capable of creating innumerable *asura*s like him. Kālī in her fight with him held him aloft, pierced him with a spear and drank every drop of blood that gushed from his wound and thus managed to kill him. Kālī is represented in art as a black, half-naked woman of terrible aspect, with claws and tusks, wearing a garland of skulls, her tongue hanging out and mouth dripping blood. The reason why Kālī is painted black is because of her supposed mastery over time. Śiva as the god of destruction is identical with the all-devouring time and his distinguishing colour is white. In contrast to him Kālī represents the dark abysmal void which is above time, space and causation. The consort of Śiva is known by many names of which the most familiar are Satī, Pārvatī, Umā, Devī, Durgā, Kālī, Bhavānī and Annapūraṇā. As Pārvatī and Umā she is generally worshipped together with her consort and sons, but in the more active aspects she is worshipped alone. As the Śaivas worship the great god in the form of the *liṅgam* the Śāktas worship his consort as *yoni*. The combined form of *yoni* and *liṅgam* representing sexual union is also worshipped. The Śāktas elevate her to the position of the primal mother from whom everything proceeds, who pervades everything and is coterminous with the Supreme Being himself, who is without beginning or end and is vaster than the universe. [*Hindu Mythology*, T.R.R. Iyengar; *Hindu Dictionary*, T. Rengarajan, *South Indian Images*, T.N. Srinivasan]

**Kālikā**: The goddess Kālī.

**Kāliya**: A serpent king who had five heads, and dwelt in a deep pool of the Yamunā with numerous attendant serpents. His mouth vomitted fire and smoke, and he laid waste all the country round.

**Kalki**: [The white horse] Viṣṇu's tenth incarnation which is yet to come. According to a Hindu legend the end of the world will be brought about by Viṣṇu in his *avatāra* as Kalki. In the *Viṣṇu*

*Purāṇa*, the need for destroying the world and building it anew is thus vividly described:

> The kings of the earth will be of churlish spirit, violent temper, and ever addicted to falsehood and wickedness. They will inflict death on women, children and cows; they will seize the property of subjects, be of limited power and will, for the most part, rapidly rise and fall; their lives will be short, their desires insatiable, and they will display but little piety.

**Kāma, Kāmadeva**: [The god of love] In the *R̥gveda* desire is said to have been the first movement that arose in the One after it had come into life through the power of fervour or abstraction. 'Desire first arose in It, which was the primal germ of mind; (and which) sages, searching with their intellect, have discovered in their heart to be the bond which connects entity with non-entity.' 'It is well known,' observes Dr. Muir, 'that Greek Mythology connected Eros, the god of love, with the creation of the universe somewhat in the same way.' 'This Kāma or desire, not of sexual enjoyment, but of good in general, is celebrated in a curious hymn of the *Atharvaveda*, which exalts Kāma into a supreme god and creator: Kāma was born the first. Him neither gods, nor fathers, nor men have equalled. Thou art superior to these and for ever great.' In another part of the same Veda, Kāma appears to be the first desire, then the power that gratifies the desire. Kāma is also in the same Veda often identified with Agni and when 'distinguished from each other, Kāma may be looked upon as a superior form of the other deity'. According to the *Taittirīya Brāhmaṇa*, he is the son of Dharma, the god of justice, by Śraddhā, the goddess of faith, but according to the *Harivaṁśa* he is son of Lakṣmī. Another account represents him as springing from the heart of Brahmā. A fourth view is that he was born from water, wherefore he is called Iraja,'the water-born'; a fifth is that he is Ātmabhū, 'self-existent', and therefore he is called Aja, 'unborn' or Ananyaja, 'born of no other'. Soon he came to be invested with parenthood and in the

*Taittirīya Brāhmaṇa*, he is described as the son of Dharma. In the later *Harivaṁśa*, he is the offspring of Lakṣmī, the goddess of wealth, and also the son of Viṣṇu and Lakṣmī in their incarnations of Kr̥ṣṇa and Rukmiṇī. He is styled as the son of Brahmā and as having risen from the waters and hence christened Ira-Raja. Kāma became more humanised in the Purāṇas. They depict how Kāma fell a victim to Śiva's wrath. The demon Tāraka distressed all the gods so much that they all desired to slay him but they realised that such a feat could only be achieved by a son of Śiva, who at that time, in the deepest grief over the demise of his wife Satī, had become insensate to all emotions. The gods tried their best to coax Kāma to inspire Śiva with love and, after great persuasion, Kāma took the great risk of shooting one of his arrows at the insensate and implacable Śiva, who on being thus disturbed in his deep meditation, was roused to fury. In his anger Śiva opened his third eye and from it a flame attacked Kāma in such a manner that reduced him to ashes. Before this actually took place Kāma, writhing in pain, which he could not suffer, flung himself into the Kālindī river to obtain some relief but the moment he fell into it, its waters dried up from the heat of the flame of Śiva's third eye. In utter desperation, he roamed about in various places to the great sorrow of his wife, Rati who searched for him in vain. Indeed it is said that all spouses, whose wives had left them, went after Kāma and swore at Śiva for causing this irreparable loss. At last Rati, having given up the search for her husband, Kāma approached Pārvatī, the wife of Śiva. She placed her case before her and entreated her to come to her rescue. Pārvatī moved by the entreaties of Rati prophesied that Kāma would be born as Kr̥ṣṇa's son, Pradyumna whom a demon Śambara would seize and hurl into the ocean. In its waters Pradyumna would penetrate a huge fish's body which would get caught and be served as food for the demon Śambara. When that fish would be ripped open the child Pradyumna would come cut alive and he would be brought up secretly in that demon's house where he would ultimately destroy Śambara. So Pārvatī advised Rati to secure a position in Śambara's household. When Pradyumna was six days old Śambara managed to have him pilfered from his mother's lying-in chamber and flung him into the sea, for Śambara had heard from the sage Nārada that the child would one day destroy him. But, without any one being aware of his existence, the child Pradyumna had come to stay again in Śambara's house under the tender care of his wife Māyāvatī, who had been advised by Nārada that she should nurse him with the greatest care as he would one day be an honour to the world. She loved the child very fondly and in due course began to love him all the more. When Pradyumna grew up, he wondered why Māyāvatī loved him so passionately and slowly he came to know of his own antecedents. On hearing of his past life and the cruelties of Śambara, Pradyumna flew into a rage one day and fought with that demon and killed him in a fight. Then with Māyāvatī, Pradyumna flew to heaven to the abode of Kṛṣṇa and Rukmiṇī where Nārada told them again that they were none else but Kāma and Rati who had regained their old forms as had been foretold by Pārvatī herself.

In the Purāṇas his wife is Rati, the goddess of desire. He inspired Śiva with amorous thoughts of Pārvatī while he was engaged in penitential devotion, and for this offence the angry god reduced him to ashes by fire from his central eye. Śiva afterwards relented and allowed Kāma to be born again as Pradyumna, son of Kṛṣṇa and Rukmiṇī or Māyā, 'delusion'. He has a son name Aniruddha, and a daughter, Tṛṣā. He is lord of the *apsaras*es or heavenly nymphs. He is armed with a bow and arrows: the bow is of sugar-cane, the bowstring a line of bees and each arrow is tipped with a distinct flower. He is usually represented as a handsome youth riding on a parrot and attended by nymphs, one of whom bears his banner displaying the *makara* or a fish on a red ground.

The mysterious origin of Kāma and the universal operation of the passion he inspires have accumulated upon him a great variety of names and epithets. Among his names are Īśāna, Kañjana and Kiṅkira, Mada, Rāma or Ramaṇa and Smara. As produced in the mind or heart he is Bhavaja and Manoja. As

Pradyumna, son of Kṛṣṇa, he is Kārṣṇi, and as son of Lakṣmī he is Mayī. As reduced to ashes by Śiva, he is Anaṅga, 'the bodiless'. He is Abhirūpa, 'the beautiful'; Darpaka and Dīpaka, 'the inflamer'; Gadayitnu, Gṛdhu and Gṛtsa, 'lustful' or 'sharp'; Kāmanā and Kharu, 'desirous'; Kandarpa, 'the inflamer of Brahmā'; Kantu, 'the happy'; Kālakeli, 'the gay or wanton'; Māra, 'destroyer'; Mayī, 'delude'; Madhudīpa, 'the lamp of honey or of spring'; Muhira, 'the bewilderer'; Murmura, 'the crackling fire'; Rāgavṛnta, 'the stalk of passion'; Rūpāśtra, 'the weapon of beauty'; Ratanarica, 'the voluptuary'; Samantaka 'the destroyer of peace'; Saṁsāraguru, 'the teacher of the world'; Smara, 'remembrance'; Śṛṅgārayoni, 'source of love'; Titha, 'fire'; Vana 'the handsome'. From his bow and arrows he is called Kusumāyudha 'armed with flowers'; Puṣpadhanu, 'whose bow is flowers'; and Puṣpaśara, 'whose arrows are flowers'. From his banner he is known as Makaraketu, and from the flower he carries in his hand he is Puṣpaketana.

He is represented as either standing, carrying in his hands a bow of sugar-cane and arrows made of flowers, or as seated on his favourite vehicle, parrot with Rati by his side. Śiva is known as Kāmantakamūrti in the aspect of destroying Manmatha — represented standing or seated on a swan as also Rati. In sculpture both are represented as well-built persons with a very charming look and graceful disposition as Kāma is the Hindu god of love. Some kind of worship of god Kāma is prevalent. In Bengal, where his images are not made, he is invoked during marriages for the general happiness of the couple and the progeny. [*A Classical Dictionary of Hindu Mythology and Religion*, J. Dowson]

**Kāmadhenu**: The cow which grants desires, belonging to the sage Vasiṣṭha. She was produced at the churning of the ocean. She was presented to him as a fee for having officiated during the *mart-manthana*. This divine cow was milk white, endowed with the power of granting all desires. She had a lovely woman's face and the body of a well-formed cow. She had a calf called by various names — Nadinī, Rohiṇī, Sabalā, Surabhi and Kāmaduh. While Kāmadhenu was with Vasiṣṭha in his hermitage, king Viśvāmitra came on one of his visits and was so amazed at the capacities of this celestial cow, which fed his entire army with everything which they wanted, that he wanted to take her away. But Vasiṣṭha would not part with her at any cost and when the king tried to take her away by force, thinking Vasiṣṭha had no power to withstand Viśvāmitra's army, multitudes of invincible warriors came forth from that divine cow and destroyed the entire battalion of Viśvāmitra, who was so astounded that he forsook his throne and became a hermit. Later when he became a sage he came to see Vasiṣṭha and thanked him and Kāmadhenu for showing him the path to real power. Later Kāmadhenu stayed with the fiery sage Jamadagni. Like another Viśvāmitra, Kārttavīrya visited the hermitage of Jamadagni and on hearing of this divine cow took her away forcibly in spite of her protests. When Jamadagni's son Paraśurāma, on returning to his hermitage, came to hear of this theft, he pursued Kārttavīrya, slew him and returned with Kāmadhenu. Subsequently Kāmadhenu was captured by a demon, Tāraka, who was gifted with the boon of invulnerability, which he had acquired through penance from Brahmā. From him also Kāmadhenu was rescued and she remained with Indra while Viṣṇu took birth in his incarnation as Kṛṣṇa. Subsequently she remained with the *sapta-ṛṣi*s and the belief is that she is still with them. There are some variations of this legend. According to some versions Kāmadhenu's daughter Nandinī was presented to Vasiṣṭha as his *dakṣiṇā*, and that it was Nandinī who went through her adventures with Jamadagni, Kārttavīrya, Tāraka, Indra and at last went back to her mother, Kāmadhenu and the *sapta-ṛṣi*s. [*A Classical Dictionary* of *Hindu Mythology and Religion*, J. Dowson]

**Kāmākṣī**: A form of Devī worshipped at Kāmarūpatīrtha in Assam.

**Kandarpa**: The Hindu cupid.

**Kapardin**: An epithet of Śiva, when he is depicted with a specific type of knot of hair. It is also applied to one of the Rudras.

**Kapila**: An epithet of Sūrya.

**Karāli**: 'Dreadful, terrible.' In Vedic times one of the seven tongues of Agni, but in later days a name of the terrible consort of Śiva.

**Kardama**: According to the *Mahābhārata* and *Rāmāyaṇa* he is one of the Prajāpatis who sprang from Brahmā. According to other authorities he or another sage of the same name was a son of Dakṣa or a son of Pulaha.

**Kārttikeya**: The god of war and the planet Mars, also called Skanda. He is said in the *Mahābhārata* and *Rāmāyaṇa* to be the son of Śiva and to have been produced without the intervention of a woman. Śiva cast his seed into fire, and the Ganges afterwards received it; Kārttikeya was the result; hence he is called Agnibhū, and Gaṅgaja. The Pleiades (Kr̥ttikā) fostered him and hence he has six heads and the name Kārttikeya. His paternity is sometimes assigned to Agni; Gaṅgā and Pārvatī are variously represented to be his mother. He was born for the purpose of destroying Tāraka, a *daitya* whose austerities had made him formidable to the gods. He is represented riding on a peacock called Paravani, holding a bow in one hand and an arrow in the other.

Śiva who used to lead the celestial hosts gave up his military career and took to practising austerities, and the gods, without a general, were defeated by the *asura*s and driven out of their kingdom. Indra became a wanderer in the forests, and one day while he was meditating on how to regain his kingdom he heard the cry of a damsel in distress. He proceeded to the spot from where the voice came and there saw the demon Keśin trying to do violence on a beautiful girl. On seeing Indra, Keśin fled and the girl, whose name was Devasenā, asked Indra to find a husband for her. Indra took her to Brahmā and requested him to provide a martial husband for her who should also lead the celestial hosts. Brahmā agreed and decided that Agni should have a son by the water of the Ganges. At the time, the seven great *r̥ṣi*s were performing a sacrifice, and while Agni issued forth from the sacrificial fire, he saw the wives of the *ṛṣi*s and fell in love with all of them. But as they were married, respectable women, Agni kept his desire to himself and repaired to a forest to cool his passion. Svāhā, daughter of Dakṣa, saw him and fell in love with him, but he loved her not. Svāhā, by her divine power, knew that Agni was in love with the wives of the *ṛṣi*s and disguising herself as the wife of one of the *ṛṣi*s approached Agni. The virtuous god hesitated for some time, but temptation proving too strong he yielded at last. Svāhā departed but came again in the guise of another *ṛṣi*'s wife. Thus she managed to visit him six times and get six germs of Agni. These were deposited in a golden reservoir which being worshipped by the *ṛṣi*s generated a son. Kumāra (Kārttikeya) was born with six heads, a double number of ears, twelve eyes, arms and feet, one neck and one belly. When he came of age he married Devasenā and regained the celestial kingdom from the *asura*s.

The *Śiva Purāṇa* states that he was born of the fiery energy of Śiva, in a forest of grass and became the commander of the army of the gods in their battle against the demon Tāraka and that he rent asunder, with his fierce arrows, the mountain Krauñca. This was the time when Śiva was living without a spouse, Satī having destroyed herself in Dakṣa's sacrificial fire. Tāraka was well aware of Śiva's ascetic leanings and was over-confident that the god would not marry again. So, after receiving the boon from Brahmā, he became so arrogant that Indra was forced to yield to him the white eight-headed horse Ucchaiśravas; Kubera gave up his thousand sea-horses; the *ṛṣi*s were compelled to resign the cow Kāmadhenu that yielded everything that could be wished; the sun in dread gave no heat and the moon in terror remained always at full; the winds blew as Terrace dictated. So the tyrannical *asura* had to be destroyed and for this purpose it was necessary to make Śiva marry. Satī was reborn as Umā, the daughter of the Himālayas, and began to practice devotion to propitiate Śiva and marry him. But this god sat immersed in meditation and was insensible to the supplications of the devotee. Indra, becoming desperate, asked Kāma, the god of love, to proceed to Kailāsa and by his art raise sexual desire in Śiva. Kāma reluctantly undertook the mission as it was pretty certain that anyone who disturbed the great god in his meditation would not get away with it. He, however, proceeded with his wife Rati, and friend Vasanta to Kailāsa, where he saw the great god seated on a tiger skin with his eyes closed, hands resting on the thighs, lost in meditation and calm and majestic as an ocean without a ripple to disturb its surface. Wind itself dared not disturb the god, and the leaves of the trees were still. There was perfect silence and quiet all around and the courage of the god of love failed him. At that movement Umā came in the neighbourhood and, while gathering flowers, she showed an excellent profile to Mahādeva, and Kāma, emboldened by her beauty, shot his arrow laden with love. The shaft struck Mahādeva and he woke up from his meditation, as if suddenly troubled by a storm. He looked for the cause of the disturbance of his *samādhi* and saw the god of love sinking away with his bow and arrows. Śiva in his wrath opened his third eye and burnt Kāma to ashes. The shaft of Kāma had no other effect than that of disturbing Śiva, and Umā had to practices severe austerities for years before she was married to him. Even after the marriage the couple had no progeny and the gods in their distress sent Agni to Mahādeva as their spokesman. Agni reached Kailāsa at an opportune moment when Śiva had just left his wife. Assuming the shape of a dove he managed to get a germ of Mahādeva and with it proceeded to Indra. But unable to support the germ, he dropped it in the Ganges, on the banks of which river arose a boy, beautiful as the moon and bright as the sun, who was called Agnibhuva, Skanda and Kārttikeya. It happened that six daughters of as many *rājā*s, coming to bath, saw the boy and each called him her son, and offering the breast, the child assumed to himself six mouths and received nurture from each; whence he is called Ṣaṣṭimātrīya. But in fact, the child had no mother for he came from his father alone. In course of time a conflict ensued between Kārttikeya and Tāraka in which the demon was slain. The sixth day of the lunar month, *ṣaṣṭi* is held very sacred to him and the *ṣaṣṭi* day in the month of Aiyappasi is said to be his birthday.

The images of Subrahmaṇya are various types. There are representations of this deity as standing or seated, single or with his two consorts Valliamman and Devayāṇī. It is laid down as a rule that if the figure is a solitary seated one, it should have only two arms; if a standing one, four and lastly if it is seated upon a peacock, it may have six, eight or twelve arms. The sitting posture is recommended for representing the *yoga bera*, the standing posture for the *bhoga bera* and the figure seated on vehicles for *dhyāna bera*, for meditation and concentration. The image with two arms is said to be *sāttvika*, one with four arms *rājasika* and one with more arms than four *tāmasika* in nature. The symbols usually carried by this deity are the Śakti, a discus, noose, *akṣamālā*, a bunch of peacock feathers while the front lower hands are in *abhaya* and *varada* poses. He carries a flag with *kukkuṭa* ensign and his vehicle is a peacock.

He has many titles. As a warrior he is called Mahāsena, Senāpati, Siddhasena, 'leader of the *siddha*s', and Yudharaṅga. He is also Kumāra, 'the boy'; Guha 'the mysterious one'; Śaktidhara, 'spear-holder'; and in the south he is called Subrahmaṇya. He is Gaṅgāputra, 'son of the Ganges'; Sarabhu, 'born in the thicket'; Tārakajit 'vanquisher of Tāraka'; Dvādaśa-kara and Dvādaśākha, 'twelve-handed' and 'twelve eyed'; and Ṛjukāya 'straight-bodied'. [*Hindu Mythology*, T.R.R. Iyengar; *A Classical Dictionary of Hindu Mythology and Religion*, J. Dowson; *South Indian Images*; T.N. Srinivasan]

**Kātyāyaṇī**: A name of Durgā.

**Kaumodakī**: The mace of Kṛṣṇa, presented to him by Agni when engaged with him in fighting against Indra and burning the Khāṇḍava forest.

**Kavyas**: A class of *pitṛ*s.

**Kedāreśa**: A name of god Śiva.

**Kelikila**: A demi god attendant upon Śiva.

**Keśava**: A name of Viṣṇu.

**Ketu**: The descending node in astronomy, represented by a dragon's tail; also a comet or meteor and the ninth of the planets. He is said to be a *dānava*, and son of Vipracitti and Siṁhikā. He is also called Akaca, 'hairless'; Aśleṣabhava, 'cut-off'; and Muṇḍa, 'bald'.

Ketu is a terrible-looking deity, having the head of a serpent with the body of a man. He is also a śūdra hailing from Kuśadvīpa, having an ugly face with two arms folded in *añjalī* pose.

**Kinnaras**: 'What men?' Mythical beings with the form of a man and the head of a horse. They are celestial choristers and musicians dwelling in the paradise of Kubera on Kailāsa. They sprang from the toe of Brahmā with the *yakṣa*s but, according to others, they are the sons of Kāśyapa. They are also called Aśvamukhas; Turaṅgavaktras, 'horse-faced'; and Mayus.

**Kiriṭin**: A title of Indra.

**Koṭavī, Koṭarī, Koṭṭavī**: [A naked woman] A mystical goddess, the tutelary deity of the *daitya*s, and mother of Bāṇa, the demon. The name is sometimes applied to Durgā.

**Kratu**: One of the Prajāpatis, and sometimes reckoned among the great *ṛṣi*s and mind-born sons of Brahmā. The *Viṣṇu Purāṇa* says that his wife Sanmati brought forth the 60,000 Vālikhilyas, pigmy sages no bigger than a joint of the thumb.

**Kṛṣṇa**: [Black] The name occurs in the *Ṛgveda* but without any relation to the great deity of later times. The earliest mention of Kṛṣṇa, the son of Devakī, is in the *Chāndogya Upaniṣad* where he appears as a scholar. There was a *ṛṣi* of the name who was a son of Viśvaka. There was also a great *asura* so named who, with 10,000 followers, committed fearful devastation until he was defeated and skinned by Indra. In another Vedic hymn, 50,000 Kṛṣṇas are said to have been slain, and it is added in another that his pregnant wives were slain with him that he might leave no posterity. This is supposed to have reference to the *rākṣasa*s or to the dark-coloured aborigines of India.

The modern deity Kṛṣṇa is the most celebrated hero of Indian mythology, and the most popular of all the deities. He is said to be the eighth *avatāra* of Viṣṇu or rather a direct manifestation of Viṣṇu himself. Kṛṣṇa was of the Yādava race, being descended from Yadu, one of the sons of Yayāti. The Yādavas of old were a pastoral race, and dwelt on the river Yamunā in Vṛndāvana on the western side and in Gokula on the other. In those days, Kaṁsa, *rājā* of the Bhojas, having deposed his father, Ugrasena ruled in the city of Mathurā. Ugrasena had a brother named Devaka and Devaka had a daughter named Devakī who married Vasudeva, son of Śūra, also a descendant of Yadu. Kaṁsa himself was driving the bridal car when a voice thundered from the sky: 'Fool, the eighth child of the damsel you are now driving shall take away your life.' Kaṁsa was greatly alarmed and was about to slay Devakī when Vasudeva interceded on her behalf and implored him to spare the lady, and added that he would give over her children to Kaṁsa as soon as they were born. Kaṁsa spared the lady but put her and her husband under guard. Six children were born to Devakī and Kaṁsa destroyed the little innocents one after another. Devakī conceived for the seventh time. The embryo was Lakṣmaṇa who, from his celestial abode, had descended to the earth to keep Rāma company. Viṣṇu by his divine power transferred the embryo from the womb of Devakī to that to Rohiṇī, another wife of Vasudeva, and a report of miscarriage was sent to Kaṁsa. Rohiṇī gave birth to the child and he was called Balarāma. Devakī conceived for the eighth time. The embryo grew and Kaṁsa strengthened the guard on Devakī. On the eve of the night the child was to be born, the lord appeared to Vasudeva and told him: 'Tonight will Devakī deliver her child. Take it hence to Yaśodā, wife of Nanda, the herdsman. She too will give birth to a child. . . .' Vasudeva was asked to leave his child by her side and bring hers to Devakī. At midnight Kṛṣṇa was born. The guards were fast asleep and the door of the prison stood wide open. Vasudeva took the child and fled towards Nanda's home. The great serpent Śeṣa went before him as a guide. The Yamunā was in floods but on Vasudeva's approach the waters receded. He crossed the river and reached Nanda's house, gained Yaśodā's apartments without anyone seeing him, and exchanging the babies returned safely to his prison. The guards now woke up and hearing the cry of the newborn babe sent word to Kaṁsa. He rushed to Devakī's bedchamber and seized the child. But while raising it to dash it on a stone, the babe escaped into the sky and exclaimed: 'Fool I am Yoganidrā, the great illusion. The child that is destined to kill you is born and is alive and well.' Kaṁsa took fright and shut himself up in his private apartments. Fearing no more harm from Vasudeva and Devakī, he set them free. Vasudeva took his son Balarāma also to Nanda and asked him to bring him up with Kṛṣṇa. Lest Kaṁsa should try to harm the children, he asked Nanda to leave Mathurā and repair to Gokula where there were plenty of pastures and waters for the cattle. And Nanda with the children went to Gokula and lived there among his kinsmen, all cowherds. Kaṁsa, finding no way of distinguishing the child destined to kill him, ordered a general massacre of children. Pūtanā, a female fiend, on sucking whose breast children died instantly, offered Kṛṣṇa her breast. Kṛṣṇa took it and sucked so hard that Pūtanā died on the spot. Now it appeared fairly certain to Kaṁsa that Kṛṣṇa was the child destined to destroy him, and a demon was sent to kill him. Kṛṣṇa was wandering alone in the woods when the demon appeared; he caught the demon by the leg and dashed his head against a rock. Another demon assuming the form of a huge raven caught Kṛṣṇa in his beak, but the boy grew hot and the raven released his hold. Thereupon Kṛṣṇa stamped its beak with his foot. Yet another demon came as a huge serpent and swallowed Kṛṣṇa, but the latter grew to such proportions inside the reptile's stomach that its belly burst open and the serpent died. Nor were Kṛṣṇa's activities confined to combating the powers of evil sent against him by Kaṁsa. He was full of childish tricks and played many practical jokes on the milkmaids. He stole butter and milk, and when questioned, accused someone else. He organised children's raids into the orchards of cowherds who were full of complaints against him. Once, while the village girls were bathing in a stream, he stole their clothes, hid himself in a tree and made them come to him naked. He used to delight the girls by playing on his flute, and dancing. He also cleared the countryside of many demons that haunted it. The serpent Kāliya that lived in the river Kālindī skirting the pastures of Gokula was a menace to the herdsmen and cattle, and Kṛṣṇa made him depart from the river. One day in a buoyant mood he took the mountain Govardhana and held it as an umbrella over Gokula to save the village from excessive rain caused by Indra. Reports of the prowess of Kṛṣṇa reached Kaṁsa and he devised a grand plan for killing the boy. He sent Akrūra, one of the few virtuous men in the kingdom, to Gokula with a polite invitation to Balarāma and Kṛṣṇa to come over to Mathurā and witness some athletic sports he was organising. Akrūra delivered the message but acquainted the boys of the evil designs of Kaṁsa and asked them not to accept the invitation. But Kṛṣṇa allayed his apprehensions and accepted the invitation. The two boys then proceeded to Mathurā. On their way a demon named Keśin, in the pay of Kaṁsa, assumed the form of a horse and attacked the boys. But Kṛṣṇa fearlessly approached the horse and thrusting his hand into its mouth, caused the animal to swell and burst. Balarāma and Kṛṣṇa then proceeded. They were clad in poor clothes, and desired to put on better ones before entering the city. On the outskrits of Mathurā they met Kaṁsa's washerman who refused to lend them clothes. Kṛṣṇa killed the washerman and the two boys put on the clothes of Kaṁsa, and thus dressed in finery, they entered Mathurā. The lists were prepared and the day for sports was fixed. Two fierce wrestlers were commanded by Kaṁsa to kill Balarāma and Kṛṣṇa by fair or foul means and as an additional precaution an elephant was kept in readiness to trample the boys to death if the wrestlers failed in their attempt. But Kṛṣṇa slew not only the wrestlers and the elephant, but vanquishing Kaṁsa's guards also slew the demon-king. Kṛṣṇa then released Ugrasena, Kaṁsa's father, and installed him as king of Mathurā. Thereafter, Balarāma and Kṛṣṇa took up their abode in Mathurā with their parents Vasudeva and Devakī. After some years, Mathurā was attacked by two demon-kings, friends of Kaṁsa, and, unable to defend the city, Kṛṣṇa and the people deserted Mathurā and built Dvārakā, an impregnable fortress that could be defended by women. From here Kṛṣṇa fought his enemies and regained Muthurā. As the virtual ruler of Dvārakā, Kṛṣṇa fought and killed many evil kings, of whom Śiśupāla is particularly worthy of note, and will receive our attention later. These kings had ravished many women and kept them imprisoned in their palace, and Kṛṣṇa to save them the fate of growing into old maids, married them himself. They were sixteen thousand in number. In addition to these, Kṛṣṇa married eight other ladies of whom Rukmiṇī, the daughter of Bhīṣmaka, king of Vidarbha, is considered the incarnation of Lakṣmī. Kṛṣṇa was the friend and counsellor of the Pāṇḍava princes and in the conflict between them and the Kauravas helped them with his advice as he was prevented by a vow from taking active part in the combat. He served as the charioteer of Arjuna and on many occasions, it was Kṛṣṇa's excellent horsemanship that saved that hero from death. In fact, he was considered the man behind the scene, who directed the military operations for the Pāṇḍavas and Gāndhārī, the mother of Kauravas, filled with grief at the loss of her beloved sons, cursed Kṛṣṇa and predicted that he and the whole Yadu race, of whom he was a member, would perish even as the Kauravas did. The history of Kṛṣṇa's birth as given in the *Mahābhārata* and followed by the *Viṣṇu Purāṇa*, is that Viṣṇu plucked out two of his own hairs, one white and the other black. These two hairs entered the wombs of Rohiṇī and Devakī; the white hair became Balarāma and the black hair became Kṛṣṇa. His reputed father, Vasudeva, was brother of Kuntī, the wife of Pāṇḍu and so Kṛṣṇa was cousin of the three elder Pāṇḍava princes. The *Mahābhārata* gives two summaries of his exploits, of which the following are abridgements. While Kṛṣṇa was growing up as a high-souled boy in the tribe of cowherds, the force of his arms was rendered famous by him in the three worlds. He slew the king of the Hayas, dwelling in the woods of the Yamunā. He slew Pralambha, Naraka, Jambha and Pitha, the great *asura*, and Muru. He overthrew and slew Kaṁsa who was supported by Jarāsandha. With the help of Balarāma he defeated and destroyed Sunaman, brother of Kaṁsa and king of the Śūrasenas. He carried off the daughter of the king of the Gāndhāra at a *svayaṁvara*, and princes were yoked to his car. He secured the death of Jarāsandha and slew Śiśupāla. He overthrew Śaubha, the flying city of the *daityas* on the shore of the ocean. He conquered the Aṅgas and Baṅgas, and numerous other tribes. Entering the ocean filled with marine monsters, he overcame Varuṇa. In *pātāla* he slew Pañcajana, and obtained the divine shell *Pāñcajanya*. With Arjuna he propitiated Agni in the Khāṇḍava forest and obtained the fiery weapon, the discus. Mounted on Garuḍa, he alarmed Amarāvatī, the city of Indra, and brought away the Pārijāta tree from thence. In another passage, Arjuna rehearses some of Kṛṣṇa's exploits. He destroyed the Bhoja kings in battle and carried off Rukmiṇī for his bride. He destroyed the Gāndhāras, vanquished the sons of Nagnajit, and released King Sudarśana whom they had bound. He slew Pāṇḍya with the fragment of a door, and crushed the Kaliṅgas in Dantakura. Through him the burnt city of Benāres was restored. He killed Ekalavya, king of the Niṣādas and the demon Jambha. With the aid of Balarāma he killed Sunaman, the wicked son of Ugrasena and restored the kingdom to the latter. He conquered the flying city of Śaubha and the king of the Śālvas, and there he obtained the fiery weapon Śataghni. Naraka, son of the earth, had carried off the beautiful jewelled earrings of Aditi to Prāgjyotiṣa, the impregnable castle of the *asuras*. The gods headed by Indra were unable to prevail against Naraka, so they appointed Kṛṣṇa to slay him. Accordingly he killed Muru and the *rākṣasa* Ogha, and finally he slew Naraka and brought back the earrings.

Kṛṣṇa married Rukmiṇī, daughter of the *rājā* of Vidarbha and the betrothed of Śiśupāla. An incident now occurred which brought him two more wives. A Yādava chief named Śatrājit had a beautiful gem called *syamantaka*, which Kṛṣṇa wished to possess. Śatrājit, for the sake of security, gave the gem into the charge of his brother Prasena, and Prasena was killed in the forest by a lion, which carried off the jewel in his mouth. Jāmbavat, the king of the bears, killed this lion. Śatrājit suspected Kṛṣṇa of taking the jewel, and he, to clear himself, went out into the forest, ascertained the manner of Prasena's death, fought with Jāmbavat, and recovered the jewel. Kṛṣṇa then married Jāmbavatī, the daughter of Jāmbavat, and Satyabhāmā, the daughter of Śatrājit.But the number of his wives was practically unlimited for he had 16,000 wives and a hundred or so besides, and he had 180,000 sons. By Rukmiṇī he had a son Pradyumna and a daughter Cārumatī. His son by Jāmbavatī was Śāmbha and by Satyabhāmā he had ten sons. Indra came to visit Kṛṣṇa at Dvārakā, and implored him to suppress the evil deeds of the demon Naraka. Kṛṣṇa accordingly went to the city of Naraka, killed the demon Muru who guarded the city, and then destroyed Naraka himself. Kṛṣṇa next went to pay a visit to Indra in *svarga*, taking with him his wife Satyabhāmā. At her request he requited the hospitality shown him by carrying off the famed Pārijāta tree which was produced at the churning of the ocean. The tree belonged to Śacī, wife of Indra, and she complained to her husband. Indra drew out his forces and tried to recover it but was defeated by Kṛṣṇa. Praydumna, son of Kṛṣṇa, had a son named Aniruddha with whom a female *daitya*, Uṣā, daughter of Bāṇa, fell in love. She induced a companion to carry off the young man, and Kṛṣṇa, Balarāma and Pradyumna went to rescue him. Bāṇa, with the whole *daitya* host, and assisted by Śiva and Skanda, the god of war, encountered them. Kṛṣṇa 'with the weapon of yawning, set Śiva agape', and so overpowered him. Skanda was wounded. Bāṇa maintained a fierce combat with Kṛṣṇa and was severely wounded but Kṛṣṇa spared his life at the intercession of Śiva and Aniruddha was released.

There was a man named Pauṇḍraka, who was a Vāsudeva. Upon the strength of the identity of this name with that of Vasudeva, the father of Kṛṣṇa, this man Pauṇḍraka assumed the insignia and title of Kṛṣṇa, and he had the king of Kāśī for an ally. Kṛṣṇa slew Pauṇḍraka and he hurled his flaming discus at Benāres and destroyed that city. Such are the principal incidents of the life of Kṛṣṇa as given in the *Harivaṁśa* and the Purāṇas.

Kṛṣṇa played a very important role in the *Mahābhārata*. He befriended the Pāṇḍavas, was present during the *svayaṁvara* of

Draupadī, decided that she had been justly won by Arjuna, visited the Pāṇḍavas at Indraprastha, hunted with them in the Khāṇḍava forest and helped Arjuna to elope with his sister Subhadrā. He witnessed the fatal gambling match in which the Pāṇḍavas lost everything and had to suffer a long period of exile. He helped Draupadī in retaining her *sārī*, which the shameless Duḥśāsana had torn in the open assembly of the Paṇḍavas and Kauravas. When the crucial moment of an inevitable conflict came between the two parties, he advocated peace between the Pāṇḍavas and Kauravas. When their representative came to ask for his assistance in the great battle, he refused to take any active part in the struggle itself but he offered them the choice of either his personal attendance or that of his forces. The thoughtless Duryodhana accepted Kṛṣṇa's forces. Kṛṣṇa offered his service to Arjuna as his charioteer. Before the battle actually commenced, Arjuna hesitated to commence the fight in which he would have to slay so many of his relatives and other people. Kṛṣṇa preached to him the vital lesson of *Gītā*: asking him to do his duty and not to concern himself with the fruits thereof, that the battle was never won by the strong always, and how in every age when wickedness prevails the good triumphs over it. He would manifest himself to uphold the good and destroy the wicked. Encouraged by this stimulating and divine exhortation, Arjuna finally decided to fight and in the ensuing battle, he witnessed the defeat of Droṇa by Yudhiṣṭhira, conquest of Duryodhana by Bhīma and the fall of the great Bhīṣma at the hands of Arjuna. He accompanied the victorious Pāṇḍavas to Hastināpura where he attended their *aśvamedha* sacrifice. At last he returned to Dvārakā, where on the appearance of a certain sign, he prohibited the use of wine and directed the people to proceed to Prabhāsa. He agreed to propitiate the deity there for a day and permitted the use of wine for one day. A brawl occurred in which his son Pradyumna was slain in his presence and all the Yādava chieftains perished. A legend relates how this event took place. A Yādava boy desiring to play a practical joke on the sage Nārada dressed up Śāmba, a son of Kṛṣṇa, as a pregnant woman and took him to the holy man and asked, 'What child will this woman give birth to?' 'To an iron rod,' said the angry sage, 'and it will be the cause of the destruction of your race'. The boys took the words of Nārada as a joke but Śāmba began to show actual signs of pregnancy. In due time he delivered an iron rod and king Ugrasena ordered it to be ground to powder. Though a small portion of the rod could not be broken, all of the material was thrown into the sea. The dust of the futal material was washed ashore and grew into rushes. The unbroken piece was swallowed by a fish which was caught by a fisherman. The fisherman sold the piece of iron found in the belly of the fish to a hunter named Jarā and the latter made it into an arrow point. The gods informed Kṛṣṇa that as his work was done, he should ascend to his home. But wishing to save his people from destruction, Kṛṣṇa advised them to leave Dvārakā and migrate to a place called Prabhāsa. The citizens started for Prabhāsa but on their way halted by the seashore and indulged in liquor and merry making. A quarrel broke out between two drunkards and it soon spread to the whole camp. Kṛṣṇa's brother Balarāma left this scene of strife and going to a tree nearby died under its shade while Kṛṣṇa himself, being mistaken for a deer by the hunter named Jarā, was shot and killed by him. His funeral obsequies were performed by Arjuna at Dvārakā and some time later Dvārakā was swallowed by the sea. Kṛṣṇa has many appellations derived from his family relations, exploits, and personal characteristics, and there are many which apply both to the full deity, Viṣṇu and to this incarnation of Viṣṇu. For genealogy, see 'Candravaṁśa'.

Some of his forms and representations are as follows:

1. ***Santānagopāla***: He is represented as a nude baby lying on its back sucking the toe of the right leg, while the other leg is bent inwards. The figure of child Kṛṣṇa may also lie on a leaf of the sacred *asvattha* tree — *ficus religiosa*. Images of this type are to be seen in many temples.

2. ***Bālakṛṣṇa***: The image of Bālakṛṣṇa is depicted as a

child crawling with his right hand holding a ball of butter and the left resting straight down. The image is nude with artistic headdress — having the hair dressed in kondai with peacock plumes and peculiar juvenile jewels.

3. ***Navanītanṛtya Kṛṣṇa***: Here the image is represented as a small three-year-old child standing with the left leg bent at the knee and the right one lifted up slightly to rest on a lotus bloom. It will have a ball of butter in the right hand and the left hand will be stretched out to represent the ecstasy of a dancing child. The image will have numerous jewels that are usually worn by children.

4. ***Kāliyamardana Kṛṣṇa***: It is almost same as Navanītanṛtya Kṛṣṇa but having the Kāliya serpent under the left leg and the right foot resting on the uplifted hood of the snake. The outstretched left hand holds the tail portion of the serpent.

5. ***Govardanadhara Kṛṣṇa***: The image is represented as a boyish image holding the mountain Govardhana by the right hand little finger and the left hand hanging in *kaṭaya* pose. The body is bent in *tribhaṅga* pose.

6. ***Gaṇagopāla***: This is one of the common representations of Kṛṣṇa where he is playing on his flute. Erect or in *tribhaṅga* pose, the image is that of a boy standing and holding the flute in the two hands and the right leg bent at the knee. Sometimes a cow is shown by his side. The image has peculiar head ornaments like the peacock feathers, or is sometimes with the *krīṭam*. Images of certain forms of Veṇugopāla have more hands than two — four with *śaṅkha* and *cakra* or eight which Pañcarātrāgama calls Madanagopāla, holding in addition to *śaṅkha*, and *cakra*, a *padma*, sugar-cane and an arrow of flowers, i.e., *puṣpa-bāṇa*.

7. ***Rājagopāla***: This is another representation of Kṛṣṇa as the monarch of cowherds, having a whip in the right hand and resting the left hand on a stick. Sometimes

Rukmiṇī and Satyabhāmā are represented as standing on either side.

8. ***Rādhākṛṣṇa***: Rādhākṛṣṇa is the representation of Kṛṣṇa as a grown-up youth with Rādhā by his side.

9. ***Gopīvastraharaṇakṛṣṇa***: It is a rare type of boyish Kṛṣṇa shown as seated on a pinnai tree with the *sārīs* of the *gopīs*, which he had taken from them. Round the tree trunk are shown the *gopīs* standing nude begging for their *sārīs*.

10. ***Rukmināthan***: This is the form of Kṛṣṇa as a grown-up man with Rukmiṇī by his side as is represented in temples. Both the images have only two hands, both of which are held at the loins. They are bent at the elbow and placed on the hips.

11. ***Pārthasārathī***: or charioteer to Arjuna. This form is rare and is represented as seated image with the right hand in a *mudrā*, and the left one holding the reins of the horses. In some images there are four hands with *śaṅkha* and *cakra* in the upper ones, as for instance the image in the original shrine of Pārathasārthī.

**Kṛttikās**: The Pleiades. The six nurses of Kārttikeya, the god of war. They have been compared to the constellation Pleiades. According to a legend, once Agni was being served with a sacrificial oblation and among those serving him were the seven wives of the seven sages. On seeing them Agni became enamoured of them and he was desirous of visiting them. His wife Svāhā, by divine power, immediately came to know of Agni's evil intention and decided to forestall him. She assumed the form of each of the wives in turn excepting that of Arundhatī who, owing to her extraordinary virtues, could not be so impersonated, and became accessible to Agni. Thus, she is said to have visited Agni six times and the germs which she obtained from her contact with him, she placed in a golden reservoir which, on being worshipped by the seven sages, in course of time brought forth the god Kārttikeya. [*See* 'Karttikeya']

**Krodha, Krodhavaśa**: One of the many daughters of Dakṣa and sister-wives of Kāśyapa. She was the mother 'of all sharp-toothed monsters, whether on the earth, amongst the birds, or in the waters, that were devourers of flesh'.

**Kṣemagaurīśvara**: A name of Śiva.

**Kumāra**: A name of Skanda, god of war.

**Kumāras**: Mind-born sons of Brahmā, who declining to create progeny, remained ever boys and ever pure and innocent. There were four of them, Sanatkumāra, Sananda, Sanaka and Sanātana; a fifth Ṛbhu, is sometimes added.

**Kumārī**: [Applied to Durgā] One of the Sapta-Mātṛkās, the others being Vārāhī, Brahmāṇī, Māheśvarī, Vaiṣṇavī, Indrāṇī, and Cāmuṇḍī. She is represented with six faces and twelve arms. Her vehicle is the peacock.

**Kumuda**: A Nāga or serpent king whose sister, Kumudvatī, married Kuśa, son of Rāma.

**Kūrma avatāra**: The tortoise incarnation of Viṣṇu when the ocean of milk was churned by the *deva*s and *asura*s to get the divine nectar *amṛta*. Viṣṇu took the shape of a tortoise to form the support for the Mandāra mountain, which was used as the churning stick. As an image, this *avatāra* is represented as a half-man and half-tortoise. The upper portion representing the man aspect has four hands similar to Matsya *avatāra*. The lower half is in the shape of a tortoise. [*See* 'Avatāra'] [*South Indian Images*, T.N. Srinivasan]

**Kuśa**: One of the twin sons of Rāma and Sītā. After the death of Rāma his two sons Kuśa and Lava became kings of the southern and northern Kośalas, and Kuśa built Kuśasthalī in the Vindhyas, and made it his capital.

**Kuśāmba**: Son of Kuśa and a descendant of Pururavas. He was engaged in devout penance to obtain a son equal to Indra and that god was so alarmed at his austerities, that he himself became incarnate as Gādhi, son of Kuśāmba.

**Kuṣmāṇḍas**: 'Gourds'. A class of demi-gods or demons in the service of Śiva.

**Kusumāyudha**: A name of Kāma or Cupid as the bearer of the bow.

**Kubera**: In the Vedas, a chief of the evil beings or spirits living in the shade; a sort of Pluto, and called by his patronymic Vaiśravana. Later he is Pluto in another sense, as god of wealth and chief of the *yakṣa*s and *guhyaka*s. He was son of Viśravas by Idavida, but he is sometimes called son of Pulastya, who was father of Viśravas. This is explained by the *Mahābhārata* according to which Kubera was son of Pulastya, but that sage being offended with Kubera for his adulation of Brahmā reproduced the half of himself in the form of Viśravas and had Rāvaṇa and other children. Kubera's capital city is Alakā in the Himālayas, and his garden Caitraratha on Mandāra, one of the spurs of mount Meru, where he is waited upon by the *kinnara*s. Some authorities place his abode on mount Kailāsa in a place built by Viśvakarmā. He was half brother of Rāvaṇa and according to the *Rāmāyaṇa* and *Mahābhārata*, he once had possession of the city of Laṅkā in Ceylon, which was also built by Viśvakarmā, and from which Rāvaṇa expelled him. The same authority states that he performed austerities for thousands of years, and obtained the boon from Brahmā that he should be immortal, one of the guardian deities of the world and the god of wealth. So he is regent of the north, and the keeper of gold and silver jewels and pearls, and all the treasures of the earth, besides nine particular Nidhis, or treasures, the nature of which is not well understood. Brahmā also gave him the great self-moving aerial car Puṣpaka.

In that marvellous city of Alakā there were lovely gardens in which hunger was unknown. Ravishing damsels also frequented it. Once a demon Virādha paid excessive attention to a celestial beauty Rambhā and he was cursed by Kubera to remain in the shape of a fiend till he was released from that form when he came into contact with Rāma. While roaming in the forests Rāma and Lakṣmaṇa were attacked by this fiend Virādha, but when the brothers found that it was irksome to slay Virādha, with their weapons, they buried him alive in a tomb in the earth and therefrom he arose in his original shape. Kubera has also been said to have a daughter named Mīnākṣī. Some other legends about him can be found in the Purāṇas. He attacked Kṛṣṇa while the latter was taking away the Pārijāta tree but was outwitted by Satyabhāmā. Kubera, therefore, retreated in fear. Later, realising the real greatness and divinity of Kṛṣṇa, Kubera handed over Kṛṣṇa his own capital Alakā, together with the eight treasures. His wife is Yakṣī, Carvī or Kauverī, daughter of the *dānava* Mura. His sons are Maṇigrīva and Nalakūbara and his daughter Mīnākṣī. Kubera is the regent of the north. Kubera completes the lists of the regents of the cardinal points. There are regents for the other four points of the heavens, but they are differently mentioned. His body is covered with ornaments. Kutanu signifies 'vile body', referring to his ugliness. He is also called Dhanapati, 'lord of wealth'; Iccavasu, 'who has wealth at will'; Yakṣarāja 'chief of the Yakṣas'; Mayūrāja, 'king of the *kinnaras*'; Ratnagarbha, 'belly of jewels'; 'Rājarāja', 'king of kings'; and Nararāja, 'king of men'. From his parentage he is called Vaiśravana, Paulastya, and Aidavida. As an especial friend of Śiva he is called Īśasakhī.

Kubera has always been commemorated in literature. In *Devī Māhātmya* it is related how Kubera gave to the goddess Caṇḍī a drinking cup filled with wine, while the other deities granted to her various gifts. In the *Gītā*, Kṛṣṇa declares that of the *rākṣasas*, he was the lord of wealth. Kubera has been depicted as fat, ugly, deformed in body, with three legs, eight teeth and adorned with ornaments. He is also represented as riding on a horse with two treasures personified as Śaṅkhanidhi and Padmanidhi who are said to flank him on either side. According to Hemādri, he rides on a horse with his wife Ṛddhi, who has also other names, seated on his left thigh, and his two treasures stand on either side of him. Kubera is also known by the patronymic, Vaiśravana. [*A Classical Dictionary of Hindu Mythology and Religion*, J. Dowson; *Hindu Mythology*, T.R.R. Iyengar]

# L

**Lakṣmī**: The word occurs in the *R̥gveda* with the sense of good fortune, and in the *Atharvaveda* the idea has become personified in females both of a lucky and unlucky character. Lakṣmī, according to *Viṣṇu Purāṇa*, was born out of the sea of milk when it was churned for ambrosia, when she threw the garland that she had in her hands over the shoulders of Viṣṇu and was wedded to him.

The rise of Lakṣmī from the sea is thus described:

Her eyes oft dared, O'er the liquid way,
With golden light embalmed the darkling main;
Wind those firm breasts, whence all our comforts well,
Rose with enchanting swell;
Her loose hair with the bounding billows played,
And caught in charming toils each pearly shell
That idling, throughout the surge forest strayed
When ocean suffered a portentous change
Tossed with convulsion strange;
With streams, rocks, woods — by gods and demons whirled
While round his craggy sides the mad spray curled?
Huge mountain, by the passive tortoise borne.
Then stole, but not forlorn,
Shipped in a flower that balmy sweets exhaled,
Over dulcet waves of cream pad-mala sailed
So name the goddess, from her lotus blue.
Or Kampala, if more auspicious deemed
With many petal wings the blossom flew,
Till on the shore it stopped — the heaven — loved shore,
Bright with unvalued store
Of gems marine, by mirthful Indra wore; But she, (what brighter gem, had shone before?)

No bride for old Maricha's frolic son,
On azure Hair fixed her props' ring eyes.
Love bade the bridegroom rise;
Straight over the deep, then dimpling smooth he rushed
And toward the unmeasured snake's stupendous bed
The world's great mother, not reluctant led;
All nature glowed whenever she smiled or blushed
The king of serpents hushed
His thousand heads, where diamond and mirrors blazed
That multiplied her image as he gazed.

Some Purāṇas speaks of Lakṣmī as a daughter of the sage Bhṛgu. On account of a *ṛṣi*'s curse on Indra, the celestials had to leave their kingdom and Lakṣmī took asylum in the milk-ocean which, when the memorable churning took place, gave her up to the gods again. The *Mārkeṇḍeya Purāṇa* gives yet another account of the origin of Lakṣmī and the consorts of Brahmā and Śiva. According to this account, Māyā, the primal mother, assumed three transcendent forms in accordance with the three *guṇa*s, and each of them produced a pair of divinities: Brahmā and Lakṣmī, Maheśa and Sarasvatī, Viṣṇu and Kālī. After whose marriage Brahmā and Sarasvatī formed the mundane egg which Maheśvara and Kālī divided into halves and Lakṣmī preserved from destruction. She is represented as the daughter of the sage Bhṛgu and Khyāti who grew up into an extremely lovely and accomplished woman. She had heard of the glories of Nārāyaṇa and was bent on marrying him. So she undertook a very severe penance for an extremely lengthy period at the end of which Indra appeared. But when she prayed in response to a request for a boon, asking him to reveal himself in the form of Viṣṇu, he was not able to comply with her prayers. So later Viṣṇu himself became manifest to her and she married him as she had desired. So he has come to be known as her husband, Śripati, while she herself was called Mūlaśrī.

In the Purāṇas details about her vary. When she issued forth from the ocean of milk, the sages were overjoyed and the celestial nymphs were delirious with ecstasy, and they danced in front of her. Then the divine elephants, taking the immaculate waters from the ocean itself in golden pitchers, poured them over her in her honour. The ocean presented her with a celestial garland of unfading flowers, and the great architect of the gods, Tvaṣṭṛ, adorned her with ornaments of incalculable worth. But the demons made her sick with their obnoxious presence and her disgust with them made them miserable. So they tried to steal the pitcher of nectar. Viṣṇu, transforming himself into a lovely woman, distracted them while the pitcher with the nectar was wrenched from them by the gods who drank it and became immortal. Unlike her sister-in-law Durgā, Lakṣmī is renowned for virtues we consider feminine. She is ever devoted to her husband and is represented in pictures as sitting on the serpent and as massaging the feet of her lord. When Viṣṇu descended to the earth in his various incarnations, Lakṣmī accompanied him. In the Rāmacandra *avatāra* Lakṣmī incarnated herself as Sītā. As Rukmiṇī she became the principal wife of Kṛṣṇa. In spite of this devotion and constancy, Lakṣmī, in her character of the goddess of wealth, is spoken of as fickle. The very turning wheels of fortune no doubt inspired the idea. She is said to reside permanently on the chest of the lord over his right nipple. Normally Lakṣmī as a consort of Viṣṇu is called Upayanaciar, the other one being Bhūdevī who is represented as a standing figure in *dvibhaṅga* pose, holding a lotus in her right hand and the left one hanging down in *gajakarma* pose. But as an individual deity she is always represented as a seated image on a well-formed *padmapīta* and in *padmāsana*. She has four arms, the lower two ones being in *abhaya* and *varada* poses, while the back ones carry a lotus bud in each one of them. She is richly decked with *kirīṭa* and other jewels and decorations and has a pleasing appearance. The *Taittirīya Saṁhitā*, as explained by the commentator, makes Lakṣmī and Śrī to be the two wives of Āditya, and the *Śatapatha Brāhmaṇa* describes Śrī as issuing forth from Prajāpati. Lakṣmī, in later times, is the goddess of fortune, wife of Viṣṇu and mother of Kāma. The origin ascribed to her by the *Rāmāyaṇa* is the one commonly received. According to this legend she sprang, like Aphrodite, from the froth of the ocean, in full beauty, with a lotus in her hand, when it was churned by the gods and the *asuras*. Another legend represents her as floating on the flower of a lotus at the creation. With reference to this origin, one of her names is Kṣīrābdhitanayā, 'daughter of the sea of milk'; from her connection with the lotus she is called Padmā. According to the Purāṇas,

> Her first birth was as the daughter of Bhr̥gu by Khyāti. It was at a subsequent period that she was produced from the sea at the churning of the ocean. . . . When Hari was born as a dwarf, Lakṣmī appeared from a lotus. When he was born as Rāma of the race of Bhr̥gu, she was Dharaṇī. When he was Rāghava, she was Sītā. And when he was Kr̥ṣṇa she became Rukmiṇī. In the other descents of Viṣṇu she is his associate.

One version of the *Rāmāyaṇa* also affirms that 'Lakṣmī, the mistress of the worlds, was born by her own will, in a beautiful field opened up by the plough' and received from Janaka the name of Sītā.

Lakṣmī is said to have four arms, but she is the symbol of beauty, and is generally depicted as having only two arms. In one hand she holds a lotus. She has no temples, but being goddess of abundance and fortune, she continues to be assiduously courted, and is not likely to fall into neglect. The *Viṣṇu Purāṇa* traces out certain points with regard to worshipping of Lakṣmī. It says that from her favourably inclined stare men obtain wives, children, friends, harvest, wealth, health, strength, power, victory, happiness; these are easy of attainment to those upon whom she smiles. She is the mother of all beings; Hari is their father, and this world, whether animate or inanimate. In another passage in the same Purāṇa, it is stated that as Viṣṇu is all-pervading, so also is she omnipresent. Viṣṇu is meaning, she is speech. Hari is polity; she is prudence. Viṣṇu understands; she is intellect. He is righteousness; she is devotion. He is the creator;

she is the creation. Hari is supporter of the earth; she is the earth. The deity is content; the eternal Lakṣmī is resignation. He is the desire; she is the wish. Viṣṇu, who is one with all things, is the wide extended space; Śrī is the heavens. The lord of Śrī is the moon; she is his unfailing light. He is the wind, which blows everywhere; she is called the moving principle of the world. The wielder of the mace is resistance; the power to oppose is Śrī. Hari is the lord of the entire lamp; Lakṣmī is the light. Viṣṇu, the tree round which she, the mother of the world, clings as the creeping vine. The god who is armed with the mace and the discus is the day; she is the night. He, the bestower of blessings, is the bridegroom; the lotus-throne goddess is the bride. The god is one with all male; the goddess one with all female rivers. The lotus eyed deity is the standard; the goddess seated on the lotus the banner. Nārāyaṇa, the master of the world, covetousness, he who knows what righteousness is; Lakṣmī is cupidity. Govinda is love, and Lakṣmī his gentle spouse is pleasure. But why thus diffusely enumerate their presence? It is enough to say in a word that of god's animals and men, Hari is all that is called male, Lakṣmī is all that is termed female. Lakṣmī is believed to have assumed different incarnations appearing as divine or mortal to suit the *avatāras* of Viṣṇu. When he was born as Hari in the dwarf incarnation, the son of Aditi, she manifested herself as Padmā from the lotus. When he was born as Paraśurāma or Jāmadagnya, she was Dharaṇī.

Other names of Lakṣmī are Hīrā and Indirā. Being Hari's beloved, she is Haripriyā and as having born from the ocean, Jaladhijā. As the goddess of fortune, she is Cañcalā or Lolā, 'the fickle' and being the protector of the universe, Lokamātā. She has also been associated with heaven, the house, traders and battle and in each case she is endowed with a suitable name. In paradise she is Svarga-Lakṣmī, in the home she is Gr̥aha-Lakṣmī, with the traders she is Vāṇijya-Lakṣmī and in the war Vijaya-Lakṣmī. Gaja-Lakṣmī is one of the common forms of Lakṣmī where two elephants are shown standing on either side of the goddess with their trunks uplifted over the head of Lakṣmī, pouring water from the pots held in their trunks. In another image she is seated high on the lotus pedestal, having only two hands and holding a lotus flower in each. She has two female attendants on either side and behind them are two majestic elephants pouring water over the head of Lakṣmī. According to *Viśvakarmāśāstra*, she is a young handsome girl, wearing all ornaments and having in her lower right hand a vessel, in the upper right hand a *gadā*, in the lower left hand the *kheṭaka* while the lower left hand holds a bilva fruit. The *Padma Purāṇa* mentions eight *śakti*s of Viṣṇu: the Aṣṭa-Lakṣmī who are named Śrī, Bhū, Sarasvatī, Prīti, Kīrti, Śānti, Tuṣṭi and Puṣṭi. As the names clearly show, these goddesses represent respectively wealth, earth, learning, love, fame, peace, pleasure and strength and these are essential for the welfare of the world. All these goddesses have four hands, hold lotus flowers in the two upper ones, and exhibit *abhaya* and *varada* postures in the two lower hands. Another conception of Aṣṭa-Lakṣmī is the conception of them as Gaja-Lakṣmī, designating victory; Rājya-Lakṣmī, representing royal possession; Dhānya-Lakṣmī, the prosperity of the fields; Vijaya-Lakṣmī, signifying powers; Saubhāgya-Lakṣmī, indicating comfort; Dhana-Lakṣmī, indicating possession of wealth; Gaja-Lakṣmī, when associated with two elephants and Mahā-Lakṣmī, the consort of Viṣṇu as the bestower of all that mankind needs. [*Hindu Mythology*, T.R.R. Iyengar; *A Classical Dictionary of Hindu Mythology and Religion*, J. Dowson]

**Lakṣmaṇa**: A son of King Daśaratha and Sumitrā and twin brother of Śatrughna.

**Lalitā**: [A deity, a *śakti*] She is generally known as the *devī* and has been eulogized in the *Devī Bhāgavatam*, *Devī-Māhātmya*, *Brahmavaivaratta Purāṇa*, and *Skanda Mahāpurāṇa*. She is also known by other names, namely, Ambā, Bṛhad-Ambā, Kālī, and Kalyāṇī. *Lalit* means lovely, charming and elegant. Book IV of the *Brahmāṇḍa Purāṇa* deals almost entirely with the legend. Ādi Śaṅkarācārya wrote a commentary on the Lalitā Triśati, addressing her with three hundred names of the Triśati and thus endowing her with special significance. There is a legend about her in the *Brahmāṇḍa Purāṇa*. In the remote past there was an *asura* called Tāraka who, owing to his excessive power and courage, not only mastered the universe, but even began pestering the gods. In a meeting over which Viṣṇu presided, they decided to depute Manmatha, the god of love, to Śiva and his consort Gaurī, because Tāraka was afraid of none excepting Kumāra, who was to be born as the offspring of that divine couple. As both of them were engrossed in meditation and would not be excited, Manmatha was entrusted with the task of inciting in them the instinct of sex. Manmatha went to the Himālayan heights and finding Śiva deeply absorbed in meditation, he shot at him with one of his flower shafts. Śiva was disturbed and thus, enraged opened his third eye. The fire, which issued from it, instantaneously reduced Manmatha to ashes. On seeing this, one Gaṇeśvara called Citrakarman, who was a clever craftsman and artist painted the picture of a man out of the ashes of Manmatha. When Śiva saw this, that figure was filled with life and light. Citrakarman, overjoyed on seeing his painting come to life, embraced him and directed him to meditate on Śiva by uttering and repeating the Śatarudrīya. Śiva being pleased with this deep devotion, granted him unparalleled power in the world for six thousand years. Brahmā the creator, on learning of this, was disturbed and muttered '*bhaṇḍa, bhaṇḍa*' and so that painted figure, which had become instinct with life, came to be known as Bhaṇḍa, but having been born out of Rudra's wrath, assumed animus nature and began to behave like a demon. The *asura* architect Maya built for him a capital called Śoṇitapura and its high priest Śukra anointed him as the emperor of the entire world. The gods began to feel his hand of oppression and through Viṣṇu dispatched Mayamohinī to disillusion Bhaṇḍa, but as his preceptor Śukra had warned him in time about this ruse, she failed in her mission. Then Nārada advised Indra, the god of the gods, to perform a penance in honour of Parāśakti, who alone could thwart Bhaṇḍa. So Indra propitiated the Devī with all kinds of meat in a sacrifice and out of the sacrificial fire arose a beautiful Mahādevī, who was the embodiment of the Trimūrti. When she volunteered to overcome Bhaṇḍa, the gods praised her eloquently as the mother and father of the universe. The 2gods were greatly pleased and, as Brahmā thought that her supremacy could become fruitful if she were married, she was wedded to Kāmeśvara. This is why she came to be called Kāmeśvarī. The wedding was celebrated on a grand scale and Nārada while departing reminded her of her great mission. Lalitā set out on her great mission and Bhaṇḍa, in his city of Śūnyaka, situated on the Mahendra hill on the sea coast, became alarmed. He immediately convened a council meeting in his council hall and a decision was arrived at to fight her. He called forth his commander-in-chief, Kuṭilākṣa to get ready. He posted valiant warriors at the key points of the capital and set a commander called Durmada to oppose Lalitā but she, in a terrific combat, slew him. On hearing this Bhaṇḍa directed his commander-in-chief Kuṭilākṣa to depute Kuraṇḍa, an expert in *citra-yuddha* and *kūṭa-yuddha*, signifying warfare by illusion and craft. In this fight Kuraṇḍa was killed and this made Bhaṇḍa fight Lalitā but they shared a similar fate and their heads were cut off. Bhaṇḍa, who was much disturbed by these reverses, ordered Kuṭilākṣa to send the seven Balhaka brothers, renowned for their courage and power but they too were slain by Tiraskarṇikā. Utterly discomfited and disheartened by these reverses, Bhaṇḍa again summoned his council and it was decided to entrust the rear attack to Bhaṇḍa's younger brother, Viśaṅga, with the aid of an army. In the terrific onslaught which resulted, both Viśaṅga and Kuṭilākṣa were routed and they retreated. Then commenced the last and the mightiest of all battles, which lasted for four days. On the first day, thirty sons of Bhaṇḍa offered to fight and capture Lalitā but they were outwitted and trounced by her nine-year-old daughter Kumārikā, who slaughtered all of them. At this tremendous loss, Bhaṇḍa was heart-broken but his younger brothers Viśaṅga and Viśukra and his officer, Kuṭilākṣa, consoled him. Then Viśukra volunteered to fight on the second day, but he was thwarted by Mahāgaṇapati and for this great achievement he was granted the special favour of being worshipped first before all the other gods. On the third day Bhaṇḍa decided to send two of his brothers Viśaṅga and Viśukra to face their foe. In a face-to-face and hand-to-hand combat both of them were slain. Bhaṇḍa, now blind with rage, determined to fight Lalitā with a force of all able-bodied men in his capital Śūnyaka. On the last day of the battle one side against the other, for final victory, used all kinds of weapons. At last on seeing the leader Bhaṇḍa, Lalitā hurled her *mahākāmeśvarāstra* at Bhaṇḍa and he fell fighting on the battlefield. Then Lalitā with her hosts set Bhaṇḍa's capital Śūnyaka on fire and destroyed everything and everyone therein including women and children. On the achievement of this great victory, there was universal rejoicing on earth and in heaven. The gods led by Brahmā, Viṣṇu and Rudra complimented Lalitā on her grant triumph. Brahmā, on behalf of the other gods, prayed to Lalitā to restore Manmatha to Rati so that Śiva might embrace his wife and give birth to Kumāra, who alone could vanquish the other *asura* Tāraka. She agreed to this and Rati and Manmatha were married. Thereafter Lalitā went to reside at Śrīnagara. [*Hindu Mythology*, T.R.R. Iyengar; *Glossary of Hinduism*, T. Rengarajan; *Epics, Myths, and Legends of India*, P. Thomas; *South Indian Images*, T.N. Srinivasan]

**Lava**: One of the twin sons of Rāma and Sītā. He reigned at Śrāvastī. He was brother of Kuśa who ruled the kingdom after disappearance of Rāma.

**Liṅga**: [The male organ, the phallus] The symbol under which Śiva is universally worshipped. It is of comparatively modern introduction and is unknown to the Vedas, but it receives distinct notice in the *Mahābhārata*. 'The emblem — a plain column of stone or sometimes a cone of plastic mud — suggests no offensive ideas. The people call it Śiva or Mahādeva, and there's an end.' In the *Śiva Purāṇa* and in the *Nandī Upapurāṇa*, Śiva is made to say, 'I am omnipresent, but I am especially in twelve forms and places.'

The twelve great *liṅga*s are as follows:

1. Somanātha — 'Lord of the moon'.
2. Mallikārjuna — 'The mountain of Śrī'.
3. Mahākāla.

4. Oṁkāra.
5. Amareśvara — 'God of gods'.
6. Vaidyanātha — 'Lord of physicians'.
7. Rāmeśvara — 'Lord of Rāma'.
8. Bhīma Śaṅkara
9. Viśveśvara — 'Lord of all'.
10. Tryambaka — 'Tri-ocular'.
11. Gautameśa — 'Lord of Gautama'.
12. Kedāreśa — Deity represented as a shapeless mass of rock.

By the time of the *Mahābhārata* the worship of the *liṅgam* and *yoni* had come to be recognised as orthodox. The superior merit of sex worship is thus maintained in the *Mahābhārata*:

> He whose *Lingam* Brahmā, Viṣṇu and Indra worship is the most eminent. Since children bear not the mark of the lotus, but are marked with the male and the female organs, therefore offspring is derived from Maheśvara. All women produced from the nature of Devī as their cause are marked with the female organ, and all males are manifestly marked with the *liṅgam* of Hara. He who asserts any other cause than Īśvara, that there is any female not marked by Devī in the three worlds including all things movable and immovable, let that fool be thrust out. Know everything, which is male to be Īśvara, and all that is female to be Venā, for this whole world movable and immovable is pervaded of these two bodies.

According to H. H. Wilson, in his introduction to his translation of the *Viṣṇu Purāṇa*, he says, 'The *Liṅga* is two-fold, external and internal. The ignorant who need a visible sign worship Śiva through a mark or type which is the proper meaning of the word *liṅga* — of wood or stone, but the wise look upon this outward emblem as nothing and contemplate in their minds the invisible inscrutable type which is Śiva himself. Whatever may have been the origin of this form of worship in India the notions upon which it was founded according to the impure fancies of European writers, are not to be traced even in the *Śiva Purāṇa*. Various forms of the *liṅga* are worshipped from the crude uncut conical gneiss, usually believed to be self-born, to the highly polished hand-made *liṅga* with ornamental shaft and pedestal with several facets. But the most general form has a circular receptacle on a high monolithic pedestal known as *panivattam*, with a side during *abhiṣekam*. The worship of the *liṅgam* was popularised in its present form by Śaṅkara, the Hindu revivalist who was in crusade against Buddhism. Now bell metal, iron and brass are used to make *liṅga*s.

1. ***Ratnaja***: This type of *liṅga* was made of precious stones like quartz, topaz, emerald and ruby. At present, *liṅga*s in India are not manufactured with this material. In general, the worship of this type of *linga* is done daily two times, and specific materials must be used for *abhiṣekam*. This is because otherwise the *liṅgam* loses its precious powers.

2. ***Dāruja:*** This type of *liṅga* was displayed at the entrance of the temples. It was made of wood or of specific wood material. This type of *liṅga* is found in village temples. Certain types of oils are used for *abhiṣekam* and no water is used, since the wood them loses its strength. In general, oil is used once a week or depending upon the condition of the temples, customs and traditions.

3. ***Śailaja***: This type of *liṅga* is usually made of stone and it is found in all Śaivite temples located either in villages or cities. Here the priest always worships with the help of oil and water. In specific functions they use different type of materials for *abhiṣekam*.

4. ***Kṣaṇika***: It is identical to Mṛṇmaya, but it is made of cooked rice and used for temporary worship — it remains for a few hours and after the worship is over, it is immersed in waters. In general this type of system was in practice only in villages where it was practised by only a specific group of the community. What was

popularly unashamed sex worship among the aborigines had to be symbolised and explained. This was generally adopted by kings and later on only certain temples practised it when the belief was incorporated into Hinduism. Hence we find many myths in the Purāṇas explaining how the worship originated. There is the story which says that when *Brahman* and Viṣṇu started arguing about each other's importance there appeared before them Śiva in the form of the *liṅgam*. In another myth it is related that while Śiva, after the death of Satī, was wandering like a lunatic he happened to pass through a forest where the wives of some hermits saw him and asked him about the cause of his madness. Śiva told them that he had a loving wife whose death he was mourning. A gay young lady did not believe him and expressed astonishment as to how any woman could ever marry such an emaciated ill-looking fellow and laughed at his story. The infuriated deity caught the woman and ravished her. Her husband came on the scene and imprecated a curse by the power of which Śiva came to be worshipped in the form of the organ of his lust. A third story is that when the sage Bhr̥gu went on a visit to Śiva he was made to wait outside for a long time as Śiva was making love to his wife, and the sage, tired of waiting, cursed Śiva to be worshipped as the *liṅgam*. Yet another account is that Śiva and Pārvatī in a romantic adventure strayed into a forest where some *r̥ṣis* were practising austerities and were seen naked. The pious men imprecated a curse by which Śiva came to be worshipped as the *liṅgam*. *Liṅgam*s are of different shapes and the uninitiated would not understand their significance at all. It is sometimes comparative and negative praise to the Hindus, says Moor, that the emblems under which they exhibit the elements and operation of nature are not externally indecorous. Unlike the abominable relative of Egypt and Greece, we see the phallic emblem in the Hindu pantheon without offence, and know not till the information be extorted that we are contemplating a symbol whose prototype is indelicate. The external decency of the symbols and the difficulty with which their recondite allusions are discovered both offer evidence favourable to the moral delicacy of the Hindu characters. Prof. Wilson, in his introduction to his translation of the *Viṣṇu Purāṇa*, says that the *liṅga* is two-fold: external and internal. The ignorant who need a visible sign worship Śiva through a mark or type which is the proper meaning of the word *liṅga* — of wood or stone, but the wise look upon this outward emblem as nothing and contemplate in their minds the invisible inscrutable type which is Śiva himself. Whatever may have been the origin of this form of worship in India, the notions upon which it was founded according to the impure fancies of European writers, are not to be traced even in the *Śiva Purāṇa*.

There are various types of *liṅga*s primarily according to their mobility: *cala* and *acala*, which means movable and immovable. The movable type of *liṅga* is used during car festivals and other local functions, while the immovable is used during specific festivals. This type of practice was introduced in Vaiṣṇavism by Rāmānujan but in Śaivites it was introduced by Śaṅkarācārya.

The movable type of *liṅga* is made of different kinds of materials.

5. ***Mṛṇmaya***: The *liṅga* is made of earth material like clay which is baked and formed in the shape of a *liṅga*. This is a movable and temporary *liṅga* used in Śaivite temples. The worship of this *liṅga* is done in villages during the *Śivarātri* festival. The *liṅga* is not used in temples which have certain historical value.

6. ***Lohaja***: This type of *liṅga* is made of costly materials like gold, sliver, copper bell metal, iron, lead and brass. This type of *liṅga* is worshipped on a specific time and

date and during this day, certain customs which have been practised over generation are followed.

Ratnaja, Dāruja, Śailaja and Kṣaṇika are all movable types of *lingas*. Similarly *acala* or *sthāvara liṅgas* which are immovable are of several varieties and can be found at certain places. As per the Department of Archaeology, this type of *liṅga* was worshipped by kings and due to certain natural calamities it was designated as *svayambhuva liṅga*. It is different from other *liṅgas*, because of its shape and dimension. The other *liṅgas* have been made recently with specific dimensions but these are of an entirely different type. This type of *liṅga* was displayed only in temples and museums.

7. ***Daivata***: This *liṅga* has divine origin and some special peculiarities. It is found now only in Rāmanāḍ, Kedārnāth and Benāres. It should be worshipped with proper Śaiva Āgamas and it is found in certain temples only.

8. ***Gāṇaptya***: This *liṅga* is believed to have been set-up by Śaivāgamas. There is no specification about this *liṅga* in the *Liṅga Purāṇa*. The origin of this *liṅga* is mentioned only in ancestral stories.

9. ***Ārṣa***: This type of *liṅga* was worshipped by *ṛṣis* at certain times. Their worship is entirely different from general worship. They do not use any type of material and the worship is only through penance. It is specified only in *Śiva Purāṇa* and in no other Purāṇa.

10. ***Āsura***: This type of *liṅga* is worshipped by *asuras* in order to gain certain power.

11. ***Rākṣasya***: This *liṅga* is worshipped by demons to gain certain powers to overcome *devas*.

12. ***Bāṇa***: This *liṅga* is found in the reservoirs of rivers. The people living on the riverside worship this *liṅga* and they have the custom of worshipping it during fishing activities.

**13.** ***Mānuṣa***: This *liṅga* is set by human hands.

In addition to the simple varieties of *liṅga*s there are also some peculiar varieties. *aṣṭottaśata liṅga*s are those on whose shaft would be carved 108 small *liṅga*s. Similarly there are *sahasra liṅga*s having 1001 *liṅga*s carved on the shaft. These are common in important Śiva temples. If the *liṅga* instead of a smooth surface has a number of faces, which may be from four to even sixty-four in number such *liṅga*s are known as *dhara liṅga*s. There are a few specimens of peculiar *liṅga*s, which are in the shape of a male holding a vase in his left hand and with right hand raised in *abhaya-mudrā*. The faces are said to represent Vāmadeva, Tatpuruṣa and Aghora and such *liṅga*s are considered very sacred. There is a famous *mukha-liṅga*. The *liṅga* as a symbol is placed on the head in the images of Mahā-Lakṣmī and is held in the hand by Bhūtamālā, a Śiva-Śakti goddess and the mother of goblins. The Liṅgāyatas concentrate on the time of worship of the *liṅga* and distinguish between the *prāṇa-liṅga*, which they call the life force, and the *bhava-liṅga*, which is *para-Brahman* that directs the life source. In the *Liṅga Purāṇa* there are eleven thousand couplets. This is believed to have been so-called by Brahmā himself. It depicts the importance of the *liṅga* and is full of mystical, spiritual and legendary material. [*Hindu Mythology*, T.R.R. Iynegar; *South Indian Images*, T.N. Srinivasan]

**Lokapālas**: Supporters or guardians of the world. The guardian deities who preside over the eight points of the compass, i.e., the four cardinal and four intermediate points of the compass. The guardian deities of the (eight) directions — *dikpāla*s.

1. Indra, east
2. Agni, south-east
3. Yama, south
4. Sūrya, south-west
5. Varuṇa, west

6. Vāyu, north-west
7. Kubera, north
8. Soma, north-east

Nirṛti is by some substituted for No.4 and Pṛthivī or Śiva, especially in his form Īśāna, for No. 8. Each of these guardian deities has an elephant that takes part in the defence and protection of the respective quarter, and these eight elephants are themselves called *lokapāla*s. Indra's elephant at the east is Airāvata. He is also called Abhramataṅga, 'elephant of the clouds'; Arkasodara, 'brother of the sun'; Nāgamālā, 'the fighting elephant'; Ṣaḍadana, 'always in rut'; and Madambara, 'covered with ichor'. His wife's name is Abhramu. Agni's elephant at the south-east is Puṇḍarīka and his female Kapila. Yama's at the south is Vāmana and his female Piṅgalā. Sūrya's at the south-west is Kumuda and his female is Anupamā. Varuṇa's at the west is Añjana, whose female is Añjanāvatī. Vāyu's at the north-west is Puṣpadanta whose female is Śubhadantī. Kubera's at the north is Sārvabhauma and Soma's elephant at the north-east is Supratīka. The two other females are Añjanā and Tāmrakarṇī whose spouses are doubtful. Añjanāvatī is sometimes assigned to Supratīka. In the *Rāmāyaṇa* Indra's eastern elephant is called Virupākṣa, Varuṇa's elephant at the west, Saumanasa, Yama's at the south is Mahāpadma and, Kubera's at the north is Himapaṇḍara [*A Classical Dictionary of Hindu Mythology and Religion*, J. Dowson]

**Lokamātā**: The mother of the world. This was one of the titles of the goddess Lakṣmī.

**Lokeśa**: [Lord of the world] An epithet of Brahmā.

# M

**Mādhava**: Name of Viṣṇu.

**Mādhavī**: A name of Lakṣmī.

**Madhukasā**: Noted granddaughter of the Maruts. She was the mother of the Ādityas. As she is believed to have sprung from the elements and to represent life of all beings, and is the source of immortality, she is worshipped by all.

**Madhusūdana**: 'Slayer of Madhu.' Name of Kṛṣṇa.

**Madirā**: A name of Vāruṇī, wife of Varuṇa, and goddess of wine. This goddess seems to have been worshipped in the fourth century BC.

**Mahādeva**: 'The great god.' A name of Śiva. One of the Rudras.

**Mahādevī**: 'The great goddess.' A name of Devī, the wife of Śiva.

**Mahā-Gaṇapati**: 'The great Gaṇapati.' In the *Bramāṇḍa Purāṇa*, it is related how, on the second day of the battle with the *asuras*, Lalitā turned her face towards Kāmeśvara, also called Gaṇanātha and Gajānana. He responded by rising to the occasion and after paying his respects to her, he too joined the fray and completely routed Viśuka on the same night. Mahāgaṇapati, aided by six Vighna *nāyaka*s who were the masters of the seven crore Herambas, entered the fray and smashed the *asura* hosts. Unable to counteract Gaṇeśvara single-handedly Viśuka, finding that his life was in danger, fled. Lalitā was pleased with these exploits and gave him a boon that Mahāgaṇapati can be seen in the Madurai temple. [*Hindu Mythology*, T.R.R. Iyengar]

**Mahākāla**: 'Great time.' 1. A name of Śiva in the destructive character. 2. One of the twelve great *liṅga*s.

**Mahākacca**: A deity representing the ocean.

**Mahākālī**: 'The great Kālī.'

**Mahālakṣmī**: The great Goddess Lakṣmī.

**Mahāpuruṣa**: 'The great or supreme male'; the supreme spirit. A name of Viṣṇu.

**Mahārājikas**: A class of inferior deities, 236 or 220 in number.

**Mahāśāstā**: Name of a village deity who is also called Aiyanar. He was son of Śiva and Viṣṇu. [See *Varāha Purāṇa*]

**Mahāsena**: A name of Kārttikeya.

**Mahāyogī**: Name of Śiva.

**Mahendra**: A name of Indra. One of the seven mountain ranges of India.

**Maheśvara**: A name of Śiva.

**Maghavan**: [A deity] A Vedic name for the generous giver of bounties to priest. As mentioned in the *Ṛgveda*, this is also the epithet *par excellence* which has been applied to Indra, the god of rain as noted therein. This epithet survived not only in the post-Vedic literature, and later Saṁhitās, but is occasionally seen in inscriptions like the Mandasor stone inscription of Yaśodharman and Viṣṇuvardhana. Maghavan is depicted in this epigraph as a 'deity pouring out cloud-full of rain' implying that he continued to be considered a god of rain. This deity may be compared to the deity called Timireśvara, who was also a god of rain and drought. [*Hindu Mythology*, T.R.R. Iyengar; *A Classical Dictionary of Hindu Mythology and Religion*, J. Dowson]

**Makhavat**: A name of Indra.

**Mallikārjuna**: A name of Śiva. One of the great *liṅga*s.

**Manasā**: A Hindu goddess, who is alleged to have been the sister of serpent Vāsukī, wife of Jaratakaru, a sage. She is also called Viṣahara as she is supposed to be a destroyer of poison. The branch of a tree, a water pot or an earthen snake image generally represents her. According to the *Mahābhārata* her marriage with Jaratkaru took place in a strange manner. After a life of severe penance, pilgrimage and suffering, Jaratkaru became extremely emaciated. During his wanderings he beheld a number of human beings suspended with their heads down from a tree over a steep abyss and a rat was gnawing at a rope suspending them. He discovered that they were his ancestors, who revealed to him that all their sufferings were on account of lack of progeny and he could save them by getting married and having progeny. When they implored him to take a wife, he was moved and agreed provided that the woman's parents consented to give her to him of their own accord. When Vāsukī heard about this he offered his sister whom Jaratkaru married and she bore him a son named Āstīka, who rescued his ancestors and also prevented the extermination of the serpent race. [*Epics, Myths and Legends of India*, P. Thomas; *Hindu Mythology*, T.R.R. Iyengar]

**Mandāra**: The great mountain which the gods used for the churning of the ocean.

**Maṅgala**: The planet Mars identified with Kārttikeya, the god of war. He is represented as a person with four arms of red hue, riding on a sheep, wearing a red necklace, and red clothes. He was son of Śiva and the Earth, and as son of the Earth he is called Aṅgāraka, Bhauma, Bhūmiputra and Mahisuta. He is also called Śivagharmaja, 'born of the sweat of Śiva'; Gaṅganolmuka, 'the torch of the sky'; Lohita, 'the red'; Navārci, 'the nine rayed'; Cara, 'the spy'; Ṛṇantaka, 'ender of debts', 'patron of debtors'. It is the belief that if one is born under the influence of this planet, he will be plagued with anxiety and is liable to be wounded with serious weapons.

**Maṇibhadra**: The chief of the *yakṣa*s and guardian of travellers.

**Manmatha**: A name of Kāma, the god of love.

**Manu**: [The man] This name belongs to fourteen mythological progenitors of mankind and rulers of the earth, each of whom holds sway for the period called a *manvantara*, the age of a Manu period of no less than 4,320,000 years.The first of these Manus was Svayambhuva, who sprang from Svayambhū, the self-existent. The self-existent, as identified with Brahmā the creator, divided himself into two persons, male and female. From this pair was produced the male Virāj, and from him sprang the Manu Svayambhuva. As the acting creator, this Manu produced the ten Prajāpatis called also *mahṛṣis*. According to another account, this Manu sprang from the incestuous intercourse of Brahmā with his daughter and wife, Śatarūpā. Brahmā created himself Manu, 'born of and identical with his original self, and the female portion of himself he constituted Śatarūpā', whom Manu took to wife. The law-book commonly known as Manu is ascribed to this Manu, and so also is a *sūtra* work on ritual bearing the same name. The Manu of the present age is the seventh, named Vaivasvata, 'sun born', who was the son of Vivasvat, the sun and he is a kṣatriya by race. He is also called Satyavrata. There are various legends about his having been saved from a great flood by Viṣṇu or Brahmā. The name of the fourteen Manus are: Auttamī, Bhautya, Brahmasāvarṇa, Cākṣuṣa, Dakṣasvaraṇa, Dharmasāvarṇa, Raivata, Raucya, Sāvaraṇa, Sāvarṇa or Rudrasāvarṇa, Svārociṣa, Svāyambhuva, Tāmasa and Vaivasvata.

The sons of Manu Vaivasvata were Ikṣavāku, Nābhāga or Nṛga, Dhṛṣṭa, Śaryāti, Nariṣyanta, Prāṁśu, Nābhāganediṣṭa, Karuṣa and Pṛṣadra. But there is some variety in the names.

With the seventh Manu,Vaivasvata is connected the very curious and interesting legend of the deluge. The first account of this is found in the *Śatapatha Brāhmaṇa*, of which the following is a summary: One morning, in the water which was brought to Manu for washing his hands, he caught a fish which spake, and said, 'Take care of me and I will preserve thee.' Manu asked, 'From what wilt thou preserve me?' The fish answered, 'A flood will carry away all living beings; I will save thee from that.' The fish desired Manu to keep him alive in an earthen vessel, to remove him to a dyke as he grew larger and eventually to the ocean, 'so that he might be beyond the risk of destruction'. The fish grew rapidly, and again addressed Manu, saying, 'After so many years the deluge will take place; then construct a ship and pay me homage, and when the waters rise, go into the ship and I will rescue thee.' Manu did as he was desired. He built the ship, conveyed the fish to the ocean and did him homage. The flood rose, and Manu, fastened the cable of the ship to the fish's horn. Thus he passed over the northern mountain. The fish then desired Manu to fasten the ship to a tree, and to go down with the subsiding waters. He did so, and found that the flood had swept away all living creatures. He alone was left. Desirous of offspring, he offered sacrifice and engaged in devotion. A woman was produced, who came to Manu and declared herself his daughter. 'With her he lived, worshipping and toiling in arduous religious rites, desirous of offspring. With her he begat the offspring which is the offspring of Manu.'

The story, as told in the *Mahābhārata*, represents Manu as engaged in devotion by the side of a river, and the fish craving his protection from the bigger fish. Manu placed the fish in a glass vase, but it grew larger and larger till the ocean alone could contain it. Then it warned Manu of the coming flood, and directed him to build a ship and to embark with the seven *r̥ṣis*. He did so, and fastened his ship to the horn of the fish. Then, according to the rendering of Professor Williams,

Along the ocean in that stately ship was borne the lord of men, and through
Its dancing, tumbling billows and its roaring waters; and the bark,
Tossed to and fro by violent winds, reeled on the surface of the deep,
Staggering and trembling like a drunken women: land was seen no more,
Nor far horizon, nor the space between; for everywhere around.
Spread the wild waste of waters, reeking atmosphere, and boundless sky.
And now, when all the world was deluged, nought appeared above the waves
But Manu and the seven sages, and the fish that drew the bark.
Unwearied thus for years on years that fish pulled on the ship across

The heaped up waters, till at length it bore the vessel to the peak
Of Himavan; then, softly smiling, thus the fish addressed the sage:
'Haste now to bind the ship to this high crag.

Know me, the lord of all,
The great creator Brahmā, mightier than all might, omnipotent.
By me, in fish-like shape, have you been saved in dire emergency.
From Manu all creation, gods, asuras, men, must be produced;
By him the world must be created, that which moves and moveth not.'

[*Hindu Mythology*, T.R.R. Iyengar; *A Classical Dictionary of Hindu Mythology and Religion*, J. Dowson]

**Marīci**: Chief of the Maruts. Name of one of the Prajāpatis. He is sometimes represented as springing direct from Brahmā. He was father of Kāśyapa and one of the seven great *ṛṣi*s.

**Mārttaṇḍa**: [The sun god] It is derived from Mārttaṇḍa, whom Aditi, the wife of Kāśyapa, brought forth.

**Maruts**: Maruts are storm deities who held an important place in Vedic times. In one hymn of the *Ṛgveda* they are said to be one hundred and eighty in number, in another twenty-seven. The Purāṇas speak of them as forty-nine. In the *Rāmāyaṇa* it is related that Diti, mother of the *asura*s, sorrowed on the death of her sons at the hands of the celestials and propitiated her husband Kāśyapa who granted her boon by which Diti conceived. But Indra, coming to know of it, stole to her apartments and treated her in a very indelicate and barbarous manner, dividing the foetus with his tremendous weapon, *vajra*, into forty-nine pieces; which, at the request of the afflicted Diti, were transformed by Indra into the Maruts or winds. The leader of the Maruts is called Marut, Vāyu or Pavan, who is often mentioned in the Purāṇas as the god of physical strength. A scholiast on the Veda says that after their birth from Diti, as above told, Śiva and Pārvatī beheld them in great affliction, and the latter asked Śiva to transform the lumps of flesh into boys; he accordingly made them boys of like form, like age, and similarly accoutre, and gave them to Pārvatī as her sons, whence they are called the sons of Rudra. Other legends are that Pārvatī, hearing the lamentations of Diti, entreated Śiva to give forms to the shapeless births, telling them not to weep, and another that he actually begot them in the form of a bull on Pr̥thivī, the earth, as a cow. All these legends have manifestly been invented to explain those passages of the Vedas, which make the Maruts the sons of Rudra. The world of the Maruts called Māruta is the appointed heaven of vaiśyas.

The Maruts occupy a prominent place in the *R̥gveda*, thirty-three hymns being addressed to them alone, seven to them with Indra, and one each to them with Agni and Pūṣan. They form a troop and are mentioned in the plural only. Yet they can only be treated as a unity because they represent one phenomenon and allow for no individual names. They are the sons of Rudras whence they are called Rudras. Their mother is the cow Pr̥ṣṇi, probably the mottled storm cloud. They are also said to be born from the laughter of lightning. Agni is said to have fashioned them and Vāyu is once said to have engendered them in the wombs of heaven. They are called the heroes of heaven. They are brothers of equal age, of equal birth, of one mind and one abode. The leading feature of the Maruts is their brilliance. They are compared to the sun and fire in brilliance. They are also intimately connected with lightning that serves the purpose of their lances. They have axes of gold. They are sometimes armed with bows and arrows like their father Rudra and are once said to bear the bolt like Indra. One verse giving a vivid description of the deities says that they have spears on the shoulders, anklets on their feet, golden ornaments on the breasts, fiery lightning in their hands and golden helmets upon their head. They ride on golden cars drawn by tawny steeds that are often described as spotted. But they are also said to have yoked the winds as steed to the poles of their cars. The Maruts are great, mighty, young, ongoing, terrible like lions, but also playful like children. The noise made by them is thunder and the roaring of winds. They cause the mountains to quake. They rend trees and devour the forests. One of their main functions is to shed rain. The rain shed by them is often figuratively called milk and ghee. The Maruts are several times called singers. While singing they make the sun shine, and while blowing their pipe they cleave the mountain. Though primarily representing the sound of the winds, their songs are also conceived as a hymn of praise. Thus they are compared with priests and are addressed as priests when in the company of Indra. The Maruts are constantly associated with Indra, who accomplishes all his exploits, particularly the slaying of Vr̥tra, in their company. Occasionally the overthrow of Vr̥tra and the winning of cows are attributed to them independently. Like their father Rudra they are sometimes implored to ward off the lightning from their worshippers and to begin healing remedies. [*Hindu Mythology*, T.R.R. Iyengar; *A Classical Dictionary of Hindu Mythology and Religion*, J. Dowson]

**Mātaṅga**: Hindu goddess.

**Mātarisvan**: The aerial being who is represented in the *R̥gveda* as bringing down fire for the Bhr̥gus. Mātarisvan is not celebrated in any hymn of the *R̥gveda*. The name is found there only twenty-seven times. Mātarisvan is very intimately connected with Agni. Mātarisvan is said to have brought Agni to Bhr̥gu. In the later Saṁhitās and *Brāhmaṇas* and the subsequent literature Mātarisvan became a designation of wind. The transition is based on a passage of *R̥gveda* where it is said that Agni, when as Mātarisvan he was formed in his mother, became the swift flight of wind. Mātarisvan, who brings fire from the heaven to the earth, has been compared to the Greek Prometheus. He was probably a personification of the Agni who descends to the earth in the form of lightning. According to Oldenberg he is an Indian Prometheus without any divine nature other than the bringing down of fire. [*R̥gveda*; *Vedic Index*, Macdonell and Keith]

**Mātr̥gaṇas**: In the historic period the number of the divine mothers or Mātr̥gaṇas is often given as eight, nine or sixteen. But originally they appear to have been counted as seven, their names usually associated with the gods of the Hindu pantheon. They are Brāhmaṇī, Māheśvarī, Kaumārī, Vaiṣṇavī, Vārāhī, Indrāṇī and Cāmuṇḍī. In the *Devī-Māhātmya* account of the fight of the Devī with the *asuras* the number of the Mātr̥kās is given as nine, by the addition of two names Śivadūtī and Narasiṁhī. In some other texts the number rises to sixteen with Gaurī in the beginning. In the *Mahābhārata* we come across numerous Mātr̥kās associated with Skanda. They had access into Jainism and other religious systems also. In the Purāṇas they are regarded as the offshoots of the goddess Kauśikī. Some of them like Vaiṣṇavī and Kālikā are often identified with Devī herself.

There are different versions of the origin of the Māṭrkās in the Purāṇas. According to one myth when Śiva's *triśūla* pierced the heart of the demon Andhaka, each drop of the latter's blood created a demon. This made Śiva highly angry and from his body emerged the goddess, Yogeśvatī and, at the same time, Vaiṣṇavī, Brahmāṇī, Kaumārī, Indrāṇī, Māheśvarī, Cāmuṇḍā and Vārāhī emanated from the bodies of Viṣṇu, Brahmā, Kumāra, Indra, Maheśvara, Yama and Varāha respectively. They drank and drained all the blood that fell from Andhaka's body. According to another story when Śumbha sent Raktabīja to fight against Devī, the latter uttered a fearful war cry and Brahmāṇī, Māheśvarī, Kaumārī, Vārāhī, Vaiṣṇavī and Nāraṣiṁhī emerged from her mouth. The seventh, formerly Cāmuṇḍā, had already emerged from Devī's body when she was engaged in a war with Ruru, a general of Śumbha. Each drop of the blood that fell from the body of Raktabīja was drunk by Cāmuṇḍā alone. The *Varāha Purāṇa* says that Yogeśvarī is the symbol of lust, Māheśvarī of anger, Vaiṣṇavī of agreed, Kaumārī of attachment, Brahmāṇī of Pride, Aindrī of jealously, Cāmuṇḍā of depravity and Vārāhī of envy. The iconographic features of the various Māṭrkās resemble those of the gods they represent. Brahmāṇī is four-armed and four-headed, has swan as her *vāhana*, and bears a water pot from which she sprinkles water with Kuśa. Māheśvarī is seated on a bull and wears a *jaṭā-mukuṭa* and a crescent. Brahmāṇī is red-coloured and four-armed, carries a *śakti* and is seated on a *mayūra*. Vaiṣṇavī resembles Viṣṇu and Vārāhī, a boar with the vehicle of the latter being the buffalo and she is armed with a club and a wheel. Indrāṇī is many-eyed, golden-coloured, carries a thunderbolt, a spear and a club, and her *vāhana* is the elephant. Cāmuṇḍā is three-eyed, fleshless and bony, is clad with tiger-skin and is seated on a corpse. [*Hindu Mythology*, T.R.R. Iyengar; *Epics, Myths and Legends of India*, P. Thomas]

**Māṭrs**: 'Mothers.' The divine mothers. These appear to have been originally the female energies of the great gods, as Brahmāṇī of Brahmā, Māheśvarī of Śiva, Vaiṣṇavī of Viṣṇu, Indrāṇī or Aindrī of Indra and so on. The number of them was seven or eight or sixteen, but in the later mythology they have increased out of number. They are connected with the Tantra worship, and are represented as worshipping Śiva and attending upon his son Kārttikeya. The following extract from the *Devī-Māhātmya* of the *Mārkaṇḍeya Purāṇa* describes the assembling of the Māt̥rs to combat the demons: 'The energy of each god, exactly like him, with the same form, the same decoration, and the same vehicle came to fight against the demons. Brahmāṇī: The *śakti* of Brahmā, girt with a white cord and bearing a hollow gourd, and on a car yoked with swans. *Māheśvarī*: Māheśvarī came riding on a bull, and bearing a trident with a vast serpent for riding and a crescent for a gem. *Kaumārī*: Kaumārī bearing a lance in her hand, and riding on a peacock, being Ambikā in the form of Kārttikeya, came to make war on the children of Diti. *Vaiṣṇavī*: The Śakti, named as Vaiṣṇavī, is represented as sitting on an eagle, and bearing a conch, a discus, a club, a bow and a sword in her several hands. *Nārasiṁhī*: Nārasiṁhī is an embodied form of Narasiṁha. *Aindrī*: Aindrī bears a thunderbolt in her hand and rides on the king of elephants and in every respect looks like Indra, with a hundred eyes. *Candrikā*: Candrikā, who sprung from the body of Devī and who was surnamed as Aparājitā, looks horrible and howling like a jackal with head encircled by dusky braided locks. Some scholars omit

Candrikā and insert Kauverī, the energy of Kubera, the deformed god of wealth.

| *Name of goddess* | *Vāhana* |
|---|---|
| Aindrī | Elephant |
| Brahmāṇī | Swan |
| Cāmuṇḍā | Corpse |
| Kaumārī | Peacock |
| Māheśvarī | Bull |
| Vaiṣṇavī | Eagle |
| Vārāhī | Buffalo |

[*Glossary of Hinduism*, T. Rengarajan; *Epics, Myths and Legends of India*, P. Thomas]

**Mauneyas**: A class of *gandharva*s, sons of Kāśyapa who dwelt beneath the earth, and were sixty million in number. They overpowered the *nāga*s and compelled them to flee to Viṣṇu for assistance, and he sent Purukutsa against them who destroyed them.

**Maya**: A *daitya* who was the architect and artificer of the *asura*s, as Viśvakarmā was the artificer of the *asura*s or gods. He was son of Vipracitti and father of Vajrakāma and Mandodarī, wife of Rāvaṇa. He dwelt in the Devagiri mountains not very far from Delhi, and his chief works were in the neighbourhood of that city, where he worked for men as well as *daitya*s. The *Mahābhārata* speaks of a palace he built for the Pāṇḍavas. In the *Harivaṁśa* he appears frequently both as victor and vanquished in contests with the gods. [*Glossary of Hinduism*, T. Rengarajan; *Epics, Myths and Legends of India*, P. Thomas]

**Mayadevī**: Wife of the demon Śambara. She brought up Pradyumna, the son of Kṛṣṇa, and subsequently married him. Pradyumna is represented as being a revived embodiment of Kāma, the god of love, and in accordance with this legend

Mayadevī is identified with his wife Rati, the Hindu Venus. [*Hindu Mythology*, T.R.R. Iyengar]

**Mayu**: The bleater, bellower. The *kinnara*s are called Māyus.

**Medhātithi**: Name of a Kāṇva who was a Vedic *ṛṣi*. There is a legend in one of the Upaniṣads that he was carried up to heaven by Indra in the form of a ram, because the god had been pleased with his austerities.

**Medinī**: The earth.

**Merusāvarṇas**: The ninth, tenth, eleventh and twelfth Manus, said to be the mind-engendered sons of a daughter of Dakṣa by himself and the three gods Brahmā, Dharma and Rudra, to whom he presented her on Mount Meru. The signification of the appellation Meru is obvious; that of Sāvarṇa or Sāvarṇī signifies that they were all of one caste. [*A Classical Dictionary of Hindu Mythology and Religion*, J. Dowson]

**Mitra**: Mitra is so closely associated with Varuṇa that only one single hymn of the *Ṛgveda* is addressed to him alone. The information supplied by this hymn is naturally scanty. He is a king to whom the five clans yield submission. His most prominent characteristic is that he marshalled men by sounding his voice. The epithet 'Yatayajjana', 'arraying men together' is peculiarly his. Savitṛ is said to become Mitra because of his laws and Viṣṇu is said to make his three steps by the laws of Mitra. These statements indicate that Mitra regulates the course of the sun. In the *Atharvaveda* Mitra at sunrise is contrasted with Varuṇa in the evening and in the *Brāhmaṇa*s, Mitra is connected with day, Varuṇa with night. The conclusion therefore is irresistible that Mitra is a solar deity and it is corroborated by the *Avesta* where Mitra is undoubtedly a sun god. Just as the Vedic Mitra is associated with Varuṇa, the Avestic Mitra is closely associated with Ahura Mazda, the Iranian successor of *asura*. The etymology of the name is uncertain, but it means friend even in the *Ṛgveda*. The Avestic Mitra is also regarded as the guardian of faithfulness. Mitra also seems to have been the sun god in his aspect as a benevolent power of nature. [*Hindu Mythology*, T.R.R. Iyengar]

**Moon**: In Hindu mythology the moon is a male deity. One of his names is Soma and in the Vedas the word is used as the name of a planet from which the drink Soma was extracted. In the Purāṇas, the moon is generally called Candra, in another account he is said to be the son of Sūrya. A third story is that he is the son of Atri. In the *Viṣṇu Purāṇa* the moon is said to receive *amṛta* from the sun and distribute it among the gods, men, animals and plants. The radiant sun supplies the moon, when reduced by the draughts of the gods to a single *kāla*, with a single ray, and in the same proportion as the ruler of the night is exhausted by the celestials it is replenished by the sun, the plunderer of the waters, for the gods Maitreya drink the nectar and ambrosia accumulated in the moon during half of the month, and from this being their food they are immortal. Thirty-six thousand three hundred divinities drink the lunar ambrosia. In this manner the moon with its cooling rays nourishes the gods in the light fortnight, the *pitṛ*s in the dark fortnight, and vegetables, with the cool nectary aqueous atoms it sheds upon them; and through their development it sustains men, animals and insects while, at the same time, gratifying them by its radiance.

The Hindus have a lunar zodiac divided into twenty-seven mansions called *nakṣatra*s. They are said to be Dakṣa's daughters whom Candra married. Of these wives Candra was particularly fond of Rohiṇī, the fourth daughter of Dakṣa and the other wives grew jealous of this partiality and complained to their father. Dakṣa argued with his son-in-law who proved incorrigible and, in his anger, Dakṣa cursed Candra with a consumption that continued fifteen days at the end of which the ailing god repented and Dakṣa restored him to health in as many days. The meaning of the myth is obvious.

The Candravaṁśa derives its name from the moon. Candra's criminal passion for Tārā, wife of Bṛhasapati, the preceptor of the gods, led him into a good deal of trouble. He performed the *rājasūya* sacrifice and secure from all harm by its power abducted Tārā. In vain did Bṛhaspati entreat and the seven *ṛṣi*s preach.

The bold sinner refused to return the lady and Bṛhaspati appealed to Indra who decided to reclaim his preceptor's wife by force. Candra was informed of Indra's intentions and he entered into an alliance with the *asura*s. There was an indecisive action, but Brahmā made a last appeal to reason and asked Candra to return the lady to Bṛhaspati. The moon had by now grown somewhat tired of Tārā and he sent her back to Bṛhaspati. But the lady was found pregnant and Bṛhaspati would not accept her till the birth of the child. At Brahmā's command Tārā gave birth to the child immediately, but seeing the beauty and splendour of the babe both Candra and Bṛhaspati claimed him. Tārā was then asked to name the father of the child and after a good deal of coaxing she admitted that Candra was his father. The enraged Bṛhaspati immediately cursed Tārā and she was reduced to ashes. However, she was revived and after the purification ceremony Tārā was received back by Bṛhaspati.

Varuṇa is the father of Candra (because of his birth from the sea, the moon is said to be a son of Varuṇa, the sea god). Lakṣmī is Candra's sister and she requested Pārvatī to influence her husband to do something for her brother. Pārvatī's suit was successful and Śiva wore Candra on his forehead. Thus ornamented Mahādeva went to a feast of the gods. [*Hindu Mythology*, T.R.R. Iyengar; *Glossary of Hinduism*, T. Rengarajan]

**Mṛtyu**: 'Death.' A name of Yama, the god of the dead.

**Muṇḍa**: 'Bald.' An appellation of Ketu. Name of a demon slain by Durgā.

**Mukhāgni**: 'Fiery-faced.' Spirits or goblins with faces of fire. Perhaps meteors.

**Murāri**: 'The foe of Mura.' An appellation of Kṛṣṇa.

# N

**Nāgas and Nāgadevatās**: The Nāgas are, according to the Purāṇic authorities, a race of serpents that inhabited the *pātāla-loka*. The *Mahābhārata* and the *Varāha Purāṇa* give the origin of the Nāgas. Kāśyapa begot the seven serpents beginning with Vāsukī. Their progeny increased and the world was flooded with serpents to the great detriment of man. The latter complained to Brahmā about the hardship caused to them by the serpents. They were cursed by the imprecations of their mother who banished them to the *pātāla-loka* with the command that they should not bite any human beings except those who were predestined to die a premature death and those who were really bad. We learn from the *Mahābhārata* that the Nāgas were the sons of Kadru and Kāśyapa, that they induced their stepmother Vainateya to fetch for them the *amṛta* preserved in the kingdom of Indra, that they were made to grant freedom to Vinatā and her sons — from the voluntary bondage they had entered Vinatā into under Kadru, that they were deprived of the *amṛta* brought down by Garuḍa when Indra carried away the *amṛta* once again to his abode, and that by licking the *kuśa* grass on which the vessel of *amṛta* was placed they had their tongues split into two. In another account India was inhabited by a race of men who went by the name Nāgas and they are said to have formed the majority of persons who joined the newly started Buddhist religion. Some scholars of Mālābār are inclined to believe that the modern Nāyars of Mālābār might be descendants of the early Nāgas, a name that in modern times might have been corrupted into Nāyars. They are believed to have been born of the *pañcamī tithi* of the bright half of the month of *Śrāvaṇa* and the whole of India offers *pūjā*s to the Nāgas on this day except the brāhmaṇas in southern India. The Marāthī and the Kannaḍa women observe the previous days, the *caturthī* also as sacred to the Nāgas — a practice which is nowhere else observed. It is a common sight all over India to witness Nāga-worship in anticipation of being blessed with children and celebration of the *Nāgapratiṣṭhā* ceremony with great pomp and at considerable expenditure.

The image of Nāgadeva should have three eyes; four arms and a beautiful countenance of red colour. The image should have *karaṇḍa-mukuṭa* on its head and all other ornaments on its person and should be standing upon a *padmapīṭha*. The hands of the front arms should be kept in the *varada* and *abhaya* poses, while the hands at the back should each have a snake in it. Over the head of Nāgarāja should be a hood of a five-headed cobra and he should be draped in white clothes. The *Śilparatna* adds that Nāgas should be half-human and half-serpentine in shape — the lower part below the navel being that of a snake. Their heads must be covered with hoods having one, three, five or seven heads and they should have split tongues like those of snakes. . . . In their hands they must carry a sword and a shield respectively. The *Māyāśilpa* gives a detailed description of the seven great Nāgas: Vāsukī, Takṣaka, Karkoṭa, Padma, Mahāpadma, Śaṅkhapāda and Kulika, of them, the collar of Vāsukī is pearl white and that of *svastika*; the collar of Karkoṭa is black and on his hood there are three white stripes; Padma is of the rosy hue of the lotus flower with a white streak and adorned with coral ornaments; the collar of Mahāpadma is white with the mark of *triśūla* on his hood; that of Saṅkhapāda is yellow with a white streak on his hood; and the collar of Kulika is also red and the hood bears the mark of the crescent moon. All these seven great serpents have two tongues and two arms and a hood with seven heads held over their human heads and bearing on them a gem. They must all be clad in one or three coats and carry in their hands an *akṣamālā* and a *kamaṇḍalu*. [*Hindu Mythology*, T.R.R. Iyengar; *Epics, Myths, and Legends of India*, P. Thomas; *India in the Vedic Age*, P.L. Bhargava]

**Nairṛta**: He is the lord of the south-western quarter, and the chief of the demons. He rides on a human being, wielding the mace and the javelin. He is also described as having in his two hands a sword and a shield, and riding on an ass, causing terror to the fiends, demons and all evil spirits. An image of this deity may be seen in Śaivite temples. [*Hindu Mythology*, T.R.R. Iyengar]

**Nairṛti** [A brāhmaṇa goddess] This is another name of the deity Jyeṣṭhā, the eldest sister of Lakṣmī mentioned in the *Padmottara khaṇḍa*. But unlike Lakṣmī, Nairṛti is portrayed as dark, with hanging lips, pendant breasts and a huge stomach. Sometimes she holds lotuses in both her hands. She is extremely fond of blood and on her banner are two crows. Her hair is curly and parted in the *visa bandana* fashion. In her image in Śaivite temples, she is made to wear a *sārī* which trails down to her feet, as she sits with her feet stretched down to the earth — as though she is sitting in a chair, holding in her right hand a staff while her left one rests on her thigh. To her right is seated her bull-faced son and like his mother, he also holds a staff in his right hand and his left one rests on his thigh. On her left side is seated a feminine figure believed to be her daughter but she is depicted as fair. To the right and left of the main deity are two feminine dwarfs, evidently her attendants. She is supposed to be the goddess of misfortune. Her residence is in the *pīpal* tree, which is therefore not touched except on Saturdays, when she is believed to be visiting her sister; and hence the tree is on that day considered auspicious. Her disciples are goblins, fiends and all evil spirits. Whenever she is represented in red, she is Raktajyeṣṭhā. Her images are often installed outside villages. [*A Classical Dictionary of Hindu Mythology and Religion*, John Dowson; *Glossary of Hinduism* , T. Rengarajan]

**Nakṣatras:** The stars have been deified in the Hindu system of life. There were 27 *nakṣatra*s which then increased to 28. Claimed to have been the daughters of Dakṣa, they were married to Soma. Their names have been noted as follows Aśvinī, Anurādhā, Ārdrā, Āśleṣā, Bharaṇī, Citrā, Dhaniṣṭhā, Hastā, Jyeṣṭhā, Kṛttikā, Maghā, Mṛgaśīrsā, Mulā, Punarvasu, Pūrva-bhādrapadā, Pūrvaphālgunī, Pūrvāṣāḍhā, Puṣyā, Revatī, Rohiṇī, Satabhiṣā, Śravaṇā, Svāti, Uttara-bhādrapadā, Uttarāphālgunī, Uttarāṣaḍhā, Vaiśā. [*Dictionary of Hinduism*, T.R.R. Iyengar]

**Nandī**: The bull of Śiva. The *Vāyu Purāṇa* makes him the son of Kāśyapa and Surabhi. The name of the tawny-coloured dwarf, a follower of Śiva, occurs in the *Rāmāyaṇa*. There he is stated to be Nandīkeśvara, another manifestation of Śiva. It is related in the *Rāmāyaṇa* that Rāvaṇa went to Śravaṇa, the birthplace of Kārttikeya, and on his way through the mountains he beheld a formidable, dark dwarf called Nandīśvara, who was a follower of Mahādeva or rather that deity himself in another body. This being desired Rāvaṇa to halt as Śiva was sporting in the mountain, and none, not even a god, could pass. Rāvaṇa asked derisively who Śiva was and laughed contemptuously at Nandīśvara, who had the face of a monkey. Nandīśvara retorted that monkeys having the same shape as himself and of similar energy should be produced to destroy Rāvaṇa's race. In reply to this menace, Rāvaṇa threatened to pull up the mountain by its roots and let Śiva know his own danger. So he threw his arms round the mountain and lifted it up, which made the hosts of Śiva tremble and Pārvatī quake and cling to her husband. Śiva then pressed down the mountain with his great toe, and crushed and held fast the arms of Rāvaṇa who uttered a loud cry, which shook all creation. Rāvaṇa's friends counselled him to propitiate Śiva, and he did so for a thousand years, with hymns and weeping. Śiva then released him and said that his name should be Rāvaṇa — from the cry which he had uttered.

At the entrance into many important temples of Śiva in southern India, one meets with a pair of images of which one is a male figure and the other female, one of the consorts of the former. The male figure is shaped exactly like that of Śiva in the aspect of *candra-śakramūrti*. It is seen standing upon a *padmāsana* and carrying in its back by hands the *paraśu* and the *mṛga*. But unlike the figure of *candra-śakramūrti* which keeps its front hands in the *varada* and the *abhaya* poses, that of Adhikārananadin has them folded on the chest in the *añjalī* pose.

Three different accounts are available in the *Mahā Purāṇa*. He was the son of the*ṛṣi* Salaṅkāyana. When Salaṅkāyana was without a son, he underwent penance under a *śāl* tree in a place called *śālagrāma*. Appreciating his austerities Viṣṇu appeared before him and asked him to request for any boon he desired. The *ṛṣi* prayed that he may be blessed with a son of great virtue. Immediately after this request was made a person sprang up who was like Śiva in every manner. He was given the name Nandīkeśvara. The Purāṇa adds that this was the forty-ninth birth of Nandīkeśvara. A second account of the birth of Nandīkeśvara states that in the *tretā-yuga*, a *ṛṣi* named Śilāda was performing a severe penance on the peak called Muñjavan on the Mandāra mountain. Śiva was pleased by his penance. The *ṛṣi* intended to satisfy Brahmā also who was desirous of Śiva taking a human incarnation. After sometime Śilāda was engaged in a sacrifice. A lad proceeded from the room in which *ṛṣi* Śilāda was performing the *yajña*. He looked precisely like Śiva, with a *jaṭā-mukuṭa* on his head, three eyes and four arms. He was carrying in his hands the *śūla*, the *ṭanka*, the *gadā* and the *vajra*. Śilāda became pleased with the fulfilment of his desire with the appearance of this, his son, born not by human agency and Śiva gave the lad the name 'Nandī' and disappeared. Then Śilāda and his son Nandī repaired to their former *āśrama*. There the boy lost his superhuman form and became quite like any ordinary mortal. Though feeling sorry for the change Śilāda performed on his son the usual ceremony *upanayaṇa*, when the boy attained the seventh year of age; the boy soon became well-versed in the Vedas. Sometime later when two *ṛṣi*s named Mitra and Varuṇa came to the *āśrama* of *ṛṣi* Śilāda as his guests they gazed intently at Nandī and perceived through their mental vision that the life of the boy was to come to an end in a year's time. They informed this sad news to the father of the boy. His father the *ṛṣi*, sank in despair on hearing the prognostication of his guests and swooned. But Nandīkeśvara, though internally perturbed, began to meditate upon Śiva so intently that the latter appeared to him and took him in his arms. Forthwith the boy was changed into a being endowed with three eyes, ten arms and an appearance which exactly resembled Śiva's. The latter blessed this metamorphosed Nandī with freedom from old age and death and also appointed him as the head of his *gaṇa*s and married him to the daughter of the Maruts.

Nandīkeśvara is the chamberlain of Śiva, chief of his personal attendants and carries a staff of office. He is guardian of all quadrupeds. He is also called Śalaṅkāyana, and he has the appellation of Nāndīdeha and Tāṇḍavatālikā, because he accompanies with music the *tāṇḍava* dance of his master. [*South Indian Images*, T.N. Srinivasan; *South Indian Images*, S.H. Kṛṣṇa, *Glossary of Hinduism*, T. Rengarajan]

**Nandī-mukha**s: A class of *pitṛ*s concerning whose character there is a good deal of uncertainty.

**Nandinī**: The cow of plenty belonging to the sage Vasiṣṭha, said to have been born of Surabhi, the cow of plenty that was produced at the churning of the ocean.

**Nārada**: A *ṛṣi* to whom some hymns of the *Ṛgveda* are ascribed. He is one of the Prajāpatis, and also one of the seven great *ṛṣi*s. The various notices of him are somewhat inconsistent. The *Ṛgveda* describes him as 'of the Kāṇva family'. He is described in the *Bhāgavatam* as the third *avatāra* of Kṛṣṇa himself, mind-born son of the Creator, free to enter and leave heaven or earth at will to appear in all the ages of human history, and above age and death. Nor does he appear as a common man at his numerous appearances. So glorious is he that Puṇḍarīka thought he must be either the sun or Agni, god of fire or Indra, the king of God, when he came to teach the great devotee the power of the holy name. The *Harivaṁśa* describes him thus: His complexion is like a flaming fire, his eyes as the morning sun, and the *Mahābhārata* compares him to a sacred fire into which libations are poured. Jean Hegerbert says he is 'possessed of immeasurable calmness, his whole personality redolent with the sweetness of divine love, graceful with the wisdom gained from leaving *māyā* as a bird leaves the nest, and mischievous in the mood of knowing all things to be but the place of the creator'. This writer goes on that the great *ṛṣi* wanders through creation playing his *vīṇā* and he sings to its accompaniment the glories of god. With God's holy name always on his tongue and his *vīṇā* always in his hand, Nārada moves blissfully about the garden of his Lord's creation, ever ready to help those in need, ever ready to comfort those in trouble, to warn those in danger, to teach those in ignorance. Always he does what he knows to be the creator's will, even when he may be misjudged by the narrow views of men as meddlesome and strife-producing. Another authority states that he sprang from the forehead of Brahmā and the *Viṣṇu Purāṇa* makes him a son of Kāśyapa and one of Dakṣa's daughters.

In the *Mahābhārata* and some Purāṇas it is stated that he frustrated the scheme which Dakṣa had formed for peopling the earth, and consequently incurred that patriarch's curse to enter again the womb of a woman and be born. Dakṣa, however, relented at the solicitation of Brahmā and consented that Nārada should be born again of Brahmā and one of Dakṣa's daughters; he was hence called Brahmā and Devabrahmā.

In some respects he bears a resemblance to Orpheus. His mother was a servant girl and was fortunate to be employed in the house of a brāhmaṇa, where she had the chance to wait upon seers as the guests of her master. The little boy, when still too young to understand what these seers said, used to sit and listen to their talk and songs about god and the life of the spirit during the four rainy months. He was also privileged to eat their holy leavings and so to share some things of their pure physical life. Even as a child of under five he came to love this holy society, and the seers themselves admired the silent reverence of the little boy and let him listen to their hymns. So in time Nārada's mind was purified and he longed to live in the same holy way as these great seers and, like them, to realise his oneness with the lord. They encouraged him in this good desire and taught him some things of the inmost secrets of the spiritual way. His mother loved him dearly and took great care of him so that it was not possible for him to follow the seers to the forest when the rains came to an end. But his time was very near. One night she went out to milk her master's cows and trod upon a snake. She died of its bite and Nārada was left free to follow the inner vocation of his soul — 'to depart in search of god' as he himself said afterwards. In perfect calmness of mind the little boy of five set out alone for the northern forests, and there like a later Dhruva sat under a big tree to meditate on God. He had only partial success. At times great light dawned upon him but it was swiftly followed by a darkness the more intense by contrast. The brief bliss gave place to wretchedness and he was soon in despair. At this hour of need the lord came to him, and he heard a voice: 'Nārada, you will not see me again in this birth, but in your next you will come to me.'

Nārada is the inventor of the *vīṇā* and was chief of the *gandharva*s. He also went down to the infernal regions and was delighted with what he saw there. In later times he is connected with the legend of Kr̥ṣṇa. He warned Kaṁsa of the imminent incarnation of Viṣṇu, and he afterwards became the friend and associate of Kr̥ṣṇa.

The *Nārada-pañcarātra* relates that Brahmā advised his son Nārada to marry, but Nārada censured his father as a false teacher, because devotion to Kr̥ṣṇa was the only true means of felicity. Brahmā then cursed Nārada to lead a life of sensuality, in subjection to women, and Nārada retorted the curse, condemning Brahmā to lust after his own daughter and to be an object unworthy of adoration.

Nārada has the appellations, Kalikāraka, 'strife-maker'; Kapivaktra, 'monkey faced'; and Piśūṇa, 'messenger or spy'.

In ancient days we learn that he went to Badarikāśrama Adarikārāma in the Himālayas to worship the twin-*avatāra* of Viṣṇu, Nara-Nārāyaṇa. He then worshipped and was told of the supreme, self *paramātmā*, who is to be adored by all, even the *avatāra*s. He went flying to the white island over the primeval sea of milk. There he found white men all of whom worshipped the one god. He took to the use of a *mantra* there and after singing a hymn saw Nārāyaṇa himself in the universal form, as Kr̥ṣṇa later showed Himself to Arjuna. From him he learned about his identity with Kr̥ṣṇa, the source, maintainer and goal of all to him. Also he revealed the history of past and further *avatāras*. And this story of his visit is called the *pañcarātra* by some. Another visit he once made to the *āśrama* of Nārāyaṇa and this led to his being taught by Sanandana as to how it is possible that Kṛṣṇa, who is beyond all qualities, yet has qualities that human minds can conceive. When Viṣṇu came to the earth in the form of Haṁsa the swan, Nārada went to him for instruction and was by him initiated into *yoga*. In the *Chāndogya Upaniṣad* we hear how Sanatakumāra progressively taught him the nature of the real self. From his own father Brahmā he learned much of the science of the self and of the way creation was brought about. He acknowledged that Viṣṇu, Nārada's own favourite deity, was far superior to himself. Brahmā then related the story of Viṣṇu's *avatāras* and taught the whole of the *Bhāgavatam* to him, which he was later to pass on to Vyāsa, its great author. At the end of the *dvāpara* age, when disheartened by the disappearance of Kṛṣṇa from earth he went to Brahmā, he was given the great sixteen letter *mantra* — the best way to cross over the ills of the new age. It was to Brahmā also he took the other seers when they asked him about true *saṁnyāsa* and received from him the laws in our *Nāradaparivrājakopaniṣad*. Once when he saw the miseries of hell Nārada went to Śaṅkara to get an explanation of the horror. From him he learned to worship Viṣṇu and so get the *parama-siddhi* which frees one from all fear and danger. Another time when he went to Śaṅkara on the Mandarācal mountain, he learned of the greatness of many holy places, many *mantras*, and indeed was taught the whole of the ancient religion, once again. From Vāsudeva himself he learned how to prepare and apply the Vaiṣṇava mark. Once he was taught by the same god a severe lesson in humility and had to learn how even the greatest may fall unaware. It happened in this way. The god of love tempted Nārada in vain with his wiles, and Nārada rather boasted of this to Śaṅkara who at once warned him not to speak in that way before his son. But in his pride of chastity Nārada could not control his tongue; he brought out the story before Hari who at once decided to humiliate that pride. Then Hari created a wonderful palace, with a king Śīlanidhi and his exquisitely beautiful daughter Viśvamohinī, who was about to be married by her own choice of the spouse. Nārada saw the girl and fell madly in love with her. He went off and asked Hari for such beauty as would infallibly make her choose him beyond all other. Hari promised to do his best for Nārada and so made him absolutely hideous as a monkey, while the poor sage imagined himself endowed with matchless beauty. He went to the *svayaṁvara* and so did Hari himself. This girl did not even once look at Nārada and chose Hari as her husband. Nārada went off furious and puzzled. When he saw his own reflection in the water he was deeply humiliated and enraged at what he thought was Hari's treachery towards him. He told the deity that he in turn would lose a bride some day and that is how he, as Rāma, lost Sītā in the forest. Learning how the whole court was but a play of Hari and had no existence outside Him, Nārada came to his senses. He begged him to cancel his foolish angry words, but Hari would not do that, and only told Nārada to find consolation in repeating Śaṅkara's name. He was author of three hymns in the *Ṛgveda*, two in honour of Soma and one to Indra.

When at the beginning of all things earthly the gods and demons strove for mastery, it was Nārada who reported the death of Jamba to his kindred and so heightened the tempo of the war. It was he again who sent Hiraṇyākṣa on the road to doom by telling him where Varāha was to be found. It was he who induced the gods to compete with Nala for the hand of his beloved Damayantī, for the *Mahābhārata* tells us, that he was always fond of strife. In Indra' s court he so praised Pururava that Urvaśī fell in love with the hero thus described, and thereby precipitated his destiny. He warned Sāvitrī that her beloved Satyavān would die within a year if she married him and so increased the heroine's love and unselfishness so that she faced this sorrow and overcame it by winning back her husband even from the very hands of death himself. At the churning of the primal ocean of milk by gods and demons, when the former were able to destroy the latter and were willing to do so at once, it was Nārada who held their hand, for without preserving the balance between good and evil the play of god would come to a sudden end. It was he also who advised the true and just king Harīścandra to ask Varuṇa for a son whose birth led him and his wife to much sorrow, testing the king's goodness to the utmost. The greatness of Nārada is sung by the Lord himself in the very highest terms, when in the *Gītā* he declares Nārada to be the greatest of all the divine seers, not hesitating to call him the same as himself in the words. 'Among the divine seers, Nārada.' Nor dare we think of him as a mythical figure of the remote or fancied past, like his lord with whom he is thus declared to be one. Nārada is here and now everywhere, accessible to those who see him as a Guru ready even now as of yore to sing to them too the glories of the Universal Lord, ready to inspire their tongues and pens with the same divine message which sang itself through his lips and the thrilling wires of his *vīṇā* one in his hand.' Vyāsa had written the Vedas, the Sūtras, the Purāṇas and yet felt a certain lack, a certain dissatisfaction with his work, as though it were defective in some way. He sat in despondency on the banks of the River Sarasvatī and there Nārada, the divine seer, visited him. Hearing his complain, Nārada said it was because Vyāsa had so far written only of *karma* and *jñāna* and had not yet sung glorious praise of god; for his love and devotion to him alone can give true happiness. He then bade Vyāsa write the *Bhāgavatam* which would be the crown of all the scriptures, and for his own happiness to sing incessantly the name and glories of the lord as he himself was ever doing. He then related his earlier lives and explained how the lord was always in front of his eyes as a friend and companion while his *vīṇā* was always in tune with the primeval *OṀ*, the mystic word of the universe. On his advice Vyāsa related the story of the *Bhāgavatam* to Śukra and he to Parīkṣit and so it came to the present form from the first narration of it by Brahmā to Nārada. While the recital was going on Nārada himself visited the devoted king Parīkṣit personally to see that the *Bhāgavatam* was being recited to him. When the little boy Dhruva went off in dudgeon to the forest to do *tapas* against his father's partiality, Nārada went there and advised him to give up this hard effort in which even strong men could not succeed, and so he strengthened the child's determination. He then gave him the great *mantra*, '*oṁ namaḥ vāsudeva*', and sent him off to repeat that at Madhuban, near Bṛndāvan, on the river Yamunā. Then Nārada went off to reassure the sorrowing father of the boy that Dhruva was safe and would bring great glory to the royal house. Long afterwards Nārada sang three verses in Dhruva's honour to the descendant of king Pṛthu, another *avatāra* of Viṣṇu. When king Citraketu was inconsolable at the loss of his long desired only son, Nārada went there with *ṛṣi* Aṅgiras and they made the dead boy sit up and explain to his astonished father that the relationship was essentially false, merely the accident of one out of many lives. This convinced Citraketu who worshipped both *ṛṣi*s as his *guru*s. Nārada gave him a hymn dedicated to Viṣṇu, which he should meditate upon. By use of this Citraketu saw the deity Śeṣa and gained liberation. To exhaust the effect of his rudeness once to Śaṅkara, the former king was sent to earth as the great demon Vṛtra who was with great difficulty killed by Indra and even in death was a firm devotee of the lord. Once Nārada met the 10000 sons of Dakṣa whom their father had sent to do *tapas* and produce children. Nārada sent them off as *saṁnyāsīs* to acquire divine wisdom instead and he did the same with a second batch of 1000 sons. Then he went straight to the outraged father, and calmly received his furious curses. On this, or another, occasion Dakṣa condemned him to perpetual restless wandering on earth with his *vīṇā* always in hand, which was no sorrow to Nārada. When *ṛṣi* was once the guest of king Śṛṅgaya, he fell in love with the king's daughter, but as Nārada asked her first she rather naturally accepted him. In his jealous rage Pārvatī swore that Nārada should no longer be able to enter Heaven freely but he replied that Pārvatī himself would never be able to go save in his company. Later some brigands murdered this king's sons because gold continually came from his body and they cut him up to get at the supply. Nārada restored the boy to life at the same time pointing out the folly of the father's avarice desiring such a dangerous gift for his son. Another time Nārada went to

King Pṛthu's great sacrifice and there pointed out the great folly of sacrifices, warning those who take pride in such displays that the slain beasts await them after death to punish them for their cruelty. He then told a long story of a hunter king and what happened to him when he died. He taught the greatness of vows to King Pṛthu. It was the arrogance of wealth he punished in Nalakūbara and Maṇigrīva, sons of Kubera, god of wealth, when he found them bathing naked with women one day in a river and turned them into trees. Thus they should remain until the baby Kṛṣṇa should liberate them. As trees they learned to be humble and do service to all. It was Nārada who taught the great demon Vṛka to worship Śiva. The deity then gave the demon the boon that he should destroy anyone by putting his palm on the other's head. This caused great trouble among the gods, until Viṣṇu cunningly led Vṛka to put his palm on his own head. In a cave on Gandhamādana mountain Nārada taught Priyavrata, son of Manu, the divine wisdom. Manu himself came there with Brahmā. Eager to lead the boy back home to rule mankind and on Brahmā's advice Priyavrata agreed to put to such a use that divine wisdom which Nārada had given him. Indra in the war of heaven against Hirayaṇkaśipu, the demon king, captured the demon's wife and was dragging her off to heaven as a prisoner. Nārada rescued her and courteously put her up in his *āśrama*. There he gave her daily instruction in spiritual truths, and though she learned very little her unborn son Prahalāda listened with his whole heart and mind and thus even before his birth became a firm devotee of god.

In the *Rāmāyaṇa* he plays a great. During the *tretā-yuga*, just before the *svayaṁvara* of Sītā, Nārada went to Janaka's capital and there met the young princess on the road. He blessed her and promised that she would see there her future lord who was eternally her lord. In the garden there she saw Rāma and she at once loved him and was delighted when the choice could fall on him in public. Nārada was very a close friend of Kṛṣṇa. The *Kṛṣṇa Upaniṣad* tells us that when the supreme lord came down to earth to remove its burden of demon-rulers many of the greatest souls in the heaven came with him to share the glory of his work and that Nārada became incarnate as Sudāmā, one of Kṛṣṇa's boy playmates. But in addition to this incarnate form, Nārada played an important role in the great story through his own proper divine form: as the eternal singer urging on the powers of evil to their destruction and encouraging the powers of good in their hours of trial. Nārada was one of the great writers upon law. His textbook called *Nāradīya Dharmaśāstra* has been translated into English. In the *Nārada Purāṇa* where Nārada has described the duties which were observed in the *Bṛhad-kalpa* that is called the Nāradīya having 25000 stanzas. But the only copy that Wilson analysed contained not more than 3000 stanzas. [*A Classical Dictionary of Hindu Mythology and Religion*, J. Dowson; *Hindu Mythology*, T.R.R. Iyengar; *Glossary of Hinduism*, T. Rengarajan; *Epics, Myths and Legends of India*, P. Thomas]

**Nara-Nārāyaṇa**: Two ancient *ṛṣi*s, sons of Dharma and Ahiṁsā. The names are sometimes applied to Kṛṣṇa and to Kṛṣṇa and Arjuna. The *Vāmana Purāṇa* has a legend about them, which is alluded to in the drama of *Vikramorvaśī*. Their penances and austerities alarmed the gods, so Indra sent nymphs to inspire them with passion and disturb their devotions. They were intimate friends from ancient times and were supposed to have performed severe penances in Badrikāśrama. Their origin is thus explained. The waters were called *naraḥ*, because they were the offspring of Nara and, as they were his first residence, he was named Nārāyaṇa. He was known as Nārāyaṇa who was no other than Brahmā himself. In the Purāṇas, when Brahmā lost his fifth head, mention is made of Nara form of Nārāyaṇa, who contended with him as the fashioner of the universe, the source of unborn life, the supreme Nārāyaṇa, saying had he not willed it the universe would not have come into existence. Nārāyaṇa took a flower and placed it on his thigh. Immediately there sprung from it a beautiful nymph whose charms far excelled those of the celestial nymphs, and made them return to heaven filled with shame and vexation. Nārāyaṇa sent this nymph to Indra with them, and from her having been produced from the thigh (*uru*) of the sage, she was called Uravaśī.

Nārāyaṇa is also known from his combined form of Śaṅkara Nārāyaṇa, the former representing Śiva and the latter, Viṣṇu. This dual form is also called Harihara. In sculpture this type of image shows two halves, the left portraying Viṣṇu and the right one Śiva. Viṣṇu stands to the left on his vehicle, Garuḍa and to the right is Śiva's vehicle Nandī, the bull. Viṣṇu holds the typical conch, pearl necklace, the *Śrīvatsa* mark, and his characteristic earring. To the right stands Śiva with his skull-garland of bones, the holy river Gaṅgā, the serpent coil-earring and the trident. A temple to this deity can be seen in Tamil Nadu. In the Āgamas, within the flaming orb of the sun, is recognised the trinity, thus: Nārāyaṇa with the golden body who becomes Brahmā in the morning, Maheśvara in the noon and Viṣṇu in the evening. In the composite form he is represented in sculpture with three faces, six arms and two legs. Such an image can be seen in Tamil Nadu. [*A Classical Dictionary of Hindu Mythology and Religion*, J. Dowson; *South Indian Images*, S.H. Kr̥ṣṇa]

**Narasiṁha**: An *avatāra* of Viṣṇu. [See 'Avatāra']

**Nārāyaṇa**: 1. The son of Nara, the original man, and often identified with Nara. 2. The creator Brahmā who, according to Manu, was so-called because the waters were his first *ayana* or place of motion. The name is found for the first time in the *Śatapatha Brāhmaṇa*. The name as commonly used applies to Viṣṇu, and is that under which he was first worshipped. According to Manu, He having felt desire and willing to create various living beings from his own body, first created the waters and threw into them a seed. That seed became a golden egg of lustre equal to the sun; in it he himself was born as Brahmā, the parent of all worlds. The waters are called Nara because they are sprung from Nara; and as they were his first sphere of motion, he is therefore called Nārāyaṇa. Being formed by that First Cause, imperceptible, eternal, both existent and non-existent, that male is celebrated in the world as Brahmā. After dwelling for a year in the egg, the glorious being by his mere thought split it into two. Having divided his own body into two parts, the lord became male in one half and female in the other; and in her he created Virāj: 'Know thou that I whom that Male Virāj himself created am the creator of this entire world.' Sir William Jones has summarised the hymn of Nārāyaṇa as:

Spirit of spirits, who through every part
Of space expanded, and of endless time,
Beyond the stretch of labouring thought sublime
Had'st uproar into beauteous order start,

Before heaven was thou art;
Ere spheres beneath us roll'd, or spheres above,

Ere earth in firmamental ether hung,
Thou sat'st above; till, through thy mystic love,
Things unexacting to existence sprung,
And graceful descant sung.

What first impelled thee to exert thy might?
Goodness unlimited. What glorious light
Thy power directed? Wisdom without bound,
What proved it first? It guides my fancy right;
Oh, rise from cumbrous ground

My soul in rapture drowned
That fearless it may soar, on wings of fire;
For thou, who only know'st. Thou only can' st inspire
Wrapped in eternal solitary shade

The impenetrable gloom of light intense,
Imprevious, inaccessible, immense,
Ere spirits were infused or forms displayed,
Brahmā his own mind surveyed.
As mortal eyes (thus finite we compare with infinite)

In smoothest mirrors gaze;
Swift, at his look, a shape supremely fair,
Leaped into being with a boundless blaze
Those fifty suns might daze

Primeval Maya was the goddess named,
Who to her sire, with love divine inflame;
A casket gave with rich idea filled
From which this gorgeous universe he framed;

For, when the almighty wills
Unnumbered worlds to build,
From unity, diversified he sprang,
While gay creation laughed and procreant nature rang

First an all-potent, all-pervading sound
Bade flow the waters — and the waters flowed
Exulting in their measureless abode,
Diffusive, multitudinous, profound

Above, beneath marooned
Then o'er the vast expanse primordial wind
Breathed gently, till a lucid bubble rose,
Which grew in perfect shape, an egg refined;

Created substance no such luster shows,
Earth no such beauty knows.
Above the warring waves it danced elate,
Till from its bursting shell with lovely state

A form cerulean flutter o'er the deep
Brightest of beings greatest of the great;
Who, not as mortals steep,
The eyes in dewy sleep,
But heavenly pensive on the lotus lay,
That blossomed at his touch and shed a golden ray.
Hail, primal blossom, hail empyreal gem.

Kamal or padma, or whatever high name
Delight the, say, what four-formed godhead came
With graceful stole and beamy diadem
Forth from thy verdant stem?

Full gifted Brahmā, rapt in solemn thought
He stood, and round his eyes fire daring threw;

But whilst his view-less origin he sought
One plane he saw of living waters blue

Their sprang nor saw nor knew
Then in his parent stalk again retired.
With restless pain for ages, he inquired,
What were his powers, by whom and why conferr'd?

With doubts perplexed with keen impatience fired
He rose, and rising heard,
Through unknown, all-knowing word
Brahmā no more invasions research persists;

My veil, thou can'st not move — go, bid all worlds exist
Hail, self -existent, in celestial speech
Nārāyaṇa, from thy wat'ry cradle named;
Or venamala may, sing unblessed,

With flowery braids, those to thy sandals reach
Whose beauties who can teach?
Or high pitamber clad in yellow robes
Than sunbeams brighter, in meridian glow,

Those weave their heaven-spun light o'er circling globes?
Unwearied, lotus-ey'd with dreadful blow
Dire evil's constant foe
Great Patmanatha, o'er thy cherished world . . .

To black despair and deep destruction hurl'd
Such views my senses dim,
My eyes in darkness swim,
What eye can bear the blaze, what utterance tell

Thy deeds with silver trump or much wreathed shell,
Omniscient spirit, whose all ruling power
Bids from each sense bright emanations beam,
Glows in the rainbow, sparkles in the stream,

Smiles in the bud and glistens in the flower
That crowns each vernal bower
Sighs in the gale and warbles in the throat
Of every bird that hails the bloom

Or tells his love in many a liquid note,
While envious artist so much the rival string.
Till rocks and forests ring;
Breathes in rich fragrance from the sandal grove,

Or where the precious musk-deer playful rove,
In dulcet juice from clustering fruit distils,
And burns salubrious in the tasteful . . .
Thy present influence fills;

Thy will inspirits all, thy sovereign Maya reigns
Blue crystal vault and elemental fire _
That in the ethereal fluid blaze and breaths.
The tossing main, whose snaky branches wreathe

This pensive orb with intertwisted gyres
Mountains, whose radiant spires,
Presumptuous rear, their summits to the skies,
And blend their emerald hue, with sapphire light;

Smooth mead and lawn that glow with varying dyes
Of dew-bespangled leaves and blossoms bright
Hence vanish from my sight
Delusive pictures unsubstantial shows

My soul absorbs one only being knows,
Of all perceptions one abundant source
Whence every object every moment flows;
Hence planets learn their course;
But suns and fading worlds I view no more
God only I perceive, god only I adore.

[*Epics, Myths and Legends of India*, P.Thomas]

**Nāsatya**: One of the celestial twins, the Aśvins. It may not be generally applicable to them in the plural as maintained by some scholars, because the two gods are mentioned in the Vedas as Nāsatya and Basra. In imagery they are represented as having the form of a horse, excepting their faces. They are found together, seated on a lion seat. They show the *abhaya-mudrā* with the right hand while the left one holds a book supposed to be dealing with medicine. To their right are the healing herbs while to their left are two sages, one of whom is Dhanvantari. [*Hindu Mythology*, T.R.R. Iyengar; *Glossary of Hinduism*, T. Rengarajan]

**Naṭarāja**: Naṭarāja means 'the lord of the stage' . The idea is that the world is a stage, a puppet-show with vision of life and activity through the power of the ill-pervading Amman or god, 'the unseen lord of the stage who will not dance when thou causes him to dance, and who will not sing when thou causes him to sing', says a poet-philosopher. But for the inner *ātman*, the entire world will be mere *jaḍa*, the *ātman* being the real teacher of human mind. Naṭarāja is meant to represent teacher or *guru*. There are two kinds of *guru*s — the apparent and the real, the seen and the unseen. The former is the teacher, who instructs the disciples and takes him along the path — this is what we usually mean by the word *guru*; but teaching is really the growth from within.

Naṭarāja is represented with a little drum in one of the right hands. It is meant to express the idea that God holds the cause of all the worlds, i.e., all the world is in his hands. To the *gaṇa* the world exists only if he chooses and not otherwise. The deer on one side is the mind because the latter leaps, and jumps from one thing to another as wildly as that animal. The *ātman* is far beyond the reach of the deer-like mind; and so the deer in the picture is placed near the legs. Naṭarāja wears the skin of a tiger which he himself slew. *Ahaṁkāra* or the skin of egoism is that tiger. It is beastly and ferocious and fiercely fights when attacked, but it has to be killed and Naṭarāja, the *guru*, alone can kill it. From his head flows the Ganges which is not cool and refreshing and blissfulness of the *ātman*. One foot is planted over and crushes the giant Muyalaka, i.e., *mahāmāyā*, the endless illusion which is the cause of birth and death, while the other foot is raised upward and represents the *turīya* state which is beyond and above the three states of waking, dreamless and dream and leaves behind the mind, *Māyā* and the world. The second right hand representing the idea of peace indicates the blessed calmness which is the glorious privilege of wisdom. In one of the left hands is held Agni. The idea is that the truth of the *guru*'s teaching can only be fully understood on practical realisation in experiences. The place of the dance, the theatre is Thillaivanaman, i.e., the body of the individual as well as the cosmos spoken of as *vanam* or forest on account of the multitude of its components. The platform in that theatre is the cremation ground, where all passions and the names and forms that constitute the vision of the world have been burnt away, and what is left is pure consciousness devoid of attachment to anything outside and devoid of illusion. In all Śaiva temples, there will be a separate shrine for Naṭarāja usually facing south, but the famous shrine at Cidambaram is noted for this particular form. In rare forms of Naṭarāja, the position of the dancing leg is changed — called '*kaal marina nadanam*' (a Tamil version) which means 'when the right leg is straight and the left leg uplifted, and extended just the opposite way'.

1. ***Sandhyātāṇḍava***: This is another pose of Śiva's dance where the demon Apasmāra is left out.
2. ***Umātāṇḍava***: In this aspect Umā is represented as standing on the left side of Śiva, who has only two arms.
3. ***Gaurītāṇḍava***: This is same as Umātāṇḍava pose but one where Nandīkeśvara is standing on the right side of Śiva.
4. ***Kālikātāṇḍava:*** Here Śiva is shown as having only two eyes with eight arms carrying trident, noose, kettledrum, skull, fire, and bell in addition to two in *abhaya* and *varada* poses.
5. ***Tripuratāṇḍava***: Here Śiva has sixteen hands carrying several weapons, with Gaurī and Skanda standing on either side.
6. ***Saṁhāratāṇḍava***: Here Śiva looks fierce with eight arms, having different weapons, which include the garland of skulls.
7. ***Lalitātāṇḍava***: This is a peculiar pose of Śiva's dance

in which he is represented as having four or eight arms and both the legs are placed on the pedestal in a graceful form — each bent slightly inwards.

8. ***Ūrdhvatāṇḍava***: In this particular aspect the right leg of Śiva is raised upwards to the level of the head, while the left is placed on the back of Apasmāra. This image has sometimes sixteen hands, possessing several weapons.

Āgamas mention as many as one hundred and eight different *nṛtya* poses of Śiva, but many of them are not in iconographical pieces. The various poses of dancing, according to Bharatanāṭyam, illustrating the several *mudrās* of the science, are sculptured at the entrance of the eastern *gopuram* of Naṭarāja temple at Cidambaram. [*Hindu Mythology*, T.R.R. Iyengar; *South Indian Images*, T.N. Srinivasan]

**Navagrahas**: The nine planets with the sun as their head are important deities allied to both astronomy and astrology. They are highly respected as every pious Hindu believes that the life of an individual goes on with ups and downs depending on the position of these nine planets. The individual horoscope is cast according to their position at the time of birth of each person.

1. ***Sūrya*:** See 'Sūrya'.
2. ***Candra*:** See 'Candra'.
3. ***Budha*:** See 'Budha'.
4. ***Maṅgala*:** Chevy is a kṣatriya of Avanti, son of the Earth and sage Bhardvāja. He is represented as wearing red garments. He is situated next to Sūrya on the eastern side, having four arms — carrying in them a *daṇḍa* and *śakti* and with two hands in *abhaya* and *varada* poses. His vehicle is a goat.
5. ***Guru*:** See Bṛhaspati.
6. ***Śukra*:** Śukra is likewise a *Brahman*, born of Bhṛgu, and a native of Bhojakaṭa. He stands on the northern

side of Sūrya, is white in complexion and has as Bṛhaspati, a *pustaka* and *kamaṇḍalu* in his hands, which are four in number. The other two are in *abhaya* and *varada* poses. Sometimes he is shown as carrying Niśi, a treasure, in one of his hands, as he is the lord of wealth.

7. ***Śani*:** See 'Śani'.
8. ***Rāhu*:** See 'Rāhu'.
9. ***Ketu*:** See 'Ketu'.

[*Hindu Mythology*, T.R.R. Iyengar; *Epics, Myths and Legends of India*, P. Thomas]

**Nīladevī**: [Goddess] Nīladevī is the third consort of Viṣṇu and is very seldom represented singly. She is shown as one of the consorts of Viṣṇu when the god is depicted in the *param* aspect as he is conceived as the Lord of Vaikuṇṭha. She is seated on the left side of Viṣṇu along with Bhūdevī on the coils of Ādiśeṣa.

**Nīlakaṇṭha**: [Blue throat] An epithet of Śiva.

**Nimi**: Son of Ikṣvāku and founder of the dynasty of Mithilā. The sage Vasiṣṭha cursed him to lose his corporeal form and he retorted the imprecation upon the sage. Both abandoned the bodily condition. Vasiṣṭha was born again as the issue of Mitra and Varuṇa, but 'the corpse of Nimi was preserved from decay by being embalmed with fragrant oils and resins, and it remained as entire as if it were immortal'. The gods were willing to restore him to bodily life but Nimi declined, declaring that the separation of soul and body was so distressing that he would never resume a corporeal shape and become liable to it again. 'To this desire the gods assented, and Nimi was placed by them in the eyes of all living creatures, in consequence of which their eyelids are ever opening and shutting.' — *Viṣṇu Purāṇa*. A wink of the eye is called *nimiṣa*, and the legend was probably built upon the resemblance of the two words. [*Hindu Mythology*, T.R.R. Iynegar]

**Nirṛti**: [Death, decay] Death personified as a goddess, sometimes regarded as the wife and sometimes as the daughter of Adharma. One of the Rudras.

# O

**Oṁ**: A word of solemn invocation, affirmation, benediction and consent, so sacred that when it is uttered no one must hear it. The word is used at the commencement of prayers and religious ceremonies, and is generally placed at the beginning of books. It is a compound of the three letters *a*, *u*, *ṁ* which are typical of the three Vedas, and it is declared in the Upaniṣads, where it first appears, to have a mystic power and to be worthy of the deepest meditation. In later times the monosyllable represents the Hindu triad or union of three gods, ***a*** being Viṣṇu, ***u*** Śiva and ***ṁ*** Brahmā. This monosyllable is called Udgītha.

**Oṁkāra**: The sacred monosyllable *oṁ*. Name of one of the twelve great *liṅga*s.

# P

**Padmā**, **Padmāvatī**: A name of Lakṣmī, who is also known as Padmālaya — who dwells in a lotus — and by other names. The lotus is a symbol of Viṣṇu and he is often associated with that flower.

**Pākaśāsana**: A name of Indra, and of Arjuna as descended from Indra.

**Pālakapya**: An ancient sage who wrote upon medicine and is supposed to have been an incarnation of Dhanvantari.

**Pañcacūḍā**: A name of Rambhā.

**Pāñcajanya**: Kṛṣṇa's conch formed from the shell of the sea-demon, Pāñcajana.

**Pañcānana**: [Five-faced] An epithet applied to Śiva.

**Parameṣṭhin**: [Who stands in the highest place]. A title applied to any superior god and to some distinguished mortals. A name used in the Vedas for a son or a creation of Prajāpati?

**Paraśurāma**: [Rāma with the axe]. He was the sixth incarnation of Viṣṇu; the fifth son of Jamadagni and Reṇukā. He was the descendant of Bhārgava paternally and Kuśika maternally. One day while her children were roaming in the forest, collecting fruits to eat, Reṇukā went to a river for her bath and there she saw Citraratha, Prince of Mṛttikāvat, and his wife. When she saw them sporting in the water with a flower-garland, she became excited and let fall her seed in the stream and returned to the hermitage in a disturbed state of mind. Jamadagni, on discovering this, was furious and wanted that she should die for this offence. When his sons returned home, he ordered them one after another to slay their mother but all excepting Paraśurāma refused. So Jamadagni cursed them to become idiots. Then Paraśurāma, on being asked, with his axe, which god Śiva had granted to him, cut off his mother's head. On seeing this act of obedience, Jamadagni, being pleased, requested his son to ask for boons.

Paraśurāma prayed for the restoration of his mother to life, with no remembrance of her death, her purification from all defilement, the revival of his brothers to normalcy and invincibility in single combat for himself. All these boons were granted. Paraśurāma soon got an opportunity of testing the last gift. Once again, when the sons of Jamadagni had gone as usual to the woods, the great king Kārttavīrya Sahasrabāhu of the Haihayas, who had been blessed by god Dattātreya with a thousand arms and a golden chariot, which he could use for going anywhere he wished to, arrived at Jamadagni's hermitage. Kārttavīrya, drunk with his power, had oppressed everyone, including the sage Jamadagni, so that in response to an appeal from them, Viṣṇu, with Indra, decided to destroy Kārttavīrya and his party. Reṇukā, in her husband's absence, treated the royal guest and his party with all due honour and hospitality. But he was mean enough to take away with him the divine cow, Kāmadhenu despite the protests of Reṇukā and her people. Paraśurāma returned home and hearing what had happened, he assailed Kārttavīrya and overthrew him in battle. The sons of the king avenged their father's death by attacking the hermitage and slaying Jamadagni. When Paraśurāma saw his father's dead body, his wrath knew no bounds and he vowed to exterminate the entire kṣatriya race. In order to fulfil his vow of extirpation, he cleared the earth twenty-one times of the kṣatriyas, because they had all hidden themselves and their children among other castes in order to escape from his anger. When he had rid the earth of the kṣatriyas, whose tyranny he wanted to eliminate, their widows in order to maintain the lineage are alleged to have approached brāhmaṇas with whom they cohabited and thus revived the kṣatriya race. He is claimed to have manifested himself in the *tretā-yuga* and, after filling the lake and some tanks with the blood of the kṣatriyas whom he had slaughtered, he bestowed the earth on Kāśyapa. Finally he retired to the Mahendra hill, and Arjuna is said to have met him there. The theory that Paraśurāma had created Mālābar is untenable. After miraculously reclaiming the west coast from the rage of the ocean he cut fissures in the *ghāṭ*s with blows from his axe. He is said to have bestowed this country upon brāhmaṇas whom he had brought from north India. Paraśurāma has been worshipped, though not like other deities, probably owing to his alleged matricide. [See Avatāra] [*A Glossary of Hinduism*, T. Rengarajan]

**Pārijāta**: The tree produced at the churning of the ocean, and the delight of the nymphs of heaven, perfuming the world with its blossoms. It is related that once Nārada brought a flower of this tree to Dvārakā and presented it to his friend Kṛṣṇa. He waited to see to which of his wives Kṛṣṇa gave the flower. The flower was given to Rukmiṇī and Nārada went straight to Satyabhāmā and made a show of sorrow. On her inquiring why he was not in good cheer, the sage told Satyabhāmā that he had presented Kṛṣṇa with a flower of the Pārijāta tree thinking that she was his favourite wife and he would present it to her, but was grieved to find that Kṛṣṇa had given it to Rukmiṇī. Satyabhāmā's jealousy was roused and she asked Nārada what could be done to spite Rukmiṇī. The sage advised her to ask Kṛṣṇa to bring the Pārijāta tree itself from heaven and plant it near her house. After giving this advice he went back to the celestial region and told Indra to guard the Pārijāta tree carefully as thieves were about. When Kṛṣṇa came to Satyabhāmā she reviled him for cheating her. 'You pretend that I am your favourite wife, but treat me as Rukmiṇī's handmaid', she said, and asked him what made him present the Pārijāta flower to Rukmiṇī. Kṛṣṇa immediately proceeded to Amarāvatī, stole into Indra's grove and started uprooting the tree. The king of the gods came upon the scene and caught the thief red-handed; but seeing who his despoiler was, he allowed him, after some show of resistance, to take the tree to Satyabhāmā by presenting Kṛṣṇa with a flower of the Pārijāta tree. It was kept in Indra's heaven, and was the pride of his wife Śaci. But when Kṛṣṇa visited Indra in *svarga*, his wife Satyabhāmā induced him to carry the tree away, which led to a great fight between the two gods and their adherents, in which Indra was defeated. The tree was taken to Dvārakā and planted there, but after Kṛṣṇa's death it returned to Indra's heaven. [*Hindu Mythology*, T.R.R. Iyengar; *A Classical Dictionary of Hindu Mythology and Religion*, J. Dowson]

**Parjanya**: A Vedic deity, the rain god or rain personified. Three hymns in the *R̥gveda* are addressed to this deity, and one of them is very poetical and picturesque in describing rain and its effects. The name is sometimes combined with the word *vāta*, 'wind', *Parjanya-vāta* referring probably to the combined powers and effects of rain and wind. In later times he was regarded as the guardian deity of clouds and rain and the name was applied to Indra. He is mentioned in the *R̥gveda* and the *Atharvaveda*. He is noted for shedding rain, producing and nourishing vegetation. His spouse is the earth and he was also connected with deities like the Maruts, Agni and Indra. He is addressed as the procreative and stimulating fructifier, resembling Indra in this respect in the R̥gvedic hymns. He is empowered with the strength of splitting trees, destroying cloud demons withholding rain with the roar of a lion — alluding to thunder, commanding the winds to blow or cease, the lightning to fall, plants to shoot up, the flowers to blossom and the vegetation to grow. Prayers are made to him to shower his rains as though he were another Indra, thereby to swell the rivers, moisten the skies and bring nourishment to the earth, and yield drinking water to the thirsty cattle. This tradition was carried on in the Purāṇas in which also he is depicted as the deity holding his sway over the clouds and controlling the showers. This name is also applied to one of the Ādityas. The rainy weather is beautifully described in a stanza addressed to Parajanya:

> The winds blow forth; to earth the quivering lightnings
> fall.
> The plants shoot up; with moisture streams the realm
> of light
> For all the world abundant nourishment is born,
> When by Parjanya earth is fertilized with seed.

[*R̥gveda*; *Atharvanaveda*; *Vedic Index* Macdonell and Keith]

**Pārvatī**: A name of the wife of Śiva. She is also known as Gaurī or Umā, and she is represented as a standing or seated figure with two hands, one of these either holding a lotus flower or held in *kaṭaka* pose and the other hanging lose by the side. But she is also represented with four hands, carrying a *pāśa* and an *aṅkuśa* in the upper hands and the lower ones in *abhaya* and *varada* poses. In these *sāttvik* forms, she has a pleasing appearance and, as *Suprabhedāgama* says, she has prominent large breasts and is adorned with all ornaments. [*A Glossary of Hinduism*, T. Rengarajan]

**Paśupati**: [Lord of creatures] A name of Rudra. In the *Mahābhārata*, Paśupati is 'lord of animals' to whom are sacred the five kinds of animals — kine, horses, men, goats and sheep. He delights in bloody sacrifices and it was for him that Jarāsandha kept the captive princes, 'sprinkled for slaughter and devoted as victims like beasts' which so roused the ire of Kṛṣṇa. Paśupati is identified with Rudra as Bhūpati or lord of dreadful forms; in the *Śatapatha Brāhmaṇa* the name is given to Agni, and again, in the *Mahābhārata*, to Varuṇa as part of Rudra. When Arjuna sought the Pāśupata weapon from Śiva, he found the deity attended by his *bhūta*s. The name of Paśupati occurs in the Rudra hymn as an epithet of Rudra. Thus, in older writings we have the term identified with the fiercer form of Śiva which leads the worshippers to offer blood to please the deity. He is represented in the *yogic* posture with eyes in *śāmbhavī mudrā*. He is sitting on a low throne flanked by antelopes. His two arms, covered with bangles, are outstretched and his hands rest on his knees. He wears a number of necklaces and a pair of horns meeting in a tall fan-shaped head-dress crowns his head. A separate class of devotees known as Pāśupatas who were guided by instruction supposed to have been written by Śiva himself prospered at the time of Śaṅkarācārya and bore as their sectarian mark a *liṅga* on the forehead, breast, arms and navel. They existed even so late as the time of Mādhava, who records that Pāśupata taught the *mantra* worship of Śiva [*Mahābhārata; Hindu Mythology,* T.R.R. Iyengar]

**Pavana**: [Wind] The god of the wind.

**Pitṛs**: [Patres, the fathers, the Manes] This name is applied to three different classes of beings: 1. The Manes of departed forefathers, to whom *piṇḍa*s (balls of rice and flour) and water are offered at stated periods. 2. The ten Prajāpatis or mythical progenitors or the human race. 3. According to a legend in the *Harivaṁśa* and in the *Vāyu Purāṇa* the first *pitṛ*s were the sons of the gods. Brahmā cursed the gods to become fools when they offended Brahmā by neglecting to worship him; but upon their repentance, he directed them to apply to their sons for instruction. Being taught accordingly the rites of expiation and penance by their sons, they addressed them as fathers; whence the sons of the gods were the first *pitṛ*s. The account given of the *pitṛ*s is much the same in all the Purāṇas. 'They agree in distinguishing them into seven classes, three of which are without form or composed of intellectual, not elementary substance, and assuming what forms they please, and four are corporeal. When the Purāṇas come to the enumeration of the particular classes, they somewhat differ and the accounts in all the works are singularly imperfect.' The incorporeal *pitṛ*s, according to one enumeration, are the Vairājas, Agniṣvātas and Barhiṣads. The first of these seem also to be called Subhasvaras, Somasads and Saumyas. The corporeal are the Sukālas or Sukālins, Aṅgirasas, Susvadas and Somapas. The Sukālas are also called Manasas; the Somapas are also called Uṣmapas; the Aṅgirasas seem also to be called Haviṣmats, Havirbhujas and Upahūtas; and the Susvadhas are apparently the same as the Ājyapas and Kāvyas. The Vairājas are the Manes of great ascetics and anchorites, the Agniṣvātas as are the *pitṛ*s of the gods, the Barhiṣads of demons, the Somapas of brāhmaṇas, the Haviṣmats of kṣatriyas, the Ājyapas of vaiśyas, and the Sukālins of the śūdras; but one authority, the *Harivaṁśa* makes the Somapas belong to the śūdras and the Sukālins to the brāhmaṇas, and there appears to be good reason for this. Dr. F. Hall gives other names from various authorities: Raśmipas, Phenapas, Sudhavats, Gārhapatyas, Ekaśṛṅgas, Caturvedas and Kālas. Besides these there are the

Vyamas, fumes, the *pitṛ*s of the barbarians. The *Ṛgveda* and Manu make two independent classes, the Agnidagdhas and the Anagnidagdhas, those who when alive kept up (or did not keep up) the household flame and presented (or did not present) oblations with fire. The *Viṣṇu Purāṇa* makes the Barhiṣads identical with the former, and the Agniṣvātas with the latter. Yama, the god of the dead, is king of the *pitṛ*s and Svadhā, 'oblation' is sometimes said to be their mother, but also at times their wife. [*A Classical Dictionary of Hindu Mythology and Religion*, J. Dowson]

**Pitṛpati**: [The lord of the Manes]. Yama, judge of the dead.

**Planets:** The planets are said to be nine. They are Candra, Ravi, Śukra, Rāhu, Ketu, Bṛhaspati, Maṅgala, Budha and Śani. [*See* 'Navagraha']

**Pracetas:** 1. One of the Prajāpatis. 2. The ten Pracetases were sons of Prācīnabarhiṣ and great-grandsons of Pṛthu and, according to the *Viṣṇu Purāṇa*, they passed ten thousand years in the great ocean, deep in meditation upon Viṣṇu, and obtained from him the boon of becoming the progenitors of mankind.

**Prahlāda**: A *daitya*, son of Hiraṇyakaśipu and father of Bali. Hiraṇyakaśipu, in his wars with the gods, had wrested the sovereignty of heaven from Indra and dwelt there in luxury. His son Prahlāda, while yet a boy, became an ardent devotee of Viṣṇu, which so enraged his father that he ordered the boy to be killed; but not the weapons of the *daitya*s, the fangs of the serpents, the tusks of the celestial elephants, nor the flames of fire took any effect, and his father was constrained to send him back to his preceptor, where he continued so earnest in performing and promoting the worship of Viṣṇu that he eventually obtained final exemption from existence. According to some accounts it was to avenge Prahlāda as well as to vindicate his own insulted majesty that Viṣṇu became incarnate as the Narasiṁha, 'man-lion' and slew Hiraṇyakaśipu. After the death of his father, Prahlāda became king of the *daitya*s and dwelt in Pātāla; but, according to the *Padma Purāṇa*, he was raised to the rank of Indra for life, and finally united with Viṣṇu. The *Padma Purāṇa* carries the story farther back to a previous birth. In this previous existence Prahlāda was a brāhmaṇa named Somaśarman, fifth son of Śivaśarman. His four brothers died and obtained union with Viṣṇu, and he desired to follow them. To accomplish this he engaged in profound meditation, but he allowed himself to be disturbed by an alarm of the *daitya*s, and so was born again as one of them. He took the part of his race in the war between them and the gods, and was killed by the discus of Viṣṇu. After that he was born again as son of Hiraṇyakaśipu. [*A Classical Dictionary of Hindu Mythology and Religion*, J. Dowson]

**Prajāpati:** [Lord of creatures] A progenitor, creator. In the Veda the term is applied to Indra, Sāvitrī, Soma, Hiraṇyagarbha, and other deities. In *Manu-smṛti* the term is applied to Brahmā as the active creator and supporter of the universe; so Brahmā is the Prajāpati. It is also given to Manu Svayambhuva himself, as the son of Brahmā and as the secondary creator of the ten *ṛṣi*s or mind-born sons of Brahmā from whom mankind has descended. It is to these ten sages, as fathers of the human race, that the name Prajāpati most commonly is given. They are Marīci, Atri, Aṅgiras, Pulastya, Pulaha, Kratu, Vasiṣṭha, Pracetas or Dakṣa, Bhṛgu and Nārada. According to some authorities the Prajāpatis are only seven in number, being identical with the seven great *ṛṣi*s. The number and names of the Prajāpatis vary in different authorities; the *Mahābhārata* mentions twenty-one.

In the institutes of Manu we are told that Brahmā divided his own substance and became half-male and half-female, or nature active and passive; and from that female he produced Virāj. Virāj by austerities produced the first Manu named Svayambhuva who produced ten the beings called Prajāpatis, lords of creatures. These Prajāpatis represent morality, deceit, charity, patience, pride, piety, ingenuity, emulation, humanity and reason respectively. [*Hindu Mythology*, T.R.R. Iyengar; *Glossary of Hinduism*, T. Rengarajan]

**Prakāśas**: Messengers of Viṣṇu, also called Viṣṇudūtas.

**Pramathas**: A class of demi-gods or fiends attendant upon Śiva.

**Pṛthā**: A name of Kuntī.

**Prasūti**: A daughter of Manu and wife of Dakṣa.

**Pṛthivī**: The earth or wide world. In the Vedas the earth is personified as the mother of all beings, and is invoked together with the sky. According to the Vedas there are three earths corresponding to the three heavens, and our earth is called Bhūmi. Another name of the earth is Urvī, 'wide'. In the *Viṣṇu Purāṇa* she is represented as receiving her name from a mythical person named Pṛthu, who granted her life and so was to her as a father. [*Vedic Index*, Macdonell and Keith]

**Pulaha**: One of the Prajāpatis and great *ṛṣi*s.

**Pulastya**: One of the Prajāpatis or mind-born sons of Brahmā and one of the great *ṛṣi*s. He was the medium through which some of the Purāṇas were communicated to man. He received the *Viṣṇu Purāṇa* from Brahmā and communicated it to Parāśara, who made it known to mankind. [*Viṣṇu Purāṇa*]

**Puloman**: A *dānava* and father of Śaci, wife of Indra. He was killed by Indra when he wished to curse that deity for having ravished his daughter.

**Puṇḍarīkākṣa**: [The lotus-eyed] A name of Viṣṇu.

**Puṇyaśloka**: An appellation applied to Kṛṣṇa.

**Pururavas**: In the Vedas, a mythical personage connected with the sun and the dawn, and existing in the middle region of the universe. According to the *Ṛgveda*, he was son of Ilā, and a beneficent pious prince, but the *Mahābhārata* says: 'We have heard that Ilā was both his mother and his father. The parentage usually assigned to him is that he was son of Budha by Ilā, daughter of Manu, and grandson of the moon.' [*Ṛgveda*; *Mahābhārata*]

**Puruṣa**: A name of Brahmā.

**Pūṣan**: The name 'Pūṣan' etymologically means 'prosper' as derived from the root *puṣ* and the primary idea is that of 'nourisher' or providence. The prosperity he confers is connected with light and this is emphasised by his exclusive epithet 'glowing'. The deity of this name is frequently mentioned in the Vedas, but he is not of a distinctly defined character. Many hymns are addressed to him. The *Taittirīya Brāhmaṇa* says, 'When Prajāpati formed living creatures Pūṣan nourished them.' Pūṣan is celebrated in eight hymns of the *R̥gveda*, five of which occur in the sixth *Maṇḍala*. His name is mentioned about 120 times. In two hymns he is lauded with Soma and Indra respectively. The account given in Böhtlingk and Roth's dictionary and adopted by Dr. Muir is as follows:

> Pushan is a protector and multiplier of cattle and of human possessions in general. As a cowherd he carries an oxgoad, and he is drawn by goats. In the character of a Solar deity, he beholds the entire universe, and is a guide on roads and journeys and to the other world. He is called the lover of his sister Surya. He aids in the revolution of day and night and shares with soma the guardianship of living creatures. He is invoked along with the most various deities, but most frequently with Indra and Bhaga.

He is a patron of conjurers, especially of those who discover stolen goods, and he is connected with the marriage ceremonial, being besought to take the bride's hand and bless her.

In the *Nirukta*, and in works of later date, Pūṣan is identified with the sun. He is also called the brother of Indra, and is enumerated among the twelve Ādityas. Pūṣan is toothless, and feeds upon a kind of gruel, and the cooked oblations offered to him are of ground materials; hence he is called Karambhad. The cause of his being toothless is variously explained. According to the *Taittirīya Saṁhitā*, the deity Rudra, being excluded from a certain sacrifice, shot an arrow at the offering and pierced it. A portion of this sacrifice was presented to Pūṣan, and it broke his teeth. Pūṣan is the lord of all things moving and stationary. As an aspect of the sun, he is called the wooer of night and the lover of dawn. The gods are said to have given him to the sun maiden Sūrya as a groom man. He is therefore sought in the wedding hymn to take the bride's hand and lead her to the chariot in which the Aśvins are prayed to conduct her to her husband's home. In the *Mahābhārata* and in the Purāṇas the legend takes a more definite shape. 'Rudra, of dreadful power, ran up to the gods present at Dakṣa's sacrifice, and in his rage knocked out the eyes of Bhaga with a blow and, incensed, assaulted Pūṣan with his foot, and knocked out his teeth as he was eating the *puroḍāsa* offering.' In the Purāṇas it is not Śiva himself but his manifestation, the Rudras who disturbed the sacrifice of the gods and knocked Pūṣan's teeth down his throat. Pūṣan shares many of his attributes with other gods. He is called *asura* and is described as strong, vigorous, wise and liberal. Like the Aśvins he is termed wonder-worker and like Agni he is called Nārāśaṁsa, 'praised of men'. The characteristic epithets of Pūṣan are glowing, bringing prosperity, losing no cattle, losing no goods, protector of cattle and guardian of paths. As guardian of roads he is besought to remove the danger, the wolf, and the way layer from the path. In this connection he is called son of deliverance. He is twice called deliverer. In the *Atharvaveda* he is called upon to deliver from sin. As knower of ways he can make hidden goods manifest and easy to find. He keeps cattle from falling into pits, brings them home unhurt and drives back the lost. Pūṣan is called Aghriṇī, 'splendid'; Dasra, Dasma, and Dasmavarcas, of wonderful appearance of power; and Kapardin. [*A Classical Dictionary of Hindu Mythology and Religion*; J. Dowson; *Hindu Mythology*, T.R.R. Iyengar]

**Puṣpa-Danta**: [Flower-teeth] One of the chief attendants of Śiva. He incurred his master's displeasure by listening to his private conversation with Pārvatī and talking of it afterwards. For this he was condemned to become a man and so appeared in the form of the great grammarian Kātyāyana.

# R

**Rādhā**: The favourite mistress and consort of Kṛṣṇa while he lived as Gopāla among the cowherds in Vṛndāvana. She was wife of Ayanaghoṣa, a cowherd. She is considered by some to be an incarnation of Laṣmī and worshipped. Some have discovered a mystical character in Rādhā and consider her as the type of the human soul drawn to the ineffable god, Kṛṣṇa or as that pure divine love to which the fickle lover returns. [*A Classical Dictionary of Hindu Mythology and Religion*, J. Dowson]

**Rādhikā**: A diminutive and endearing form of the name Rādhā.

**Rāghava**: Descendant of Raghu, a name of Rāma.

**Rāhu**: Rāhu and Ketu are in astronomy the ascending and descending nodes. Rāhu is the cause of eclipses, and the term is used to designate the eclipse itself. He is also considered as one of the planets, as king of meteors and as guardian of the south-west quarter. Mythologically Rāhu is a *daitya* who is supposed to seize the sun and the moon and swallow them, thus obscuring their rays and causing eclipses. He was son of Vipracittī and Siṁhikā, and was called by his metronymic Sainhikeya. He had four arms, and his lower part ended in a tail. He was a great mischief-maker, and when the gods had produced the *amṛta* by churning the ocean, he assumed a disguise and impersonating as one of them drank some of it. The sun and the moon detected him and informed Viṣṇu who cut off his head and two of his arms, but as he had secured immortality his body was placed in the stellar sphere, the upper parts represented by a dragon's head, being Rāhu, the ascending node, and the lower parts, represented by a dragon's tail, being Ketu, the descending node. Rāhu wreaks his vengeance on the sun and the moon by occasionally swallowing them. The *Viṣṇu Purāṇa* says, 'Eight black horses draw the dusky chariot of Rāhu, and once harnessed are attached to it forever. On the Parvans (nodes of lunar and solar eclipses) Rāhu directs his course from the sun to the moon, and back again from the moon to the sun. The eight horses of the chariot of Ketu, swift as the wind, are of the dusky red colour of lac or of the smoke of burning straw'.

Rāhu is represented as fearful in appearance: black in colour having the head of a man with the body of a serpent, having two arms folded in *añjalī* pose. Rāhu is called Abhrapiśāca, 'the demon of the sky'; Bharaṇibhū, 'born from the asterism Bharaṇī'; Graha, 'the seizer'; Kabandha, 'the headless'. [*A Classical Dictionary of Hindu Mythology and Religion*, J. Dowson; *Hindu Mythology*, T.R.R. Iyengar]

**Rāma**, **Rāmacandra**: Eldest son of Daśaratha, a king of the solar race, reigning at Ayodhyā. This Rāma is the seventh incarnation of the god Viṣṇu, and made his appearance in the world at the end of the *tretā-yuga*. His story in full length is the grand subject of the *Rāmāyaṇa*. King Daśaratha was childless, and performed the *aśvamedha* sacrifice with scrupulous care, in the hope of obtaining offspring. His devotion was accepted by the gods and he was promised four sons. At the time the gods were in great terror and alarm at the deeds and menaces of Rāvaṇa, the *rākṣasa* king of Laṅkā, who had obtained extraordinary power in virtue of severe penances and austere devotion to Brahmā. In their terror the gods appealed to Viṣṇu for deliverance, and he resolved to become manifest in the world with Daśaratha as his human father. Daśaratha was performing a sacrifice when Viṣṇu appeared to him as a glorious being from out of the sacrificial fire, and gave to him a pot of nectar for his wives to drink. Daśaratha gave half of the nectar to Kauśalyā, who brought forth Rāma with a half of the divine essence, a quarter to Kaikeyī, whose son Bharata was endowed with a quarter of the deity, and the fourth part to Sumitrā, who brought forth two sons Lakṣmaṇa and Śatrughna, each having an eighth part of the divine essence. The brothers were all attached to one another, but Lakṣmaṇa was more especially devoted to Rāma and Śatrughna to Bharata. The two sons of Sumitrā and the pairing off of the brothers have not passed without notice. The version of the *Rāmāyaṇa* given by Wheeler endeavours to account for these circumstances. It says that Daśaratha divided the divine nectar between his senior wives, Kauśalyā and Kaikeyī, and that when the younger, Sumitrā asked for some, Daśaratha desired them to share their portions with her. Each gave her half, so Sumitrā received two quarters and gave birth to two sons: 'from the quarter which she received from Kauśalyā she gave birth to Lakṣmaṇa, who became the ever-faithful friend of Rāma, and from the quarter she received from Kaikeyī, she gave birth to Śatrughna, who became the ever-faithful friend of Bharata'. The account is silent as to the superior divinity of Rāma, according to it all four brothers must have been equals as manifestation of the deity.

The four brothers grew up together at Ayodhyā, but while they were yet young, the sage Viśvāmitra sought the aid of Rāma to protect him from the *rākṣasa*s. Daśaratha, though very unwilling, was constrained to consent to the sage's request. Rāma and Lakṣmaṇa then went to the hermitage of Viśvāmitra, and there Rāma killed the demoness Tāḍakā, but it required a good deal of persuasion from the sage before he could be induced to kill a female. Viśvāmitra supplied Rāma with celestial arms, and exercised a considerable influence over his actions. Viśvāmitra afterwards took Rāma and his brothers to Mithilā to the court of Janaka, king of Videha. This king had a lovely daughter named Sītā, whom he offered in marriage to anyone who could bend the wonderful bow that had once belonged to Śiva. Rāma not only bent the bow but also broke it, and thus won the hand of the princess, who became a most virtuous and devoted wife. Rāma's three brothers also were married to a sister and two cousins of Sītā. This breaking of the bow of Śiva brought about a very curious incident, which is probably an interpolation of a later date, introduced for sectarian purposes. Paraśurāma, the sixth incarnation of Viṣṇu, the brāhmaṇa, exterminator of the kṣatriyas, was still living upon earth. He was a follower of Śiva, and was exasperated at the breaking of that deity's bow. Notwithstanding that he and Rāma were both incarnation of Viṣṇu, he challenged Rāma to a trial of strength and was discomfited, but Rāma spared his life because he was a brāhmaṇa.

Preparations were made at Ayodhyā for the inauguration of Rāma as successor to the throne. Kaikeyī, the second wife of Daśaratha, and mother of Bharata, was her husband's favourite. She was kind to Rāma in childhood and youth, but she had a spiteful hump-backed female slave named Mantharā. This woman worked upon the maternal affection of her mistress until she aroused a strong feeling of jealousy against Rāma. Kaikeyī had a quarrel and a long struggle with her husband, but he at length consented to install Bharata on the throne and to send Rāma into exile for fourteen years. Rāma departed with his wife Sītā and his brother Lakṣmaṇa, and travelling southwards, he took up his abode at Citrakūṭa in the Daṇḍaka forest, between the Yamunā and Godāvarī. Soon after the departure of Rāma his father Daśaratha died and Bharata was called upon to ascend the throne. He declined, and set out for the forest with an army to bring Rāma back When the brothers met, there was a long contention. Rāma refused to return until the term of his father's sentence was concluded, and Bharata declined to ascend the throne. At length it was arranged that Bharata should return and act as his brother's vicegerent. As a sign of Rāma's supremacy, Bharata carried back with him a pair of Rāma's shoes and these were always brought out ceremoniously when business had to be transacted. Rāma passed ten years of his banishment moving from one hermitage to another, and went at length to the hermitage of the sage Agastya, near the Vindhya mountains. This holy man recommended Rāma to take up his abode at Pañcavaṭī, on the river Godāvarī and the party accordingly proceeded yonder. This district was infested with *rākṣasa*s, and one of them named Śūrpanakhā, sister of Rāvaṇa, saw Rāma and fell in love with him. He repelled her advances, and in her jealousy she attacked Sītā. This so enraged Lakṣmaṇa that he cut off her ears and nose. She brought her brothers Khara and Dūṣaṇa with an army of *rākṣasa*s to avenge her wrong, but they were all destroyed. Smarting under her mutilation and with *spretae injuria formae*, she repaired to her brother Rāvaṇa in Laṅkā, and inspired him by her description with a fierce passion for Sītā. Rāvaṇa assumed the form of a religious mendicant and lulled Sītā's apprehensions until he found an opportunity to declare himself and carry her off by force to Laṅkā. Rāma's despair and rage at the loss of his faithful wife were terrible. He and Lakṣmaṇa went in pursuit and tracked the ravisher. On their way they killed Kabandha, a headless monster, whose disembodied spirit counselled Rāma to seek the aid of Sugrīva, king of the monkeys. The two brothers accordingly went on their way to Sugrīva and after overcoming some obstacles and assisting Sugrīva to recover Kiṣkindhā, his capital, from his usurping brother Bālin, they entered into a firm alliance with him. Through this connection Rāma got the appellations of Kapiprabhu and Kapiratha. He received not only the support of all the forces of Sugrīva and his allies, but also the active aid of Hanumān, son of the wind and minister and general of Sugrīva. Hanumān's extraordinary powers of leaping and flying enabled him to do all the work of reconnoitering. By superhuman efforts their armies were transported to Ceylon by 'Rāma's bridge', and after many fiercely contested battles the city of Laṅkā was taken, Rāvaṇa was killed and Sītā was rescued. The term of exile was now over.

The recovery of his wife filled Rāma with joy, but he was jealous of her honour, received her coldly, and refused to take her back. She asserted her purity in touching and dignified language, and determined to prove her innocence by the ordeal of fire. She entered the flames in the presence of men and gods, and Agni, god of fire, led her forth and placed her in Rāma's arms unhurt. Rāma then returned taking with him his chief allies to Ayodhyā. Reunited with his three brothers he was solemnly crowned and began a glorious reign, Lakṣmaṇa being associated with him in the government.

Ten thousand years Ayodhyā, blest,
With Rāma's rule, had peace and rest.
No widow mourned her murdered mate,
No house was ever desolate.
The happy land no murrain knew,

The flocks and herds increased and grew.
The earth her kindly fruits supplied,
No harvest failed, no children died.
Unknown were want, disease, and crime,
So calm, so happy was the time.

The sixth section of the *Rāmāyaṇa* here concludes; the remainder of the story is told in the Uttara-kāṇḍa, a subsequent addition.

But once again trouble started. A washerman in the kingdom beat his wife suspected of adultery, and drove home the point by observing that he was not a fool like Rāma to believe that a wife who had been kept years by another man was pure. The treatment, which Sītā had received in captivity, was better than might have been expected at the hands of a *rākṣasa*. She had asserted and proved her purity, and Rāma believed her, but jealous thoughts would cross his sensitive mind, and when his subjects blamed him for taking back his wife, he resolved, although she was pregnant, to send her to spend the rest of her life at the hermitage of Vālmīki. There she was delivered of her twin sons Kuśa and Lava, who bore upon their persons the marks of their high paternity. When they were about fifteen years old they wandered accidentally to Ayodhyā and were recognised by their father, who acknowledged them and recalled Sītā to test her innocence. She returned and in a public assembly declared her purity and called upon the earth to verify her words. It did so. The ground opened and received the daughter of the furrow, and Rāma lost his beloved and only wife. Unable to endure life without her, he resolved to follow, and the gods favoured his determination. Time appeared to him in the form of an ascetic and told him that he must stay on earth or ascend to heaven and rule over the gods. Lakṣmaṇa with devoted fraternal affection endeavoured to save his brother from what he deemed the noxious visit of time. He incurred a sentence of death for his interference, and was conveyed bodily to Indra's heaven. Rāma with great state and ceremony went to the river Sarayū, and walking into the water was hailed by Brahmā's voice of welcome from heaven and entered into the glory of Viṣṇu.

Rāma has been interpreted as the son of Daśaratha, a friend of Indra, and the incarnation of Viṣṇu, the sun god. His story has been conceived as the development of an early zodiacal legend, according to which he dwells in Ayodhyā and, on attaining nineteen years, he leaves it at his father's behest for the Daṇḍaka forest and for Laṅkā, wandering for fourteen years. On reaching Laṅkā on or near the equator, he annihilates the demons, whose king was Rāvaṇa. Finally after thirty-three years he returns to the kingdom of the gods of Ayodhyā. This feat is repeated in every cycle of thirty-three years which has been considered the real *kalpa* magnified in the Purāṇas and the *siddhānta* as into 432,000 years.

**Genealogy of Rāma**

Ikṣvāku

| | | |
|---|---|---|
| Vikukṣī | Pṛṣadasva | Āyutāyus |
| Kakutstha | Haryasva | Ṛtuparṇa |
| Aneanas | Sumanas | Sarvakāma |
| Pṛthu | Tridhanvan | Sudāsa |
| Ārdra | Trayāruṇa | Saudāsa |
| Yuvanāśva | Hariścandra | Asmaka |
| Śrāvasta | Rohitāśva | Mūlaka |
| Bṛhadaśva | Hārīta | Daśaratha |
| Kuvalayāsva | Cuñcu | Ilavila |
| Dṛḍhaśva | Vijaya | Viśvasaha |
| Haryaśva | Ruruka | Khaṭvāṅga |
| Nikumbha | Vṛka | Dīrghabāhu |
| Sanhataśva | Bahuka | Raghu |
| Kṛsaśva | Sagara | Aja |
| Prasenajit | Asmañajas | Daśaratha |
| Yuvanāśva | Dilīpa | Rāma |
| Māndhātṛ | Bhagīratha | — |

| | | |
|---|---|---|
| Purukutsa | Śruta | — |
| Trasadasyu | Nābhāga | — |
| Sambhūta | Ambarṣa | — |
| Anaraṇya | Sindhudvipa | — |

[*A Classical Dictionary of Hindu Mythology and Religion*, J. Dowson; *Hindu Mythology*, T.R.R. Iyengar; *A Study of the Ramāyaṇas*, A. Sarkar]

**Rāmeśvara**: [Lord of Rāma] Name of one of the twelve great *liṅgas* set-up, as is said, by Rāma at Rāmeśvaram, which is a celebrated place of pilgrimage and contains a most magnificent temple.

**Ranneśa**: A sun god. A sun deity is called by this name near Puṣkara.

**Rati**: [Love, desire] The Venus of the Hindus, the goddess of sexual pleasures, wife of Kāma. When he was reduced to ashes by a furious glance from Śiva through his third eye, when he dared to tempt Śiva under the directives of the gods, she was beside herself with irreconcilable grief and anguish. So she prayed to Pārvatī, Śiva's consort, to plead with her to restore Kāma back to life. Pārvatī consoled Rati that Kāma would be born again as the son of Kṛṣṇa and be called Pradyumna, that he would be carried away by a demon, Śambara, who would throw him into the sea in order to be drowned but that child would enter the bowels of a huge fish, which would be caught and brought into Śambara's kitchen. There it would be cut open and the child would come out alive. So Pārvatī advised Rati to proceed to Śambara's house and work there as a maidservant until this event should occur and when Pradyumna arrived, to bring him up so that when he had grown up, he might destroy the demon, Śambara. She is also called Revā; Kāmī; Pṛthī; Kāmapatnī, 'wife of Kāma'; Kāmakalā, 'part of Kāma'; Kāmapriyā, 'beloved of Kāma'; Rāgalatā, 'vine of love'; Māyāvatī, 'deceiver'; Kelikilā, 'wanton'; and Subhāṅgī, 'fair-limbed'. [*Glossary of Hinduism*, T. Rengarajan]

**Raucya**: The thirteenth Manu.

**Raudra**: A Descendant of Rudra. A name of Kārttikeya, the god of war.

**Ravi**: The sun.

**Reṇukā**: Daughter of king Prasenajīt, wife of Jamadagni, and mother of Paraśurāma. A sight of the cannibal endearments of King Citraratha and his wife inspired her with impure thoughts and her husband, perceiving that she had 'fallen from perfection' desired her sons to kill her. Rūmanvat, Suṣena, and Vāsu, the three seniors, declined, and their father cursed them so that they became idiots. Paraśurāma, the fourth son, cut off her head, which act so gratified his father that Jamadagni promised him whatever blessings he desired. Among other things, Paraśurāma asked that his mother might be brought back to life in ignorance of her death and in perfect purity. He also desired that his brothers might be restored to their senses. All this Jamadagni bestowed. She was also called Koṅkanna. [*Hindu Mythology*, T.R.R. Iyengar; *A Classical Dictionary of Hindu Mythology and Religion*, J. Dawson]

**Revā**: A name of Rati.

**Revanta**: A Son of Sūrya and Saṁjñā. He was also known as Vāhana probably because he had a horse for his vehicle. According to the *Viṣṇu Purāṇa* his mother conceived him when she had adopted the form of a mare to escape from her husband's excessive warmth and Sūrya, who too had become a horse, followed her. In that shape she gave birth to three children, the first two being the divine Aśvins and the third being Revanta. He was also worshipped, according to Varāhamitra, in north-eastern India. He is chief of the Guhyakas and is also called Hayavāhana. [*Hindu Mythology*, T.R.R. Iyengar]

**Revatī**: Daughter of king Raivata and wife of Balarāma. She was so beautiful that her father, thinking no one upon earth worthy of her, repaired to the god Brahmā to consult him about a husband. Brahmā delivered a long discourse on the glories of

Viṣṇu, and directed Raivata to proceed to Dvārakā where a portion of Viṣṇu was incarnate in the person of Balarāma. While Raivata was in heaven ages had elapsed without his knowledge. When he returned to earth, he found the race of men dwindled in stature, reduced in vigour, and enfeebled in intellect. He went to Balarāma and gave him Revatī, but that hero, beholding the damsel of excessively lofty height, shortened her with the end of his ploughshare, and she became his wife. She had two sons. Revatī is said to have taken part with her husband in his drinking bouts. [*A Classical Dictionary of Hindu Mythology and Religion*, J. Dowson]

**Ṛbhu**: [Clever, skilful] An epithet used for Indra, Agni and the Ādityas. In the Purāṇic mythology, Ṛbhu was a son of the Supreme Brahmā who from his innate disposition was of a holy character and acquainted with true wisdom. His pupil was Nidāgha, a son of Pulastya, and he took special interest in his instruction, returning to him after two intervals of a thousand years to instruct him further in true wisdom. The *Viṣṇu Purāṇa*, 'originally composed by the *ṛṣi*, was communicated by Brahmā to Ṛbhu'. [*A Glossary of Hinduism*. T. Rengarajan]

**Ṛddhi**: [Prosperity] The wife of Kubera, god of wealth. The name is also used for Pārvatī, the wife of Śiva. She was also called Citriṇī. In iconographical representations of Kubera, she is made to sit on his left thigh, when he rides. [*Hindu Mythology*, T.R.R. Iyengar]

**Rohiṇī**: (1) Daughter of Kaśyapa and Surabhi, and mother of horned cattle including Kāmadhenu, the cow which grants desires. (2) Daughter of Dakṣa and fourth of the lunar asterisms, the favourite wife of the moon. (3) One of the wives of Vasudeva, the father of Kṛṣṇa and mother of Balarāma. She was burned with her husband's corpse at Dvārakā.

Kṛṣṇa himself also had a wife so-called, and the name is common. [*Hindu Mythology*, T.R.R. Iyengar]

**Rohita**: [Red] A red horse, a horse of the sun or of fire. A deity celebrated in the *Atharvaveda*, probably a form of fire or the sun.

**Rudra**: [A howler or roarer; terrible] In the Vedas Rudra has many attributes and many names. He is the howling terrible god, the god of storms, the father of the Rudras or Martus, and is sometimes identified with the god of fire. In the Vedas the Rudras are mentioned as storm deities and companions of Indra. The functions and nature of the Purāṇic Rudras are incomprehensible. According to the *Viṣṇu Purāṇa* Rudra sprang up half-male, half-female from the forehead of Brahmā. 'Separate yourself', Brahmā said to him; obedient to which command Rudra became two-fold, disjoining his male and female natures. His male being he again divided into eleven persons of whom some were agreeable, some hideous, some fierce, some mild, and he multiplied his female nature manifold, of complexions black and white. Rudra is celebrated in only three entire hymns in part of another, and in one conjointly with Soma, while his name occurs about 75 times in the *R̥gveda*. In view of his later development, however, his importance cannot be minimised. His anthropomorphism is fairly advanced and he is credited with hands, arms, and firm limbs. He has beautiful lips and wears braided hair. His shape is dazzling and he is multiform. He shines like the brilliant sun or like gold. He is adorned with golden ornaments and wears a glorious multiform necklace. Rudra is regarded in the *R̥gveda* as exalted, strongest of the strong, swift, and unsurpassed in might. He is young and unaging. He is the great *asura* of heaven, a lord and father of the world. By his rule and universal dominions he is aware of the deeds of men and gods. He is bountiful, easily invoked and auspicious. He holds the thunderbolt in his arm and carries a bow and arrows, which are strong and swift. He sits on a car-seat. The hymns addressed to Rudra often express fear of his terrible shafts and deprecation of his wrath. He is implored to avert his bolt when he is incensed and not to injure their children and their cows. But though terrible when incensed, he otherwise bestows blessings and produces welfare for man and beast. His healing powers are mentioned frequently. He carries in his hand choice remedies and his hand is restorative and healing. He is the greatest physician of physicians and by his auspicious remedies his worshipper hopes to live a hundred years. Rudra in the *R̥gveda* is closely associated with the Maruts. He is their father. The Maruts for this reason are sometimes called Rudras or Rudriyas. But Rudra is never associated, as Indra is, with the warlike exploits of the Maruts, for he does not fight with the demons. The evidence of the *R̥gveda* does not clearly show the physical basis of Rudra. In a passage of the *R̥gveda*, Rudra is one of the several deities identified with Agni. He is also identified with Agni in the *Atharvaveda*, the *Taittirīya Saṁhitā* and the *Śatapatha Brāhmaṇa*. Rudra therefore seems to represent an aspect of fire, probably lightning as accompanied by storms. This would account for his deadly shafts and for his being the father of the Maruts who are armed with lightning and are said to be born 'from the laughter of lightning'. On the one hand he is a destructive deity who brings diseases upon men and cattle and upon the other he is beneficent. Rudra afterwards developed into the god Śiva. It is worthy of note that Rudra is first called Mahādeva in the *White Yajurveda*. The supremacy of Rudra-Śiva was reiterated in the *Śatapatha Brāhmaṇa*, where in he is called the son of Uṣas and after his birth was granted eight names by Prajāpati. Four of them indicated his destructive nature, namely Rudra, Sarva, Ugra and Śani while the other four, Bhava, Paśupati, Mahādeva and Īśāna denoted his beneficent nature. In spite of these distinct aspects of his nature, his feature was better commemorated, especially during the period of the *Gr̥hyasūtra*, when the bull sacrifice was performed outside the village, oblations were offered to his wives Bhavānī, Indrāṇī, Sāvarṇī and Rudrāṇī, for he was the greatest of the protectors and had to be appeased at all costs to save their menfolk and their cattle. In the Upaniṣads his supremacy became unquestioned. In all Upaniṣads he is identified with the Supreme Being, and gradually, as in the *Kaṭha Upaniṣad*, through a legend he was associated with Śakti, Umā-Haimavatī. Applied to the god Śiva, the name of Rudra generally designates him in his destructive character. In the *Bṛhadāraṇyaka Upaniṣad* the Rudras are ten vital breaths with the heart as eleventh. Though Brahmā had overcome the demons, the gods took that credit for themselves and, while they were gloating amongst themselves over this triumph, they saw before them a spirit, and they were curious to know its strength. Agni went forth and when asked about its might, it laid down a blade of grass and suggested Agni to burn it but he could not succeed. Like him Vāyu also failed and Indra, ongoing ahead, instead of that spirit saw a lovely woman who revealed that she was Brahmā. This legend has been interpreted to imply that, this time, the ancient Vedic deities had lost their supremacy and that Brahmā as Rudra-Śiva with his consort Umā-Haimavatī had come to be recognised as the supreme god and goddess. In the epics like *Mahābhārata*, this supremacy was sustained. This is best exemplified in the *Vana Parva* wherein Arjuna is represented as proceeding to the Himālayas for gaining the blessings of god Śiva and therefore practising severe penance there. Thereupon Arjuna prayed to Śiva, offered flowers to him and to Arjuna's surprise they appeared on that Kirāta's head. Arjuna, now realising that the Kirāta could be no other than Śiva himself, submitted to him. Śiva was convinced of Arjuna's sincere devotion and granted him boons, among which Pāśupatāstra was one. This supremacy of Śiva is repeated in the *Droṇa Parva* (*Mahābhārata*) wherein again Arjuna and Kṛṣṇa, going to the Himālayas, prayed for the Pāśupata weapon which they were told would be found hidden in a lake. Again in the *Sauptika Parva*, it is related how Aśvatthāman, after appeasing Śiva, obtained from him an invincible sword and, as Śiva himself entered his body, he became so powerful that he penetrated the Pāṇḍava camp at night and slew everyone including the children of the Pāṇḍavas. In the *Anuśāsana Parva* (*Mahābhārata*) again Kṛṣṇa reminds his audience that Rudra was the supreme deity, who should not under any circumstance be displeased. In response to the continued severe austerities of Upamanyu, Śiva manifested himself, riding on his mighty ox, accompanied by Brahmā on one side, also seated on his vehicle the swan, and by Nārāyaṇa on the other, riding on his Garuḍa. The Purāṇas show this supremacy of Mahādeva or Śiva, one of the epithets given to Rudra, the others being Īśvara, Bhagavata and Maheśvara. The *Vāyu Purāṇa* echoes the legend related in the *Mahābhārata*, which records that once Kṛṣṇa told Yudhiṣṭhira how on one occasion Brahmadeva had directed Śiva to cease creation and that, as the latter hid himself in the water for a considerable time, nothing was created. It then became incumbent on Brahmā to create a new Prajāpati, who brought into existence numerous beings which, in their ravenous hunger, proceeded to devour their own creator. In fright, he fled to Hiraṇyagarbha, who pacified them with two types of food. Subsequently Mahādeva emerging from his watery hideout found a new creation and realising that his procreative function, ineffective, severed his generative organ which he planted on the earth and went to the mountain for his penance. The *Vāyu Purāṇa*, repeating this legend, relates how Brahmadeva had requested Nīlalohita to commence creation, which he did by recollecting his spouse with the result that numerous beings were born, but they were deathless like their maker. Finding that he had completed his task, he devoted himself to the execution of the Pāśupata emblem. In the *Viṣṇu Purāṇa* the god Rudra is said to have sprung from the forehead of Brahmā, and at the command of that god to have separated his nature into male and female, then to have multiplied each of these into eleven persons, some of which were white and gentle and others black and furious. Rudra is represented through *Śilpasāra* in sixteen varieties of such images while the *Karaṇāgama* points to twenty-five of them. Hemādri depicts Rudra as riding on a bull with five faces, all depicting a mild mien excepting the one on the right side of his central face. He is described as a god having ten arms and wearing a garland of skulls. There are different types of such images, known as Rudra *mūrtis*, which have the following features — four hands, the two upper ones holding in each the kettledrum and the deer, while the two lower ones displaying the *varada* and *abhaya mudrās*. He is represented with three eyes, one in the forehead and two in their natural places, interpreted to symbolise fire, the sun and the moon. His costume is a tiger skin worn above the waist, with an undergarment and a scarf. He wears the typical ornaments like the girdle, wristlet, finger-rings, armlets, anklets and the sacred thread and on his matted hair is visible the face of the holy Gaṅgā flowing through it from the right side. Elsewhere it is said that the eleven Rudras were sons of Kaśyapa and Surabhi, and in the *Viṣṇu Purāṇa* it is said that Brahmā desired to create a son and that Rudra came into existence as a youth. He wept and asked for a name. Brahmā gave him the name Rudra, but he wept seven times more, and so he obtained seven other names: Bhava, Sarva, Īśāna, Paśupati, Bhīma, Ugra and Mahādeva. Other Purāṇas agree in this nomenclature. These names are sometimes used for Rudra or Śiva himself, and at other times for the seven manifestations of him, sometimes called his sons.

In the post-Vedic period Rudra became the third member of the Hindu trinity, with Śiva as his most popular name. He came to be regarded as the destroyer of the universe when it requires to be created anew. The germs of this development are found in the *Ṛgveda*. A common epithet of Rudra in post-Vedic literature is Tryambaka which is applied to him once even in the *Ṛgveda*. The original meaning of the word seem to have been 'one having three mothers' in allusion to the three-fold division of the universe. Later, however, the word came to be interpreted as 'one having three eyes'. His comparison to a white bull in the *Ṛgveda* in order to describe his complexion and power led the post-Vedic priests to make the white bull his vehicle. In fact, the history of this deity as reflected in the numerous epithets which were piled on him by later works beginning with the *Atharvaveda* and the *Yajurveda* seems to reveal the fusion of diverse ideas. Thus he is called Paśupati, Śaṅkara, Nīlagrīva, Nīlalohita, Kṛttivāsa, Giricara and Pinākabhṛt. It is clear that the rise of Rudra's popularity in the later Vedic period resulted in his absorbing the characteristics of some non-Āryan deities and his consequent acceptance as a god to be worshipped by several nomadic non-Āryan tribes living on plunder and pilferage. That seems to be the reason why this deity is called the patron of thieves, robbers and highwaymen in the *Vājasaneyī Saṁhitā*. In the *Śatapatha Brāhmaṇa* Rudra is mentioned as the son of Uṣas; and, after he was born, Prajāpati gave him, as he grew up, eight names, seven of which are the same as those given above from the *Atharvaveda* regards the seven as different though allied gods though once Rudra is identified with Paśupati. The character of Rudra appears in a much more developed form and is distinguished from its opposite, the malignant. He is called Girīśa or Giritra, 'lying on a mountain', probably because the thunderbolt that he hurls springs from a cloud, which is often compared to a mountain and in which he was believed to dwell. [*Hindu Mythology*, T.R.R. Iyengar; *A Classical Dictionary of Mythology and Religion*, J. Dowson; *South Indian Images*, N. Srinivasan; *Rāmāyaṇa*; *Mahābhārata*; *Vaisnavism, Saivism and Minor Religious Systems,* Bhandarkar]

**Rudrāṇī**: Name of goddess Durgā in a corporeal form. She is the beloved of Śiva.

**Rukmiṇī**: Daughter of Bhīṣmaka, king of Vidarbha. According to the *Harivaṁśa* she was sought in marriage by Kṛṣṇa with whom she fell in love. But her brother Rukmi was a friend of Kaṁsa whom Kṛṣṇa had killed. He therefore opposed him and thwarted the match. Rukmiṇī was then betrothed to Śiśupāla, king of Cedi, but on her wedding day as she was going to the temple, Kṛṣṇa saw her, took her by the hand and carried her away in his chariot. They were pursued by her intended husband and by her brother Rukmi, but Kṛṣṇa defeated them both, and took her safely to Dvārakā where he married her. She was his principal wife and bore him a son, Pradyumna. By him also she had nine other sons and one daughter. These other children were Cārudeṣṇa, Sudeṣaṇa, Cārudeha, Suṣeṇa, Cārugupta, Bhadracāru, Cāruvinda, Sucāru and the very mighty Cāru, and daughter Cārumati. At Kṛṣṇa's death she and seven other of his wives immolated themselves on his funeral pyre. [*A Classical Dictionary of Hindu Mythology and Religion*, J. Dowson]

# S

**Śaci**: Wife of Indra.

**Sādhyas**: According to the *Nirukta* the word 'Sādhyas' means a ray of lights. The gods who abide in the sky and absorb water and the other liquids are said to be Sādhyas. They are said to be adorable even to the gods. The Sādhyas are twelve in number; according to *Agni Purāṇa,* they are Mana, Manta, Prāṇa, Nara, Apāna, Vīryavān, Vinirbhaya, Nārāyaṇa, Vṛṣa and Prabhi. These are said to be the sons of Dharma and were great souls. The images of the Sādhyas should be represented upon *padmāsana*s and as carrying in their hands the *akṣamālā* and the *kamaṇḍalu*. Energy should be produced to destroy Rāvaṇa's race. In reply to this, Rāvaṇa threatened to pull up the mountain by its roots and let Śiva know his own danger. So he threw his arms round the mountain and lifted it up, which made the hosts of Śiva tremble and Pārvatī quake and cling to her husband. Śiva then pressed down the mountain with his great toe, and crushed and held fast the arms of Rāvaṇa who uttered a loud cry which shook all creation. Rāvaṇa's friends counselled him to propitiate Śiva and he did so for a thousand years with hymns and weeping. Śiva then released him, and said that his name should be Rāvaṇa from the cry, which he had uttered. The origin of this story is sufficiently manifest; it has been built up on the name Rāvaṇa to the glorify Śiva by a zealous partisan of that deity. Incensed at the insult offered to him he cursed Rāvaṇa that being possessing the same shape as himself and of similar energy would destroy the race of Rāvaṇa. The *Viṣṇudharmottara* gives the following description of Nandīkeśvara. He should have three eyes and four arms and red complexion. His garments should be made of tiger skin, in one of his hands there should be the *triśūla* and in another the *bhiṇḍī*; a third hand should be held over his head and the fourth held as though he is commanding a hose of people. His gaze should suggest that he is seeing objects at a great distance and regulating the large crowd of devotees resorting to offer worship of Śiva. He is more often represented as a bull than as a bull-faced being or as a duplicate of Śiva. [*Hindu Mythology*, T.R.R. Iyengar; *Glossary of Hinduism*, T. Rengarajan; *A Classical Dictionary of Hindu Mythology and Religion*, J. Dowson]

**Sahasrākṣa**: [Thousand-eyed] An epithet of Indra.

**Śakra**: A name of Indra.

**Sākinī**: A feminine demon attendant on Durgā.

**Sakrāṇī**: Wife of Indra.

**Śakti**: The wife or the female energy of a deity but especially of Śiva, namely, Sarasvatī, Lakṣmī, and Pārvatī in their benign aspects while the fierce ones are Kālī and Durgā. The worshippers are known as Śāktas. There can be little doubt that the Śakti or female forms are due to a popularising of the Sāṅkhya idea of Puruṣa and Prakṛti. The early conception of the supreme Puruṣa or spirit as being without qualities gave rise to a theory to account for the creation and the existence of the sexes which makes the exhibition of the creative power to be due to the union of the wish with the deity himself. Later on the followers of the Sāṅkhya system of philosophy made a distinction between nature and the supreme spirit. The former, which they call Prakṛti, is held to be the eternal matter and origin of all things, independent of the supreme spirit but co-existent with him as Śakti, his personified energy. Thus, from the union of power and will or spirit and matter all things were produced, and as each of these creatures of the creator possess a portion of the supreme spirit, they have a double character, male and female. The Prakṛti-khaṇḍa of the *Brahmavaivartta Purāṇa* devotes itself to an explanation of the forms of *prakṛti*, which are also identified with Māyā, the goddess of illusion. In that work *pra* means pre-eminent; *kṛti* means creating; that goddess who was pre-eminent in creating called Prakṛti. Again, *pra* means best, or is equivalent to satiate, 'the quality of purity'; *kṛti* 'implies middling', the quality of passion and time or worse, that of 'ignorance'. She who is invested with all power is identifiable with the three properties and as the principal was divided into five portions —

Durgā, the *śakti* of Mahādeva, Lakṣmī, the *śakti* of Viṣṇu, Sarasvatī, also the *śakti* of Viṣṇu, Sāvitrī, the *śakti* of Brahmā and mother of the Vedas and Rādhā, the mistress of Kṛṣṇa. The category has since been modified and extended to include portions of parts of the primitive *prakṛti*, whilst all woman-kind are included in the third category as containing portions or parts of the deity and are divided into good middling and bad, according as they derive their origin from each of the three qualities inherent in the primitive *prakṛti*. In the *Sāmaveda* occurs the verses: 'He felt not delight being alone. He wished another and instantly became such. He caused his own self to fall in twain and thus became husband and wife. He approached her and thus were human beings produced'. It is precisely in this form that Śiva appears in some very early sculptures under the title of Ardhanārīśvara — on the right side male and on the left side female. An account of the third-century records the following description of this form: In a very high mountain, situated pretty nearly in the middle of the earth there was . . . a large natural cave in which was to be seen a statue ten or perhaps twelve cubits high, standing upright with its hands folded crosswise and the right half of its face, its right arm and foot, in a word its whole right side was that of a man a very hard and sound wood'. This Śākta cult has been fully dealt with in many of the Tāntric works of which 64 are mentioned in the famous work *Saundaryalaharī*. All of them are connected with the worship of one divinity or the other.

These Tantras have been taken to be no other than what came to be known in the Tamil country as the Agars, some of which appear to have contained certain heretical treatises which pertained to the Kuala school. The chief peculiarity of the Tantras is the prominence they give to the female energy of the deity, his active nature being personified in the person of his *śakti*. There are a few Tantras which make Viṣṇu's wife the object of devotion, but the great majority of them are devoted to one of the manifold forms of Śakti of Śiva, and they are commonly written in the form of a dialogue between these two deities.

Devī, as the *śakti* of Śiva, is the special energy concerned with sexual intercourse and magical powers and these are the leading topics of the Tartars. Each Śākta has a two-fold nature, white and black, gentle and ferocious. The Umā and Gaurī are gentle forms of the *śakti* of Śiva, while Durgā and Kālī are her fierce forms.

The *śakti* cult is not traceable in the Vedas; still the traits of motherland apparently prevailed in Vedic thought. Several goddesses are mentioned therein. All these would indicate the existence of the concept of motherhood and aspects of *śakti* or power in the Vedic period. But whether this concept could be equated with that of the Mother goddess is a problem which requires further examination. In the later Upaniṣadic works it clearly refers to the *śakti* cult. Both the *Kaulopaniṣad* and *Tarakopaṇisad* specifically allude to *śakti* worship but their precise dates cannot be determined. In the *Śāktopaniṣad*s, which discuss about the various forms of Devī, like *Bhavanopaṇisad*, *Saubhāgya-lakṣmīupaniṣad*, *Tripuratāpnīyopaniṣad* and others. In the *Devīupaniṣad* dedicated to Ādividyā, Devī says, 'I am of the nature of *Brahman*. From me is the world of the nature of Prakṛti, and Puruṣa void and non-void. I am pleasure and pain. I am the quintuplicated and non-religious element. In short I am the entire Universe.' In the *Rāmāyaṇa*, wherein the sage Viśvāmitra teaches Rāma and his brother Lakṣmaṇa the *mantra*s Bala and Atibala, which enshrined the secrets of the new weapons, the expression has been claimed to exemplify the types of knowledge of superhuman efficiency. The terms have also been supposed to be reminiscent of Śākta literature terminology in which can be seen Śākta literary works. Śaktis may be found depicted iconographically in any one of the three aspects — the calm, the terrible or the ugliest as distinguished by the circumstances under which they are worshipped. When ordinarily represented as the consorts of the gods, they are mild and of pleasing appearance and have only two hands, in one of which they hold a lotus or *nīlotpalam* bud. More often the goddesses have independent existence, when they are represented as mild.

The Vaiṣṇavite goddesses being few in number are mostly of *sāttvika* type, but the Śaivite goddesses are more often very wild, fearful and even grotesque. Before passing on to the consideration of the several types of the *śakti* goddess it must be noted that they are in general associated with mystic charms or geometrical figures known as *cakras*, with conventional geometrical designs and mystic symbols. Associated with these *yantras* or *cakras*, *śakti* goddesses are considered to be very powerful and according to the incantations used, they are said to be benefic or malefic in their benefaction to the devotees. Śakti has also been represented as a person. In earlier versions Śakti is claimed to have defeated Viśvāmitra in a debate and consequently the latter went to Jamadagni and, after learning from him the Śaśapurī, he avenged himself on Śakti by burning him in a forest. In the *Jaiminīya Brāhmaṇa*, Śakti is recorded as a son of Vasiṣṭha who was flung into fire by the Viśvāmitra. He has, as Śakti, been depicted as a priest and the eldest son of Vasiṣṭha who had once cursed Kalmāṣapāda for having struck him with a whip for not giving him the right of way in a forest. The king immediately became a demon and the first victim of his hunger was the sage himself, whom he devoured. Andhakāsura brought drops of blood from his body; each drop assumed the shape of the demon when it touched the ground. So Śiva and the gods were much handicapped. To prevent the blood-drops from touching the ground, the Devas sent their Śaktis seven in number to catch them and in the meantime Śiva killed the *asura*. The seven deities, known as Brahmāṇī, Māheśvarī, Kaumārī, Vaiṣṇavī, Vārāhī, Indrāṇī and Cāmuṇḍī, are the female creations of the deities Brahmā, Maheśvara, Kumāra, Viṣṇu, Varāha, Indra and Yama. They are formed with the same weapons and, in general features, resemble the corresponding gods from whom they are derived. [*Glossary of Hinduism*, T. Rengarajan; *A Classical Dictionary of Hindu Mythology and Religion*, J. Dowson]

**Śāligrāma**: In the place of idols which possess certain well-defined anatomical features, worship is also offered to other objects which may be described as shapeless, of which the most important are the *śāligrāma*s and the *bāṇaliṅga*s which the Vaiṣṇavites and the Śaivites respectively hold in high esteem. A *śāligrāma* at least, according to geological notion, is believed to be a finite siliceous much-eroded ammonite shell found only in the Himālayan rivers and more especially in the river Gaṇḍakī, one of the tributary of the Ganges, which flows through Nepal. It is usually a rounded, well-polished stone, having at times one or several holes with visible spiral grooves inside them, resembling the *cakra*. It is on account of this peculiar configuration that a *śāligrāma* is considered as the symbol of Viṣṇu. To strengthen this relationship, the *Varāha Purāṇa* cites a legend according to which the goddess Gaṇḍakī, personifying the river of the same name, prayed to Viṣṇu, who appeared in the stream Gaṇḍakī as *śāligrāma*s and ordained that every one worshipping the *śāligrāma* stone would attain the same benefits as would accrue by worshipping the lord himself in other forms. Such forms became the replica of Viṣṇu and though *śāligrāma*s do not come precisely under the purview of the present study, it would be interesting to know something about them. There are a few treatises dealing with the characteristics and varieties of these sacred stones as several *mūrti*s or forms are to be distinguished among the *śāligrāma*s. The symbol of coitus is indicated by the *liṅga* inserted in its receptacle, the *argha* or *yoni*. A ring at the bottom of a pillar is also indicative of the union of the two principles. This purpose, the number and size of the opening, of the spirals and the colour of the *śāligrāma* are taken into account to distinguish them. *Śāligrāma*s, though normally jet black in colour, are also of other colours. The common specimen have one of these hues: brownish, black deep brown, deep green, red and even white. The size of the *śāligrāma* is an important factor. While some are very small, just the size of a pea, several *śāligrāma*s are very big, almost gigantic in size. Usually it is believed that in ordinary households, a *śāligrāma* should be of medium size which can be held conveniently in one's palm. The opening, its size and nature also account for the sanctity of the *śāligrāma*s. *Śāligrāma*s with small openings, with a definite number of spirals, are the most sought for by householders for their daily *pūjā*. There are innumerable varieties of *śāligrāmas* — as many as about one hundred and twenty *muhūrtas*. Some *śāligrāmas* which are of lighter colour are said to represent *vyūha* forms of Viṣṇu-Vāsudeva, Saṁkarṣaṇa and Aniruddha. Small broken ones are called *sudarśanas* if they contain at least one complete spiral and such of those *śāligrāmas* that are merely spherical with no openings or *cakras* are called Hiraṇyagarbhas. [*Hindu Mythology*, T.R.R. Iyengar; *South Indian Images*, T.N. Srinivasan]

**Saptarṣis**: The *saptaṛṣis* (seven great *ṛṣis*), with the six Pleiads as their wives, are represented by the seven stars of the constellation of the Great Bear. To reconcile the difficulty of six women being considered the wives of seven men, the following explanation is given. The seven *ṛṣis* with their seven wives lived together in the North Pole. Agni happened to see the ladies and fell in love with them but he knew they were virtuous women and hence wandered about the world to cool his passion when Svāhā, daughter of Dakṣa, fell in love with him when she saw him. She came to know of his passion for the *ṛṣis*' wives and assuming the form of each of the wives in turn had relations with him six times. This was witnessed by some wandering celestials who circulated slanderous rumours about the wives of the *ṛṣis*, who drove them away from their original abode to the position of the Pleiads. Arundhatī, wife of Vasiṣṭha, was not suspected and was allowed to remain with her husband. She is the small star seen near the constellation of the Great Bear. The Pleiads, we have already noticed, nursed Kārttikeya, the god of war, and in that myth they are mentioned as the daughters of six *rājās*. The story has parallel in Greek mythology according to which Bacchus, the god of wine, was nursed by the Pleiads all of whom, when he came to power, he translated to the heaven. The Greek account says the Pleiads were originally seven, but due to a quarrel one of the sisters left for the North Pole, and she is Arundhatī of the Hindus. Most of the legends connected with the *ṛṣis* are found in the *Rāmāyaṇa*. They lived in the great forests practising austerities and were the friends or family priests of Daśaratha and Rāma. They enjoyed great occult powers and travelled through the three worlds at will. In the *tretā-yuga* in which Rāma lived good men were like gods and the celestials conversed with mortals, and hence the apparent confusion of mortals with celestials. The *ṛṣis* and some of the legends connected with them are as follows:

1. ***Kaśyapa***: The sage is noted for his prolific nature. Many *deva*s were born of him by his wife Aditi of whom the twelve Ādityas are the most prominent. He is the father of most of the *asura*s too who were born of his wife Diti and hence called *daitya*s. Garuḍa, the *vāhana* of Viṣṇu, was born of his third wife,Vinatā. Most of the popular mansions are, in some accounts, spoken of as the daughters of Kaśyapa. According to *Mahābhārata*, the *Rāmāyaṇa* and the Purāṇas, he was the son of Maricī, the son of Brahmā and he was father of Vivasvat, the father of Manu, the progenitor of mankind. The *Śatapatha Brāhmaṇa* gives a different and not very intelligible account of his origin thus: "Having assumed the form of a tortoise Prajāpati created offspring. That which he created he made (*akarot*); hence the word *kūrma* (tortoise). Kaśyapa means tortoise; hence men say, 'All creatures are descendants of Kaśyapa'. . . ."

2. ***Viśvāmitra***: A celebrated sage, who was born a kṣatriya but by intense austerities raised himself to the brāhmaṇa caste, and became one of the seven great *ṛṣi*s. According to the *Ṛgveda* he was son of a king named Kuśika, a descendant of Kuśa, but later authorities make him the son of Gāthin or Gādhi, king of Kānyakubja, and a descendant of Puru; so Viśvāmitra is declared in the *Harivaṁśa* to be 'at once a Paurava and a Kauśika' by lineage. According to some, Gādhi was of the Kuśika race, descended from Kuśika. Viśvāmitra is called Gādhija and Gāndhinandana, 'son of Gādhi'. The story of Viśvāmitra's birth, as told in the *Viṣṇu Purāṇa*, is

that Gādhi had a daughter named Satyavatī, whom he gave in marriage to an old brāhmaṇa of the race of Bhṛgu named Ṛcika. The wife being a kṣatriya, her husband was desirous that she might bear a son having the qualities of a *Brahman*, and he gave her a dish of food, which he had prepared to effect this object. He also gave her mother a dish intended to make her conceive a son with the character of a warrior. At the instigation of the mother the dishes were exchanged, so the mother gave birth to Viśvāmitra, the son of a kṣatriya with the qualities of a brāhmaṇa and Satyavatī bore Jamadagni, the father of Paraśurāma, the warrior brāhmaṇa and destroyer of the kṣatriyas.

The most noteworthy and important feature in the legends of Viśvāmitra is the active and enduring struggle between him and the brāhmaṇa *ṛṣi* Vasiṣṭha, a fact that is frequently alluded to in the *Ṛgveda* and is supposed to typify the contentions between the brāhmaṇas and the kṣatriyas for superiority. Both these *ṛṣi*s occupy a prominent position in the *Ṛgveda*. Viśvāmitra being the *ṛṣi* of the hymns in the third *maṇḍala*, which contains the celebrated verse Gāyatrī, and Vasiṣṭha of those of the seventh. Each of them was at different times the *purohita* of king Sudās, a position of considerable importance and power, the possession of which stimulated if it did not cause their rivalry. The two sages cursed each other, and carried their enmity into deeds of violence. Viśvāmitra's hundred sons are represented as having been eaten up by the breath of Vasiṣṭha. On the other hand, the hundred sons of Vasiṣṭha were, according to one legend, eaten by King Kalmāṣapāda, into whom a man-eating *rākṣasa* had entered under the influence of Viśvāmitra or, according to another legend, they were reduced to ashes by Viśvāmitra's curse, 'and reborn as degraded outcasts for seven hundred births'. The *Aitareya Brāhmaṇa* states that Viśvāmitra had a hundred sons, but that when he adopted his nephew Śunaḥśephas he proposed to make him the eldest of his sons. Fifty of them assented, and them Viśvāmitra blessed that they should abound in cattle and sons; the other and elder fifty dissented, and them he cursed 'that their progeny should possess the furthest ends' and from them have descended many of the border tribes and most of the *dasyus*. The *Mahābhārata* has a legend of Viśvāmitra having commanded the river Sarasvatī to bring his rival Vasiṣṭha that he might kill him, and of having turned it into blood when it flowed in another direction and carried Vasiṣṭha out of his reach.

Viśvāmitra's relationship to Jamadagni naturally places him in a prominent position in the *Rāmāyaṇa*. Here the old animosity between him and Vasiṣṭha again appears. He as a king paid a visit to Vasiṣṭha's hermitage, and was most hospitably entertained; but he wished to obtain Vasiṣṭha's wondrous cow, the Kāmadhenu, which had furnished all the dainties of the feast. His offers were immense, but were all declined. The cow resisted and broke away when he attempted to take her by force, and when he battled for her, his armies were defeated by the hosts summoned up by the cow, and his hundred sons were reduced to ashes in a movement by the blast of Vasiṣṭha's mouth. A long and fierce combat followed between Vasiṣṭha and Viśvāmitra, in which the latter was defeated; the kṣatriya had to submit to the humiliation of acknowledging his inferiority to the brāhmaṇa, and he therefore resolved to work out his own elevation to the Brāhmaṇical order.

While he was engaged in austerities for accomplishing his object of becoming a brāhmaṇa he became connected with King Triśaṅku. This monarch was a descendant of king of Ikṣavāku, and desired to perform a sacrifice in virtue of which he might ascend bodily to heaven. His priest, Vasiṣṭha, declared it to be impossible, and that priest's hundred sons, on being applied, refused to undertake what their father had declined. When the king told them that he would seek some other means of accomplishing his object, they condemned him to become a *cāṇḍāla*. In this condition he had resort to Viśvāmitra, and he, taking pity on him, raised him to heaven in his bodily form, notwithstanding the opposition of the sons of Vasiṣṭha. The *Harivaṁśa* version of this story is different. Triśaṅku, also called Satyavrata, had attempted the abduction of the young wife of a citizen. For this his father banished him, and condemned him to 'the performance of a silent penance for twelve years'. During his exile there was a famine, and Triśaṅku succoured and supported the wife and family of Viśvāmitra, who were reduced to the direst extremity in that sage's absence. Vasiṣṭha, the family priest, had done nothing to assuage the wrath of the aggrieved father, and this offended Triśaṅku. At the end of his penance, being in want of meat, he killed Vasiṣṭha's wonder-working cow and partook of her flesh; for this act Vasiṣṭha gave him the name of Triśaṅku, 'guilty of three sins'. Viśvāmitra was grateful for the assistance rendered by Triśaṅku, and gave him the choice of a boon. He begged that he might ascend bodily to heaven. Viśvāmitra then installed Triśaṅku in his father's kingdom, 'and in spite of the resistance of the gods and of Vasiṣṭha he exalted the king alive to heaven'.

The *Mahābhārata* and the *Rāmāyaṇa* tell the story of Viśvāmitra's amour with Menakā. His austerities had so alarmed the gods that Indra sent this *apsaras* to seduce Viśvāmitra 'by the display of her charms and the exercise of all her allurements'. She succeeded, and the result was the birth of Śakuntalā. Viśvāmitra at length became ashamed of his passion, and 'dismissing the nymph with gentle accents, he retired to the northern mountains, where he practised severe austerities for a thousand years'. He is also said to have had an amour with the nymph Rambhā. The result of the struggle between Vasiṣṭha and Viśvāmitra is thus told in the *Rāmāyaṇa*: 'Vasiṣṭha, being propitiated by the gods, became reconciled to Viśvāmitra, and recognised his claim to all the prerogatives of a brāhmaṇa *ṛṣi*. Viśvāmitra, too, having attained the Brāhmaṇical rank, paid all honour to Vasiṣṭha. The *Rāmāyaṇa* gives many particulars of Viśvāmitra's connection with Rāma. It was Viśvāmitra who prevailed upon king Daśaratha to send his son Rāma for the protection of the brāhmaṇas from the attacks of Rāvaṇa and his *rākṣasa*s. He acted as his *guru*, and returned with Rāma to Ayodhyā, where the prince obtained the hand of Sītā.

In the *Mārkaṇḍeya Purāṇa* and other Purāṇas the story is told of Viśvāmitra's implacable persecution of king Hariścandra, one result of which was that Vasiṣṭha and Viśvāmitra cursed each other so that they were turned into birds, and fought most furiously till Brahmā put an end to the conflict, restored them to their natural forms, and compelled them to be reconciled.

3. ***Atri***: A *ṛṣi*, son of Ūrva and grandson of Bhṛgu. His wife Aruṣī describes him in the *Mahābhārata* as son of the sage Cyavana. From his race he is called Bhārgava. The *Mahābhārata* relates that a king named Kṛtavīrya was very liberal to his priests of the race of Bhṛgu, and that they grew rich upon his munificence. After his death, his descendants who had fallen into poverty begged help from the Bhṛgus but met with no liberal response. Some of them buried their money and when this was discovered the impoverished kṣatriyas were so exasperated that they slew all the Bhṛgus down to the children in the womb. One woman concealed her unborn child in her thigh, and the kṣatriyas, being informed of this, sought the child to kill it, but the child issued forth from its mother's thigh with lustre and blinded the persecutors. As it was

produced from the thigh the child received the name of Aurva. The sage's austerities alarmed both gods and men and he for a long time refused to mitigate his wrath against the kṣatriyas, but at the persuasion of the *pitṛ*s, he cast the fire of his anger into the sea, where it became a being with the face of horse called Hayaśiras. While he was living in the forest he prevented the wife of king Bāhu from burning herself with her husband's corpse. Thus he saved the life of her son, with whom she had been pregnant for seven years. When the child was born he was called Sagara; Aurva was his preceptor, and bestowed on him the *āgneyāstra* or fiery weapon with which he conquered the barbarians who invaded his country. Aurva had a son named Ṛcika, who was father of Jamadagni. The *Harivaṁśa* gives another version of the legend about the offspring of Aurva. The sage was urged by his friends to beget children. He consented, but he foretold that his progeny would live by the destruction of others. Then he produced from his thigh a devouring fire, which cried out with a loud voice, 'I am hungry; let me consume the world'. The various regions were soon in flames, when Brahmā interfered to save his creation, and promised the son of Aurva a suitable abode and maintenance. The abode was to be at Baḍavatmukha, the mouth of the ocean; for Brahmā was born and rests in the ocean, and he and the newly-produced fire were to consume the world together at the end of each age, and at the end of time to devour all things with the gods, *asura*s and *rākṣasa*. The name Aurva thus signifies, shortly, the submarine's fire. It is also called Baḍavānala and Samvarttaka. It is represented as a flame with a horse's head, and is also called Kākadhvaja, from carrying a banner on which there is a cow.

4. ***Vasiṣṭha***: [Most wealthy.] A celebrated Vedic sage to whom many hymns are ascribed. According to Manu he

was one of the seven great *ṛṣis* and one of the ten Prajāpatis. There was a special rivalry between him and the sage Viśvāmitra, who raised himself from the kṣatriya to the brāhmaṇa caste. Vasiṣṭha was the possessor of a cow of plenty called Nandinī, who had the power of granting him all things he desired; hence his name. A law book is attributed to him, or to another of the same name. Though Vasiṣṭha is classed among the Prajāpatis who sprang from Brahmā, a hymn in the *Ṛgveda* and the commentaries thereon assign him a different origin, or rather a second birth, and represent him and the sage Agastya to have sprung from Mitra and Varuṇa. The hymn says, 'Thou, O Vasiṣṭha, art a son of Mitra and Varuṇa, born a brāhmaṇa from the soul of Urvaśī. All the gods placed in the vessel there the drop which had fallen through divine contemplation.' The comment on this hymn says, 'When these two Ādityas beheld the *apsaras* Urvaśī at a sacrifice their seed fell from them. It fell on many places, into a jar, into water, and on the ground. The *muni* Vasiṣṭha was produced on the ground, while Agastya was born in the jar.'

There is a peculiar hymn attributed to Vasiṣṭha in the *Ṛgveda*, beginning 'protector of the dwelling', which the commentators explain as having been addressed by him to a housedog which barked as he entered the house of Varuṇa by night to obtain food after a three-day fast. By it the dog was appeased and put to sleep, 'wherefore these verses are to be recited on similar occasions by thieves and burglars'. In the same Veda and in the *Aitareya Brāhmaṇa*, Vasiṣṭha appears as the family priest of King Sudās, a position to which his rival Viśvāmitra aspired. This is amplified in the *Mahābhārata* where he is not the priest of Sudās but of his son Kalmāṣapāda, who bore the patronymic Saudāsa. It is said that his rival Viśvāmitra was jealous and wished to have this office for himself, but the king preferred Vasiṣṭha.

Vasiṣṭha had a hundred sons, the eldest of whom was named Saktr̥. He, meeting the king in the road, was ordered to get out of the way, but he civilly replied that the path was his, for by the law a king must cede the way to a brāhmaṇa. The king struck him with a whip, and he retorted by cursing the king to become a man-eater. Viśvāmitra was present, but invisible, and he maliciously commanded a man-devouring *rākṣasa* to enter, and his first victim was Saktr̥. The same fate befell all the hundred sons, and Vasiṣṭha's grief was boundless. He endeavoured to destroy himself in various ways. He cast himself from the top of Mount Meru, but the rocks he fell upon were like cotton. He threw himself into the sea with a heavy stone tied to his neck, but the waves cast him on dry land. He plunged into a river swollen by rain, but although he had bound his arms with cords the stream loosened his bonds and landed him unbound on its banks. From this the river received the name of Vipāśā. He threw himself into another river full of alligators, but the river rushed away in a hundred directions, and was consequently called Śatadru. Finding that he could not kill himself, he returned to his hermitage, and was met in the woods by King Kalmāṣapāda, who was about to devour him, but Vasiṣṭha exorcised him and delivered him from the curse he had borne for twelve years. The sage then directed the king to return to his kingdom and pay due respect to brāhmaṇas. Kalmāṣapāda begged Vasiṣṭha to give him offspring. He promised to do so, and 'being solicited by the king to beget an heir to the throne, the queen became pregnant by him and brought forth a son at the end of the twelve years'.

Another legend in the *Mahābhārata* represents Viśvāmitra as commanding the river Sarasvatī to bring Vasiṣṭha, so that he might kill him. By direction of Vasiṣṭha the river obeyed the command, but on approaching Viśvāmitra, who stood ready armed, it promptly carried away Vasiṣṭha in another direction.

The enmity of Vasiṣṭha and Viśvāmitra comes out very strongly in the *Rāmāyaṇa*. Viśvāmitra ruled the earth for many thousand years as king, but he coveted the wondrous cow of plenty, which he had seen at Vasiṣṭha's hermitage, and attempted to take her away by force. A great battle followed between the hosts of king Viśvāmitra and the warriors produced by the cow to support her master. A hundred of Viśvāmitra's sons were reduced to ashes by the blast of Vasiṣṭha's mouth, and Viśvāmitra, being utterly defeated, abdicated and retired to the Himālaya. The two met again after an interval and fought in single combat. Viśvāmitra was again worsted by the Brāhmaṇical order, and resolved to work out his own elevation to the Brāhmaṇical order so as to be upon equality with his rival. He accomplished his object and became a priest and Vasiṣṭha suffered from his power. The hundred sons of Vasiṣṭha denounced Viśvāmitra for presuming, though a kṣatriya, to act as a priest. This so incensed Viśvāmitra that he 'by a curse doomed the sons of Vasiṣṭha to be reduced to ashes and reborn as degraded outcasts for seven hundred births'. Eventually, Vasiṣṭha, being propitiated by the gods, became reconciled to Viśvāmitra, and recognised his claim to all the prerogatives of a brāhmaṇa *ṛṣi*, and Viśvāmtira paid all honour to Vasiṣṭha.

A legend in the *Viṣṇu Purāṇa* represents Vasiṣṭha as being requested by Nimi, a son of Ikṣavāku, to officiate at a sacrifice which was to last for a thousand years. The sage pleaded a prior engagement to Indra for five hundred years, but offered to come at the end of that period. The king made no remark and Vasiṣṭha taking silence as assent, returned as he had proposed. He then found that Nimi had engaged the *ṛṣi* Gautama to perform the sacrifice, and this so angered him that he cursed the king to lose his corporeal form. Nimi retorted the curse, and in consequence the vigour of Vasiṣṭha entered into the vigour of Mitra and Varuṇa. Vasiṣṭha, however, received from them another body when their seed had fallen from them at the sight of Urvaśī.

In the *Mārkaṇḍeya Purāṇa*, he appears as the family priest of Hariścandra. He was so incensed at the treatment shown to that monarch by Viśvāmitra, that he cursed that sage to be transformed into a crane. His adversary retorted by dooming him to become another bird, and in the form of two monstrous birds, they fought so furiously that the course of the universe was disturbed and many creatures perished. Brahmā at length put an end to the conflict by restoring them to their natural forms and compelling them to be reconciled.

According to the *Viṣṇu Purāṇa,* Vasiṣṭha had for wife Ūrjā, one of the daughters of Dakṣa, and by her he had seven sons. The *Bhāgavata Purāṇa* gives him Arundhatī for wife. The *Viṣṇu Purāṇa* also makes him the family priest of the house of Īkṣavāku; and he was not only contemporary with Ikṣvāku himself, but with his descendants down to the sixty-first generation. 'Vasiṣṭha, according to all accounts, must have been possessed of a vitality altogether superhuman', for it appears that the name Vasiṣṭha is 'used not to denote merely a person belonging to a family so-called, but to represent the founder of the family himself as taking part in the transactions of many successive ages'. 'It is clear that Vasiṣṭha, although he is frequently designated in post-Vedic writings as a brāhmaṇa, was, according to some authorities, not really such in any proper sense of the word, as in the accounts which are given of his birth he is declared to have been either a mind-born son of Brahmā, or the son of Mitra and Varuṇa and the *apsarsas* Urvaśī, or to have had some other supernatural origin.' Vasiṣṭha's descendants are called Vāsiṣthas and Vāśkalas.

5. ***Gautama***: He is reputed to be the *guru* of Indra and we have already noticed the peccadillos of the king of the gods, with Gautama's wife Ahalayā. On one occasion the six *ṛṣis* plotted against Gautama and his wife, and persuaded Gaṇeśa to appear before Gautama in the form of a cow and provoke him. Gautama was provoked; he struck the cow with a blade of grass and the cow died. This had the desired effect and Gautama fell into the snare of his brothers.

6. ***Jamadagni***: He was the father of Paraśurāma and the husband of Reṇukā. The sons of Kārttavīrya killed him and this made Paraśurāma swear undying vengeance on all kṣatriyas.

7. ***Bharadvāja***: This *ṛṣi* had his hermitage in the forests of Daṇḍaka and is mentioned in the *Rāmāyaṇa* as a great friend and well-wisher of Rāma. During the exile of this prince he often visited the hermitage of Bharadvāja. After Rāma's conquest of Laṅkā Bharadvāja bestowed a boon on the prince by which all the trees from Bharadvāja's hermitage to Ayodhyā stood in bloom.

[*Hindu Mythology*, T.R.R. Iyengar; *Epics, Myths, and Legends of India*, P. Thomas]

**Śaramā**: In the *Ṛgveda* the dog of Indra and mother of the two dogs called, after their mother, Śarameyas, who each had four eyes, and were the watchdogs of Yama. Śaramā is said to have pursued and recovered the cows stolen by the Paṇis, a myth which has been supposed to mean that Śaramā is the same as Uṣas, the dawn, and that the cows represent the rays of the sun carried away by night. [*Hindu Mythology*, T.R.R. Iyengar; *Ṛgveda*]

**Śarameyas**: The two children of Śaramā, Indra's watchdog; they were the watchdogs of Yama and each had four eyes. They have been compared with the Greek Hermes.

**Śaraṇyu**: [The fleet runner] A daughter of Tvaṣṭṛ. She has been identified with the Greek Erinnys. The beginning of this myth is in a hymn of the *R̥gveda*, which says, '(1) Tvaṣṭr̥ makes a wedding for his daughter. (Hearing) this the whole world assembles. The mother of Yama, the wedded wife of the great Vivasvat, disappeared. (2) They concealed the immortal from mortals. Making of like appearance, they gave her to Vivasvat. Śaraṇyu bore the two Aśvins, and when she had done so she deserted the two twins.' In the *Nirukta* the story is expanded as follows: 'Śaraṇyu, the daughter of Tvaṣṭr̥, bore twins to Vivasvat, the son of Aditi. She then substituted for herself another female of similar appearance, and fled in the form of a mare. Vivasvat in like manner assumed the shape of a horse and followed her. From their intercourse sprang two Aśvins, while Manu was the offspring of Sāvarṇa (or the female of like appearance).' The *Br̥haddevatā* has another version of the same story: 'Tvaṣṭr̥ had twin children, Śaraṇyu and Triśiras. He gave Śaraṇyu in marriage to Vivasvat to whom she bore Yama and Yamī, who also were twins. Creating a female like herself without her husband's knowledge and making the twins over in charge to her, Śaraṇyu took the form of a mare and departed. Vivasvat, in ignorance, begot on the female who was left Manu, the royal *r̥ṣi*, who resembled his father in glory; but discovering that the real Śaraṇyu, Tvaṣṭr̥'s daughter, had gone away, Vivasvat followed her quickly taking the shape of a horse of the same species as she. Recognising him in that form, she approached him with the desire of sexual connection, which he gratified. In their haste his seed fell on the ground, and she being desirous of offspring, smelled it. From this act sprang the two Kumāras, Nāsatya and Dasra, who were lauded as Aśvins. [*Hindu Mythology*, T.R.R. Iyengar; *India in the Vedic Age*, P.L. Bhargava]

**Sārasvata**: In the *Mahābhārata*, the *r̥ṣi* Sārasvata is represented as being the son of the personified river Sarasvatī. In a time of great drought he was fed with fish by his mother and so was enabled to keep up his knowledge of the Vedas, while other brāhmaṇas were reduced to such straits for the means of subsistence that study was neglected and the Vedas were lost.

When the drought was over, the brāhmaṇas flocked to him for instruction, and 60,000 acquired a knowledge of the Vedas from him. 'This legend,' says Wilson, 'appears to indicate the revival or, more probably, the introduction of the Hindu ritual by the race of brāhmaṇas, or the people called Sārasvata,' who dwelt near the Sarasvatī river. Sārasvata brāhmaṇas still dwell in the Panjab and are met with in many other parts.

**Sarasvatī**: [Watery, elegant.] In the Vedas, Sarasvatī is primarily a river, but is celebrated in the hymns both as a river and a deity. The Sarasvatī river was one boundary to Brahmāvartta, the home of the early Āryans, and was to them, in all likelihood, a sacred river, as the Ganges has long been to their descendants. As a river goddess Sarasvatī is lauded for the fertilising and purifying powers of her waters, and as the bestower of fertility, fatness and wealth. Her position as Vāc, the goddess of speech, finds no mention in the *Ṛgveda*, but is recognised by the *Brāhmaṇas* and the *Mahābhārata*. Dr. Muir endeavours to account for her acquisition of this character. He says, 'When once the river had acquired a divine character it was quite natural that she should be regarded as the patroness of the ceremonies which were celebrated on the margin of her holy waters, and that her direction and blessing should be invoked as essential to their proper performance and success. The connection into which she was thus brought with sacred rites may have led to the further step of imagining her to have an influence on the composition of the hymns which formed so important a part of the proceedings, and of identifying her with Vāc, the goddess of speech'.

Sarasvatī is known from the early period mainly as the goddess of speech and wisdom. In *Manu-sumṛti*, offerings to her are prescribed for the expiation of falsehood. Although Macdonell thinks that in the *Ṛgveda* she is nothing more than a river-goddess, there are also passages in that work which clearly connect her with wisdom and instruction. According to Banerjee the fact that Vedic learning developed on the banks of Sarasvatī seems to have played some part in making her the goddess of learning. In the 10th *maṇḍala* of *Ṛgveda*, she is described as the embodiment of the *śakti* principle. In the *Vājasaneyī Saṁhitā*, however, Sarasvatī's connection with speech becomes quite clear when she communicates vigor to Indra by her speech. In the *Brāhmaṇa*s and chiefly in the *Śathapata Brāhmaṇa*, she is repeatedly described as the personification of speech. In the *Āśvalāyana* script she is repeatedly described as the intelligence, which is personified as a newborn child. In the *Pāraskara* script also she is requested to bestow insight and intelligence upon her worshippers. In the later mythology, she becomes the only accepted goddess of learning. In the Epics, she is called the tongue of Viṣṇu and in the *Mahābhārata* she gets the highly flattering title 'the mother of the Vedas'. As the presiding deity of learning it was natural that Sarasvatī became the goddess of arts and music. The *vīṇā* became her special instrument. In the *Kāmasūtra* of Vātsyāyana, the Nāgarakas flock every fortnight to the temple of the goddess Sarasvatī to witness dramatic performances. But the personality of Sarasvatī has other aspects also. In the *Śatapatha Brāhmaṇa* she often appears as a healer-goddess. Her conception as a healer and physician may be traced to a Vedic passage where she, along with the Aśvins, is said to have refreshed Indra. According to the *Kathāsaritsāgara* of Somadeva the ladies of Pāṭaliputra used the potent drugs of Sarasvatī to cure some sick people. Sarasvatī is represented in the *Śatapatha Brāhmaṇa* as a deity of prosperity also. In this connection one may recall that as a river-goddess in the *Ṛgveda*. Sarasvatī has been described as yielding riches of every kind and is invoked to give health, plenty and nourishment. In the passage of the *Mahābhārata*, Sarasvatī is associated with the science of judicature. In later times Sarasvatī, the wife of Brahmā, is the goddess of speech and learning, inventories of the Sanskrit language and Devanāgarī letters, and patroness of the arts and sciences. In *Ṛgveda* she describes herself thus, 'I range with the Rudras, with the Vāsus, with the Ādityas and with the Viśvadevas. I uphold both the sun and the ocean, the firmament (Indra) and fire, and both the Aśvins.' I support the moon and the sun. I grant wealth to the honest votary who performs sacrifice, offers oblations, and satisfies me, who am the queen, the conferer of wealth, the possessor of knowledge and the first of such as merit worship, present everywhere and provider of all beings. He who eats food through he sees whom or me breathe or who hears, through me yet know me not am lost; hear then the faith, which I pronounce. Even I declare this self who is worshipped by gods and men; I make strong whom I choose, I make him Brahmā holy and wise for Rudra, I bend the bow top, slay the demon, foe of Brahmā; for the plea I make war on their foes, and I pervade heaven and earth. I bore the father on the head of this and my origin is in the midst of the ocean, and therefore do I pervade all beings, and touch this heaven with my form. Originating all beings I pass alike the breeze, I am above this heaven, beyond this earth, and what is the great one that am I.' Gāyatrī is considered a synonym for Sarasvatī; one myth speaks of her as the second wife of Brahmā. In a sacrifice Brahmā performed, he, as a married god, had to do certain rites together with his wife but Sarasvatī was found absent. A messenger was sent to call her and she told him that she was busy in her toilet and Brahmā could very well wait for some time. The messenger conveyed Sarasvatī's message to Brahmā and the god in his wrath asked some of the assembled gods to find another wife for him. They brought to him Gāyatrī, the daughter of a sage, and Brahmā married her and performed the rites. On the belated arrival of Sarasvatī there was a terrible row. Gāyatrī, however, pacified her by her eloquence and agreed to occupy a position subordinate to her. In certain accounts Gāyatrī is said to be the only wife of Brahmā, and Sarasvatī of Gaṇeśa. She is usually represented with four hands and has as her *āyudha*s, an *akṣamālā* and a bundle of *cadjan* leaves. Usually her lower right hand is in *vyākhyāna mudrā* and in the other she carries a lotus at times. She wears the *kirīṭa*, the *yajñopavīta* and other ornaments. Sometimes she is represented as playing on a *vīṇā*. She usually wears white-coloured garments, is without any superfluity of limbs and not unfrequently of a graceful figure, wears a slender crescent on her brow and sits on a lotus — Wilson. The same authority states that 'the Vaiṣṇavas of Bengal have a popular legend that she was the wife of Viṣṇu, as were also Lakṣmī and Gaṅgā. The ladies disagreed; Sarasvatī, like the other prototype of learned ladies Minerva, being something of a termagant, and Viṣṇu finding that one wife was as much as he could manage, transferred Sarasvatī to Brahmā and Gaṅgā to Śiva and contented himself with Lakṣmī alone. Sarasvatī is seated upon a white lotus, and is of white complexion and draped in white clothes. She has four hands. In one of the right hands she holds an *akṣamālā*, and the right hand is in the pose called *vyākhyāna-mudrā* and in the left hand she carries respectively a book and a white lotus. Surrounding her there are standing a number of *muni*s or sages engaged in worshipping her. She wears a *yajñopavīta* on her person and has the *jaṭā-mukuṭa* on the head; otherwise also she is decked with various ornaments. The *Viṣṇudharmottara* tells us that Sarasvatī should be standing upon a white lotus and further substitutes the *kamaṇḍalu* in the place of the lotus in one of the right hands and makes the right hand with the *vyākhyāna mudrā* carry, instead of *vīṇā*, the bamboo stem. In her standing posture she should be concidered as a *sambhaga* image. The *Aṁśumadbhedāgama* says that the *kuṇḍala*s of Sarasvatī should be made of rubies but the *Pūrva-karaṅgama* prescribes for her ear-rings of pearl. Sarasvatī is described in the *Sūta Saṁhitā* of the *Skanda Purāṇa* as a female figure having a *jaṭā-mukuṭa* on her head, in which a crescent moon is inserted. Her neck is of blue colour and she has three eyes. The *Devī-Māhātmya* of the *Mārkaṇḍeya Purāṇa* describes in her hands *aṅkuśa*, a *vīṇā*, an *akṣamālā* and a *pustaka*. In relation to the sculptures and castings of goddesses in south India, it may be observed that in groups consisting of a god and two goddesses on either side, the goddess on the right is seen wearing the *kūca-bandha*, just as is worn by the Nambūdarī women of Kerala under the name of *mulaikkachchu* or breast band, and that the goddess on the left does not wear such a bodice. This is a noteworthy peculiarity. It may be particularly noticed in relation to the group of images consisting of Viṣṇu and his consorts Bhū and Śrī. Other names of Sarasvatī are Bhāratī, Brāhmī, Pūtkarī, Śāradā, and Vāgīśvarī. The river is now called Sarsuti. It falls from the Himālayas and is lost in the sands of the desert. In ancient times it flowed on to the sea. A passage in the *Ṛgveda* says of it, 'She who goes on pure from the mountains as far as the sea.' [*A Classical Dictionary of Hindu Mythology and Religion*, J. Dowson; *Hindu Dictionary*, T. Rengarajan; *Epics, Myths and Legends of India*, P. Thomas]

**Śārṅga**: The bow of Kṛṣṇa.

**Sarva**: A Vedic deity; the destroyer. Afterwards a name of Śiva and one of the Rudras.

**Śaśada**: [Hare-eater] A name given to Vikukṣi.

**Śaśi**: The moon, so-called from the marks on the moon being considered to resemble a hare.

**Śatakratu**: The god of a hundred rites. Indra.

**Śatarūpā**: [The hundred formed.] The first woman. According to one account she was the daughter of Brahmā, and from their incestuous intercourse the first Manu, named Svayambhuva, was born. Another account makes her the wife, not the mother, of Manu. The account given by Manu is that Brahmā divided himself into two parts, male and female and from them sprang Manu. She is also called Sāvitrī.

**Sātavāhana**: A name by which Śālivāhana is sometimes called.

**Satī**: A daughter of Dakṣa and wife of Rudra, i.e., Śiva. The *Viṣṇu Purāṇa* states that she abandoned her body in consequence of the anger of Dakṣa. She then became the daughter of Himavatī and Menā. She was named as Umā and married Śiva. The authorities generally agree that she died or killed herself in consequence of the quarrel between her husband and father, and the *Kāśī Khaṇḍa*, a modern work, represents that she entered the fire and became a Satī.

**Satrājit**: Son of Nighna. In return for praise rendered to the sun he beheld the luminary in his proper form, and received from him the wonderful *syamantaka* gem. He lost the gem, but it was recovered and restored to him by Kṛṣṇa. In return he presented Kṛṣṇa with his daughter Satyabhāmā as wife. There had been many suitors for this lady's hand, and one of them named Satyadhanvan, in revenge for her loss, killed Satrājit and carried off the gem, but he was afterwards killed by Kṛṣṇa.

**Śatrughna**: [Foe-destroyer] Twin brother of Lakṣmaṇa and half-brother of Rāma in whom an eighth part of the divinity of Viṣṇu was incarnate. His wife was Śrutakīrti, cousin of Sītā. He fought on the side of Rāma and killed the *rākṣasa* chief, Lavaṇa.

**Satyabhāmā**: Daughter of Satrājit and one of the four chief wives of Kṛṣṇa. She had ten sons, Bhānu, Subhānu, Svarbhānu, Prabhānu, Bhānumat, Candrabhānu, Bṛhadbhānu, Atibhānu, Śrībhānu and Pratibhānu. Kṛṣṇa took her with him to Indra's heaven, and she induced him to bring away the *pārijāta* tree.

**Satyadhṛti**: Son of Saradvat and grandson of sage Gautama. According to the *Viṣṇu Purāṇa* he was father by the nymph Urvaśī of Kṛpa and Kṛpī.

**Satyavrata**: A king of the solar race, descended from Ikṣavāku. He was father of Hariścandra, and is also named Vedas and Triśaṅku. According to the *Ramāyaṇa*, he was a pious king, and was desirous of performing a sacrifice in virtue of which he might ascend bodily to heaven. Vasiṣṭha, his priest, declined to perform it, declaring it impossible. He then applied to Vasiṣṭha's sons, and they condemned him to become a *cāṇḍāla* for his presumption. In his distress and degradation he applied to Viśvāmṭira, who promised to raise him in that form to heaven. Viśvāmitra's intended sacrifice was strongly resisted by the sons of Vasiṣṭha, but he reduced them to ashes, and condemned them to be born again as outcasts for seven thundered births. The wrathful sage bore down all other opposition, and Triśaṅku ascended to heaven. Here his entry was opposed by Indra and the gods, but Viśvāmitra in fury declared that he would create another Indra, or the world should have no Indra at all. The gods were obliged to yield and it was agreed that Triśaṅku, an immortal, should hang with his head downwards and shine among some stars newly called into being by Viśvāmitra.

The *Viṣṇu Purāṇa* gives a simpler version. While Satyavrata was a *cāṇḍāla* and the famine was raging, he supported Viśvāmitra's family by hanging deer's flesh on a tree on the bank of the Ganges, so that they might obtain food without the degradation of receiving it from a *cāṇḍāla*; for this charity Viśvāmitra raised him to heaven. According to the *Harivaṁśa*, Satyavrata or Triśaṅku, when a prince, attempted to carry off the wife of a citizen, in consequence of which his father drove him from home nor did Vasiṣṭha, the family priest, endeavour to soften his father's decision. The period of his exile was a time of famine and he greatly succoured the wife and family of Viśvāmitra, who were in deep distress while the sage was absent far away. He completed his twelve years' exile and penance, and being hungry one day, and having no flesh to eat, he killed Vasiṣṭha's wondrous cow, the Kāmadhenu, and ate thereof himself and gave some to the son of Viśvāmitra. In his rage Vasiṣṭha gave him the name Triśaṅku, as being guilty of three great sins. Viśvāmitra was gratified by the assistance that Satyavrata had rendered to his family; he installed him in his father's kingdom and in spite of the resistance of the gods and of Vasiṣṭha, exalted the king alive to heaven.

**Śaubhari**: A devout sage who, when he was old and emaciated, was inspired with a desire of offspring. He went to king Māndhātṛ, and demanded one of his fifty daughters. Afraid to refuse and yet unwilling to bestow a daughter upon such a suitor, the king temporised, and endeavoured to evade the request. It was at length settled that, if any one of the daughters should accept him as a bridegroom, the king would consent to the marriage. Śaubhari was conducted to the presence of the girls, but on his way he assumed a fair and handsome form so that all the girls were captivated and contended with each other as to who should become his wife. It ended by his marrying them all and taking them home. He caused Viśvakarmā to built for each a separate palace, furnished in the most luxurious manner, and surrounded with exquisite gardens, where they lived a most happy life, each one of them having her husband always present with her, and believing that he was devoted to her and her only. By his wives he had a hundred and fifty sons; but as he found his hopes and desires for them to daily increase and expand, he resolved to devote himself wholly and solely to penance and the worship of Viṣṇu. Accordingly, he abandoned his children and retired with his wives to the forest.

**Savarṇā**: Wife of the sun. The female of like appearance whom Saraṇyu, wife of Vivasvat, substituted for herself when she fled. Manu was the offspring of Savarṇā. This is the version given in the *Nirukta*. In the *Viṣṇu Purāṇa*, Savarṇā is daughter of the ocean, wife of Prācīnabarhiṣ, and mother of the ten Pracetasas.

**Savitṛ**: Savitṛ is celebrated in eleven entire hymns of the *Ṛgveda* and in parts of others, his name being mentioned about 170 times. He is pre-eminently a golden deity. His eyes, hands, tongue, and arms are all golden, his hair is yellow and he wears a tawny garment. He has a golden car, with a golden pole, which is drawn by two radiant steeds. Savitṛ has mightily golden splendour which he diffuses illuminating heaven, earth and air. He raises aloft his strong golden arms with which he arouses and blesses all beings and which extend to the ends of the earth. He travels through the air on dusty paths, and is implored to convey the departed souls to the place where the righteous dwell. Like Sūrya he drives away bad dreams, evil spirits and sorcerers. Savitṛ is often distinguished from Sūrya as when he is said to impel the sun or to declare men sinless to the sun or when he is implored to strengthen the worshipper when the sun has risen. But in other passages it is hardly possible to keep the two deities apart. Savitṛ is connected with the evening as well as the morning, for he brings all beings to rest and awakens them. Savitṛ's special epithet is Bhaga or dispenser, which is often applied to him in the hymns. In fact, one hymn of the *Ṛgveda* is devoted chiefly to the praise of this deity under the name of Bhaga, where he is also called Bhagavān. Like many other gods he is also called *asura*. He observes fixed laws. Indeed sometimes he is extolled as the supreme god as when Indra, Varuṇa, Mitra, Aryaman and Rudra do not dare to break his laws. In one stanza he is besought to stimulate the thoughts of the worshippers who meditate on his excellent glory. This is the famous Savitr̥ stanza, which has been a Morning Prayer in India since the very ancient times. As the upholder of moral law it is Savitr̥ who, in the hymn of the gambler, inspires the latter to desist from gambling and to plough his tillage. The word Savitr̥ is derived from the root *su*, to stimulate. He is thus the great stimulator of life and motion in the world. His name Bah occurs in the form of Bhaga [*Hindu Mythology*, T.R.R. Iyengar; *Epics, Myths and Legends of India*, P. Thomas; *A Classical Dictionary of Hindu Mythology and Religion*, J. Dowson]

**Sāvitrī**: 1. The holy verse of the Veda, commonly called Gāyatrī. 2. A name of Śatarūpā, the daughter and wife of Brahmā, who is sometimes regarded as a personification of the holy verses. 3. Daughter of King Aśvapati, and lover of Satyavān, whom she insisted on marrying, although she was warned by a seer that he had only one year to live. When the fatal day arrived, Satyavān went out to cut wood, and she followed him. There he fell dying to the earth, and she, as she supported him, saw a figure, which told her that he was Yama, king of the dead, and that he had come for her husband's spirit. Yama carried off the spirit towards the shades, but Sāvitrī followed him. Her devotion pleased Yama, and he offered her any boon except the life of her husband. She extorted three such boons from Yama, but still she followed him, and he was finally constrained to restore her husband to life. [*Hindu Mythology*, T.R.R. Iyengar]

**Śeṣa**: King of the serpent race and of the infernal regions called *pātāla*. A serpent with a thousand heads which is the couch and canopy of Viṣṇu whilst sleeping during the intervals of creation. Sometimes Śeṣa is represented as supporting the world, and sometimes as upholding the seven hells. Whenever he yawns he causes an earthquake. At the end of each *kalpa* he vomits venomous fire which destroys all creation. When the gods churned the ocean they made use of Śeṣa as a great rope, which they twisted round the mountain Mandāra, and so used it as a churn. He is represented clothed in purple and wearing a white necklace, holding in one hand a plough and in the other a pestle. He is also called Ananta, 'the endless', as symbol of eternity. His wife was named Anantaśīrṣā. He is sometimes distinct from Vāsukī but generally identified with him. In the Purāṇas he is said to be the son of Kaśyapa and Kadru, and according to some authorities he was incarnate in Balarāma. His hood is called Maṇidvīpa, 'the island of jewels', and his palace, Maṇibhitti, 'jewel-walled'. Śeṣa is usually shown as a standing human figure with the two hands folded in *añjalī* pose and having the five-headed sainthood spread over his keratin. The image of Śeṣa is always installed in Vaiṣṇavite shrines and taken out at the time of festivals along with Garuḍa. [*Hindu Mythology*, T.R.R. Iyengar]

**Siddhas**: A class of semi-divine beings of great purity and holiness, who dwell in the regions of the sky between the earth and the sun. They are said to be 88,000 in number.

**Siṁhikā**: A daughter of Dakṣa and wife of Kaśyapa; also a daughter of Kaśyapa and wife of Vipracittī.

**Śiradhvaja**: An epithet for Janaka.

**Śiśumāra**: [A porpoise] The planetary sphere, which as explained by the *Viṣṇu Purāṇa*, has the shape of a porpoise, Viṣṇu being seated in its heart, and Dhruva or the pole star in its tail. 'As Dhruva revolves, it causes the sun, moon, and other planets to turn round also; and the lunar asterisms follow in its circular path, for all the celestial luminaries are, in fact, bound to the polar star by aerial cords.'

**Sītā**: [A Furrow] In the Veda, Sītā is the furrow or husbandry personified, and worshipped as a deity presiding over agriculture and fruits. In the *Rāmāyaṇa* and later works she is daughter of Janaka, king of Videha and wife of Rāma. The old Vedic idea still adhered to her, for she sprang from a furrow. In the *Rāmāyaṇa* her father Janaka says, 'As I was polishing my field, there sprang from the plough a girl, obtained by me while cleansing my field, and known by name as Sītā. This girl sprung from the earth grew up as my daughter.' Hence she is styled Ayonija, 'not born from the womb'. She is said to have lived before in the *kṛta* age as Vedavatī, and to be in reality the goddess Lakṣmī, in human form, born in the world for bringing about the destruction of Rāvaṇa, the *rākṣasa* king of Laṅkā, who was invulnerable to ordinary means, but doomed to die on account of a woman. Sītā became the wife of Rāma who won her by bending the great bow of Śiva. She was his only wife, and was the embodiment of purity, tenderness, and conjugal affection. She accompanied her husband in his exile, but was carried off from him by Rāvaṇa and kept in his palace at Laṅkā. There he made many efforts to win her to his will but she continued firm against all enticement, threat and terrors, and maintained a dignified tranquillity throughout. When Rāma had slain the ravisher and recovered his wife, he received her coldly, and refused to take her back, for it was hard to believe it possible that she had retained her honour. She asserted her purity in touching language, and resolved to establish it by the ordeal of fire. The pile was raised and she entered the flames in the presence of gods and men, but she remained unhurt and the god of fire brought her forth and placed her in her husband's arms. Notwithstanding this proof of her innocence, jealous thoughts passed through the mind of Rāma and after he had ascended his ancestral throne at Ayodhyā, his people blamed him for taking back a wife who had been in the power of a licentious ravisher. So, although she was pregnant, he banished her and sent her to the hermitage of Vālmikī, where she gave birth to twin sons, Kuśa and Lava. There she lived till the boys were about fifteen years old. One day they strayed to their father's capital. He recognised and acknowledged them and then recalled Sītā. She returned and publicly declared her innocence. But her heart was deeply wounded. She called upon her mother earth to attest her purity, and it did so. The ground opened, and she was taken back into the source from which she had sprung. Rāma was now disconsolate and resolved to quit the mortal life.

Sītā had the appellations of Bhūmija, Dharaṇīsuta and Pārthivī, all meaning 'daughter of the earth'. [*A Classical Dictionary of Hindu Mythology and Religion*, J. Dowson; *Hindu*

*Mythology*, T.R.R. Iyengar; *A Glossary of Hinduism*, T. Rengarajan; *Epics, Myths and Legends of India,* P. Thomas; *Hinduism*, Goldstücker]

**Śiva**: The name Śiva is unknown to the Vedas, but Rudra, another name of this deity, and almost equally common, occurs in the Veda both in the singular and plural and from these, the great deity Śiva and his manifestations, the Rudras have been developed. In the *Ṛgveda*, the word Rudra is used for Agni, and the Maruts are called his sons. In other passages he is distinct from Agni. He is lauded as the lord of songs, the lord of sacrifices, who heals, remedies, is brilliant as the sun; the best and most bountiful of gods, who grants prosperity and welfare to horses and sheep, men, women and cows; the lord of nourishment, who drives away disease, dispenses remedies, and removes sin; but, on the other hand he is the wielder of the thunderbolt, the bearer of bow and arrows, and mounted on his chariot is terrible as a wild beast, destructive and fierce.' In the Vedas the following account of Rudra's origin is given. The Lord of beings was a householder and Uṣā was his wife. A boy was born in a year. The boy wept. Prajāpati said to him, 'Boy, why dost then weep since thou hast been born after toil and austerity?' The boy said, 'My evil has not been taken away, and a name has not been given to me. Give me a name.' Prajāpati said, 'Thou art Rudra.' He was Rudra because he wept — from *rud,* 'to weep'. Many hymns of the *Ṛgveda* are addressed to Rudra. 'What can we utter to Rudra', runs one, 'the intelligent, the strong, the most bountiful, which shall be most pleasant to his heart, so that Aditi may bring Rudra's healing to our cattle and men and kine, and children? We seek from Rudra, the lord of songs, the lord of sacarifice, who possesses healing remedies, his auspicious favour; from him who is brilliant as the sun, who shines like gold, who is the best and most bountiful of the gods.' In the *Yajurveda* there is a long prayer called Śatarudriya which is addressed to him and appeals to him under a great variety of epithets. He is 'auspicious not terrible', 'the deliverer, the first divine physician'; he is, 'blue-necked and red-coloured, who has a thousand eyes and bears a thousand quivers', and in another hymn he is called 'Tryambaka, the sweet-scented increaser of prosperity', and 'a medicine for kine and horses, a medicine for men and a (source of) ease to rams and ewes.' In the *Atharvaveda* he is still the protector of cattle, but his character is of a fierce god who is besought to betake himself elsewhere, and not to assail mankind with consumption, poison and celestial fire. The *Brāhmaṇa*s tell that when Rudra wept at his birth and his father, Prajāpati, asked the reason, he was told that he wept because he had not received a name. His father gave him the name of Rudra (from the root *rud*, 'weep'). They also relate that at the request of the gods he pierced Prajāpati because of his incestuous intercourse with his daughter. In another place he is said to have applied to his father eight successive times for a name and to have received in succession the names, Bhava, Sarva, Paśupati, Ugradeva, Mahādeva, Rudra, Īśāna and Asani. In the Upaniṣads his character is further developed. He declares to the inquiring gods, 'I alone was before (all things) and I exist and I shall be. No other transcends me. I am eternal and not eternal, discernible and undiscernible, I am Brahmā and I am not Brahmā'. Again it is said, 'He is the only Rudra, he is Īśāna, he is divine, he is Maheśvara, he is Mahādeva.' 'There is only one Rudra; there is no place for a second. He rules this fourth world, controlling and productive; living beings abide with him, united with him. At the time of the end he annihilates all worlds, the protector.' 'He is without beginning, middle or end, the one, the pervading, the spiritual and blessed, the wonderful, the consort of Umā, the supreme lord, the three-eyed, the blue-throated, the tranquil. . . . He is Brahmā, he is Śiva, he is Indra; he is undecaying, supreme, self-resplendent; he is Viṣṇu, he is breath, he is the spirit, the supreme lord; he is all that hath been or that shall be, eternal. Knowing him, a man overpasses death. There is no other way to liberation.'

In the *Rāmāyaṇa* Śiva is a great god, but the references to him have more of the idea of a personal god than of a supreme divinity. He is represented as fighting with Viṣṇu, and as receiving worship with Brahmā, Viṣṇu and Indra, but he acknowledges the divinity of Rāma, and holds a less exalted position than Viṣṇu. The *Mahābhārata* also gives Viṣṇu the highest honour upon the whole. But it has many passages in which Śiva occupies the supreme place, and receives the homage and worship of Viṣṇu and Kr̥ṣṇa. 'Mahādeva', it says, 'is an all-pervading god yet is nowhere seen, he is the creator and the lord of Brahmā, Viṣṇu and Indra, whom the gods, from Brahmā to the Piśācas, worship.' The rival claims of Śiva and Viṣṇu to supremacy are clearly displayed in this poem and many of those powers and attributes are ascribed to them which were afterwards so widely developed in the Purāṇas. Attempts also are made to reconcile their conflicting claims by representing Śiva and Viṣṇu, Śiva and Kr̥ṣṇa, to be one, or, as it is expressed at a later time in the *Harivaṁsa*, there is 'no difference between Śiva who exists in the form of Viṣṇu, and Viṣṇu who exists in the form of Śiva'.

In the Purāṇas while Rudra is used as a synonym of Śiva, he is also spoken of as a son of Brahmā. One myth relates that Brahmā by severe austerities propitiated Śiva who was requested to be born of Brahmā. Śiva, having already given the promise of granting any boon Brahmā desired, agreed, and added a curse by which the first of the Triad lost his fifth head. The Purāṇas distinctly assert the supremacy of their particular divinity, whether it is Śiva or whether it is Viṣṇu, and they have developed and amplified the myths and allusions of the older writings into numberless legends and stories for the glorification and honour of their favourite god. In the *Bhāgavata Purāṇa*, Śiva, on learning of Umā's death, became so furious that, through the agency of Vīrabhadra, whom he had created from a lock of his own hair, had Dakṣa, Bhr̥gu and their sacrifice destroyed. Then in utter remorse of Umā, Śiva proceeded to the Himālayas where he became immersed in deep meditation and subsequently Umā was reborn as Pārvatī, the daughter of Himavat and Menā. In the *Vāmana Purāṇa* Śiva and Pārvatī are depicted as living together as man and wife but, as a result of Umā's death, Śiva had become utterly insensible to passion. To kindle this, the gods instigated Kāma, who was reduced to ashes with one glance from his third eye. Thus slowly the supremacy of Śiva came to be revived in the Purāṇa, which also defined his personality. In the *Bhāgavata Purāṇa*, he is called the son of Kaśyapa and Aditi, of a dark and red complexion, with triple eyes, four heads, with four hands, the back two clasping water lilies while the front ones dispensing favour and protection poses. But in the *Viṣṇu Purāṇa* he is shown as having married Saṁjñā and his brilliance was reduced by her father Viśvakarmā, as she could not withstand alluding to a reduction of his influence.

The Rudra of the Vedas has developed in the course of ages into the great and powerful god Śiva, the third deity of the Hindu triad, and the supreme god of his votaries. He is shortly described as the destroying principle but his powers and attributes are more numerous and much wider. Under the name of Rudra or Mahākāla, he is the great destroying and dissolving power. But destruction in Hindu belief implies reproduction; so as Śiva, the auspicious, he is the reproductive power which is perpetually restoring that which has been dissolved and hence he is regarded as Īśvara, the supreme lord, and Mahādeva, the great god. Under this character of restorer he is represented by the symbol of *liṅga* or phallus, typical of reproduction, and it is under this form alone, or combined with the *yoni* or female organ, the representative of his *śakti*, that he is everywhere worshipped. Thirdly, he is the Mahāyogī, the great ascetic, in whom is centered the highest perfection of austere penance and abstract meditation, by which the most unlimited powers are attained, marvels and miracles are worked, the highest spiritual knowledge is acquired and union with the great spirit of the universe is eventually gained. In this character he is the naked ascetic *digambara,* clothed with the elements or *dhurjaṭī*, loaded with matted hair and his body smeared with ashes. His first or destructive character is sometimes intensified, and he becomes Bhairava, the terrible destroyer, who takes a pleasure in destruction. He is also Bhūteśvara, the lord of ghosts and goblins. In these characters he haunts cemeteries and places of cremation, wearing serpents round his head and skulls for a necklace, attended by troops of imps and trampling on rebellious demons. He sometimes indulges in rivalry and, heated with drink, dances furiously with his wife Devī the dance called *tāṇḍava*, while troops of drunken imps caper around them. Possessed of so many powers and attributes, he has a great number of names and is represented under a variety of forms. One authority enumerates a thousand and eight names but most of these are descriptive epithets, as Trilocana, the three-eyed, Nīlakaṇṭha, the blue-throated and Pañcānana, the five-faced. Śiva is a fair man with five faces and four arms. He is commonly represented seated in profound thought with a third eye in the middle of his forehead, contained in or surmounting by the moon's crescent; his matted locks are gathered up into a coil like a horn, which bears upon it a symbol of the river Ganges, which he caught as it fell from heaven; a necklace of skulls hangs round his neck and serpents twine about his neck as a collar; his neck is blue from drinking the deadly poison which would have destroyed the world, and in his hand he holds a *triśūla* or trident called *pināka*. His garment is the skin of a tiger, a deer, or an elephant, hence he is called Kṛttivāsas; sometimes he is clothed in a skin and seated upon a tiger-skin and he holds a deer in his hand. His bull Nandī generally accompanies him. He also carries the bow *ajagava*, a drum in the shape of an hour glass, the *khaṭvāṅga* or club with a skull at the end or a cord for binding refractory offenders. His *pramatha*s or attendants are numerous, and are imps and demons of various kinds. His third eye has been very destructive. With it he reduced to ashes Kāma, the god of love, for daring to inspire amorous thoughts of his consort Pārvatī while he was engaged in penance; and the gods and all created beings were destroyed by its glance at one of the periodical destructions of the universe. He is represented to have cut off one of the heads of Brahmā for speaking disrespectfully, so that Brhamā has only four heads instead of five. His heaven is on mount Kailāsa.

Śiva has been known by several names, some of which may be noted: Aghora, Babhru, horrible; divine; Bhagavat, divine;

Bhūteśvara, god of ghosts; Candraśekhara, moon-crested; Digambara, nude with space as his robe; Gaṅgādhara, bearer of the Gaṅgā; Girīśa, mountain lord; Hara, seizer; Īśāna, ruler; Jalamūrti, whose form is water; Jaṭādhara, wearing matted hair; Kāla, time; Kapālamālin, wearing a garland of skulls; Mahākāla, great time; Maheśa, great lord; Mr̥tyuñjaya, vanquisher of death; Nīlakaṇṭha, blue-throated; Pañcānana, five-faced; Paśupati, lord of animals; Sadāśiva, auspicious; Śaṅkara, auspicious; Sarva, auspicious; Sirīśa, monarch of the hills; Smarahāra, slayer of Kāma; Śrīkaṇṭha, one with the lovely neck; Sthānu, the firm; Tryambaka, three-eyed; Ugra, fierce; Virupākṣa, of misinformed eyes; Viśvanātha, lord of all.

The images of Śiva can be roughly classified according to their *gaṇa* and disposition. The icons of Śiva are either in standing or seated poses only as there are no *mūrti*s of Śiva in reclining pose. The entire range can be divided into five divisions: *Anugraha-mūrti*s, *Nr̥tya-mūrti*s, *Saṁhāra-mūrti*s, *Śānta-mūrti*s, and *Ugra-mūrti*s.

In each group, excepting the last one, which is only one of the several forms of *nr̥tya* or dancing images, the images are either in standing or seated posture.

In *Sthānaka-mūrti*s, there are a few important types that are interesting to study.

1. ***Liṅgodbhava-mūrti***: *Lingodbhava-mūrti* is the manifestation of Śiva as *liṅga*. This is to represent the form of Śiva as he appeared to Brahmā and Viṣṇu, when both of them sought to find out the upper and lower height of Śiva's form. It is said that Brahmā as a swan flew in the air and Viṣṇu as Varāha delved deep into the depths of the earth for this purpose. The *mūrti* is represented as a four-armed figure with axe and antelope in the upper two hands, set inside a *liṅga* form. The lower portion of the legs below the ankles are shown as being hidden in the *liṅga* portion. Out of this *Liṅgodbhava-mūrti* is believed to have evolved the

*Ekapāda-mūrti* (one-footed) or the *Ekapāda-trimūrti*. In the latter Śiva's superiority is again asserted.

2. ***Ekapāda-trimūrti***: In the *Ekapāda-trimūrti* image, the deities Brahmā and Viṣṇu appear with folded hands as issuing forth from the waist of Śiva. This image can be seen in specific Śaivite temples.

3. ***Candraśekhara-mūrti***: This is the representation of Śiva having Candra or the moon as his head ornament. There are two types of this image — Kevala, when Śiva alone is represented and Umāsahita, when he has Umā at his side. According to the *Kāśyapa-śilpa* of the *Aṁśumat-tantra*, he stands on a pedestal with level feet, *samapada*, holding the antelope and the kettledrum in the arms behind the fore-arms, while the fore-arms are in *abhaya* and *varada* poses. The crescent moon decorates the *jaṭā-mukuṭa* and the deity has a very pleasing appearance.

4. ***Pāśupata-mūrti***: *Pāśupata-mūrti* is almost the same as *Candraśekhara-mūrti*, but the image has a *śūla* and an *akṣamālā* in the lower two hands instead of them being in *abhaya* and *varada* poses.

5. ***Sukhāsana-mūrti***: Śiva of a handsome type is represented as a seated *bhadrapīṭha* with left leg bent and resting on the seat while the right one is hanging. In the upper arms he carries the *paraśu* and *mṛga* while the right lower one is in *abhaya* pose and the left one in *varada* pose.

6. ***Umāsahita-mūrti***: *Umāsahita-mūrti* is the *Sukhāsana-mūrti* with Umā seated on Śiva's left side. Umā is represented as seated with two arms: in the right one she holds a lotus flower while the other is in *siṁhakaraṇa* pose or may be shown as resting on her thigh or on the *pīta* below. Sometimes the *pīta* may have a *prabhāvalī* behind the two images. If Śiva is shown as seated on the

vehicle, the *vṛṣabha*, he is called *Vṛṣabhārūḍha Umāsahita-mūrti*.

7. ***Somaskanda-mūrti***: This is perhaps one of the most common images of Śiva and also one of the oldest designs. In this particular form Śiva and Pārvatī are shown as seated with Skanda. Pārvatī is seated on the left side of Śiva, who as usual holds a *ṭaṅkā*, axe in the back arms while the front ones are in *abhaya* and *varada* poses. Between them, the young Skanda is shown standing, holding a flower in each hand.

8. ***Umā-maheśvara-mūrti***: This form is almost similar to *Somaskanda-mūrti*, but in addition to Skanda, the image of young Gaṇeśa and at times Nandī are included in the group.

9. ***Candreśvara-mūrti***: *Candreśvara-mūrti* is the form taken by Śiva to confer blessings on Candeśa. A cowherd of Seynālūr named Yajñadatta had a son named Vicaraśarman, who was asked to take the cattle to pastures for grazing. Vicaraśarman used to milk some of the cows and poured the same on small sand *liṅga*s that were in the grazing ground. Seeing this one day his father tried to kick the sand *liṅga*s and the son, in his devotional fury, cut off the legs of his father with an axe. Seeing his son's piety Śiva appeared to them and made Vicaraśarman the head of his *bhūta-gaṇa*s, naming him Candreśvara, and also ordered that all offerings intended for him should be first given to Candreśvara.

10. ***Viṣṇuānugraha-mūrti***: According to *Śiva Purāṇa* and *Śrītattvanidhi*, Viṣṇu is said to have received the *cakra* from Śiva. The representation of this type is almost similar to that of *Candreśānugraha* form excepting that Viṣṇu is shown as receiving the *cakra* from Śiva.

11. ***Nandīśānugraha-mūrti***: Nandī is one of the important adjuncts to the family of Śiva, as he is the vehicle of Śiva. Once when Nandī's tenure of life was almost coming

to an end, he prayed to Śiva for a further lease of life, so that he could continue his service to him. Śiva made him the commandant of his *gaṇa*s and blessed him with eternal life. The image is the same as in the above two forms, except that Nandī in human form with the head of a bull is shown standing between Śiva and Pārvatī, receiving their blessings.

12. ***Vigneśvarānugraha-mūrti***: Śiva blessed Vināyaka with eternal life after the head of an elephant was placed over the headless body of his son, and to signify the incident this form of *anugraha-mūrti* was evolved. In a slightly variant type Śiva and Pārvatī are shown as seated with Vināyaka standing between them with his two hands folded in *añjalī* pose, receiving his parents' blessings.

13. ***Kirātārjuna-mūrti***: *Kirātārjuna-mūrti* relates to the form of Śiva that he assumed when as a hunter he appeared before Arjuna who was doing penance, as described in the Vana Parva of the *Mahābhārata*. Then Śiva presented him with the *pāśupata-astra*. Śiva is represented with four hands, carrying the usual *āyudha*s in the upper ones and a huge bow in his lower left hand, and as accompanied by Pārvatī. Arjuna is represented as standing in front of them in the attitude of doing penance.

14. ***Rāvaṇānugraha-mūrti***: When Rāvaṇa attempted to shake the Kailāsa mountain on which Śiva and Pārvatī resided, Pārvatī became frightened and clung to Śiva praying that he might hold her from falling. Śiva pressed the mountain with his right toe and Rāvaṇa was caught under it. But later Rāvaṇa pleased Śiva by his *samagāna* and he was blessed. The iconographical representation of this form of *anugraha-mūrti* is to show Śiva and Pārvatī in *Somaskanda* form, with a representation of the great mountain under them. Rāvaṇa is shown as seated below the mountain with a *vīṇā* in hand, having ten heads and twenty hands.

15. ***Kāmantaka-mūrti***: *Kāmantaka-mūrti* portrays Śiva as the destroyer of Kāma, the Indian cupid. According to the Purāṇas Kāmadeva was deputed to disturb the penance that Śiva was doing in order that he may marry Pārvatī. This incident is said to have taken place in south India. Śiva is represented as seated with four arms and *jaṭā-mukuṭa* on head with a terrific look. He carries an *akṣamālā*. The front two hands are in *patākā-hasta* and *sūci-hasta*.

16. ***Gajasaṁhāra-mūrti***: This is to depict the incident narrated in the *Kūrma Purāṇa*: when Śiva destroyed an *asura* who came as an elephant by tearing open the belly of the animal and later wore its skin as his garment. This aspect of Śiva is well represented in the temples particularly in the *gopuram*. This form is described in detail in *Aṁśumadbhedāgama* and other Śaivāgamas. Śiva is represented as standing with either four or eight arms, carrying besides the usual weapons, *triśūla*, tusk of an elephant, *pāśa*, *ḍamaru*, *khaṭvāṅga* and other fierce *āyudha*s. The left leg is firmly planted on the head of the elephant and the right one bent and lifted up above the thigh of the other leg. The entire body of Śiva is encompassed in the oval-shaped abdomen of the elephant, its head being below and the tail above, with the four legs at corner points.

17. ***Kālāri-mūrti***: Śiva, according to *Mārkaṇḍeya Purāṇa*, kicked Kāla or Yama, the god of death, on his chest when he came to take away the life of his devotee Mārkaṇḍeya. Śiva is represented as emerging out of a *liṅga*, which Mārkaṇḍeya embraces, having his right leg on the *liṅga* and the left leg raised forward in the aspect of kicking. He has a fierce look. His right rear hand holds a trident pointed towards Yama and the other left hand a battle axe. The lower hands are in *varada* pose. The presence of the third eye on the forehead is usually well-marked in this aspect.

18. ***Tripurāntaka-mūrti***: This aspect of Śiva is connected with the episode narrated in the *Mahābhārata* where Śiva killed three demons of Tripura. For this purpose the other gods helped him by becoming one or other of his equipment. Images of Tripurāntaka going in a chariot drawn by Brahmā are common features in *gopurams*. No less than eight different descriptions are given to describe this aspect in *Aṁśumadbhedāgama*. Usually he is represented as a standing image, with the right leg firmly placed and the left one bent to signify an archer. The right forearm is in *siṁhakaraṇa* pose holding a *bāṇa*, while the left one is raised to hold a huge bow. The upper ones carry a *ṭaṅkā* or axe. He is usually represented alone, with a fierce look, protruding eyes, and *jaṭā-mukuṭa* on head.

19. ***Sarabha-mūrti***: This form is personified by Śiva to subdue the ferocious nature of Narasiṁha. Though there is no Purāṇic authority to this aspect, Śiva as Sarabha is worshipped in temples. He is represented as an animal with three legs, having the face of a lion with an outspreading mane. He has four arms, the upper ones carry the *paraśu* and the deer, while the lower ones bear *pāśa* and Agni. The front leg is raised and pinioned over the body of Narasiṁha, while the two hind legs are straight and fixed to the pedestal.

20. ***Brahmaśiraschedaka-mūrti***: The *Varāha Purāṇa* narrates the story that Śiva cut off the fifth head of Brahmā, for having officiated at the sacrifice conducted by Dakṣa. This head got stuck to the right palm of Śiva and would not fall off. Later, Śiva did penance to Viṣṇu at a place called Kaṇḍiyūr, when Viṣṇu enabled him to get rid of the skull of Brahmā. Śiva, according to *Śrī-Tattvanidhi*, is represented as a standing image with the usual weapons of *vajra* and *śūla* in the upper two hands, but carrying the skull of Brahmā in the lower right hand palm.

21. ***Bhairava-mūrti***: Śiva as the protector of the world is represented as a very fierce image with protruding eyes and a long curved teeth in the mouth protruding out from the upper lip. He is represented with strange ornaments like garlands of snakes and skulls and even in the headdress, the skull is shown. There are as many as sixty-four types of *Bhairava-mūrti*s, most of them having a ghastly appearance. Bhairava is worshipped in many Śiva temples outside the main shrine, but he is an important deity with villagers.

22. ***Vīrabhadra-mūrti***: This is the form that Śiva took when he destroyed the *yajña* of Dakṣa. He is represented in a terrific aspect, standing astride, having four or eight arms carrying deadly weapons and with a garland of skulls. He is usually shown as carrying, in his lower right arm, a massive jade with which he destroyed Dakṣa and others. Usually this form of Śiva can be seen at the entrance of the Śiva temples, facing south and alone or with Bhadrakālī by his side.

23. ***Jālandharahāra-mūrti***: The *Śiva Purāṇa* describes how Śiva destroyed Jālandhara who was born from the fire that emanated from the forehead of Śiva when he destroyed the Tripura *asura*. He is represented as a standing image, with a single pair of arms carrying an umbrella and a *kamaṇḍalu* and having a dishevelled *jaṭādhara* with the crescent moon and Gaṅgā. He has a fierce appearance here.

24. ***Aghora-mūrti***: Very rare images of this type are seen, as this aspect is considered very fierce and rather inauspicious. He is represented as a person with protruding teeth and huge round eye with garland of skulls and snakes, having ten or eight arms carrying very delay weapons with Agni Jwālā emanating from his *jaṭā-mukuṭa*.

25. ***Dakṣiṇa-mūrti***: After destroying Kāma, Śiva began to

do penance and again married Umā, who was born as Pārvatī, daughter of the Himālayas. During the period of his penance, he was conceived as a youthful teacher seated beneath a banyan tree, teaching aged *ṛṣi*s like Sanatakumāras whose doubts he cleared by his great silence. This image shows him as seated on a rock pedestal, with his right leg bent vertically at the knee and placed on the body of the demon Apasmāra while his left leg is bent across so as to rest upon the right thigh. Śiva has a very calm and pleasing countenance, depicting perfect peace, with the matted hair tied up neatly as *jaṭā-mukuṭa* and having four hands, the upper ones holding the *ḍamaru* and the *māzhu* while the right lower has a bundle of *cadjan* leaves. Under his feet are sages as also Apasmārpuruṣa, the demon. There are several different forms of *Dakṣiṇa-mūrti*, like *Yajña Dakṣiṇa-mūrti*, *Jñāna-mūrti* and *Yoga Dakṣiṇa-mūrti*. In *Yoga Dakṣiṇa-mūrti* he is represented as seated in the *yogāsana* pose with four hands: the back arms carrying *śūla* and *kapāla*, the front right hand up in a *mudrā* and the front left hand bent in the pose characteristic of an expounder of knowledge.

26. ***Kaṅkāla-mūrti***: Śiva is represented as a wandering mendicant after he cut off the head of Brahmā. This standing figure is draped in fine cloth with the left leg firmly fixed and the right one slightly bent and a bit forward, suggesting movement. He has a beautiful face and the head is well-ornamented. A serpent is shown as coiling round his loins. He has four hands: he holds a small kettledrum and a stick in the pose of beating the drum while the other right hand is in *siṁhakaraṇa* pose, touching an agile antelope, and the left one carries a bunch of peacock feathers tied to a staff. He wears a garland of skulls.

27. ***Bhikṣāṭana-mūrti***: This represents Śiva when he went

to the ṛṣis of Tāraka forest as a beautiful nude wandering mendicant. He is represented as a nude figure walking on a pair of high sandals, carrying the skull, kettledrum, antelope and trident in his hands. While many forms are in *sambhaṅga* pose, some are bent elegantly in *tribhaṅga* pose also.

28. ***Gaṅgādhara-mūrti***: *Gaṅgādhara-mūrti* represents Śiva as bearing Gaṅgā, when she came down from the heaven at the request of King Bhagīratha. Here Śiva is represented as a standing image with his feet firmly on the ground to bear the heavy weight of the waters of the Gaṅgā flowing down in great force.

29. ***Ardhanārīśvara-mūrti***: This relates to the episode of sage Bhṛgu who was doing *pradakṣiṇā*s to Śiva alone at Kailāsa. To test his adherence to his vow, Pārvatī was asked to join with Śiva's body on the right side so that Bhṛgu had to go round both of them. However the sage took the form of a beetle and bored through the composite body, going round only the Śiva portion of this *mūrti*. The image is represented as a standing figure in which one half is male and the other is female, each half having its own components, i.e., male or female characteristics, anatomical features and jewellery. Usually the image has four arms, but in rare cases, they have two or even three arms.

30. ***Harihara-mūrti***: This is a combination of the images of Śiva and Viṣṇu as described in the *Vāmana Purāṇa*. As in the case of *Ardhanārīśvara-mūrti* the two halves have characteristics of Viṣṇu and Śiva. Usually the image has four arms carrying *cakra* on one side and *māzhu* on the other side. The lower arms are in *abhaya* and *varada* pose.

31. ***Kalyāṇasundara-mūrti***: This represents Śiva and Pārvatī as they were at the time of their marriage. Here Śiva is represented as holding the right hand of Pārvatī

to represent his taking her in marriage. Here Śiva is represented as a lovely person devoid of the usual ghastly ornaments like snakes and skulls with four arms and Pārvatī as a typical bride in fine *tribhaṅga* pose.

32. ***Vīṇādhara-mūrti***: This is a fine standing image of Śiva with one leg slightly bent and resting on the head of demon Apasmāra. He has four arms, the back pair bearing the *māzhu* and the deer, while the front two ones are in the attitude of playing on the *vīṇā*, the musical instrument.

33. ***Vṛṣabhārūḍha-mūrti***: Here Śiva is represented as a standing image with Umā and the bull at the back. He has only two arms, one embracing the animal and the other bent downwards in *kaṭi-hasta* pose.

## Avatāras of Śiva's Disciples

| *Name of the Avatāra* | *Disciple* |
|---|---|
| Atri | Sarvajña, Samabuddha, Sādhya, Sarva |
| Damana | Viśoka, Vikeśa, Viśāpa, Śāpanāśana |
| Daṇḍin | Chāgala, Kumbhakarsagya, Kumbha |
| Pravanuka Dāruka | Plakṣa, Dakṣayāṇi, Ketumālin, Vaka |
| Gautama | Atri, Ugratapas, Śravaṇa, Śravista(stha) |
| Gokarṇa | Kaśyapa, Uśanas, Cyavana, Bṛhaspati |
| Guhavāsin | Utathya, Vāmadeva, Mahākāla, Mahālaya |
| Jātamālin | Hiraṇyanāman, Kauśilya, Kākśiva, Kuthumi |
| Kaṅka | Sana, Sanandana, Ṛtu, Sanatkumāra |
| Laigisavya | Sārasvata, Sumedha, Vasuvaha, Suvāhana |
| Lāṅgalin | Tulyarcis, Madhu, Piṅgākṣa, Śvetaketu |
| Lokākṣī | Sudhaman, Virāja, Śaṅkhapadrava |
| Nakulin | Kuśika, Gārgya, Mitraka, Rusta |
| Ṛṣabha | Pārāśara, Gārgya, Bhārgava, Aṅgiras |
| Sahiṣṇu | Ulūka, Vaidyuta, Śrāvaka, Aśvatayanu |
| Śikhaṇḍin | Vācaśravas, Ṛttikika, Savasa, Dṛḍhavrata |

| | |
|---|---|
| Somaśarman | Akṣapāda, Kaṇāda, Ulūka, Vatsa |
| Suhotrin | Sumukha, Durmukha, Durdama, Duratikrama |
| Śūlin | Śālihotra, Agniveṣya, Yuvanāśva, Saradvasu |
| Sutara | Dundubhi, Śatarūpā, Ṛcika, Ketumat |
| Śveta | Śveta, Śikhā, Śvetāsva, Śvetalohita |
| Śveta (2nd) | Uṣija, Vṛhaduthya, Devala, Kavi |
| Tridhāman | Balarandhu, Nira(ra)mitra, Ketuśṛṅga, Tapodhana |
| Ugras | Lambodara, Lamba, Lambākṣa, Lambakeśaka |
| Vali | Sudhaman, Kaśyapa, Vasiṣṭha, Virājas |
| Vasiṣṭha | Kapila, Āsuri, Pañcasikṣa, Vagvali |
| Vedaśiras | Kuni, Kumbahu, Kusarira, Kunetraka. |

[*Hindu Mythology*, T.R.R. Iyengar; *Epics, Myths and Legends of India*, P. Thomas; *A Classical Dictionary of Hindu Mythology and Religion*, J. Dowson; *South Indian Images*, T.N. Srinivasan; *Glossary of Hinduism*, T. Rengarajan; *Vedic Index,* Macdonnell and Keith]

**Soma**: In the Vedas, Soma is addressed as the deity representing the liquor yielding plant, Soma. Not only are all the hymns of the ninth book of *Ṛgveda*, one hundred and fourteen in number, besides a few in other places, dedicated to his honour, but also there is constant reference to him in the Vedas. Evidently at that time he was the most popular deity. Indra was an enthusiastic worshipper of Soma. In the Vedas, it is said that the plant was originally a native of the mountains where the *gandharva*s lived and the goddess Vāc, 'went to the *gandharva*s' who gave it to her. But when Vāc brought it to the gods there arouse a dispute among them as to who should have the first draught. At length this was decided by a race. Vāyu first reached the goal; Indra tried hard to win but when near the winning post proposed that they should reach it together. Vāyu said, 'Not so, I will be the winner alone.' Then Indra said, 'Let us come together, and give me one-fourth of the draught divine.' Vāyu consented to this and so the juice was shared between them.

The following is a portion of one of the hymns addressed to Soma:

This soma is a god, he cures,
The sharpest ills that man endures:
He heals the sick, the sad he cheers,
He nerves the weak, displeases their fears;
The faint with martial ardour fires,
With lofty thoughts the bard inspires
The soul room earth to heaven he lifts;
So great and wondrous is his gifts,
Men feel the god within their veins,
And cry in loud exulting strains;
We've quaffed the soma bright,
And are immortals grown;
We've entered into light,
And all the gods have known,
What mortal now can harm,
Or foremen vex us more?
Through thee, beyond alarm,
Immortal god, we soar.

From this hymn it is clear that Vedic Āryans used to indulge in drink.

[*Hindu Mythology*, T.R.R. Iyengar; *Epics, Myths and Legends of India*, P. Thomas]

**Subrahmaṇya**: A name of Kārttikeya, the god of battle. This is a name of the serpent god. An image of Subramaṇya shows the god riding on his vehicle, the peacock with six faces, three eyes and two arms, holding with one hand, a *śakti*, and with the other, a thunderbolt. He is made to wear the sacred thread, a girdle and a loincloth and has a tuft of hair and a staff like a *brahmacārī* student. The birth of Subrahmaṇya is described in several Purāṇas, the *Ramāyaṇa* and the Vana Parva of the *Mahābhārata*.

He is the son of Śiva and Umā and was born of the six mothers, the Kṛttikās and that gave him the name Ṣaṇmukha. The Purāṇas state that he was born of the fiery energy of Śiva in a forest of grass and became the commander of the army of the gods in their battle against the demon Tāraka and that he rent asunder with his fierce arrows, the mountain Krauñca. Kālidāsa also gives a lucid description of the birth of Kārttikeya in his *Kumārasambhava*. The sixth day of the lunar month *ṣaṣṭhī* is held sacred to him and the *ṣaṣṭhī* day in the month of Aiyappasi is said to be his birth day. [*Hindu Mythology*, T.R.R. Iyengar]

**Sudarśana**: The famous wheel weapon once used by Nārāyaṇa. It was transmitted to Kṛṣṇa by Agni for his assistance in defeating Indra and by wielding it, Kṛṣṇa became more powerful than the deities themselves, the demons and the serpents. It was invested with the exceptional power of returning back to its wielder like a boomerang. By it Kṛṣṇa cut the fiend Śāmba into two parts. Vṛṣaṅka (Śiva) was its first creator and he slew with it a demon dwelling within the water. [*Hindu Mythology*, T.R.R. Iyengar]

**Sūrya**: The sun or its deity. He is one of the three chief deities in the Vedas, as the great source of light and warmth but the references to him are more poetical than precise. Sometimes he is identical with Sāvitrī and Āditya, sometimes he is distinct. 'Sometimes he is called son of Dyaus, sometimes of Aditi.' Vedic Āryans loved the brighter side of the life and hence the sun was an important object of worship. The sun is thus described in the *Ṛgveda*:

To thy refulgent orb.
Behold the rays of dawn, like heralds, lead on high,
The sun, that men may see the great all knowing god.
Before the all-seeing eye, whose beams reveal his presence?
Gleaming like brilliant flames, to nation after nation
With speed, beyond the ken of mortals, thou,
O Sun Dost ever travel, conspicuous to all.
Thou dost create the light, and with it doest illume.

The universe entire; thou rises in the sight,
Of all the race of men, and all the host of heaven.
Light-giving Varuṇa, thy piercing glance does scan.
In quick succession, all this stirring, active world,
And penetrate too the broad, ethereal space,
Measuring our days and nights and spying out all creatures.

Sūrya with flaming flocks, clear-sighted god of day,
The seven ruddy mares bear on thy rushing car,
With these thy self-yoked steeds seven daughter of thy chariot.

Onward thou dost advance,
Beyond this lower gloom, and upward to light,
Would we ascend, O Sun, thou god among the gods.

Sūrya moves through the sky in a chariot drawn by seven ruddy horses. Sūrya has several wives but, according to later legends, his twin sons the Aśvins who are ever handsome and ride in a golden car as precursors of Uṣas, the dawn, were born of a nymph called Aśvinī, from her having concealed herself in the form of a mare. In the *Rāmāyaṇa* and Purāṇas Sūrya is said to be the son of Kaśyapa and Aditi, but in the *Rāmāyaṇa*, he is otherwise referred to as a son of Brahmā. His wife was Saṁjñā, daughter of Viśvakarmā, and by her he had three children, Manu Vaivasvata, Yama and the goddess Yamī or the Yamunā river. His effulgence was so overpowering that his wife gave him Chāyā for a handmaid and retired into the forest to devote herself to religion. While thus engaged, and in the form of a mare, the sun saw her and approached her in the form of a horse. Hence sprang the two Aśvins and Revanta. Sūrya brought back his wife Saṁjñā to his home, and her father, the sage Viśvakarmā, placed the luminary on his lathe and cut away an eighth of his effulgence, trimming him in every part except the feet. The fragments that were cut off fell blazing to the earth and from them Viśvakarmā formed the discus of Viṣṇu, the trident of Śiva, the weapon of Kubera, the lance of Kārttikeya, and the weapons of the other gods.

According to the *Mahābhārata*, Karṇa was his illegitimate son by Kuntī. He is also fabled to be the father of Śani and the monkey chief Sugrīva. The Manu Vaivasvata was the father of Ikṣavāku, and from him, the grandson of the sun, the Sūryavaṁśa or Solar race of kings draws its origin. In the form of a horse Sūrya communicated the *White Yajurveda* to Yājñavalkya, and it was he who bestowed on Satrājit the *syamantaka* gem. A set of terrorising *rākṣasa*s called Mahadhas made an attack upon him and sought to devour him but were dispersed by his light. According to *Viṣṇu Purāṇa* Satrājit saw him in his proper form, of dwarfish stature with a body like burnished copper and with slightly reddish eyes. Sūrya is represented in a chariot drawn by seven horses, or a horse with seven heads surrounded with rays. His charioteer is Aruṇa or Vivasvat, and his city Vivasvatī. Hemādri says that in the depiction of sun there should be the two attendant gods, Dandala Piṅgala and Ati Piṅgala on either side of the sun. His sons, Yama and the two Manus and his four wives, Rajanī, Chāyā, Svārma and Suvarcasā are also to be shown as standing by his side. It must be noted that the mystic *cakra* called the Sūrya-Yantra is closely associated with his worship, as in the case of Śakti goddess. The image of sun, according to the Āgamas, is always placed in the centre of the planets, which in all occupy the eighty cardinal points round the sun. He is shown as standing in the centripetal, facing eastward. Round red and decorated with red flowers he must be clothed with rich garments. He is shown as standing in a chariot having only one wheel. In both of his hands he carries a *padma* or lotus. The sun is represented in art as a dark red man with three eyes and four arms. The Gāyatrī is the most important *mantra* of the Vedas and it is addressed to the sun. The nature and power of the Gāyatrī are thus described: Nothing in the Vedas is superior to the Gāyatrī. No invocation is equal to the Gāyatrī, as no city is equal to Kāśī. The Gāyatrī is the mother of the Vedas and *Brāhmaṇa*s. By repeating the *mantra* a man may safeguard himself owing to the power of the Gāyatrī; by this, the kṣatriya Viśvāmitra became a *brahmarṣi* and even obtained such power as to be able to create a new world. For Gāyatrī, Brahmā, Viṣṇu and Śiva are the three Vedas. The mystic monosyllable *auṁ* is also traced to the sun and represents the solar fire as well as the Trinity. The first letter stands for the creator, the second for the preserver and the third for the destroyer. It is written inside a circle representing the orb of the sun, and the Hindus as lockets often wear its representation. The worship of the sun in India is very ancient dating back to the Vedic period; there is adequate evidence of Sūrya addressed for one object or the other. This worship continued in the time of the epics. For instance, in the *Mahābhārata*, the childless Kuntī wanted a son and prayed to Sūrya, who granted Karṇa to her. In the *Matsya Purāṇa* he is depicted as sitting on a lotus throne with lotus flowers in his hands and circumambulating the Meru mountain. His ensign is the lion and he is the lord of the planets. In other cases Sūrya is described as wearing an armour costume and headgear of a northern type although he is styled as the Lord of Kaliṅga. He is also pictured as having three eyes like Śiva, four arms, the front ones showing gift and shelter while the back ones hold water lillies. His seven horses were interpreted as the seven meters of the Vedas. The image of the sun, according to the Āgamas, is always placed in the centre of the planets which in all occupy the eight cardinal points round the sun. He is shown as standing in the centre facing eastward, round, red and decorated with red flowers. He must be clothed in rich garments and is shown as standing in a chariot having only one wheel and drawn by seven horses.

***Names of Sūrya***: Ādideva; Aditisuta; Aindhna; Aja; Alolupa; Aṅgāraka; Aṁśu; Apa; Aravindākṣa; Arhapati; Arihas; Arka; Aryaman; Caracarātman; Dehakarti; Dhanvantari; Dharmadhvaja; Dhātr̥; Dhūmaketu; Diptāśu; Dinakara; Dvādaśātman; Dvāparakālī; Gabhastimat; Graharāja; Jaṭharāgni; Jaya; Jīmūta; Jīvana; Kaivalya; Kālāgniruda; Kālī; Karmasākṣī; Kaṭha (Rudra); Kauṣitakī; Kena; Kr̥ṣṇa; Kṣuri(ka); Kuṇḍika; Lokacakṣuḥ; Manasa; Mātr̥; Mokṣadvāra; Mr̥tyu; Muhūrtta; Pitāmaha; Pitr̥; Prabhākara; Prajādhyakṣa; Prājadvāra; Prāṇdharaṇa; Praśāntātman; Pr̥thibī; Puruṣa; Pūṣa; Ravi; Rudra;

Sagara; Sahasrakiraṇa; Samvartaka; Saṁvatsarakara; Sanaiścara; Sanātana; Sarvādi; Sarvatomukha; Śāśvata; Śauri; Sāvitrī; Sighraga; Skanda; Soma; Sraṣṭr̥; Suci; Sūkṣmātman; Śukra; Suparṇa; Sūrya; Svargadvāra; Tamounda; Teja; Tejasam-Pati; Tretā; Tripiṣtapa; Tvaṣṭr̥; Vaidyutāgni; Vaiśravana; Varada; Varhi; Varuṇa; Vāyu; Vedakarttr̥; Vedāṅga; Vedavāhana; Vikarttana; Viśāla; Viṣṇu; Viśvakarmā; Viśvātman; Viśvatomukha; Vivasvat; Vr̥haspati; Vyakkavyakta; Yama; Yogin.

[*Hindu Mythology*, T.R.R. Iyengar; *A Glossary of Hinduism*, T. Rengarajan]

# T

**Tripurasundarī**: A milder deity enticed along with Lalitarājeśvarī and Ānandabhairavī. Tripurabhairavī or Tripura simply is her names as consort of Śiva, who is Tripuradāha, 'the destroyer of Tripura'. Tripura here represents the three aerial cities of the *asura*s, one of iron, one of sliver, and one of gold, which Indra with all his weapons could not destroy. In the *Mahābhārata*, Yudhiṣṭhira tells Kṛṣṇa how Rudra destroyed the three cities with a three-joint barbed arrow of which Viṣṇu was the shaft, Agni the barb, Yama the feather, the Vedas, the bow and the sacred text, the bow-string. She is a Tāntric goddess, a combination of Śiva and his Śakti also known as Kāmakalā, Aham and Para, the first of the four kinds of speech. She is associated with the metaphysical doctrine called Sambhavadarśana and is believed to be pacified by the observance of a vow in her honour. It is comprised of three types. The first in the *Mahāpadmavana*, a garden of lotuses, according to which a devotee has to fully concentrate his mind on her as sitting on Śiva's lap in such a garden, with an entirely ecstatic body and identical with one's self. The next is *Cakra-pūjā* which is the worship of a mystic circle named the Śrīkara, drawn on a piece of silk or a *burja* leaf or a gold leaf, with the feminine organ painted in the centre. When nine such circles were drawn they constituted the divine wheel. This system of worship was adopted by a class of Śākta worshippers known as the ancient Kaulas while the modern adherents went a step further and worshipped the same part of a living woman. These worshippers offered to this deity liquor, honey, fish and similar items of food. During this worship all caste distinctions were forgotten which were resumed after it was over. Apart from the sexual orgies, the goddess was also worshipped in same ways as Lalitā and Upāṅga Lalitā, the former on the first ten days and the later on the fifth day of Āśvina. [*Vaisnavism, Saivism and Minor Religious Systems*, R.G. Bhandarkar]

**Triśūla**: A trident. A symbol in the hands of deities of the Śaivas like *Umā-Tāṇḍava*, *Samahartā-Tāṇḍava*, *Candraśekhara*, *Hari-Hara*, *Kālahara-mūrti*, *Pāśupata-mūrti*, and others. It also appears in the hands of lesser village deities. It was also fixed in the ground in front of village deities and, in the image of Yama and Agni, it appears as though it were a flame. In some of Agni's images, in three of his arms, he holds flaming tridents while in his fourth hand he carries a rosary.

**Tumburu**: A Brāhmaṇical *gandharva* musician. He was credited with great merit and had two daughters, Manovatī and Sukeśā. He was afraid of Candrodakadundubhi, a *gandharva* disciple of Nārada and he accompanied that sage during his visit to Yudhiṣṭhira. He sang with Nārada, went to heaven where he witnessed the glories of Ananta and finally became the overlord of all the worlds. Still he eulogised Kṛṣṇa when he lifted up the Govaradhana mountain. His famous daughters known as the Pañcacūḍas are believed to preside over the months of Caitra and Māgha.

**Tvaṣṭṛ**: Tvaṣṭṛ, like Mātarisvan, is not celebrated in any hymn of the *Ṛgveda*, but his name occurs about sixty-five times in this Veda. In the *Naighaṇṭuka*, he is mentioned among the celestial and aerial as well as the terrestrial gods. His characteristic feature is the iron axe, which he bears in his hand and which marks him out as the skilled artificer. He is, therefore, also called left-handed. He is the most skilful of workmen. He forges the bolt of Indra, the axe of Brahmaṇaspati and the cup out of which the gods drink. He is the shaper of all forms, human and animal. He is said to have fashioned husband and wife for each other, even from the womb. He himself is called omniform more often than any other deity in the *Ṛgveda*. The word *tvaṣṭṛ* is derived from the root *tvaṣṭṛ*, the cognate of which is found in the *Avesta*, and therefore means 'artificer'. Oldenberg considers that the god is no more than the personification of creative activity. Hilebrandt, on the other hand, thinks that he represents the sun. In the post-Vedic literature he is indeed regarded as one of the Ādityas, but this fact is of no consequence in determining his original name.

# U

**Ucchiṣṭa Gaṇapati**: This Gaṇapati is also known as Śakti Gaṇapati. This is a form of Gaṇapati in a standing posture and is worshipped by the Hindus. Among them he is represented with four hands with sweetmeat with his two hands showing the *varada* and shelter poses. His hands have varied from 2 to 18. He is shown as pot-bellied and his vehicle is the mouse, although the four arms seem to be standard.

**Umā**: Umā is mentioned as wife of Rudra or Śiva, but in the *Kenopaniṣad*, which is certainly one of the earlier Upaniṣads, the name of Umā occurs. She is called Haimavatī, or the daughter of Himavatī, but she is not mentioned in the *Kenopaniṣad* as the wife of Rudra or Śiva though in later times she was known to be so. *Brahman* conquered the enemies of the gods for them, but the gods took credit to themselves for the victory and were proud of their achievements. Agni, Vāyu and Indra were sitting together, engaged in joyous conversation, when there appeared at some distance a spirit. Agni first went out to see what it was. The spirit asked him the nature and extent of his power and laid down a blade of grass, which it asked him to burn away. Agni was not able to do this and returned baffled. Then went Vāyu, who also was not able to blow away the blade of grass; afterwards went Indra, and at his approach the spirit disappeared. Indra was disappointed, but he saw the beautiful woman of the name of Umā-Haimavatī and asked her where the spirit was. She said it was *Brahman* who had come into prominence as the supreme spirit. Since it was Umā that disclosed the nature of the spirit, it may be understood that the *Brahman* mentioned was Rudra-Śiva, and Umā was his wife. It would thus appear that she had come to be so regarded sometime before the Upaniṣad was composed. According to Śaṅkarācārya, who wrote a commentary on this Upaniṣad, it was Umā in the form of Vidyā or knowledge which appeared to Indra and, according to Sāyaṇa, 'Since Gaurī, the daughter of Himavatī is the impersonation of divine knowledge.' In the *Talavakāra Upaniṣad* the impersonation of divine knowledge is introduced in these words, 'He said to the very resplendent Umā, Haimavatī the supreme spirit, who is the object of this divine knowledge from his existing together with Umā is called Soma.' From these considerations a connection between Umā as divine knowledge, and Sarasvatī, 'the divine word', might be supposed and even etymologically with the sacred omnified word *oṁ*, but Weber points out that here are other characteristics which place the original signification of Umā in quite another light. Why is she called Haimavatī? Umā lived with her husband Rudra. She is often described in the Purāṇas as an ideal housewife, cheering Śiva with her delightful company and sweet conversation. But there were also domestic quarrels between them. One day, for instance, while Śiva was reading and explaining to his wife some abstruse philosophical point, Umā felt sleepy. When the great god wanted to ask for her approval of his interpretation of the text, he looked at her and saw her nodding. He rebuked her for being inattentive. But Umā maintained that she was really attentive and had closed her eyes to contemplate the meaning of his words, upon which Śiva asked her to repeat the last words he had uttered. Poor Pārvatī could not, and was thus caught red-handed. The angry god cursed his wife to become a fisherwoman. Immediately Pārvatī fell from Rudra to the earth as a fishermaid. Śiva, determined to forget so indifferent a wife, assumed his characteristic *yogī*'s pose and began to practise concentration. But he found it difficult to meditate, and his thoughts wandered after Pārvatī. He made some more attempts at concentration but failed. At last the thought of Pārvatī became tormenting him and he decided to regain his lost wife. He asked his servant Nandinī to become a shark and break the nets of the fishermen among whom Pārvatī lived. Pārvatī had been picked up by the chief officer among the fishermen and brought up as his daughter. She was exceedingly beautiful and when she came of age, all the young fishermen of the village wished to marry her. In the meantime the shark's activities had become quite intolerable and the worried chief declared that his daughter would be given in marriage to the person who caught the shark. Śiva was only waiting for this opportunity. He assumed the form of a fisherman and easily enough caught the shark. And then he married Pārvatī, and with her went back to Kailāsa. There were also other causes of dispute between Śiva and Pārvatī as it very often happened that Śiva wanted to curse a person whom his wife wanted to bless. On the other hand, the felicity of their domestic life is eulogised at great length in many of the Purāṇas. The married life of Śiva and Pārvatī is also shown as a faithful representation of the average human family. Pārvatī is a fond mother, a prudent though somewhat assertive wife, and, like all women, wise and childish at once. Now, we come to the terror aspect of woman as personified as Śiva's consort. In this character she is known by various names of which the most popular is Durgā. Although in essence she is said to be the energy of Śiva, the Purāṇas observe that the Durgā form of her was produced 'from the radiant flames that issued from the mouths of Brahmā, Viṣṇu and Śiva as well as from the mouths of other principal deities' for the destruction of Mahiṣa, an *asura* who had conquered the celestial kingdom and driven out the gods from there. It is said that she appeared before the gods as 'a female of celestial beauty with ten arms into which the gods delivered their weapons, the emblem of their powers'.

Weber says that

> it would have been quite natural if this state of things had not been confined to language, but had become extended to speculation also, and if the knowledge of the one, eternal Brahmā, had been sooner attained in the peaceful valleys of the Himālayas than was possible for such living in Madhyadeśa, where their minds were more occupied with the practical concerns of lives.

Such a view of Umā-Haimavatī appears, however, to be very hazardous. For not to say that in our explanations of the ancient Indian deities we act wisely when we attach greater importance to the physical than to the speculative elements we are by no means certain that Umā actually does signify divine knowledge and, moreover, her subsequent position as Rudra's wife and so Śiva's would thus be quite inexplicable. Now there is among the epithets of this latter goddess a similar one, viz., Pārvatī, which would lead us in interpreting the word Haimavatī to place the emphasis not in the Haimavatī, but upon the mountain and with this I might connect the epithets of Rudra which we have learned from the Śatarudrīya.

**Umāpati**: Husband of Umā, that is to say, Śiva.

**Uparicara**: A Vasu or demi-god who, according to the *Mahābhārata*, became king of Cedi by command of Indra. He had five sons by his wife and, by an *apsaras* named Ādrikā condemned to live on earth in the form of a fish, he had a son named Matsya and a daughter, Satyavatī, who was the mother of Vyāsa.

**Upendra**: A title given to Kṛṣṇa by Indra.

**Uṣas**: The dawn goddess is called Uṣas. The Sūkta I.48.6 says, 'O, Uṣā when you rise in the morning the flying birds do not remain in any longer.' She comes towards men from the place above the sun with the hundred chariots. *Ṛgveda* 15 says, 'O, Uṣas today with your light you have opened the portals of sky.' The *Ṛk* 3 says, 'O, Uṣas at the time of your appearance, all the biped, quadruped and the winged birds fly up at the upper end of the sky.' The *Ṛk* 4 says,' 'O Uṣas by killing darkness shining, white-coloured, the mother of sun, Uṣas has come, black-coloured has returned to its place; night and Uṣas both are friends and both are immortals. One comes after another, and one destroyer of the colour of another; in this wise they roam about by becoming brilliant.' From these Ṛgvedic verses we get the idea that morning dawn is being adored here in figurative speeches. The brilliancy of the rays of the morning dawn is expressed in allegorical language. Poetic redundancy is to be noticed here, and no anthropological data regarding the physical characteristics of the dawn-goddess are to be extracted from these expressions. Some of the most beautiful hymns of the *Ṛgveda* are addressed to the goddess Uṣas, personification of the dawn. The Vedic goddess is celebrated in 20 hymns of the *R̥gveda*, and mentioned more than 300 times. The *Naighaṇṭuka* mentions the names of Uṣas in the list of celestial as well as aerial deities. As the name of the goddess is identical with that of the natural phenomenon which she represents the personification is but slight, the phenomenon of dawn being always present in the poet's mind while addressing the goddess.

Uṣā is the finest creation of Vedic poetry and no figure is more charging than she in the religious lyrics of any other literature. Decked in gay attire and clothed in light, she appears in the east and is an unveiler of charms. Rising resplendent as from a bath, she comes with light driving away the darkness, and removing the black robe of night. She is ever young though ancient. She lists up the ends of the sky and opens the gates of the heaven. Her brilliant rays appear like herds of cattle. She awakens every living being to motion. When Uṣas shines forth, the birds fly up from their nest and men seek their work. She wards off evil spirits and drives away bad dreams. She discloses the treasures concealed by darkness and distributes them bountifully. She is borne of a shining car, drawn by ruddy steeds or kine, which probably represent the red rays of the morning. As the golden goddess rises, she awakens the sweet notes of the birds. Uṣas is closely associated with Sūrya who follows her as a lover. She thus comes to be spoken of as a wife of Sūrya. She is also called sister of Nakta, and their names are often conjoined as a dual compound. She is constantly called the daughter of Dyaus. As the sacrificial fire is kindled at dawn, Uṣas is often associated with Agni. She is also connected with Aśvins, the twin gods of early morning. She is characteristically bountiful and she travels in a shining chariot drawn by seven ruddy cows. One of the hymns addressed to Uṣas runs as follows:

Hail ruddy Ushas, golden goddess, borne,

Upon thy shining car, thou comest like,
A lovely maiden by her mother decked,
Disclosing coyly all thy hidden grace,

To our admiring eyes; or, like a wife.

Unveiling to her lord with conscious pride,
Beauties which, as he gazes, lovingly,
Seem fresher, fairer, each succeeding morn,
Through years and years, thou hats lived on and yet.

Thou'rt every young. Thou art, the breath and life,
Of all that breathes, and lives, awaking day by day,
Myriad of prostrate sleepers, as from death,
Causing the birds to flutter in their nest.

And rousing men to ply with busy feet,
They're daily duties and appointed tasks,
Toiling for wealth or pleasure or renown.

The name of Uṣas is derived from the root *was*, to shine. She is identical with the *Usha* of *Avesta*, the *Eos* of Greece, and the *Aurora* of Rome. [*Hindu Mythology*, T.R.R. Iyengar; *A Classical Dictionary of Hindu Mythology and Religion*, J. Dowson]

# V

**Vāc**: [Speech] In the *Ṛgveda*, Vāc appears to be the personification of speech by whom knowledge was communicated to man. Thus, she is said to have 'entered into the *ṛṣi*s' and to make whom she loves terrible and intelligent, a priest and a *ṛṣi*. She was generated by the gods and is called 'the divine Vāc', 'queen of the gods', and she is described as 'the melodious cow who milked forth sustenance and water', 'who yields us nourishment and sustenance'. The *Brāhmaṇa*s associate her with Prajāpati in the work of creation. In the *Taittirīya Brāhmaṇa* she is called the mother of the Vedas and 'the wife of Indra who contains within herself all worlds'. In the *Śatapatha Brāhmaṇa* she is represented as entering into a sexual connection with Prajāpati who, being desirous of creating, connected himself with various spouses, and among them, 'through his mind, with Vāc' from whom he created the waters; or, as this last sentence is differently translated, 'He created the waters from the world of speech.' In the *Kaṭhaka Upaniṣad* this idea is more distinctly formulated; Prajāpati was this universe. Vāc was a second to him. He associated sexually with her; she became pregnant; she departed from him; she produced these creatures; she again entered into Prajāpati. In the *Aitareya Brāhmaṇa* and the *Śatapatha Brāhmaṇa* there is the story of the *gandharva*s having stolen the *soma* juice, or, as one calls it, 'King Soma', and that as the *gandharava*s were fond of women, Vāc was, at her own suggestion, 'turned into a female' by the gods and *ṛṣi*s and she went to recover it from them. In the *Atharvaveda*, she is identified with Virāj and is the daughter of Kāma. 'That daughter of thine, O Kāma, is called the cow, she whom sages denominate Vāc-Virāj.' The *Mahābhārata* also calls her 'the mother of the Vedas'. 'A voice derived from Brahmā entered into the ears of them all; the celestial Sarasvatī was then produced from the heavens.' Here and 'in the later mythology, Sarasvatī was identified with Vāc, and became under different names the spouse of Brahmā, and the goddess of wisdom and eloquence, and is invoked as a muse', generally under the name of Sarasvatī but sometimes as Vāc. The *Bhāgavata Purāṇa* recognises her as 'the slender and enchanting daughter' of Brahmā, for whom he had a passion and from whom mankind was produced, that is the female Virāj. Sarasvatī, as wife of Brahmā and goddess of wisdom, represents perhaps the union of power and intelligence, which was supposed to operate in the work of creation. According to the *Padma Purāṇa*, Vāc was daughter of Dakṣa, wife of Kaśyapa, and mother of the *gandharva*s and *apsaras*.

**Vāhana**: [A vehicle] Most of the gods are represented as having animals as their *vāhana*s. It is a symbol associated with deities in the Hindu system of gods and goddesses.

| *Name of the God / Goddess* | *Vāhana* |
|---|---|
| Agni | Ram |
| Aiyanār | Elephant and horse |
| Bhairava | Dog |
| Bhūtamātā | Lion |
| Brāhmī | Swan |
| Budha | Lion |
| Cāmuṇḍā | Lion |
| Caṇḍakhaṇḍa | Lion |
| Candeśa | Bull |
| Caṇḍī | Lion |
| Candra | Horse/ten-yoked chariot |
| Gaṇapati | Rat |
| Gaṅgā | Crocodile |
| Gāyatrī | Swan |
| Govindabhairva | Garuḍa |
| Herambagaṇapati | Lion |
| Indra | Elephant and horse |
| Kālarāti | Ass |
| Kālayama | Buffalo |

| | |
|---|---|
| Kāmadeva | Crocodile |
| Kaumārī | Peacock |
| Ketu | Vulture |
| Kubera | Horse |
| Mahā Gaurī | Elephant |
| Mahā-Kālī | Owl |
| Māhendrī | Elephant |
| Māheśvarī | Bull |
| Mahiṣāsura Mardinī | Lion |
| Kubera | Lion |
| Nairṛta | Lion |
| Pracaṇḍa | Elephant |
| Pratyaṅgirā | Lion |
| Rāhu | Lion |
| Śani | Vulture |
| Sarasvatī | Garuḍa |
| Śītalā | Ass |
| Śiva | Bull |
| Skanda | Peacock |
| Skandamātā | Lion |
| Sūrya | Horse/seven-yoked chariot |
| Svapna Vārahī | Horse |
| Vaiṣṇavī | Garuḍa |
| Vārāhī | Buffalo, Cow |
| Varuṇa | Crocodile |
| Vāyu | Deer |
| Vindhyavāsinī | Lion |
| Viṣṇu | Garuḍa |
| Viśvakarmā | Elephant |
| Yamunā | Tortoise |

**Vahni**: Name of fire god. (See Agni)

**Vaibhrāja**: A celestial grove; the grove of the gods on Mount

Supārśva, west of Meru.

**Vaidyanātha**: 'Lord of physicians.' A title of Śiva. Name of one of twelve *liṅga*s.

**Vaijayanta**: The banner of Indra.

**Vaijayantī**: The necklace of Viṣṇu.

**Vaikuṇṭha**: The paradise of Viṣṇu.

**Vainateya**: A name of Viṣṇu's bird, Garuḍa.

**Vairājas**: Semi-divine beings or Manes unconsumable by fire, who dwell in *tapa-loka*, but are capable of translation to *satya-loka*. The Kāśī Khaṇḍa explains this term as the Manes of 'ascetics, mendicants, anchorites, and penitents, who have compiled a course of rigorous austerities'.

**Vaiśvānara**: Name of god Agni.

**Vaiśravana**: Patronymic of Kubera.

**Vaivasvata**: Name of the seventh Manu; he was son of Sūrya and father of Ikṣvāku, the founder of the Solar race of kings.

**Vajra**: The thunderbolt of Indra said to have been made of the bones of the *ṛṣi* Dadhicī. It is a circular weapon, with a hole in the centre, according to some, but other represent it as consisting of two transverse bars. It has many names: Aśani, Abhrotta, 'sky-born'; Bāhudara, 'much cleaving'; Bhidira or Chidaka, 'the splitter'; Dambholi and Jasuri, 'destructive'; Hradin, 'roaring'; Kuliśa, 'axe'; Pavi, 'pointed'; Phenavāhin, 'foam-bearing'; Śaṭkoṇa, 'hexagon'; Śāmba and Svaru.

**Vajra-Nābha**: The celebrated *cakra* (discus) of Kṛṣṇa. According to the *Mahābhārata* Agni gave it to him for his assistance in defeating Indra and burning the Khāṇḍava forest.

**Vālmīki**: The author of *Rāmāyaṇa*, which he in Vedic phase is said to have 'seen'. He himself is represented as taking part in some of the scenes he describes. He received the banished Sītā into his hermitage at Citrakūṭa, and educated her twin sons Kuśa and Lava.

**Vāmadeva**: A name of Śiva; also of one of the Rudras.

**Vāmana**: The dwarf incarnation of Viṣṇu. [See 'Vamana Purāṇa']

**Varada**: [Bestower of boons] A name of Devī; also of Sarasvatī.

**Varāha**: The boar incarnation of Viṣṇu.

**Vārṣṇeya**: A name of Kṛṣṇa as a descendant of Vṛṣṇī.

**Varuṇa**: 'The universal encompasser, the all embracer.' One of the oldest of the Vedic deities, a personification of the all-investing sky, the maker and upholder of heaven and earth. As such he is king of the universe, king of gods and men, possessor of illimitable knowledge, the supreme deity to whom especial honour is due. He is often associated with Mitra, he being the ruler of the night and Mitra the ruler of the day but his name frequently occurs alone, that of Mitra only seldom. The following hymn describes the character of the deity:

> The mighty lord of high, our deeds, as if at hand espies;
> The gods know all men do; though me would fain their deeds disguise
> Whoever stands, whomever moves, or steals from place to place,
> Or hides him in his secret cell, the gods his movement trace
>
> Wherever two together plot, and deem they are alone
> King Varuṇa is there, a third and all their schemes are known
> This earth is his; to him belong those vast and boundless skies;
> Both seas within him rest, and yet in that small pool he lies,
>
> Whoever far beyond the sky should think his way towing;
> He could not there elude the grasp of Varuṇa the king,
> His spies descending from the skies glide this entire world, around,
> Their thousand eyes all-scanning sweep to earth's remotest bound.

The ceaseless winking all he counts of every mortal's
eyes;
He wields this universal frame, as gamester throws his
dice,
Those knotted nooses which thou fling's, O god, the bad
to snare,
All liars let them overtake, but the entire truthful spare.

In later times he was chief among the lower celestial deities called Ādityas, and still he became a sort of Neptune, a god of the seas and rivers, who rides upon the *makara*. This character he still retains in his sign as a fish. He is regent of the west quarter and of one of the *nakṣatra*s or lunar mansions. According to the *Mahābhārata* he was son of Kardama and father of Puṣkara. The *Mahābhārata* relates that he carried off Bhadra, the wife of Utathya, a brāhmaṇa, but Utathya obliged him to submit and restore her. He was in a way the father of the sage Vasiṣṭha. In the Vedas Varuṇa is not specially connected with water, but there are passages in which he is associated with the element of water both in the atmosphere and on the earth, in such a way as many account for the character and functions ascribed to him in the later mythology. Dr. Muir thus sums up in the words of the hymns the functions and attributes of Varuṇa. 'The greatest cosmic functions are ascribed to Varuṇa. Possessed of illimitable resources, the divine being has meted out and upholds heaven and earth, he dwells in all worlds as sovereign ruler; indeed the three worlds are embraced with him. He made the golden and revolving sun to shine in the firmament. The wind which resounds through the atmosphere is his breath. He has opened out boundless paths for the sun, and has hollowed out channels for the rivers, which flow by his command. By his wonderful contrivance the rivers pour out their waters into the one ocean but never fill it. His ordinances are fixed and unassailable. They rest on him unshaken as on a mountain. Through the operation (of his laws) the moon walks in brightness and the stars which appear in the night sky mysteriously vanish in daylight. Neither birds flying in the air nor the rivers in their ceaseless flow can attain a knowledge of his power or his wrath. His messengers behold both worlds. He knows the flight of birds in the sky, the paths of ships on the ocean, the course of the far travelling wind, and beholds all the things that have been or shall be done. No creature can even wink without him. He instructs the *ṛṣi* Vasiṣṭha in mysteries; but his secrets and those of Mitra are not to be revealed to the foolish by the righteous'. The attributes and functions ascribed to Varuṇa impart to his character a moral elevation and sanctity far surpassing than that attributed to any other Vedic deity. In the Purāṇas, Varuṇa is sovereign of the waters and one of his accompaniments is a noose, which the Vedic deity carries for binding offenders. It is called *nāgapāśa, pulakāṅga* or *viśvajīt*. His fawn resort is Puṣpagiri, Flower Mountain, and his city, Vasudhā Nagara. He also possesses an umbrella impermeable to water, formed of the hood of a cobra, and called Abhoga. The *Viṣṇu Purāṇa* mentions an incident that shows a curious coincidence between Varuṇa and Neptune. At the marriage of the sage Ṛcika, Varuṇa supplied him with the thousand-fleet white horses which the bride's father had demanded of him. Varuṇa is of white colour and is draped in yellow garments and possesses a pacific look. His head in representations should be adorned with *karaṇḍa mukuṭa* and all other ornaments and he should be wears on his person a *yajñopavīta*. He should be represented as of strong constitution and as seated upon a fish or a crocodile. He should be shown represented as possessing two or four arms; if shown with two arms only, one hand should be in the *varada* pose and the other should be carrying a *pāśa*, if with four, one of the hands should be in the *varada* pose while the remaining ones should carry the *pāśa*, a snake and a *kamaṇḍalu*. Varuṇa's *vāhana* is a monster fish called Makara. It has the head of a deer, legs of an antelope and the body and tail of a fish. Varuṇa is not worshipped now but is propitiated before voyages. Fishermen also invoke him before venturing out into the sea. Varuṇa, when represented, should be seated in a chariot drawn by seven horses. He must be draped with white garments and adorned with ornaments set with pearls and necklaces, composed of the umbrella and on his left should be the fish banner. He should have a slightly hanging belly and four arms over his head. To the right and left respectively of Varuṇa should be standing the rivers Gaṅgā and Yamunā. Gaṅgā of moon like white colour and possessing a pretty face should be standing on a *matsya* with a *cāmara* in one hand and a *padma* in the other, and Yamunā, also possessing good looks and having the colour of the *nīlotpala* flower, should be standing on a tortoise with a *cāmara* in one hand and a *nīlotpala* in the other. Varuṇa being the lord of the ocean is represented as keeping with him the *padma*, the *śaṅkha* and a vessel containing gems — the sea being believed by the Hindus to be the repository of gems — and as being attended upon by the river goddesses.

Varuṇa's epithets are as follows: Pracetas, lord of the waters; Amburāja, lord of the waters; Jalapati, lord of the waters; Keśa, lord of the waters; Uddama, the surrounder; Pāśabhṛt, the noose-carrier; Viloma, watery-hair; Variloma, watery hair; Yadaḥpati, king of aquatic animals. [*Hindu Mythology*, T.R.R. Iyengar; *A Classical Dictionary of Hindu Mythology and Religion*, J. Dowson; *Epics, Myths and Legends of India*, P. Thomas; *Varuṇa Purāṇa*]

**Varuṇāni:** Wife of Varuṇa and goddess of wine. She is said to have sprung from the churning of the ocean. The goddess of wine is also called Mada and Surā.

**Vāstoṣpati**: [House-protector] One of the later gods of the Veda, represented as springing from Brahmā's alliance with his daughter. He was the protector of sacred rites and guardian of houses.

**Vasu**: The Vasus are a class of deities, eight in number, chiefly known as attendants upon Indra. They seem to have been in Vedic times personifications of natural phenomena. They are Apa, Dhruva, Soma, Anila, Pratyūṣa, Anala, Prabhāsa and Dhara. According to the *Rāmāyaṇa* they were children of Aditi. [*India in the Vedic Age*, P.L. Bhargava]

**Vasudeva**: Son of Śūra, of the Yādava branch of the Lunar race. He was father of Kṛṣṇa and Kuntī, the mother of the Pāṇḍava princes, was his sister. He married seven daughters of Ahuka and the youngest of them, Devakī, was the mother of Kṛṣṇa. After the death of Kṛṣṇa and Balarāma, he also died, and four of his wives burnt themselves with his corpse. So says the *Mahābhārata*, but according to the *Viṣṇu Purāṇa* he and Devakī and Rohiṇī burnt themselves at Dvārakā. He received the additional name of Anakadundubhi, because the gods, conscious that he was to be the putative father of the divine Kṛṣṇa, sounded the drums of heaven at his birth. He was also called Bhū-Kaśyapa and Dundu, 'drum'. [*Dictionary of Hinduism*, T.R.R. Iyengar]

**Vāsukī**: King of the Nāgas who live in *pātāla*. The gods and *asuras* used him as a coil round the mountain Mandāra at the churning of the ocean.

**Vasusena**: A name of Karṇa.

**Vāta**: [Wind] Generally the same as Vāyu, but the name is sometimes combined in the Veda with that of Parjanya and Parajayavāta and Vāyu are then mentioned distinctively.

**Vāyu**: [Air, wind] The god of the wind Eolus. In the Vedas he is often associated with Indra and rides in the same car with him, Indra being the charioteer. The chariot has a framework of gold that touches the sky, and is drawn by a thousand horses. There are not many hymns addressed to him. According to the *Nirukta* there are three gods specially connected with each other: 'Agni whose place is on Earth, Vāyu or Indra, whose place is in the air, and Sūrya whose place is in the heaven'. In the hymn *Puruṣa Sūtka* Vāyu is said to have sprung from the breath of Puruṣa, and in another hymn he is called the son-in-law of Tvaṣṭṛ. He is regent of the north-west quarter where he dwells.

According to the *Viṣṇu Purāṇa* he is king of the *gandharvas*. The *Bhāgavata Purāṇa* relates that the sage Nārada incited the wind to break down the summit of mount Meru. He raised a terrible storm which lasted for a year but Viṣṇu's bird Garuḍa shielded the mountain with his wings, and all the blasts of the wind god were in vain. Nārada then told him to attack the mountain in Garuḍa's absence. He did so, and breaking off the summit of the mountain he hurled it into the sea, where it became the island of Laṅkā.

Vāyu is the reputed father of Bhīma and Hanumān. And he is said to have made the hundred daughters of King Kuśanābha crooked because they would not comply with his licentious desires and this gave the name Kānyakubja, 'hump-backed damsel' to their city.

Other names of Vāyu are: Anila; Marut; Pavana; Vāta; Gandhavaha, 'bearer of perfumes'; Jālakāntara, 'whose garden is water'; Sadāgata, 'ever moving'; Satataga , 'ever moving'.

He is said in the *Mahābhārata* to be the father of Bhīma as also of Hanumān. The Mādhavas believe that their *ācārya*, Ānandatīrtha is an incarnation of Vāyu. He is depicted as a powerful person of youthful constitution, of black colour and possessing two or four arms. His eyes must be of red colour and his garments white. He should have a wavy and curved brow and be adorned with all ornaments. In his right hand it is stated that there should be a *dhvaja* and in the left hand a *daṇḍa*. It might also mean that the right hand should be held in the *patākā-hasta* pose. Some authorities prescribe the *aṅkuśa* in the right hand of this deity. His hair should be dishevelled and he may be seated either on a *siṁhāsana* or on a deer — the latter is more often met within the sculptures as the vehicle of Vāyu. He should also appear to be in a haste to move very quickly. Vāyu is said to have a shining car within a golden seat drawn by a team of ruddy steeds with which he touches the sky. Vāyu is described as beautiful, thousand-eyed, and swift as thought. Like the other gods, Vāyu is found of *soma* for which he is often invited and the first draught of which he obtains as his share, for he is the swiftest of the gods. The *Viṣṇudharmottara* states that the colour both of the body and of the garment of Vāyu should be sky blue and that he should carry in his hands the *cakra* and a *dhvaja*. Vāyu should have his mouth open. To his left seated is his consort. In the *Vāyu Purāṇa* Vāyu has 'declared the laws of duty, in connection with the *śveta kalpa* and which comprises the Māhātmya of Rudra.' It contains twenty-four thousand verses.

[*Glossary of Hinduism*, T. Rengarajan; *Vāyu Purāṇa*; *India in the Vedic Age*, P.L. Bhargava]

**Vedavatī**: The vocal daughter of the sage Kuśadhvaja, son of Bṛhaspati. She was renowned for her beauty and had set her heart on marrying none else than Viṣṇu. When Rāvaṇa tried to gain her affection, she bluntly told him of her mind and that even the deities, not to mention the *gandharva*s, had tried to win her in vain. Such stock replies once provoked the demon king Śāmba so much that he at once slew her father, but nothing could deter her from her firm resolve. Rāvaṇa renewed his suit and once touched her hair and she was so enraged by this contact that she cut off her hair and threatened to commit *satī*, so that in her next birth she might be reborn as Sītā and bring about his destruction. So she entered the blazing fire, and celestial flowers all fell around it. She who was born again as Sītā, and was the moving cause of Rāvaṇa's death though Rāma was the agent. [*Rāmāyaṇa*]

**Veda-Vyāsa**: The arranger of the Vedas. [See 'Vyasa']

**Vegavat**: Swift. A son of Kṛṣṇa.

**Vidhātṛ**: [Creator]. A name of Brahmā, of Viṣṇu and of Viśvakarmā.

**Vidyādhara (mas.), Vidyādharī (fem.)**: [Possessor of knowledge] A class of inferior deities inhabiting the regions between the earth and sky, and generally of benevolent disposition. They are attendants upon Indra, but they have chiefs and kings of their own, and are represented as intermarrying and having much intercourse with men. They are also called Kāmarūpin, 'taking shapes at will'; Khecara and Nabhaścara, 'moving in the air'; Priyamvada 'sweet-spoken'. [*A Classical Dictionary of Hindu Mythology and Religion*, J. Dowson]

**Vindhyavāsinī**: The dweller in the Vindhyas. The wife of Śiva.

**Vīrabhadra**: A son or emanation of Śiva, created from his mouth, and having, according to the *Vāyu Purāṇa*, 'a thousand heads, a thousand eyes, a thousand feet, wielding a thousand clubs, a thousand shafts; holding the shell, the discus, the mace, and bearing a blazing bow and battle-axe; fierce and terrific, shining with dreadful splendour, and decorated with the crescent moon; clothed in a tiger's skin, dripping with blood, having a capacious stomach and a vast mouth armed with formidable tusks. The object of his creation was to stop Dakṣa's sacrifice, and carry away the gods and others who were attending. He is a special object of worship in the Maharashtra country, and there are sculptures of him in the caves of Elephanṭā and Ellorā, where he is represented with eight hands. [*A Classical Dictionary of Hindu Mythology and Religion*, J. Dowson]

**Virāj**: Manu thus describes Virāj: 'Having divided his body into two parts, the Lord became with the half a male and with the (other) half a female; and in her he created Virāj. Know that I (Manu), whom that male Virāj himself created, am the creator of all this world.' One passage in the *Ṛgveda* says, 'From him sprang Virāj and from Virāj sprang Puruṣa', like as Aditi is said to have sprung from Dakṣa, and Dakṣa from Aditi. Virāj, the male half of Brahmā, is supposed to typify all male creatures; and Śatarūpā, the female half, all female forms. [*Vedic Index*, Macdonell and Keith; *Ṛgveda*]

**Virūpākṣa**: [Deformed as to the eyes]. A name of Śiva, who has three eyes. Also one of the Rudras. Also a *dānava*, son of Kaśyapa.

**Viśvaksena**: He is the commander of Viṣṇu's forces. All Vaiṣṇavites at the beginning of all auspicious occasions invoke him, just as Gaṇeśa is invoked by Śaivites. Viśvaksena is also the custodian of the personal effects of Viṣṇu and so all-important in festivals like the *Brahmotsavam*. A special festival first invokes him. He is represented as a seated image with four hands, the upper one carrying *śaṅkha* and *cakra* while the right lower hand is in *tarjanī* pose and the left one holds a heavy *gadā*. [*Dictionary of Hinduism*, T.R.R. Iyengar]

**Viṣṇu**: A Vedic deity. He is the second of the Hindu triad or Trinity. He is not pre-eminent in the Vedas in which, however, a few hymns are dedicated to him. He is depicted as taking three long steps to measure the universe, the first two being visible to humanity and the next which not even birds could transgress. To the wise, he is visible as enthroned in the loftiest station where exists a well of honey and where the deities are happy. He is also known as the friend and assistant of Indra, thus showing a subservience to him. His importance increased during the time of the *Brāhmaṇa*s, the epics and Purāṇas when he rose in estimation till he was assigned the highest position among the celestials in their firmament. As a contrast to him, Agni was relegated to the lowest status among the divinities. How Viṣṇu attained his supreme status is depicted in a legend. During a sacrifice celebrated by the gods for achieving brilliance and the satisfaction of the appetite, they decided that any one among them, who could complete the sacrifice before others, would be considered the most supreme among them. As Viṣṇu succeeded in attaining that object he was assigned that status. Viṣṇu's supremacy is depicted in the legend of the Vāmana *avatāra* as well which is first mentioned in the *Ṛgveda*, as noted earlier. This legend is repeated in the *Mahābhārata*, though briefly; barely noticed in the *Viṣṇu Purāṇa*; at some length in the *Bhāgavata Purāṇa* — all alluding to the supremacy of Viṣṇu, which he had secured in the sphere of public worship. The highest place which he had acquired in popular esteem, is again reflected in the *Kaṭha Upaniṣad*, where the end of the journey, which a mortal soul makes, has for its zenith, the goal of Viṣṇu. He was considered the goal of all immortal ecstasy — an idea from the *Ṛgveda*, as pointed out earlier. Viṣṇu worship was not evidently so popular during Āśvalāyana, so far as ritual was concerned but in the *Gṛhyasūtra*s of Āpastamba, Hiraṇyakeśin and Pārāśara, in the course of marriage rites and the execution of the *saptapadī* ceremony in particular, when everytime the bride takes one step the groom prays to the deity Viṣṇu. Though he was the youngest of the twelve Ādityas, he was the most supreme. In his incarnation as Kṛṣṇa, he was invoked by Draupadī to rescue her when she was taunted and disrobed in an open assembly by the wicked Kauravas. He responded to her appeal at once. He is worshipped by the divinities in the *tīrtha*s of Vaḍava, Lokoddhāra,

Agnidhara and Viṣṇupada. He had recovered a thousand of such *tīrtha*s, which had been captured by a demon in the form of a tortoise. That was one of his manifestations. He manifested himself in ten incarnations. He granted to Rāma, his manifold energy to conquer the demons headed by Rāvaṇa and save the world from all the evils. He assisted in raising the earth from the sea in his Varāha incarnation. As a Narasiṁha he slew the demon Hiraṇyakaśipu and preserved faith in god, and as Vāmana he rescued the three worlds from the demon Bāli. He destroyed the fierce *asura* Jambha, who invariably disturbed execution of sacrifices. Another of his incarnations was that of Rāma Jāmadagnya. On the representation of the deities that a demon had sought refuge in the bottom of the sea, he advised them to approach the sage Agastya with a request to dry it up and later fill it by appealing to Brahmā. Among his other exploits are his slaughter of the demons, Madhu and Kaiṭabha, and his filling up the Kuvalāśva with his boundless energy. He is also interpreted symbolically. He is believed to acquire a red colour in the *tretā* age, yellow in the *dvāpara* and black in *kali* age. At the close of every *yuga*, being the embodiment of manifold energy, he is believed to issue forth in the form of an all-consuming fire to destroy not only this world but also the underworld. At such moments clouds will gather in the skies, pouring forth their showers to quell four thousand of such *yuga*s and the earth will be flooded with the light of the supreme spirit as Nārāyaṇa. He will be endowed with a thousand eyes, feet, heads, and will lie on the great serpent Śeṣa which will have a thousand hoods, enveloping all space with a gloom like that of eternal night itself. His heaven is Vaikuṇṭha comprised of precious stones of every conceivable kind and there he is supposed to dwell with Lakṣmī. The ten incarnations of Viṣṇu have been interpreted astronomically. They have been held to be no other than the forms cast by the gnomon during the *dakṣiṇāyaṇa* and *uttarāyaṇa*. The strides of Viṣṇu, referred to in the *Kr̥ṣṇa Yajurveda* in terms of meters like Gāyatrī, Triṣṭubh, Anuṣṭubh and Jagatī, have been held to imply the varying lengths of a *dakṣiṇāyaṇa* and 48 *aṅgula*s on the *uttarāyaṇa*s in the month of Pauṣa. The different shapes of the gnomon shadows have been interpreted to alluding to each of the incarnations. In the Purāṇas, Viṣṇu's supremacy was maintained. In them his incarnations are sometimes described as ten, at other times as twenty-four while in some connections, they are said to be without any end. Of the ten *avatāra*s, nine have been completed while the tenth Kalki is yet to take place. The *Matsya Purāṇa* explains why Viṣṇu had to manifest himself in so many incarnations. The demons, on finding that the gods were always worsening them in battle, appealed to their preceptor Śukra. He left them to perform a mighty penance to procure from Śiva a charm that would always ensure victory to them. Until he returned they wanted a refuge and so they decided to approach Śukra's mother, Kavyā, who agreed to protect them. The gods, finding the fiends in this helpless condition, decided to destroy all of them. When Kavyā realised what the gods were about to do, she threatened Indra that she would deprive him of his sovereignty over the deities if he, with his celestial hosts, would not desist from their course. Indra, frightened and disheartened, was about to give up the proposed attack but Viṣṇu agreed to come to his help. In order to subdue both Indra and Viṣṇu, Kavyā commenced a great penance, which if completed would have upset the designs of Viṣṇu and Indra. So Indra prevailed on Viṣṇu to see that she did not complete her penance. Viṣṇu, finding his discus, decapitated her and this enraged her husband Bhṛgu so much that he cursed Viṣṇu to be born seven times in the world of men for having wilfully slain a woman. Later he modified his curse, adding that each one of such births would be for the benefit of humanity and the re-establishment of *dharma*. To these seven *avatāra*s were added more till their number was increased to ten. The names of Viṣṇu are many. Among them the most popular are Vikuṇṭhanātha or Lord of Heavan. Viṣṇu has been worshipped from a very long time. The *Viṣṇu Purāṇa* describes the benefits of his worship. He is propitiated by the observation of the Varṇa Dharma, the protection of the outcasts and the rituals associated with them, the performance of sacrifice, non-injury to living creatures, doing of good to others, leading a blameless life and purity in heart. To a person, who observes all these injunctions, not only all earthly enjoyments but also heaven and a place therein will be assured. His worship has prevailed not only in the north but also in the south, in different places and in various forms. In the *Mānasāra* he is shown as a deity with four arms, two eyes, wearing a high crown, a yellow scarf, with a *śrīvatsa* mark or symbol on his chest. He carries the discus and the conch in his upper two hands while in his lower one he holds the club and the sword or the lotus. Sometimes, his lower hands are shown in the postures of granting boons and protection. In such images Viṣṇu has usually a prominent nose, broad eyes and a smiling face. On his right and left are the deities Śrī and Mahi. Sometimes the goddess Nīladevī is depicted as seated with four hands in two of which she has lotuses. In actual imagery, out of his ten *avatāra*s generally are depicted the Varāha, Vāmana, Rāma and Kṛṣṇa — either as the cowherd or the chief hero in the Kurukṣetra battle. As preserver and restorer, Viṣṇu is a very popular deity, and the worship paid to him is of a joyous character. He has a thousand names, the repetition of which is a meritorious act of devotion. Of the thousand names of Viṣṇu, the following are some of the most common: Acyuta,unfallen, imperishable; Ananta, endless; Anantaśayana, who sleeps on the serpent; Caturbhuja, four-armed; Dāmodara, bound round the belly with a rope; Kṛṣṇa, cowkeeper; Govinda; Gopāla; Hari; Hṛṣikeśa, lord of the organs of sense; Jalaśāyin, who sleeps on the waters; Janārdana, whom men worship; Keśava, the hairy; Kirīṭin, wearing a tiara; Lakṣmīpati, lord of Lakṣmī; Madhusūdana, destroyer of Madhu; Mādhava, descendant of Madhu; Mukunda, deliverer; Murāri, the foe of Mura; Nara, the man; Nārāyaṇa, who moves in the waters; Pañcāyudha, armed with five weapons; Padmanābha, lotus-navel; Pītāmbara, clothed in yellow garments; Puruṣa, the man; Puruṣottama, the highest of men; the supreme spirit; Śārṅgin, carrying the bow *śārṅga;* Vāsudeva-Kṛṣṇa, son of Vasudeva; Vārṣṇeya, descendant of Vṛṣṇī; Vaikuṇṭhanātha, lord of Vaikuṇṭha; Yajñeśa, lord of sacrifice; Yajñeśvara, lord of sacrifice.

In addition to the popular *daśāvatāra* forms of Viṣṇu, he is also represented in many other aspects. But of these twenty-four are considered most important and are repeated in daily worship. According to the esoteric doctrines of the Vaiṣṇava schools, the supreme Lord Pravāsudeva, the primeval form of Viṣṇu, is considered to possess six excellent characteristics, knowledge, energy, strength, supremacy, heroism and brilliance and is said to be free from any evil. From him sprang four Vibhāva forms, in each of which two *guṇa*s predominating as under: Saṅkarṣaṇa — with *jñāna* and *bala,* Pradyumna — with *aiśvarya* and *vīrya,* and Aniruddha — with *śakti* and *tejas.*

From each of these four aspects of *Vibhāva-mūrti*s, *Ahirbudhnya-Saṁhitā* says that three other minor aspects emanated. Thus from Vāsudeva sprang Keśava, Nārāyaṇa, and Mādhava. From Saṅkarṣaṇa arose Govinda, Viṣṇu and Madhusūdana. Trivikrama, Vāmana and Śrīdhara sprang forth from Pradyumna, while from Aniruddha came Hṛṣikeśa, Padmanābha and Dāmodara. Thus evolved the twelve *mūrti*s from the primeval aspect of Viṣṇu, which are popularly known as *dvādaśa mūrti*s whose names are daily repeated in the *sandhyāvandanam.* From these secondary deities came out Puruṣottama, Adhokṣaja, Narasiṁha, Acyuta, Janārdana, Upendra, Hari and Kṛṣṇa. Thus, with these eight further manifestations and the four Vibhāva forms, there are twenty-four *mūrti*s of Viṣṇu each of which is worshipped in some place or other. The twenty-four *mūrti*s of Viṣṇu, according to *Rūpamaṇḍana*, along with the names of the corresponding Devīs are as follows:

| *Name of the Mūrti* | *Name of his Devī* |
|---|---|
| Keśava | Kirīṭī |
| Nārāyaṇa | Kānti |
| Mādhava | Tuṣṭi |
| Govinda | |
| Viṣṇu | |

| | |
|---|---|
| Madhusūdana | |
| Trivikrama | Śānti |
| Vāmana | Kriyā |
| Śrīdhara | Medhā |
| Ṛṣikeśa | Harṣa |
| Padmanābha | Śraddhā |
| Dāmodara | Lajjā |
| Saṅkarṣaṇa | Sarasvatī |
| Vāsudeva | Lakṣmī |
| Pradyumna | Prīti |
| Aniruddha | Rati |
| Puruṣottama | |
| Adhokṣaja | |
| Narasiṁha | Dayā |
| Acyuta | |
| Janārdana | |
| Upendra | |
| Hari | |
| Kṛṣṇa | |

But according to strict Vaiṣṇavite conception, the images of the *dvādaśa mūrti*s are conceived differently. The following is the description of these *mūrti*s according to an acknowledged authority. Of these, Keśava, shining like gold, bears four *cakra*s. The dark-complexioned Nārāyaṇa bears four *śaṅkha*s. Govinda, who shines like the moon, has four bows. Viṣṇu, who resembles the lotus-blossoms in complexion, bears four ploughs. The lotus-complexioned Madhusūdana has four clubs. The fire-complexioned Trivikrama holds four swords. Vāmana, who is effulgent like the rising sun, bears four *vajra*s; and Śrīdhara who resembles a white lotus in colour bears four maces. Padmanābha, who is radiant as the sun, has five weapons. Dāmodhara, who is red-complexioned, bears four cords. Viṣṇu is represented in art as reposing on the coils of the serpent Śeṣa, his wife sitting at his feet. The stream of a lotus shoots up from his navel, and on the blossom sits Brahmā. Viṣṇu has four hands in each of which he holds different weapons. His heaven is Vaikuṇṭha, made entirely of gold. Its circumference is 80,000 miles. All its buildings are made of jewels. The pillars and ornaments of the building are of precious stones. The celestial Ganges flows through it. In Vaikuṇṭha are also five pools containing blue, red and white lotuses. On a seat glorious as the meridian sun, sitting on white lotuses is Viṣṇu and on his right side Lakṣmī, who shines like a continued blaze of lightning and from whose body the fragrance of the lotus extends 800 miles. The *Viṣṇu Sahasranāma*, held most sacred for the worship of Viṣṇu, enumerates a thousand names. The names are described below alphabetically. Numbers written in the parentheses shows the sequence of the name appearing in *śloka*s of *Viṣṇu Sahasranāma*:

Abhiprāyāya (871)

Abhuve (437)

Acalāya (745)

Acintyāya (832)

Acyutāya (100)

Acyutāya (318)

Adbhutāya (895)

Ādhāranilayāya (950)

Adhātre (951)

Adhiṣṭhānāya (324)

Adhokṣajāya (415)

Adhṛtāya (842)

Ādidevāya (334)

Ādidevāya (490)

Ādityāya (40)

Ādityāya (563)

Adṛśyāya (304)

Agrāhyāya (56)

Agrajāya (891)

Agraṇye (218)

Ahaḥ Saṁvartakāya (232)

Ahre (90)

Ajāya (204)

Ajāya (521)

Ajāya (95)

Ajitāya (549)

Akrūrāya (915)

Akṣarāya (17)

Akṣarāya (481)

Akṣobhyāya (801)

Akṣobhyāya (999)

Amānine (747)

Amaraprabhave (50)

Ambhonidhaye (517)

Ameyātmane (102)
Ameyātmane (179)
Amitāśanāya (372)
Amitavikramāya (516)
Amitavikramāya (641)
Amoghāya (110)
Amoghāya (154)
Amṛtāśāya (813)
Amṛtāṁśūdbhavāya (283)
Amṛtapāya (504)
Amṛtavapuṣe (814)
Amṛtāya (119)
Amṛtyave (198)
Amūrtaye (830)
Amūrtimate (720)
Anādaye (941)
Anādinidhanāya (43)
Anaghāya (146)
Anaghāya (831)
Analāya (293)
Analāya (711)
Anāmayāya (689)
Ānandāya (526)
Ānandine (560)
Anantaśriye (933)
Anantajite (307)
Anantarūpāya (932)
Anantātmane (518)
Anantāya (659)
Anantāya (886)
Anarthāya (431)
Aṇave (835)
Anayāya (400)
Anekamūrtaye (721)
Anilāya (234)
Anilāya (812)
Animiṣāya (215)
Anirdeśyavapuṣe (177)
Anirdeśyavapuṣe (656)
Aniruddhāya (185)
Aniruddhāya (638)
Anirviṇṇāya (435)
Anirviṇṇāya (892)
Anīśāya (626)
Anivartine (596)
Anivṛttātmane (774)
Aniyamāya (865)
Annādāya (984)
Annāya (983)
Antakāya (520)
Anukūlāya (342)
Anuttamāya (81)
Apāṁanidhaye (323)
Aparājitāya (716)
Aparājitāya (862)
Apramattāya (325)
Aprameyātmane (248)
Aprameyāya (47)

Apratirathāya (639)
Apyayāya (900)
Araudrāya (906)
Arciṣmate (633)
Arcitāya (634)
Arhāya (873)
Arkāya (795)
Arthāya (430)
Arvindākṣāya (347)
Asaṅkhyeyāya (247)
Asammitāya (108)
Asate (479)
Aśokāya (336)
Āśramāya (852)
Aśvatthāya (824)
Atīndrāya (157)
Atīndriyāya (169)
Ātmayonaye (985)
Atulāya (355)
Auṣadhāya (287)
Āvartanāya (228)
Avidheyātmane (621)
Avijñātre (482)
Aviśiṣṭāya (309)
Avyaktāya (722)
Avyaṅgāya (129)
Avyayāya (13)
Avyayāya (31)
Ayamāya (866)
Babhrave (116)
Bahuśirase (115)
Bhagaghne (559)
Bhagavate (558)
Bhaktavatsalāya (736)
Bhānave (284)
Bhārabhr̥te (847)
Bhartre (34)
Bhāskaradyutaye (282)
Bhāvanāya (33)
Bhāvāya (7)
Bhayakr̥te (833)
Bhayanāśanāya (834)
Bhayāpahāya (935)
Bheṣajāya (578)
Bhīmaparākramāya (949)
Bhīmāya (357)
Bhīmāya (948)
Bhiṣaje (579)
Bhojanāya (142)
Bhoktre (143)
Bhoktre (500)
Bhoktre (888)
Bhrājiṣṇave (141)
Bhūgarbhāya (72)
Bhūrbhuvaḥsvastarave (967)
Bhūridakṣiṇāya (502)
Bhuṣaṇāya (629)
Bhūśayāya (628)

Bhūtabhāvanāya (9)
Bhūtabhavyabhāvannāthāya (290)
Bhūtabhavyabhavatprabhave (4)
Bhūtabhṛte (6)
Bhūtādaye (29)
Bhūtakṛte (5)
Bhūtamaheśvarāya (489)
Bhūtātmane (8)
Bhūtāvāsāya (708)
Bhūtaye (630)
Bhuvo Bhuve (942)
Bījamavyayāya (429)
Brahmajñāya (669)
Brahmakṛte (662)
Brāhmaṇapriyāya (670)
Brāhmaṇāya (667)
Brahmaṇe (663)
Brahmaṇe (664)
Brahmaṇyāya (661)
Brahmavide (666)
Brahmavivardhanāya (665)
Brahmiṇe (668)
Bṛhadbhānave (333)
Bṛhadrūpāya (272)
Bṛhate (836)
Bujagottamāya (193)
Cakragadādharāya (546)
Cakriṇe (908)
Cakriṇe (995)
Calāya (746)
Candanāṅgadine (740)
Candrāṁśave (281)
Cāṇūrāndhraniṣūdanāya (825)
Caturaśrāya (936)
Caturātmane (137)
Caturātmane (769)
Caturbāhave (766)
Caturbhāvāya (770)
Caturbhujāya (140)
Caturdaṁṣṭrāya (139)
Caturgataye (768)
Caturmūrtaye (765)
Caturvedavide (771)
Caturvyūhāya (138)
Caturvyūhāya (767)
Chinnasaṁśayāya (623)

Dakṣāya (423)
Dakṣāya (917)
Dakṣiṇāya (918)
Damanāya (190)
Damāya (861)
Damayitre (860)
Dāmodarāya (367)
Daṇḍāya (859)
Darpadāya (713)

Darpaghne (712)
Dāruṇāya (569)
Dāśārhāya (511)
Devabhṛdgurave (493)
Devakīnandanāya (989)
Devāya (375)
Deveśāya (492)
Dhāmne (211)
Dhanañjayāya (660)
Dhaneśvarāya (474)
Dhanurdharāya (857)
Dhanurvedāya (858)
Dhanvine (77)
Dhanyāya (754)
Dharādharāya (756)
Dharaṇīdharāya (235)
Dharmādhyakṣāya (135)
Dharmagupe (475)
Dharmakṛte (476)
Dharmaviduttamāya (404)
Dharmāya (403)
Dharmayūpāya (438)
Dharmiṇe (477)
Dhātava Uttamāya (46)
Dhātre (44)
Dhṛtātmane (160)
Dhruvāya (388)
Dhuryāya (329)
Dīptamūrtaye (719)
Diśāya (940)
Divaḥ Spṛśe (571)
Draviṇapradāya (570)
Dṛḍhāya (551)
Dṛptāya (714)
Duḥsvapnanāśanāya (926)
Durādharṣāya (82)
Durārighne (781)
Duratikramāya (776)
Durāvāsāya (780)
Durdharāya (266)
Durdharāya (715)
Durgamāya (778)
Durgāya (779)
Durjayāya (775)
Durlabhāya (777)
Durmarṣaṇāya (205)
Duṣkṛtighne (924)
Dyutidharāya (758)
Ekapade (772)
Ekasmai (725)
Ekātmane (965)
Gabhastinemaye (486)
Gabhirātmane (937)
Gabhīrāya (543)
Gadādharāya (997)
Gadāgrajāya (764)
Gahanāya (382)
Gahanāya (544)

Garuḍadhvajāya (354)
Gatisattamāya (566)
Ghṛtāśiṣe (744)
Gohitāya (591)
Gopataye (495)
Gopataye (592)
Goptre (496)
Goptre (593)
Govidāṁpataye (188)
Govindāya (187)
Govindāya (539)
Grāmaṇye (219)
Guhāya (383)
Guhyāya (542)
Guṇabhṛte (839)
Guptāya (545)
Gurave (209)
Gurutamāya (210)
Halāyudhāya (562)
Haṁsāya (191)
Haraye (650)
Havirharaye (359)
Haviṣe (698)
Hemāṅgāya (738)
Hetave (366)
Hiraṇyagarbhāya (71)
Hiraṇyagarbhāya (411)
Hiraṇyanābhāya (194)
Hṛṣīkeśāya (48)
Hutbhuje (879)
Hutbhuje (887)
Ijyāya (446)
Indrakarmaṇe (786)
Īśānāya (65)
Iṣṭāya (308)
Īśvarāya (37)
Īśvarāya (75)
Jagadādijāya (145)
Jagataḥ Setave (288)
Jahnave (244)
Janajanmādaye (947)
Jananāya (946)
Janārdanāya (126)
Janeśvarāya (341)
Janmamṛtyujarātigāya (966)
Jayantāya (798)
Jayāya (509)
Jetre (148)
Jitakrodhāya (462)
Jitamanyave (934)
Jitāmitrāya (524)
Jīvanāya (930)
Jīvāya (513)
Jñānagamyāya (497)
Jñānāyottamāya (454)
Jyeṣṭhāya (68)
Jyotirādityāya (564)
Jyotirgaṇeśvarāya (619)

Jyotiṣe (877)
Kālaneminighne (642)
Kālāya (418)
Kāmadevāya (651)
Kāmaghne (294)
Kāmakṛte (295)
Kāmapālāya (652)
Kāmapradāya (298)
Kāmāya (297)
Kāmine (653)
Kanakāṅgadine (541)
Kāntāya (296)
Kāntāya (654)

Kapaye (899)
Kapilāya (898)
Kapīndrāya (501)
Karaṇāya (378)
Kāraṇāya (379)
Kartre (380)
Kasmai (729)
Kathitāya (848)
Kavaye (132)
Kāya (728)
Keśavāya (23)
Keśavāya (648)
Keśighne (649)
Khaṇḍaparaśave (568)
Kramāya (80)
Kratave (448)
Krodhaghne (314)
Krodhakṛtkartre (315)
Kṛśāya (837)
Kṛṣṇāya (58)
Kṛṣṇāya (550)
Kṛtāgamāya (655)
Kṛtāgamāya (789)
Kṛtajñāya (83)
Kṛtajñāya (532)
Kṛtakarmaṇe (788)
Kṛtākṛtāya (136)
Kṛtalakṣaṇāya (485)
Kṛtāntakṛte (537)
Kṛtirātmavate (84)
Kṣamāya (442)
Kṣāmāya (443)
Kṣāmāya (854)
Kṣamiṇāṁvarāya (919)
Kṣarāya (480)
Kṣemakṛte (599)
Kṣetrajñāya (16)
Kṣitīśāya (991)
Kṣobhaṇāya (374)
Kumbhāya (635)
Kumudāya (589)
Kumudāya (807)
Kuṇḍaline (907)
Kundarāya (808)

Kundāya (809)
Kuvaleśayāya (590)
Lakṣmīvate (361)
Lakṣmyai (943)
Lohitākṣāya (59)
Lokabandhave (733)
Lokādhiṣṭhānāya (894)
Lokādhyakṣāya (133)
Lokanāthāya (734)
Lokasāraṅgāya (783)
Lokasvāmine (750)
Lokatrayāśrayāya (614)
Mādhavāya (73)
Mādhavāya (167)
Mādhavāya (735)
Madhave (168)
Madhusūdanāya (74)
Mahābalāya (172)
Mahābhāgāya (370)
Mahābhogāya (433)
Mahābhūtāya (805)
Mahābuddhaye (173)
Mahādevāya (491)
Mahādhanāya (434)
Mahādridhr̥ṣe (180)
Mahādyutaye (176)
Mahāgartāya (804)
Mahāhaviṣe (678)
Mahāhradāya (803)
Mahākarmaṇe (672)
Mahākarmaṇe (787)
Mahākośāya (432)
Mahākramāya (671)
Mahākratave (675)
Mahākṣāya (353)
Mahāmakhāya (439)
Mahāmanase (557)
Mahāmūrtaye (718)
Mahāmāyāya (170)
Mahānidhaye (806)
Maharddhaye (350)
Mahārhāya (522)
Maharṣaye Kapilācāryāya (531)
Mahāśaktaye (175)
Mahāśanāya (303)
Mahāśr̥ṅgāya (536)
Mahāsvanāya (42)
Mahātapase (122)
Mahate (841)
Mahātejase (673)
Mahāvarāhāya (538)
Mahāvīryāya (174)
Mahāyajñāya (677)
Mahāyajvane (676)
Mahejyāya (447)
Mahendrāya (268)
Maheṣvāsāya (181)
Mahībhartre (182)

Mahīdharāya (317)
Mahīdharāya (369)
Mahodadhiśayāya (519)
Mahoragāya (674)
Mahotsāhāya (171)
Mānadāya (748)
Manave (52)
Maṅgalāyaparasmai (64)
Manoharāya (461)
Manojavāya (690)
Mantrāya (280)
Mānyāya (749)
Mārgāya (365)
Mārgāya (397)
Marīcaye (189)
Medhajāya (753)
Medhāvine (78)
Medinīpataye (533)
Muktānāṁparamāyaigataye (12)
Mukundāya (515)
Nahuṣāya (312)
Naikajāya (890)
Naikakarmakr̥te (469)
Naikamāyāya (302)
Naikarūpāya (271)
Naikasmai (726)
Naikaśr̥ṅgāya (763)
Naikātmane (468)
Nakṣatranemaye (440)
Nakṣatriṇe (441)
Nandakine (994)
Nandanāya (527)
Nandāya (528)
Nandaye (618)
Nārasiṁhavapuṣe (21)
Narāya (246)
Nārāyaṇāya (245)
Nayāya (399)
Netre (222)
Neyāya (398)
Nidhaye (30)
Nigrahāya (761)
Nimiṣāya (214)
Nirguṇāya (840)
Nirvāṇāya (577)
Niṣṭhāyai (583)
Nivr̥ttātmane (229)
Nivr̥ṭṭātmane (597)
Niyamāya (161)
Niyantre (864)
Nyagrodhāya (822)
Nyāyāya (221)
Ojastejodyutidharāya (275)
Padamanuttamāya (732)
Padmagarbhāya (348)
Padmanābhāya (49)
Padmanābhāya (196)

Padmanābhāya (346)
Padmanibhekṣaṇāya (345)
Padmine (344)
Paṇāya (958)
Pāpanāśanāya (992)
Paramaspaṣṭāya (390)
Paramātmane (11)
Parameṣṭhine (419)
Parameśvarāya (377)
Pararddhaye (389)
Parāyaṇāya (585)
Parigrahāya (420)
Parjanyāya (810)
Paryavasthitāya (931)
Pavanāya (291)
Pāvanāya (292)
Pāvanāya (811)
Pavitrāya (63)
Peśalāya (916)
Prabhavāya (35)
Prabhave (36)
Prabhave (299)
Prabhūtāya (61)
Pradhānapuruṣeśvarāya (20)
Pradyumnāya (640)
Pragrahāya (760)
Prāgvaṁśāya (845)
Prajābhavāya (89)
Prajāgarāya (953)
Prajāpataye (70)
Prajāpataye (197)
Prakāśanāya (274)
Prakāśātmane (276)
Prāmāṇāya (428)
Pramāṇāya (959)
Pramodanāya (525)
Prāṁśave (153)
Prāṇabhṛte (961)
Prāṇadāya (321)
Prāṇadāya (408)
Prāṇadāya (66)
Prāṇadāya (956)
Prāṇajivanāya (962)
Prāṇanilayāya (960)
Praṇavāya (409)
Praṇavāya (957)
Prāṇāya (67)
Prāṇāya (320)
Prāṇāya (407)
Prapitāmahāya (970)
Prasannātmane (237)
Pratāpanāya (277)
Pratardanāya (60)
Prathitāya (319)
Pratiṣṭhitāya (326)
Pratyayāya (93)
Prītivardhanāya (875)
Priyakṛte (874)

Priyārhāya (872)
Pṛthave (410)
Punarvasave (150)
Puṇḍarīkākṣāya (111)
Puṇyakīrtaye (688)
Puṇyaśravaṇakīrtanāya (922)
Puṇyāya (687)
Puṇyāya (925)
Purandarāya (335)
Purātanāya (498)
Pūrayitre (686)
Pūrṇāya (685)
Purujite (506)
Purusattamāya (507)
Puruṣāya (14)
Puruṣāya (406)
Puruṣottamāya (24)
Puṣkarākṣāya (41)
Puṣkarākṣāya (556)
Puṣpahāsāya (952)
Puṣṭāya (392)
Pūtātmane (10)
Rakṣaṇāya (928)
Rāmāya (394)
Raṇapriyāya (684)
Rathāṅgapāṇaye (998)
Ratnagarbhāya (473)
Ratnanābhāya (793)
Ravaye (881)
Ravilocanāya (885)
Ṛddhāya (278)
Ṛddhāya (351)
Ṛtave (416)
Rohitāya (364)
Rucirāṅgadāya (945)
Rudrāya (114)
Śabdasahāya (912)
Śabdātigāya (911)
Sadāmarṣiṇe (893)
Sadāyogine (165)
Sadbhūtaye (702)
Sadbhyo (929)
Sadgataye (699)
Sādhave (243)
Sahasrākṣāya (226)
Sahasrāṁśave (483)
Sahasramūrdhne (224)
Sahasrapade (227)
Sahasrārciṣe (826)
Sahāya (368)
Sahiṣṇave (144)
Sahiṣṇave (565)
Sajasrajite (306)
Sākṣiṇe (15)
Śaktimatāṁ Śreṣṭhāya (402)
Sāmagāya (575)
Sāmagāyanāya (988)
Samātmane (107)

Samāya (109)
Śamāya (581)
Samayajñāya (358)
Saṁbhavāya (32)
Śaṁbhave (39)
Samīhanāya (444)
Samīraṇāya (223)
Samitiñjayāya (362)
Sāmne (576)
Saṁnyāsakr̥te (580)
Saṁpramardanāya (231)
Saṁsthānāya (386)
Saṁvatsarāya (91)
Saṁvatsarāya (422)
Saṁvr̥tāya (230)
Sanān (896)
Sanātanatamāya (897)
Sandhātre (201)
Sandhimate (202)
Saṅgrahāya (158)
Saṅkarṣaṇāyācyutāya (552)
Śaṅkhabhr̥te (993)
Saṅkṣeptre (598)
Sannivāsāya (706)
Śāntāya (582)
Śāntidāya (587)
Śāntyai (584)
Saptaidhase (828)
Saptajihvāya (827)
Saptavāhanāya (829)
Śarabhāya (356)
Śaraṇāya (86)
Sargāya (159)
Śarīrabhr̥te (349)
Śarīrabhūtabhr̥te (499)
Śarmaṇe (87)
Śārṅgadhanvane (996)
Sarvadarśanāya (94)
Sarvadarśine (451)
Sarvādaye (99)
Sarvadr̥gvyāsāya (572)
Sarvadr̥śe (199)
Sarvagāya (123)
Sarvajñāya (453)
Sarvajñāya (815)
Sarvakāmadāya (851)
Sarvalakṣaṇalakṣaṇyāya (360)
Sarvapraharaṇāyudhāya (1000)
Śarvarīkarāya (914)
Sarvasahāya (863)
Sarvaśastrabhr̥tāṁvarāya (759)
Sarvasmai (25)
Sarvāsunilayāya (710)
Sarvataścakṣuṣe (625)
Sarvatomukhāya (816)
Sarvavāgīśvareśvarāya (802)
Sarvavidbhānave (124)

Sarvavijjayine (799)
Śarvāya (26)
Sarvayogavinisṛtāya (103)
Sarveśvarāya (96)
Śaśabindave (285)
Śāstre (206)
Śāśvatasthāṇave (120)
Śāśvatasthirāya (627)
Śāśvatāya (57)
Satāṁgataye (184)
Satāṁgataye (450)
Śatamūrtaye (723)
Śatānanāya (724)
Śatānandāya (617)
Śatāvartāya (343)
Sate (478)
Satkartre (241)
Satkīrtaye (622)
Satkṛtāya (242)
Satkṛtaye (700)
Satparāyaṇāya (703)
Satpathācārāya (955)
Satrāya (449)
Śatrughnāya (412)
Śatrujite (820)
Śatrutāpanāya (821)
Sattāyai (701)
Sattvasthāya (487)
Sattvavate (867)
Sāttvikāya (868)
Sātvatāṁpataye (512)
Satyadharmaṇe (529)
Satyadharmaparākramāya (289)
Satyadharmaparāyaṇāya (870)
Satyamedhase (755)
Satyaparākramāya (213)
Satyasandhāya (510)
Satyāya (106)
Satyāya (212)
Satyāya (869)
Śauraye (340)
Śauraye (644)
Savāya (727)
Savitre (884)
Savitre (969)
Siddhārthāya (252)
Siddhasaṅkalpāya (253)
Siddhāya (97)
Siddhāya (819)
Siddhaye (98)
Siddhidāya (254)
Siddhisādhanāya (255)
Śikhaṇḍine (311)
Siṁhāya (200)
Siṁhāya (488)
Śipiviṣṭāya (273)
Śiśirāya (913)
Śiṣṭakṛte (250)

Śiṣṭeṣṭāya (310)
Śivāya (27)
Śivāya (600)
Skandadharāya (328)
Skandāya (327)
Smāvartāya (773)
Śokanāśanāya (632)
Somapāya (503)
Somāya (505)
Spaṣṭākṣarāya (279)
Sragviṇe (216)
Sraṣṭre (588)
Sraṣṭre (990)
Śreṣṭāya (69)
Śreyase (612)
Śrīdāya (605)
Śrīdharāya (610)
Śrīgarbhāya (376)
Śrīkarāya (611)
Śramaṇāya (853)
Śrīmatāṁvarāya (604)
Śrīmate (22)
Śrīmate (178)
Śrīmate (220)
Śrīmate (613)
Śrīnidhaye (608)
Śrīnivāsāya (183)
Śrīnivāsāya (607)
Śrīpataye (603)
Śrīśāya (606)
Śrīvāsāya (602)
Śrīvatsavakṣase (601)
Śrīvibhāvanāya (609)
Śṛṅgiṇe (797)
Śrutisāgarāya (264)
Stavapriyāya (680)
Stavyāya (679)
Sthānadāya (387)
Sthāṇave (28)
Sthāvarasthāṇave (427)
Sthavirāya Dhruvāya (55)
Sthaviṣṭhāya (54)
Sthaviṣṭhāya (436)
Sthirāya (203)
Sthūlāya (838)
Stotrāya (681)
Stotre (683)
Stutaye (682)
Śubhāṅgāya (586)
Śubhāṅgāya (782)
Śubhekṣaṇāya (393)
Subhujāya (265)
Śucaye (155)
Śucaye (251)
Śuciśravase (118)
Sudarśanāya (417)
Sudhanvane (567)
Sughoṣāya (458)

Suhr̥de (460)
Sukhadāya (459)
Sukhadāya (889)
Sūkṣmāya (457)
Sulabhāya (817)
Sulocanāya (794)
Sumedhase (752)
Sumukhāya (456)
Sundarāya (791)
Sundāya (792)
Śūnyāya (743)
Suparṇāya (192)
Suparṇāya (855)
Suprasādāya (236)
Surādhyakṣāya (134)
Śūrajaneśvarāya (645)
Surānandāya (186)
Surārighne (208)
Śūrasenāya (704)
Śūrāya (339)
Sureśāya (85)
Sureśvarāya (286)
Surucaye (878)
Sūryāya (883)
Suṣeṇāya (540)
Sutantave (784)
Sutapase (195)
Suvarṇabindave (800)
Suvarṇavarṇāya (737)
Suvīrāya (944)
Suvratāya (455)
Suvratāya (818)
Suyāmunāya (707)
Svābhāvyāya (523)
Svadhr̥tāya (843)
Svakṣāya (615)
Svāṅgāya (548)
Svaṅgāya (616)
Svāpanāya (465)
Svastaye (903)
Svastibhuje (904)
Svastidakṣiṇāya (905)
Svastidāya (901)
Svastikr̥te (902)
Svāsyāya (844)
Svavaśāya (466)
Svayaṁbhuve (38)
Svayaṁjātāya (986)
Tantuvardhanāya (785)
Tāraṇāya (337)
Tārāya (338)
Tārāya (968)
Tasmai (731)
Tattvavide (964)
Tattvāya (963)
Tejovr̥ṣāya (757)
Tīrthakarāya (691)
Tridaśādhyakṣāya (535)

Trikakubdhāmne (62)
Trilokadhr̥ṣe (751)
Trilokātmane (646)
Trilokeśāya (647)
Tripadāya (534)
Trisāmne (574)
Trivikramāya (530)
Tuṣṭāya (391)
Tvaṣṭre (53)
Udbhavāya (373)
Udbhavāya (790)
Udīrṇāya (624)
Udumbarāya (823)
Ugrāya (421)
Upendrāya (151)
Ūrdhvagāya (954)
Ūrjitaśāsanāya (910)
Ūrjitāya (156)
Uttāraṇāya (923)
Uttarāya (494)
Vācaspataya Udāradhiye (217)
Vācaspataye'yonijāya (573)
Vāgmine (267)
Vahnaye (233)
Vaidyāya (164)
Vaikhānāya (987)
Vaikuṇṭhāya (405)
Vājasanāya (796)
Vāmanāya (152)
Vaṁśavardhanāya (846)
Vanamāline (561)
Varadāya (330)
Varāṅgāya (739)
Varārohāya (121)
Vardhamānāya (262)
Vardhanāya (261)
Varuṇāya (553)
Vāruṇāya (554)
Vaṣaṭkārāya (3)
Vāsavānujāya (322)
Vasave (104)
Vasave (270)
Vasave (696)
Vasudāya (269)
Vāsudevāya (332)
Vāsudevāya (695)
Vāsudevāya (709)
Vasumanase (105)
Vasumanase (697)
Vasupradāya (693)
Vasupradāya (694)
Vasuretase (692)
Vatsalāya (471)
Vatsarāya (470)
Vatsine (472)
Vāyave (414)
Vāyuvāhanāya (331)
Vāyuvāhanāya (856)

Vedāṅgāya (130)
Vedavide (128)
Vedavide (131)
Vedāya (127)
Vedhase (547)
Vedyāya (163)
Vegavate (371)
Vibhave (240)
Vibhave (880)
Vidāraṇāya (464)
Vidhātre (45)
Vidhātre (484)
Vidiśāya (938)
Vidvattamāya (920)
Vihāyasagataye (876)
Vijayāya (147)
Vijitātmane (620)
Vikartre (381)
Vikramāya (79)
Vikramiṇe (76)
Vikramiṇe (909)
Vikṣarāya (363)
Vimuktātmane (452)
Vinayāya (508)
Vinayitāsākṣiṇe (514)
Vīrabāhave (463)
Vīraghne (166)
Vīraghne (741)
Vīraghne (927)
Virāmāya (395)
Viratāya (396)
Vīrāya (401)
Vīrāya (643)
Vīrāya (658)
Virocanāya (882)
Viṣamāya (742)
Viśiṣṭāya (249)
Viṣṇave (2)
Viṣṇave (258)
Viṣṇave (657)
Viśodhanāya (637)
Viśokāya (631)
Viśrāmāya (424)
Viśrutātmane (207)
Vistārāya (426)
Viśuddhātmane (636)
Viśvabāhave (316)
Viśvabhuje (239)
Viśvadakṣiṇāya (425)
Viśvadhṛṣe (238)
Viśvakarmaṇe (51)
Viṣvaksenāya (125)
Viśvamai (1)
Viśvamūrtaye (717)
Viśvaretase (88)
Viśvātmane (225)
Viśvayonaye (117)
Viśvayonaye (149)

Vītabhayāya (921)
Viviktāya (263)
Vṛddhātmane (352)
Vṛkṣāya (555)
Vṛṣabhākṣāya (594)
Vṛṣabhāya (257)
Vṛṣāhiṇe (256)
Vṛṣākapaye (101)
Vṛṣakarmaṇe (112)
Vṛṣākṛtaye (113)
Vṛṣaparvaṇe (259)
Vṛṣapriyāya (595)
Vṛṣāya (313)
Vṛṣodarāya (260)
Vyādiśāya (939)
Vyagrāya (762)
Vyaktarūpāya (305)
Vyālāya (92)
Vyāpine (467)
Vyāptāya (413)
Vyavasāyāya (384)
Vyavasthānāya (385)
Yaduśreṣṭhāya (705)
Yajñabhṛte (976)
Yajñabhuje (979)
Yajñaguhyāya (982)
Yajñakṛte (977)
Yajñāṅgāya (974)
Yajñāntakṛte (981)
Yajñapataye (972)
Yajñasādhanāya (980)
Yajñavāhanāya (975)
Yajñāya (445)
Yajñāya (971)
Yajñine (978)
Yajvane (973)
Yamāya (162)
Yasmai (730)
Yogavidāṁnetre (19)
Yogāya (18)
Yogine (849)
Yogīśāya (850)
Yugādikṛte (300)
Yugāvartāya (301)

**Viśvadevas**: [Deities] They are first mentioned in the Vedas as the preservers of humanity and the bestowers of gifts. They were generally taken to be nine, but this number has varied. In later times, they are a class of deities particularly interested in exequial offerings. The accounts of them are rather vague. They are generally said to be ten in number, by the lists vary, both as to the number and the names. They were named Vasu, Satya, Kṛtu, Dakṣa, Kāla, Kāma, Dhṛt, Kuru, Pururavas and Madravas.

Two others are sometimes added, Rocaka or Locana and Dhuri or Dhvani. [*Hindu Mythology,*T.R.R. Iyengar; *Vedic Index*, Macdonell and Keith]

**Viśvakarmā**: [Omnificent]. This name seems to have been originally an epithet of any powerful god, as of Indra and Sūrya, but in course of time it came to designate a personification of the creative power. In this character Viśvakarmā was the great architect of the universe, and is described in two hymns of the *Ṛgveda* as the one 'all-seeing god, who has on every side eyes, faces, arms and feet, who when producing heaven and earth, blows them forth with his arms and wings; the father, generator, disposer who knows all worlds, gives the gods their names, and is beyond the comprehension of mortals'. In these hymns also he is said to sacrifice himself or to himself, and the *Nirukta* explains this by a legend which represents that 'Viśvakarmā, son of Bhuvana, first of all offered up all worlds in a Sarvamedha and ended by sacrificing himself'.

In the Epic and Purāṇic periods, Viśvakarmā is invested with the powers and offices of the Vedic Tvaṣṭṛ, and is sometimes so-called. He is not only the great architect, but also the general artificer of the gods and maker of their weapons. It was he who made the Āgneyāstra or 'fiery weapon' and it was he who revealed the *Sthāpatyaveda*, or science of arctiecture and mechanics. The *Mahābhārata* describes him as 'the lord of the arts, executor of a thousand handicrafts, the carpenter of the gods, the fashioners of all ornaments, the most eminent of artisans who formed the celestial chariots of the deities, on whose craftsmen subsist, and whom, a great and immortal god, they continually worship'. In the *Rāmāyaṇa*, Viśvakarmā is represented as having built the city of Laṅkā for the *rākṣasa*s, and as having generated the ape Nala, who constructed Rāma's bridge from the continent to Ceylon. The Purāṇas make Viśvakarmā the son of Prabhāsa, the eighth Vasu, by his wife 'the lovely and virtuous Yogasiddha'. His daughter Saṁjñā was married to Sūrya, the sun; but as she was unable to endure his effulgence, Viśvakarmā placed the sun upon his lathe and cut away an eighth part of his brightness.

The fragments fell to the earth, and from these Viśvakarmā formed 'the discus of Viṣṇu, the trident of Śiva, the weapon of Kubera, the god of wealth, the lance of Kārttikeya, god of war, and the weapons of the other gods'. He is also represented as having made the great image of Jagannātha. In his creative capacity he is sometimes designated Prajāpati. He also has the following appellations: Karu, 'workman'; Takṣaka, 'woodcutter'; 'Deva-vardhika', 'the builder of the gods'; Sudhanvan, 'having a good bow'. [*A Classical Dictionary of Hindu Mythology and Religion*, J. Dowson; *Rāmāyaṇa*]

**Viśvarūpa**: [Wearing all forms, omnipresent, universal] A title of Viṣṇu.

**Viśvāvasu**: A chief of the *gandharva*s in Indra's heaven.

**Viśveśvara** The lord of all. A name of Śiva. The celebrated *liṅga*.

**Vivasvat**: Vivasvat is not celebrated in any hymn of the *R̥gveda* but his name occurs there about thirty times. Since Indra is closely associated with his abode, Vivasvat may be regarded as a deity of the aerial sphere. He is well known as the father of Yama, and in one passage he is also regarded as the father of Aśvins. His wife is said to be Śaranyu. Agni is said to be the messenger of Vivasvat. Indra is connected with Vivasvat in several passages of the *R̥gveda*. Soma is also brought into intimate relation with Vivasvat. The streams of soma flow through Śiva, having obtained the blessing of Vivasvat. The name of Vivasvat is derived from the root *vas*, the same as in Uṣas, and means brilliant. The most probable interpretation of Vivasvat seems to be that he originally represented the rising sun. In any case he is identical with the Vivanhvant of *Avesta*. Vivasvat is also the name of the first sacrificer among men and parent of Soma and the father of Manu. The two were most probably different originally but in the *R̥gveda*, it is not always easy to know which Vivasvat is meant. Later, of course, the two identified with each other. [*Hindu Mythology*, T.R.R. Iyengar; *Vedic Index*, Macdonell and Keith]

**Vivasvat**: The bright one. The sun.

**Vṛhaspati**: See 'Bṛhaspati'.

**Vṛkodara**: 'Wolf belly'. A name of Bhīma.

**Vṛṣṇī**: A descendant of Yadu, and the ancestor from whom Kṛṣṇa got the name of Vārṣṇeya.

**Vṛṣṇīs**: The descendants of Vṛṣṇī, son of Madhu, whose ancestor was the eldest son of Yadu. Kṛṣṇa belonged to this branch of the lunar race.

**Vṛtrahan**: A title of Indra.

**Vṛndā**: She was a deity who became ultimately the *tulasī* plant. She was supposed to be a companion of Kṛṣṇa in Gloom Dhaka and one day Rādhā, when she went there, found Kṛṣṇa sporting with her. She became so annoyed with Vṛndā that she cursed her to leave heaven, and to be reborn as a human being. At this Vṛndā was very much aggrieved for she was not really to be blamed in this matter and Kṛṣṇa, seeing the iniquity of this curse, mitigated it by saying that, though she would be born as a mortal, still she would be very dear to him. Consequently Vṛndā was born as a princess and although she had set her heart on marrying Kṛṣṇa, her father had her married to a demon Jālandhara who seduced Vṛndā. When she discovered that she had been outraged she cursed Viṣṇu to become a stone and hence he was turned into the *śāligrāma*, which has since become his emblem. Immediately on this seduction, Jālandhara expired on the field of battle and the gods were relieved. Finding that her husband had perished, Vṛndā too died with him and the tradition is that her body was transformed into the *tulasī* plant and that her hair became its branches and leaves. [*Epics, Myths and Legends of India*, P. Thomas]

# Y

**Yādava**: A descendant of Yadu. The Yādavas were the celebrated race in which Kṛṣṇa was born. At the time of his birth they led a pastoral life, but under him they established a kingdom at Dvārakā.

**Yadu**: Son of King, Yayāti of the lunar race, and founder of the line of the Yādavas in which Kṛṣṇa was born. He refused to bear the curse of decrepitude passed upon his father by the sage Śukra, and in consequence he incurred the paternal curse, 'Your posterity shall not possess dominions'. His posterity however prospered as he received the southern districts of his father's kingdom and his posterity prospered.

**Yajñasena**: A name of Drupada.

**Yakṣas**: A class of supernatural beings attendant on Kubera, the god of wealth. Authorities differ as to their origin. They have no special attributes, but they are generally considered as inoffensive, and so are called Punjyajanas, 'good people' but they occasionally appear as imps of evil.

**Yakṣī, Yakṣiṇī**: A female *yakṣa*. Wife of Kubera.

**Yama:** [Restrainer] Pluto, Minos. In the Vedas Yama is god of the dead, with whom the spirits of the departed dwell. He was son of Vivasvat and had a twin-sister named Yamī. Yama, the ruler of the blessed dead, is celebrated in three hymns of the tenth book of the *Ṛgveda*. There is also another, which consists of a dialogue between him and his sister Yama. Yama's name occurs about fifty times in the *Ṛgveda*. The *Naighaṇṭuka* mentions the name of Yama in the list of celestial as well as aerial deities. Yama is associated with Varuṇa, Bṛhaspati and especially Agni who, as conductor of the dead, is called his friend and priest. He is also associated with the departed fathers, especially the Aṅgirases, with whom he comes to the sacrifice to drink *soma*. He is the gatherer of the people, giving the dead man resting place and preparing an abode for him. Yama and

Yamī are by some looked upon as the first human pair, the originators of the race, and there is a remarkable hymn, in the form of a dialogue, in which the female urges their cohabitation for the purpose of perpetuating the species. Another hymn says that Yama was the first man that died, and the first that departed to the (celestial) world. 'He it was who found out the way to the home which cannot be taken away. Those who are now born (follow) by their own paths to the places whither our ancient fathers have departed.' Dr. Muir says,

> Yama is nowhere represented in the *Ṛgveda* as having anything to do with the punishment of the wicked. So far as is yet known, the hymns of that Veda contain no prominent mention of any such penal retribution. . . . Yama is still to some extent an object of terror. He is represented as having two insatiable dogs with four eyes and wide nostrils, which guard the road to his abode, and which the departed are advised to hurry past with all possible speed. These dogs are said to wander about among men as his messengers, no doubt for the purpose of summoning them to their master, who is in another place identified with death, and is described as sending a bird as the herald of doom.

In the epic poems Yama is the son of the sun by Saṁjñā and brother of Vaivasvata. Mythologically he was the father of Yudhiṣṭhira. He is the god of departed spirits and judge of the dead. A soul when it quits its mortal form repairs to his abode in the lower regions; there the recorder Citragupta reads out his account from the great register called Agrasandhānī, and a just sentence follows, when the soul either ascends to the abodes of the *pitṛ*s or is sent to one of the twenty-one hells according to its guilt or it is born again on earth in another form. Yama is regent of the south quarter, and as such is called Dakṣiṇapati. He is represented as of a green colour and clothed with red. He rides upon a buffalo, and is armed with a ponderous mace and a noose to secure his victims.

In the Purāṇas a legend is told of Yama having lifted his foot to kick Chāyā, the handmaid of his father. She cursed him to have his leg affected with sores and worms, but his father gave him a cock which picked off the worms and cured the discharge. Through this incident he is called Sīrṇapada, 'shrivelled foot'. In the *Bhaviṣya Purāṇa* there is an account of Yama's marriage with a mortal woman. He fell in love with Vijayā, the pretty daughter of a brāhmaṇa, married her and took her to Yamapurī, his abode. Here he told her not to enter the southern regions of his spacious palace. For some time Vijayā remained obedient, but afterwards curiosity overpowered her and 'thinking that Yama must have another wife' she entered the forbidden region, and there saw hell and souls in torment; and among the tormented souls was her mother. She also met Yama there and implored him to release her mother. Yama told her that the release could only be obtained by some of her relatives performing a sacrifice. The sacrifice was performed and Yama's mother-in-law was released. Yama had several wives, as Hemamālā, Suśīlā and Vijayā. He dwells in the lower world, in his city Yamapura. There, in his palace called Kālīcī, he sits upon his throne of judgement, Vicārabhū. He is assisted by his recorder and councillor Citragupta and waited upon by his two chief attendants and custodians, Caṇḍa or Mahācaṇḍa, and Kālapuruṣa. His messengers, *yama-dūta*s, bring in the souls of the dead, and the door of his judgement-hall is kept by his porter, Vaidhyata. The owl and the pigeon are mentioned as his messengers, but the two four-eyed, broad-nosed, bridled dogs, sons of Samara, are his regular emissaries. It is remarkable that though Yama rules the dead, he is not feared but loved, for the Vedic poet prays that the dead man may go to the realm of light and meet the fathers who revel with Yama in the highest heaven. The word Yama literally means 'twin'. Yama and Yamī were originally probably personifications of day and night. But in course of time the physical basis was completely obscured. The epithets of Yama are as follows: Antaka, death; Auḍumbara, fig tree; Bhīmaśāsana, terrible decrees, Daṇḍadhara, rod-bearer; Daṇḍī, rod-bearer; Dharmarāja, king of justice; Kāla, death; Kr̥tāna, finisher; Mr̥tyu, death; Pāśī, noose-carrier; Pitṛpati, lord of the manes; Preta-rāja, king of the ghosts; Samāna, settler; Śrāddhadeva, god of the exequial offerings.

The number of hells are in some accounts said to be seven, each one set apart for torturing a particular kind of sinner. The *Bhāgavata Purāṇa*, however, names twenty-eight hells and describes most of them in detail:

| *Name of the hell* | *Nature of sinners* |
|---|---|
| Andhakūpa | Killers of the blood-sucking insects |
| Andhatāmisra | Selfish people and egoists |
| Asipatravana | Heretics |
| Kālasūtra | Those guilty of Brāhmicide |
| Kṛmibhojana | Inhospitable people |
| Kumbhipāka | Cruel men |
| Raurava | Those who hurt the creatures |
| Śukramukha | Kings who oppress their subjects |
| Tāmisra | Robbers and adulterers |
| Taptasurmi | Guilty of sin of simony |
| Vajrakaṇṭaka | Those who have married, women/from other castes |

[*Hindu Mythology*, T.R.R. Iyengar; *Dictionary of Hinduism*, T.R.R. Iyengar; *Epics, Myths and Legends of India*, P. Thomas]

**Yamī**: The twin sister of Yama. In a dialogue in the *Ṛgveda* she proposed to her brother but he rejected her proposal with horror, observing that such a union would amount to incest. They also call themselves in places as the children of a *gandharva* and a water nymph. Legends alleging that she is Yama's wife, if any, cannot be given any credence especially in view of their specific dialogue in the *Ṛgveda*. [*Hindu Mythology*, T.R.R. Iyengar]

**Yamavaivasvata**: Yama as son of Vivasvat.

**Yantras**: These are important mystic diagrams with mystic letters engraved on metallic sheets, like gold, silver, copper, iron or even on paper. These diagrams are drawn as per canons laid down by the various *tantra*s and *śāstra*s and are supposed to be very powerful if worshipped properly. This sort of worship is closely associated with the Śakti cult which invokes the blessing of the universal energy, who is believed to reside both in the macrocosm and in the microcosm. The development of Śakti cult can be traced to olden days and Patañjali's famous *Yogasūtra* describing the various means of developing the inherent *śakti* in man and employing the same for the realisation of the infinite. *Yantra*s help in this direction and are worshipped for both good and bad effects depending on how they are applied. It is believed that *yantra*s are usually made and put under the pedestals of the *mūla-mūrti*s in temple at the time of their installation, so that the deities can wield great power. *Yantra*s are also known as talismans to ward off disease, misfortunes and calamities. There are several varieties of *yantra*s. The most important among them and perhaps the most widely worshipped *yantra* is the *śrīcakra* which is considered most sacred to Devī. The *śrīcakra* consists of a large number of triangles cutting one another, with straight lines crossing them in a geometrical form. The whole set is enveloped by two series of circles, each having a definite number of lotus petals. In the angular and circular portions thus formed, *bījākṣara*s are written and the whole design is engraved. Properly consecrated they form objects of worship. Similar to *śrīcakra* are several other *yantra*s. [*South Indian Images*, T.N. Srinivasan]

**Yaśodā**: Wife of the cowherd Nanda, and foster-mother of Kṛṣṇa.

**Yoganidrā**: [The sleep of meditation] Personified delusion. The great illusory energy of Viṣṇu and the illusory power manifested in Devī as Mahāmāyā, the great illusion.

**Yoni**: The cult of the Yoni is said to have originated from the place where that organ of Satī fell when Viṣṇu cut her body into pieces. Every place where a part of the body fell became sacred and a temple was built in honour of the relic. The Yoni is said to have felled in Assam from where the worship spread all over India. Thus the myth of the origin of phallus worship in Egypt and that of Yoni-worship in India can be traced to a common source although the sexes have subsequently got mixed up. The Yonijas maintain that the feminine principle is anterior and superior to the male. It is said that Śiva and Pārvatī had once a dispute between them as to the superiority of the sexes and each one created a race of men. Those whom Śiva created devoted themselves to the exclusive worship of the male deity and their intellects became dull their bodies feeble, their limbs distorted, and their complexions of different hues. The race created by Pārvatī, on the other hand, worshipped the female power and they became powerful, virile and handsome. Mahādeva was enraged at the result and was about to destroy the Yonijas when Pārvatī interceded on their behalf. The race was, however, exiled from their homeland. Men who were excommunicated due to pollution such as that supposed to be caused by going overseas were at one time made to be reborn through metallic Yoni before they were re-admitted into the Hindu fold. In the case of rich people the symbol was made of gold which was, after the ceremony, given to the brāhmaṇas. Clefts and rocks, which resemble the *yoni* and *liṅgam*, are also worshipped. Impotent men hope to gain virility by passing through such a cleft while barren women, who wish to become mothers, are particularly devoted to the worship of the *liṅgam*. While the Liṅgāyatas exclusively worship the *liṅgam* and the Yonijas the *yoni*. [*Hindu Mythology*, T.R.R. Iyengar; *Epics, Myths and Legends of India*, P. Thomas]

# Index

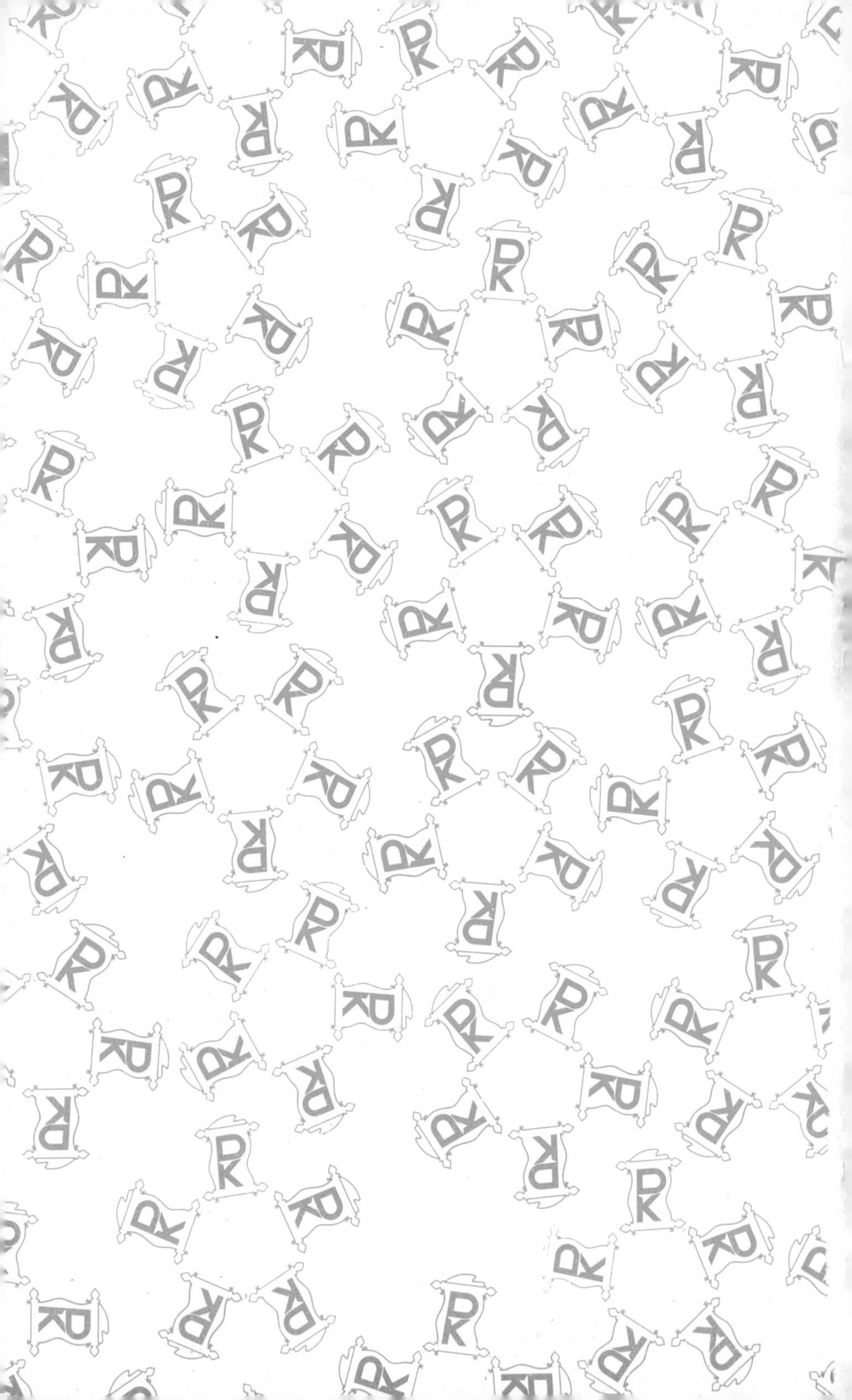

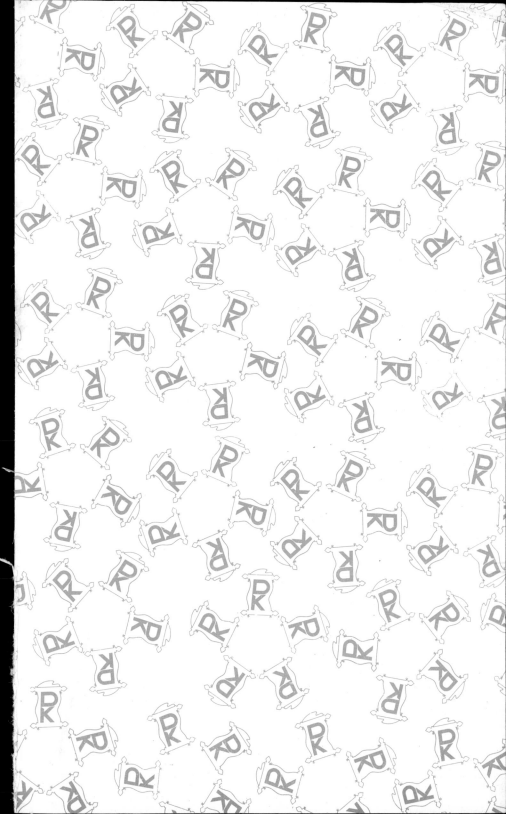